BRITISH POLITICS
IDEAS AND CONCEPTS

KEITH PYE AND RICHARD YATES

STANLEY THORNES (PUBLISHERS) LTD

First published in 1990 by:
Stanley Thornes (Publishers) Ltd
Old Station Drive
Leckhampton
CHELTENHAM GL53 0DN
England

Reprinted 1992

British Library Cataloguing in Publication Data
Pye, Keith
British politics: ideas and concepts.
1. Politics
I. Title II. Yates, Richard
320

ISBN 0-7487-0227-X

Cover illustration: (clockwise from left to right): George Washington, Margaret Thatcher, Karl Marx, Adolf Hitler, Plato.

Typeset by TA Tek Art Ltd, Croydon, Surrey
Printed and bound in Great Britain at The Bath Press

Contents

DEDICATION

This book is dedicated to our fathers: Cecil Pye and John Yates.

Introduction

It is a sobering but oft repeated thought that politics is the only profession for which absolutely no formal qualifications are required.

Our doctors, lawyers, teachers, business people and nurses all need to complete lengthy training periods before we will allow them to do so much as to fill in a form.

To be a politician, however, one needs only to be able to talk, to have the presence to be able to stand up in public, to have the confidence (some would say the gall) to be sure that one knows exactly what is good for one's fellow citizens, and, of course, increasingly in this image conscious world – to look good.

Into the hands of amateurs we entrust our futures. In Britain, unlike some States in the USA, we don't even have the opportunity of recalling those politicians who turn out not to be to our liking. Once elected they are there for the duration.

Under these conditions – in which politicians are being elected almost entirely on the basis of what party label stands beside their name on the ballot paper – we believe that it is vital that our students learn not only how political institutions work and what their 'problems' are, but also, what **ideas** and **concepts** underlie the entire system.

To their credit, various Chief Examiners – particularly Bernard Crick – have recognised this need and have amended the requirements of the A-level syllabuses accordingly. Today's students actually have to *think* about political concepts as well as know such things as the stages through which a Bill must pass.

The concepts – which, we must all recognise, used to be the preserve of degree courses – are extremely difficult. Uncertainty comes hard to students who are brought up, during earlier examination courses, on a strict diet of fact and black-and-white examples. The intellectual challenge of the concepts is bad enough without the traumatic blow to the system which comes from knowing that even their teachers don't know the 'right' answer!

This book is an attempt to meet the problem of difficulty by taking the concepts and ideas in reasonably easy stages. It meets the trauma head on – by saying to the student 'We don't know the answers but here are the main issues.'

▶▶▶▶▶▶▶▶▶▶▶▶▶▶▶▶ About the book

We ought to begin by saying what the book is not:

it is not

- a traditional politics textbook
- a comprehensive discussion of concepts or ideas
- the final word.

The objective of the book is to present concepts and ideas alongside a brief discussion of the application of those matters to issues and to institutions in British politics.

British Politics: Ideas and Concepts is designed for a wide readership. We hope that it will be of interest and value to casual readers and to those who require a reasonably detailed background in political ideas. It is likely to be of greatest value, however, to those who are studying for introductory degree-level courses and GCE A-level, although students undertaking BTEC courses at a higher level should also find it relevant.

Not all the examples relate to British politics, for modern examination papers require first and foremost that the student understand the **ideas** and the **concepts** of politics rather than the bland and otherwise empty detail of institutional structure and rules.

We have attempted to ensure that, wherever possible, British case studies and examples are used, but, where this is not possible due to the nature of the subject under consideration or where we have felt that an overseas example will illustrate the issue more clearly, then we have made use of such examples.

The book is by no means comprehensive. It is intended to be an introduction; to stimulate interest and to provide a means of getting to grips with some of the most difficult ideas in human society. The reader is referred to other, more scholarly works, if depth of study is the main objective.

The book is divided into three main sections:

A. **Concepts** Examines the concepts which are central to politics and provides some limited applications of these concepts to given case studies.
B. **Theory** Seeks to give the reader a basic introduction to theoretical work on a variety of political ideas and to illustrate these theories with the ideas of some of the major political philosophers.
C. **Institutions** Attempts to provide *initial* linkages between the theories and concepts which have gone before and the main concerns of modern British politics. Again, it should be stressed that the section is not comprehensive. The ideas are discussed alongside British institutions in a way which we hope will stimulate discussion and enable the reader to see other, perhaps more important, linkages.

The more important object of this book, though, is to try to give the reader an approach to British politics which does not begin with rules and institutions: to try to ensure that the reader begins to think of politics from the point of view of *why* rather than *how*.

Each chapter is also divided into several distinct sections:

- **Basic principles** A relatively simple set of examples and cases designed to highlight the main issues in an applied way
- **Discussing the arguments** Seeks to discuss some of the major implications of the subject at hand
- **Examination questions** Provides selected examination questions
- **Now read on . . .** Gives some interesting and relevant further reading about and around each subject.

In addition, the earlier, conceptual chapters are complemented by case studies which illustrate the concepts and which direct the reader's attention to some of the more difficult problems surrounding them.

The key word is **introduction** – we hope that students who fight shy of thinking about such difficult things as concepts will be able to get an initial grip on part of them from this book and that it will provide a base from which those who wish can branch out into deeper discussion and questioning.

The contents are *not* intended to be a comprehensive discussion of concepts and theory, *nor* are they meant to provide a full text on the detail of British political institutions. We have, rather, tried to give a broad introduction to each of these areas of study in such a way that the *links* are seen to be paramount. It is our firm belief that it is of little import if our students do not know the precise regulations surrounding Parliamentary debate but of vital interest to the future of our democracy that they comprehend the conceptual foundations of the system.

One further note is necessary. The evil spectre of *bias* raises its ugly head whenever two political words are rubbed together.

We have tried to meet this problem in the simplest possible way – by recognising it and presenting it as such to our readers. The student should realise that we are all products of our society and our training. They must understand that any author is biased towards certain viewpoints and that this will be evident to the seasoned reader.

We have attempted, where possible, to present as many points of view as possible so that, if the reader feels uneasy about a particular approach, then a different angle may be explored through other writers. In one area only did we find it almost impossible to present a 'balanced' viewpoint. The reason for this is that no amount of scholarly research would find a significant amount of good to be said for Totalitarian, Fascist or Nazi systems. For this bias we offer neither excuse nor apology.

We differ in many of our political beliefs and viewpoints, but we are both committed to the principle of democratic government and to the educated, knowledgeable and perceptive populace upon which a true democracy rests.

Acknowledgements
We should like to thank everyone who has helped us to complete this book: our students for helping to develop both our own ideas and the shape of these chapters; Sharon Yearsley in particular for reading several chapters and making valuable comments; and, of course, our respective wives – Susan, who did a sterling job of typing, and Stephanie, who put up with being a word-processing widow.

KEITH PYE
Harrogate

RICHARD YATES
Cambridge

1 Order and Disorder

Internment issue flares again at IRA outrage

By Paul Vallely and Martin Fletcher

There were renewed demands for the reintroduction of internment in Northern Ireland yesterday as all sides in the Commons united in condemnation of the murders of six soldiers in the IRA bomb attack in Lisburn, Co Antrim.

As a top-level security inquiry began into how the IRA managed to plant the bomb in an unmarked army van in the town on Wednesday evening, both the Prime Minister and Mr Tom King, the Secretary of State for Northern Ireland made clear their profound reservations about internment, last used in 1975, but made clear that the question would have to be kept under review.

The security investigation is to centre on two separate areas. It will consider how the bomb was actually attached to the unmarked army van in the heart of the town which is the province's largest army garrison.

Perhaps more significantly, it will look for a possible breach of army security in Londonderry, where the six soldiers were based.

Pressed in the Commons by Mr Anthony Marlow, Conservative MP for Northampton North, to take known terrorists "temporarily out of circulation", Mrs Thatcher said she would be "very, very reluctant" to see internment reintroduced though she understood the strength of Mr Marlow's feelings.

She told MPs that the bombing was a "terrible atrocity" made still worse by the fact that it was a great charitable occasion in which whole families had participated.

Mr King told the Commons that he could "not rule out the possibility of selective detention at some time", accepted that it had worked in the past, and made the point that the Government had retained the necessary legislative powers.

But he stressed repeatedly that internment gave the IRA a propaganda platform and could act as their most effective "recruiting sergeant".

Yesterday the Army headquarters in Lisburn released the names of the six soldiers killed.

Source: *Daily Telegraph*, 1988

A major problem for any government is how to respond to threats to law and order. Many groups which are committed to the violent overthrow of a political system engage in tactics that are aimed at provoking a strong and illiberal reaction from the state. A primary objective of the state is the maintenance of law and order, but this must be balanced against the need to guarantee various other rights for its citizens. The apparent need for a strong response on law and order issues may in itself result in a reduction of established freedoms. Liberal democracies have the difficulty, on the one hand, of allowing groups to freely express their viewpoints, but on the other, of taking adequate and effective measures to ensure social stability, and security for, its citizens.

BASIC PRINCIPLES

Definition

Rule of Law
The rule of law introduces stability and predictability by applying general rules to all, consistently. The law is upheld by an independent judiciary.

Examples

The concept of **legality** does not concern most people, but the order that results from the observance of legal rules does.

In Chapter 2 we establish that one of the primary characteristics of the state is an exclusive possession of coercive power in society. The justification for this is often claimed to be the necessity for the preservation of **Law and Order**. Without a sufficient degree of security, social organisations, political, economic, educational, etc. could not function. Order is often argued to be the greatest benefit that the state can provide, but the establishment of order is not enough, for it can be achieved by authoritarian measures or by violent repression. Order must embody what people feel to be just with the equal treatment of all persuading them to obey. So order will usually be coupled with law and especially with the concept of the **Rule of Law**.

The word 'order' is in constant and widespread use by politicians, newspapers, TV, etc. It is hard to imagine a politician, especially of the right, who would not claim to be committed to the extension of law and order as a major political objective. Certain actions are described as 'threats to order', others need to be taken to 'preserve order' and frequently, in popular usage, it is linked with law.

Examples

Soviet military intervention in Afghanistan, Czechoslovakia and Hungary, was justified in terms of a prevention of internal 'disorder', but could they be justified in terms of 'law'?

Safety, normality, stability, peace, security are all associated with order; **Disorder** is seen to threaten them and, at worst, plunge society into 'anarchy'. Yet the price that is demanded for the preservation of order may be high in terms of other factors such as liberty, freedom of speech, justice, equality, and even legality.

DISCUSSING THE ARGUMENTS

A difficult question to answer is whether, without the state to ultimately guarantee order in economic, social and political relationships, society would collapse into complete chaos?

Answers to this question have provided instances where repressive state activity is justified as necessary for the preservation of law and order. The imposition of martial law, the substitution of military for civilian rule, the suspension of civil liberties, the bypassing of established judicial practice have all been undertaken for such an end.

A Pessimistic View

Perhaps the classic exponent of the view that the state exists fundamentally to enforce order was the English political philosopher, Thomas Hobbes (1588–1679). Hobbes was strongly influenced by the English Civil War and the removal of the monarchy in the 1640s. His best known work on the role of the state was *Leviathan*, published in 1651.

Hobbes took a very pessimistic view of human nature and felt that without sufficient state power to regulate the activities of man, no one could be secure, and a war of every man against every man would result. He felt that without the state no condition of civilised society could exist and that the life of man would be 'solitary, poor, nasty, brutish, and short'.

Security for him depended upon the state having enough power to keep the peace and apply sanctions to curb man's essentially unsocial nature. He did accept, however, that resistance to the state would be admissible if the state failed to produce security and order, its sole basis for existence. The advantages of the state for the citizen were tangible in the form of peace, comfort, and security for both persons and property. This was the only basis upon which the state could be justified.

Examples

The Hobbesian view would seem to be vindicated in the internal chaos and bloodshed that has occurred with the collapse of effective government in the Lebanon in the 1980s. The inability of the state to provide security and order resulted in a war of every man against every man, with no central source of power to ensure order.

An Optimistic View

The unduly pessimistic conclusions of human nature presented by Hobbes have not gone unchallenged. It need not be assumed that a centralised body possessing a monopoly of coercive power is the only way to ensure an ordered pattern of existence. A much more optimistic view of human nature might lead to the idea of man in a condition of happy innocence obeying laws without constraint and living in peace and harmony with his fellows. Many political writers have created models for a perfect society where state imposed order has been removed and a new society created on the basis of mutual cooperation and fellowship.

Anarchists like Peter Kropotkin (1842–1921) and Socialists like William Morris (1834–96) are writers who took such an optimistic view of human nature.

William Morris (1834–96)

William Morris established himself as a successful designer and businessman before entering active politics in 1876. He was opposed to the quality of art, design and the living standards of mid-Victorian Britain. His most developed view of an alternative society was painted in *News from Nowhere* (1890). In it he presents a picture where the civilisation of Britain is gone and has been replaced by a rural society based on voluntary cooperation where handicrafts have been revived.

Definition

Order

Order, is not just a description of a particular set of social circum stances, perhaps status quo, but a value or even an ideal which may be achieved through political action.

Order will set limits on per sonal action whether self-imposed, as in a Utopian model of society, whether imposed by a popularly supported police force, as in most democratic and communist states, or strictly and brutally enforced, as in some dictatorships of left or right.

To assume that the basic function of the state is to preserve 'law and order', gives little indication of what values are being pursued.

Both writers assume that it is modern society that needs to be transformed radically to allow individual self development. They argue that man is naturally sociable and cooperative and that rules of social behaviour can be self-imposed.

Writers who seek to present alternative models of Utopian societies generally do not deny the need for an ordered society but argue that a different form of order can be created – in some cases without law. Both Kropotkin and Morris argue in this way.

The popular use of the word **anarchy** to imply the breakdown of order is confusing. Anarchy may seem to represent disorder for the current state but the final objective of Anarchists is to establish a different form of society (see Chapter 13 on Anarchism).

Order, however, is seen often in a very negative sense where, for example, a serious outbreak of disorder is stopped by military intervention. Order is in this way seen as the opposite of disorder.

DISORDER

What is disorder? To consider this question it has to be understood that one man's 'disorder' is another's 'legitimate struggle to oppose oppression'. Less dramatically it may be a resort to forms of legal protest to pressurise an intransigent government to change certain policies. However, several important questions are raised.

Questions

1 What forms of protest are legal and which are not?
2 What should a citizen do when under a legal obligation to undertake that which clashes with personal convictions?
3 How should a citizen respond when legally prohibited from doing what he or she morally feels to be right?
4 At what point is it legitimate for citizens to resort to disorder so as to resist governmental action thought to be wrong?

Scales of Disorder

The scale of the problem has to be gauged by a state faced by 'disorder'. What distinguishes legitimate protest from civil disobedience, riot, rebellion, sedition, terrorism or even revolution, where the whole framework of the state is threatened?

Dilemma of Minorities

In democratic theory it is often felt that a principle reason for the establishment of government is the protection of liberties within a given society. In this way the activity of government is accepted by the people. This is usually taken to mean that the preservation of order in society depends upon minority interests coming second to those of the majority. This is a difficult theory to sustain, however, for a minority who feel that their interests are continually disregarded in favour of majority opinion. The preservation of order, arguably, depends upon such minorities working through established procedures for the redress of their grievances. But what happens if they feel the procedures are failing to meet their needs or demanding compliance with rules they oppose fundamentally? A simple answer is for them to follow their conscience and be prepared to accept whatever the law metes out. But how should the state respond, for example, to pacifist groups during a war that may threaten the state's very existence? The difficulty is one of a *conflict of duty*.

We have a moral duty to our fellow citizens to observe what the law directs and allow others to do the same. Citizens when enjoying the benefits provided by the state (which might include freedom, liberty, justice, etc) may on occasions have to be prepared to put aside personal moral preferences for the preservation of the society in which they live. No individual can always do what he or she considers right in their own eyes, for being a member of a community there has to be at least a partial reduction in personal choice.

In most free societies the state, generally, does not produce situations that lead to widespread moral conflict with its citizens, for most obligations are negative ones. Citizens are usually required to refrain from certain forms of activity, however, the non-payment of taxes is a major and almost universal exception. If the state begins to act in a way that runs counter to widely held moral preferences, then the legitimacy of these actions may be questioned and the obligation to conform will become confused. Citizens may be compelled to obey by force of sanctions but questions about the need to resist will arise. Those who have resisted unjust and oppressive laws of tyrants may well have been threatening established order but later, come to be seen as heroes: a good example are the 'Founding Fathers' in the USA.

Types of Disorder

The right to rebel has been considered by many political philosophers since ancient times, but the appropriate degree and form of resistance required is difficult to determine. Some questions arise:

Questions

1 Is is reasonable to resist all the laws of a tyrannical regime?
2 If a legitimate government produces a law that offends a significant proportion of the electorate are they entitled to resist and to what extent?

A further problem arises when assessing which actions constitute a threat to order. A well-established, stable regime may safely be able to absorb a considerable degree of resistance from disgruntled groups, whereas other regimes may see almost any extra-legal activity as extremely dangerous. Considerable confusion exists over forms of extra-legal activity and the distinctions that can be drawn between them. They range from largely peaceful actions directed at forcing the pace of legitimate political change, to attempts to overthrow the existing political order and replace it with an alternative system.

Example

Many instances where demonstrations have turned into violent confrontations with the police have occurred in Northern Ireland. One such incident involved the violence which followed a march organised by Unionist 'Orangemen' in Londonderry in July 1986. The organisers wished the event to be peaceful, but at a final rally violence flared and police clashed with marchers.

Demonstrations

If demonstrations are legally constituted (i.e. they have been given police permission to go ahead) and are aimed at a limited objective, usually a change of government policy, and are accompanied by no great degree of violence, then they cannot be seen as a form of disorder. Such activity, nonetheless, has a record of generating violence and this may spill over into forms of civil disobedience, which will lead to a response from the forces of 'law and order'.

Example

'Animal Rights' protestors have broken into laboratories and taken away or released animals. Yet, whilst accepting that their actions are illegal, they feel themselves to be justified on the grounds that the animals were subjected to what they claim is considerable cruelty. The group feel government is unwilling to change the law and that 'conventional' lobbying has failed to produce results.

Example

In 1985 Monsignor Bruce Kent, a leading figure in the Campaign for Nuclear Disarmament in Britain, was arrested and charged with causing criminal damage after cutting the perimeter fence at an American air base in England. The action took place in the full glare of media coverage, with the police well aware of his intentions. The action was largely symbolic, but was part of CND's campaign of non-violent civil disobedience in opposition to nuclear weapons.

Direct Action

What comprises a legitimate form of action is difficult to assess, for it may be possible to see an illegal act as legitimate because it is morally defensible. Some forms of direct action are justified by their perpetrators in this way.

The forces of law and order (the police and the courts) cannot be interested in any justifications for law breaking because their role is to uphold the written laws passed down by the elected parliament. Any prosecution that may result will be on the grounds of upholding the law and punishing its transgressors.

Civil Disobedience

Activities which can be broadly categorised in this way are confused with, and sometimes associated with, other forms of non-conventional political activity. Civil disobedience is often accompanied by violence and therefore could be seen to be lawless and divorced from established political practices, leading to condemnation by, and possible counter action from, the state. However, civil disobedience should be distinguished from rebellion or revolution, for it does not usually arise from an immediate desire to bring about the overthrow of the existing political order. It aims to achieve change by attracting maximum publicity through its tactics of calculated breaches of the law. (Not necessarily the same law that the protestors may want altered.)

Other complications arise because forms of civil disobedience may be used as short term tactics by those whose ultimate aim is to remove the existing political regime. Widespread support for civil disobedience may also be an early indicator of more deep seated public discontent which could erupt into revolution.

Providing the action taken is limited to non-violent activity and does not threaten the overall stability of the state then this consequently allows for a moderate response from the authorities. Civil disobedience is usually a very public form of activity designed, as we have seen, to court maximum publicity. In some cases the intentions of the protestors will be advertised well in advance so as to attract news coverage and possibly allow the authorities to take sufficient action to minimise the likelihood of violence and disorder.

By emphasising non-violence it is intended that no threat to the state is posed, only opposition to specific policies. The difficulty for some types of non-violent protest is that there is no guarantee that the response from the state will be appropriate. Violence may be instigated by the police or other opposing factions in such campaigns.

Passive Resistance

One of the main inspirations for effective non-violent protest was the campaign in India for independence led by Mahatma Gandhi. The campaign resulted in the end of British colonial rule in 1947. Gandhi tried to impress upon his followers the need for discipline and non-violence, thus removing any legitimate excuse for a violent reaction by British authorities. A good deal of violence did occur and many were killed but the essential doctrine was still one of passive resistance.

Similar tactics were employed by the Rev. Martin Luther King and the civil rights activists in the USA in the 1960s. An orchestrated campaign of largely non-violent civil disobedience was undertaken mainly in the South, to win equal civil rights for blacks. The campaign was conducted via boycotts, sit-ins and protest marches which generated a good deal of violence in response from the police. Rev. King was arrested on several occasions. A number of ingenious ways were found to develop the concepts of 'passive resistance' and 'civil disobedience'. Black and white supporters of the Rev. King rode on buses which were supposed to be segregated, went into segregated bars and cinemas and, in one famous incident, held a demonstration march in spite of its having been banned by the authorities.

Riot and Rebellion

It is often the *level* of violence that distinguishes civil disobedience from other more serious protest. Riots are usually the violent but uncoordinated outbursts of frustrated groups in the community.

The political impact of riots is hard to ascertain. No government wishes to be seen to be 'coerced' by the actions of rioters who cause widespread damage and injury. This could be viewed as an invitation to other disgruntled groups to use such tactics against a government. It should also be noted that during riots the response of the state itself can be unpredictable and uncontrolled. Police and soldiers have to make instant judgements and take actions based on those judgements and upon their own emotional, and sometimes fearful, state of mind. A fairly short and sustained period of rioting has been effective in many parts of the world in special circumstances, usually where the regime is already extremely unstable.

Example

The riots in the St Paul's district of Bristol, Tottenham in London, and Toxteth in Liverpool in the early 1980s were due to growing tensions over relations between sections of the local community and the police in those areas.

Example

The year long miners' strike in 1984 provided many instances of violent outbursts at pit gates between police and striking miners. In many cases the miners claimed the police had instigated the violence in response to peaceful picketing. The police claimed that, at times, a campaign of organised violence was carried out against them.

▲ *Mounted police charge miners' pickets at the Orgreave coke works during the miners' strike in 1984–5.*

Example

The fall of the 'Baby Doc' Duvalier regime in Haiti in 1986 occurred as public discontent boiled over into rioting.

A more remarkable episode was the period of unrest and 'Peoples' Power' that followed the 1986 Philippine Presidential elections. It resulted in the overthrow of President Marcos, who it was claimed had rigged the election.

The student riots in France, in May 1968, were seen as a major challenge to President Charles De Gaulle. The riots undermined his political authority and he resigned the next year, after a defeat in a referendum.

In Britain, Northern Ireland has a long history of civil disorder by both Unionists and Republicans in the Province. Some of it has been spontaneous, arising from clashes between protestors and authorities, but other action has been carefully planned and executed. For example, the strikes called by Unionists in opposition to proposed power sharing policies in 1986 were followed by a sustained series of attacks on the Royal Ulster Constabulary (the police force in Northern Ireland). The whole question of maintaining law and order in Northern Ireland has been a continuing problem for British governments since the 1960s. Unionists groups have resisted, often violently, attempts to arrive at an accommodation with the Eire government and the Provisional Irish Republican Army have pursued a terrorist campaign to end British rule in the province.

Terrorism

The threat of terrorism has arisen for many governments across the world. The scope of terrorist activities covers ideologies of both extreme right and extreme left. The bombings of Italian railway stations by the extreme right

Example

In 1974 the Prevention of Terrorism Act allowed for a partial suspension of *habeus corpus* for people held under provisions of the Act. Its introduction followed the bombing of two public houses in Birmingham which led to considerable injury and loss of life. The Act allows those held to be kept in police custody for seven days instead of the customary 24 hours before being brought before a magistrate after being charged.

Several civil liberties groups have argued for its repeal, claiming not only that it is an infringement of civil rights but also ineffective, because few people have been charged with terrorist offences after being held under the provisions of the Act.

Example

An executive of the Siemens electrical group Herr K.H. Beckurts and his driver were killed when a bomb blew up his car in Munich in July 1986. The left wing Red Army Faction claimed responsibility for the terrorist act. This was the thirtieth murder claimed by, or credited to them. Their justification was that Siemens were engaged in defence contracts with the USA for missile development.

or the murder of American servicemen in Germany by left wing organisations have the same objective: the undermining of the stability of the state concerned.

The sophistication of modern weaponry and the ease of air travel have created a universal problem. Terrorist organisations receive support (diplomatic, military and financial) in many countries. In fact, some states are actually committed to the 'export' of terrorism. The cooperation of terrorist organisations by the formation of federations or groups have made their ability to threaten the stability of many countries even more effective. Which organisations can actually be classified as 'terrorist' is difficult to say, because the distinction between 'terrorist' or 'freedom fighter' depends upon who is making the distinction.

The response to terrorism in itself also can cause problems for a government. As we have tried to establish, one of the primary functions of the state is to ensure internal order and protect its citizens from external aggression. In free societies mere physical protection is not enough. The protection of values, broadly called 'civil liberties', is also given a high priority and in facing terrorism it may on occasions be necessary to curtail or modify such liberties in order for the state to respond effectively.

The need for the state to make a positive response can possibly result in over reaction and serious loss of civil liberties. This in itself can be counterproductive, for some terrorist groups hope to evoke a strong reaction so as to be able to portray the state as authoritarian and illiberal. They may also wish to generate such undesirable social conditions that their demands will be met.

Some western European nations require their citizens to carry identity cards at all times (e.g. Spain and West Germany). Would you accept the compulsory carrying of identity cards which the police could ask to see at any time as a fair price to pay in the battle to defeat terrorism? What safeguards would be necessary to stop the state misusing the system?

Tactics of Terror: Some examples	
Provocation of the state	IRA in Northern Ireland
Economic disruption	Bombings in Spanish holiday hotels by ETA in 1986
Individual assassination	Assassination of West German Federal Attorney General in 1978 (Siegfried Buback)
Intimidation by terror	Conservative party conference bombing in 1985; Bombings of Frankfurt airport 1985; Assassination of Israeli athletes at the Munich Olympics in 1976.

Revolution

Widespread terrorism, disorder, civil obedience, rebellion, etc., may all ultimately result in 'revolution'.

The process of revolution will generally involve a degree of violence. The state has a monopoly of coercive power and office holders threatened by a revolt will use the power of the state to resist.

A revolution usually involves more than a mere change of personnel in state offices. The replacement of one group of generals at the head of a military junta (a small governing group) by another group of generals, does not constitute a revolution. When this occurs it may well have little effect on the mass of people or the policies pursued by the 'junta'. This change is often referred to as a ***coup d'état*** or ***putsch***. Coups happen with remarkable regularity in some countries and may be the only real change of government that ever occurs. Some coups are described as 'palace revolutions' and are achieved with a minimum of violence because they involve only a small group of individuals. As the name implies it is confined only to those at the very top of the governing elite and comprises a transfer of the symbols of state from one group to another.

A revolution is far more widespread, involving large numbers of people and often considerable violence. The use of force means that the attitude of the military to any revolt can prove to be critical. Disagreement in the military might intensify the struggle with armed units fighting each other.

A successful outcome for the rebels will be the removal of the political system and it replacement by another. Revolution can take the form of a 'national' struggle where a country attempts to throw off the externally imposed political control of an alien power. Independence movements against colonial rule are examples. The primary objective is the claim of a people to govern themselves, even though the whole of the people may not be involved in the revolutionary struggle. The American Revolution in 1776 took this form as did the Cuban Revolution against US 'colonial' rule in 1958–9.

Another kind of revolution occurs where internal divisions, or class conflicts, within a country result in the overthrow of the political system. The idea of a 'class revolution' presents a picture of a ruling class which deliberately, or through ignorance, is out of touch with changing social forces. The new forces, by failing to be accommodated in the dominant political order, become discontented and disorder results.

The disorder is then met with repressive measures and the resulting pressure that builds up, erupts into violence and the ruling regime is overthrown. The leadership of the revolutionary movement may well be small and will need the mass of the people to counter the power of the state. New political leaders are then able to introduce widespread changes in the established economic and political order.

Examples of this kind of revolutionary activity took place in France in 1789, Russia in 1917 and China in 1947. This is not to say that revolutionary change is always accomplished quickly. It may be the result of years of political agitation and even armed resistance, but the actual period of activity prior to the revolutionary change can be fairly short. Considerable external support for the revolution may also prove critical with the rebels drawing financial and military support from other friendly countries.

Definition

Revolution
The term 'revolution' occurs in many contexts and is employed to describe fundamental and permanent change. We talk of the 'industrial revolution'; the present day 'technological revolution'; China had a 'cultural revolution' in the 1960s etc.

In political terms it is used to denote the overthrow of an existing political system and its replacement by another.

Example

The United States has given support to rebels in Nicaragua and Afghanistan and there has been Communist support for revolutionary struggles in many parts of the world, especially in South East Asia, Vietnam, Cambodia and Laos.

CASE STUDY: ORDER AND DISORDER

Handsworth, Brixton and Tottenham, 1985

During September and October 1985, a number of violent incidents occurred in British cities. The most serious was in the Handsworth district of Birmingham, and the Brixton and Tottenham areas of London. Violent clashes took place between the police and groups of local youths.

Handsworth

In September problems began to grow after a carnival, when a stabbing occurred, and later when a black man was questioned by the police over a motoring offence. Further tension was generated, it was claimed, by police action over alleged drug offences. Violence eventually broke out when firemen were attacked as they attempted to tackle a blaze in a disused bingo hall. Violence intensified as shop windows were broken, shops looted and property burned. Two local Asian residents died when their post office was fire-bombed and further violence occurred following a visit by the Home Secretary, Douglas Hurd, which was terminated when he was confronted by a hostile crowd.

The police inquiry into the disturbances concluded that they had been organised by local drug dealers and drug users who had been threatened by concerted police action in the area. An inquiry sponsored by West Midlands County Council, however, argued that social deprivation in Handsworth and tough policing provided the basis for the outbreak of disorder. A further investigation set up by Birmingham City Council and conducted by a former Labour MP, Julius Silverman, saw racial discrimination and unemployment as the major factors and ruled out an organised plot to ferment violence.

Brixton

Serious violence occurred in Brixton in South London, after a black woman, Mrs Cherry Groce, was shot by the police and partially paralysed when they entered her home searching for her son. Violence flared as the news of the shooting spread through the area. Property was damaged, shops looted, cars burned and the police attacked. A press photographer died of the injuries he received when covering the disturbances. The police claimed that attempts had been made by militants from the West Midlands to stir up trouble, but they had been unsuccessful and the Brixton troubles were a direct response to the police shooting of Mrs Groce.

Tottenham

The most serious outbreak of public disorder and violence of 1985 took place in Tottenham in North London. It followed the death of a black woman, Mrs Cynthia Jarrett, who died in her home of a heart attack as police searched it for stolen property. The next day a demonstration took place outside the local police station to protest at police action, but later in the day the protests turned to violence. Missiles and petrol bombs were thrown, at least 50 cars were set on fire, and property destroyed. The violent confrontations which took place on the Broadwater Housing Estate, between the police and, primarily, black youths, led to police officer Keith Blakelock dying of multiple stab wounds after being attacked by a mob. Another police officer was hit by a bullet and four journalists suffered shotgun wounds. There were strong reactions to the violence with some local black leaders blaming the police for deliberately provoking the situation and harassing local black youths during the previous week. The police blamed left wing activists for instigating and organising the violence. The Metropolitan Police Chief, Sir Kenneth Newman, said that 'anarchy' would not be tolerated and that the use of plastic bullets would be sanctioned in other instances where he felt no other option was available in protecting law and order.

▼ *Police in Railton Road, Brixton.*

Mr Bernie Grant, the black leader of Haringey Council, and prospective Labour Party parliamentary candidate for Tottenham, caused considerable debate by saying that the police only wanted plastic bullets because they had 'got a bloody good hiding' and he refused to condemn the actions of black youths in the violence. He did, however, add in a later statement that such violence was inexcusable.

The government's view as expressed by the Home Secretary Douglas Hurd was that the disturbance had been 'criminal' and that the use of 'CS' riot control gas and plastic bullets by the police would be supported in any future violent disturbances similar to those on the Broadwater estate.

In a debate in the House of Commons in October, the Labour Party called upon the government to set up a judicial inquiry into the disturbances of 1985. However, it was a government amendment to this motion which stressed the importance of maintaining public order and pledging fast effective action in response to violent disorder that was finally approved. The judicial enquiry motion was defeated.

THE DEVELOPMENT OF THE LAW OF RIOT

The first law concerning riot was passed in 1714 and remained on the statute book until it was replaced by the Criminal Law Act in 1967.

The Riot Act required the magistrate to read a proclamation calling upon the rioters in the Queen's name to disperse. This was known as 'reading the Riot Act'. Once the mob had been warned, troops could be called in if necessary to use force of arms to disperse them. They would be directed by the appropriate civil authorities and the degree of force used was to be proportionate to the threat posed. Not that this could be guaranteed.

A significant change in the law relating to public disorder occurred with the 1936 Public Order Act, the provisions of which remained in force until 1987. The Act was passed in response to violent demonstrations that had taken place involving the British Union of Fascists 'black shirts'.

The Act's provisions:

- It became illegal to carry an offensive weapon at a public meeting or procession.
- It became an offence to wear uniforms associated with a political organisation.
- It became an offence to use threatening, abusive and insulting words in a public place.
- Power was given to a chief constable to reroute, or lay down conditions for, a procession or demonstration if he had reasonable grounds for believing serious disorder could result.
- Power was given to a chief constable, with the approval of the local council, to prohibit the holding of all public processions for up to three months.

Even though the government denied that the bill which it introduced late in 1985 was a direct response to the violence of the autumn, the law relating to public order was changed significantly.

The Public Order Act 1986, amongst other things, created new order offences:

- Riot: an offence is committed where 12 or more people use or threaten unlawful violence. The maximum penalty is ten years imprisonment.
- Violent Disorder: committed when three or more people use or threaten violence.
- Affray: committed when a person uses or threatens unlawful violence towards another to the extent that others present would fear for personal safety.
- Threatening Behaviour: committed by the use of abusive, insulting or threatening words or behaviour, likely to lead to violence.
- Disorderly Conduct: committed by conduct of a less serious nature but where it may cause harassment, alarm or distress to others.

The Act has been criticised by civil liberties groups for failing to provide a positive right to demonstrate peacefully. Such a right has never been established in Britain. The government argued that it provided the correct balance between the right to demonstrate and the need for public order. Its critics claim that public order considerations have weighed too heavily with the government. Other criticisms are that the provisions set out in the new offences are too widely drawn especially the definitions of 'affray' and 'disorderly conduct', which give discretion to the police in considering what conduct amounts to an offence.

Questions

1 How would you classify each of the instances of disorder mentioned in the case study in terms of the categories given by the 1986 Act? Is it necessarily the case that all riots develop through every one of the five stages from disorderly conduct to riot?

2 Is it possible to distinguish between legitimate uses of civil disorder and illegitimate ones?

3 Given that a riot is occurring, which is the 'best' response to it? For example, is it 'better' to structure the response fairly exactly to the level of violence, so that the police react with no shields or protection at first and only bring these out as, and when, the rioters become more violent; or is it 'better' to respond with large numbers of well protected police fully backed up with water cannon or rubber bullets right from the start in the hope of extinguishing the riot very quickly?
4 Is justice served by sending rioters to jail for up to ten years? What alternative response to these people might there be?
5 What are the arguments for and against more potent weaponry for the police to deal with outbreaks of public disorder?

EXAMINATION QUESTIONS

1 Is there any evidence that direct action like strikes, demonstrations, or riots can influence policy making? (University of Cambridge, Politics and Government, A-Level, 1984)

2 Evaluate the claim that there is a 'right' to disobey some laws in a democracy. (AEB Government and Politics A-Level, 1986)

3 How important is the problem of public disorder? Are the present laws on public order adequate? (University of London, Government and Political Studies, 1987)

NOW READ ON . . .

P. Norton (ed.) *Law and Order in British Politics* Gower, 1984
An interesting analysis of the problems.

P. Hewitt *The Abuse of Power: Civil Liberties in the United Kingdom* Martin Robertson, 1982
A critical review of police powers on questions of law and order.

S.C. Greer *Military Intervention in Civil Disturbances* Public Law, Winter, 1983
A consideration of the legal problems of military intervention. Written after the 1982 Brixton riots.

P.W. Wilkinson *Terrorism and the Liberal State* New York University Press, 1986
A comprehensive analysis of both the ideologies and practice of terrorism.

2 The State, Nation and Sovereignty

Every State is a community of some kind, and every community is established with a view to some good; for men always act in order to obtain that which they think good. But if all communities aim at some good, the State or political community – which is the highest of all and which embraces the rest – aims at good in a greater degree than any other and at the highest good.

Aristotle: *Politics* (Book 1; Chs 1 & 2).

Basic Principles

The term 'state' is one that is often used these days without too much thought as to what it means. It is probably the most used and least understood word in our political vocabularies:

'state persecution'
'state benefits'
'state secrets'
'for the good of the state' . . .

. . . all these terms are in everyday usage, but what exactly is the **state** and how does it differ from the **government** and the **nation**?

Philosophers have spent many thousands of years pondering this question. Artistotle (whose central view is quoted above) believed that the state was the natural extension of all the other organisations to which human beings belong, such as families, villages, cities, regions, etc. Hegel, on the other hand, believed that it was the ultimate institution in all our lives . . .

. . . The State is the Divine Idea as it exists on earth.

Philosophy of Right.

. . . while those who followed Marx believed that it was merely an evil institution established by one class in order to subjugate the other classes. Lenin proposed that the state would actually disappear ('wither away') once the revolution was complete. There would, in his view, be no need for a state if the need for class domination was removed.

However, if one leaves this view aside, for the moment, and assumes that the **state** is an inevitable phenomenon, then the most important question is: does it have a life, existence or justification of its own separate from the lives of its citizens?

It seems like a silly question to modern, British ears but, if one answers it in the affirmative, it can vitally affect the lives of all who live within the confines of 'the state'.

One can begin to move towards an answer to the question if one examines the definition of a state:

Definition

The State

1 Its rules are public (as opposed to private);
2 Its authority is centralised (even if some is devolved to federal units);
3 It has a monopoly of coercive power;
4 Its geographical boundaries are determinate;
and,
5 It is sovereign.
Some would also add:
6 It is the most important institution in the lives of its citizens and that it has a right to their total devotion (up to and including giving up their lives for it).

Discussing the Arguments

The term 'state' has a particular meaning in political studies but it is often substituted or confused in popular usage with 'government' or 'nation' or 'country'. States will usually have clearly defined territorial boundaries within which some form of government exercises the powers of the state. The state is an association between its members and is entrusted with supreme authority to make and to enforce its rules. To ensure compliance it will possess a monopoly of coercive power and the right to command observance of the laws. The state will normally be seen to have certain duties towards its citizens: at the very least to protect their property and persons and to ensure internal peace and stability. It may also perform other functions such as providing social welfare.

Everyone (with only very special exceptions) is a member of a particular state even though it may be possible to change membership and, in some cases, to hold dual membership. It should not be assumed, however, that the need for the existence of the state is universally accepted. The principal belief of **Anarchism** is that people can and should exist without the need for a state (see page 162).

There is no such thing as the **modern state** – merely an immense variety of different types of states coexisting in today's world. The form that a state takes in order to exercise power differs, but in all cases it is the state which is seen to be sovereign. One form of this sovereignty was identified by Max Weber as the claim to the legitimate use of physical force within a given territory. This leads some political theorists to conclude that the state is *primarily* an instrument of coercion and Marxist analysts, in particular, see the state as a tool of coercion used by the ruling class.

The state's permanence and superiority to all other institutions within its boundaries are what distinguishes it from **government**. States often have **constitutions** within which governments have to operate. Government can, therefore, be seen as the principle agent of the state existing to facilitate the state's objectives. Governments are short term institutions which represent the state but can never replace it. In a domestic system the government can expect opposition from many sources, but opposition to the form of the state is usually seen as little short of treasonable.

States should also be distinguished from other forms of geographical entity which are, superficially, similar. Some countries have territorial boundaries and systems of government but are, nevertheless, not states. Many colonies and protectorates struggled for a long time to win independent *statehood* from their original colonial masters.

Definition

The Government . . .

. . . is temporary in the sense that each one has a finite period of time to govern even if they are non-democratic;

. . . is subservient to the state in almost all cases; (the only case in which this would not apply being one in which the government claims to be *the state, e.g. Louis XIV:* 'L'état c'est moi.')

Example

Rhodesia/Zimbabwe

When the former British colony of Southern Rhodesia declared unilateral independence in 1965 its white minority were not only claiming statehood but were also claiming statehood for only themselves. The majority of the population of that country were to be largely denied political power by a constitution which gave most of the power to the minority.

It took a prolonged period of civil strife for the black majority to gain independent statehood in their own right through an internationally recognised settlement negotiated by the British government.

New states are also created through the break up of old ones or through the creation of new ones. East Pakistan became the independent state of Bangladesh in 1972 when it seceded from Pakistan. Tanganyika and Zanzibar together created the new state of Tanzania in 1964. In the nineteenth century, modern day Italy was created from a collection of minor Italian states.

Mere statehood is also not a guarantee of acceptance by the rest of the world. There is a need for a form of legitimising by the rest of the world community which usually takes place through the process of *Recognition*. In recent times South Africa has created a number of 'independent homelands' for some of its black population which have never been recognised as separate states by the rest of the world. Similarly the Arab states of the Middle East, with the exception of Egypt, do not recognise Israel as a legitimate state. Instead they believe that the 'state' of Palestine is the rightful possessor of the land currently occupied by Israel.

Most countries have a Head of State and, often, the office can be combined with that of Head of Government (e.g. the office of the President of the United States). In Britain, the distinction between state and government is seen very clearly in the separation of the two offices: the monarch being Head of State and the Prime Minister being the Head of Government.

The importance attached to the state also varies. In western Europe it is generally the case that the state is accorded a fairly low priority and status whereas in many other countries it is regarded as the source of all true law and the target of every citizen's duty. For such countries it is often the ultimate demonstration of ones loyalty and devotion to die for the state.

The first five features of our definition of the State constitute what might be called the '**neutral state**'.

The addition of the sixth feature, however, changes the whole nature of the concept into what might be called a '**value state**'.

Even within areas which regard themselves as being neutral states, such as the UK, it is only too easy to find the state being regarded as having its own separate existence. From the 'left', one hears of the 'state' imposing taxes and penal sanctions in order to subjugate its citizens (state Capitalism) while, from the 'right', one hears of the need for a strong state or the need to recreate the days when Britain had an Empire. The State itself is seen as being sufficient justification for all sorts of action. It is given a character and is regarded as being worth protecting. The concept of the state is very rarely understood by those who use it so freely.

The tendency to impart to the state a personality and a separate existence is, to some extent, understandable. In Britain, for example, the *nature* of the state has been established over many centuries and the weight of its own history gives it a character which cannot be neutral.

While no state is ever purely neutral, one can see that there is still an important difference between the **character** of a state and giving the state itself a **personality**.

Definition

Neutral state
One which is seen as purely instrumental or mechanical and which carries out, in a neutral manner, the wishes of those who control the power systems within it.

Definition

Value state
A state which has an existence apart from and superior to that of its individual inhabitants. It is seen as having a life of its own – its own history, its own needs and its own destiny. Human life is usually seen as having a justification purely in terms of furthering the greatness and glory of the State.

Example

Personification of the State
There are many other examples but the following give a taste of this approach:
The Fatherland
Britannia rules the waves
Uncle Sam
Mother Russia
John Bull

Example

The Values of the British State:

1 It has public rules which apply to all its citizens – in theory!
Are there any reasons to believe that some of the rules apply to only one group or class of inhabitants?

2 It has a monopoly of coercive power.

But on whose behalf is that power wielded?

Many would argue that the British state has a set of very clear values which can be described in shorthand as **capitalist**. They would say that British law applies first to those without capital, second to those regarded as social inferiors (due to race, religion, class etc.) and only thirdly to those with money. In private rules this emerges very clearly –one has only to ask whether it is equally possible for those without money and those with money to obtain redress at law. Can the poor *afford* to insist on their rights?

Similarly it could be argued that the coercive power of the state is used primarily against the lower socio-economic groups: that the police enforce laws strictly against those with little money or those who are members of religious or racial minorities, but much less strictly against members of the middle and upper classes.

What evidence is there that this *is* the case? Perhaps more importantly, what *other* aspects are there to the character of the British state?

As Norman Barry (1981) said,

> *. . . the danger of anthropomorphic accounts of the state must be avoided.*

Once the state is given a life of its own, anything is possible and anything can be justified merely by referring to the higher needs and the higher authority of the state: any law can be imposed 'for the good of the state'; any person or group can be proscribed and have their freedom limited; wars can be justified as being for the 'greater glory or enhancement of the state'; and people may be put to death if they stand between the state and whatever have been established as its objectives. If the state is superior then no individual can have any rights except those granted by the state itself. The state decides how you live – and how, and when, you die.

Is there any substantive difference between the use of the term 'the Fatherland' in Hitler's Germany and the use of the term 'the Motherland' in today's Soviet Union?

Types of Neutral State

To the political scientist the neutral state can be subdivided only to the extent that it differs from others with respect to its features (1–5 in the Definition on page 21). It may have more or less of a monopoly of coercive power, or it may be more or less sovereign (it may, for example be a federal state). Most categorisations of neutral states are not, therefore, purely political but are economic (for the purist, the categories are based upon the theories of political-economy).

Several different types can be distinguished, ranging from Communist, through the varieties of Socialist, to those of Liberal states. In effect the distinction is based upon the degree to which the institutions of the state are involved in the control of people's lives. This distinction can be illustrated by a circular dimension which, while it is an academic abstraction, does demonstrate the essential links between different and apparently mutually exclusive ideas of the state:

▼ *The State and Political Philosophies*

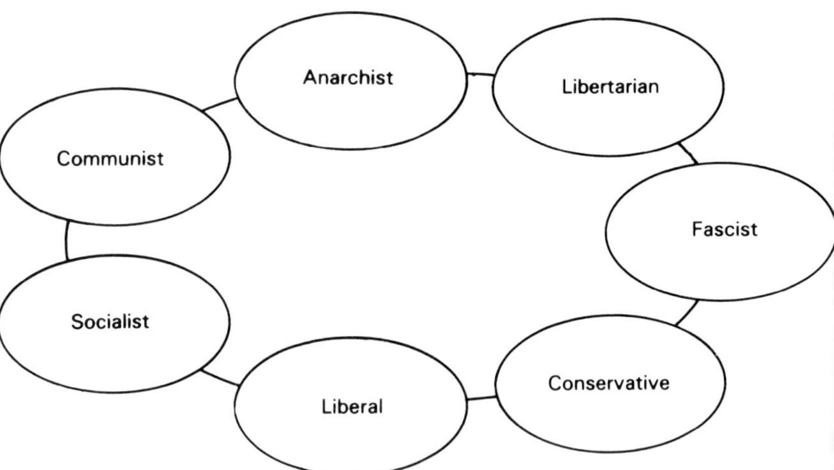

The key to this type of diagram is the extent to which the state involves itself in the lives of its people and in the economy. Anarchists view the state as an irrelevance invented by one dominant section of society in order to subjugate other sections. They would wish to see the state replaced by systems of private rules and regulations.

Definition

Private Rules
Are those in which disputes are settled not by a set of universal laws established to apply to everyone and enforced by a system of uniform courts, but by unique negotiations between individuals under commonly accepted frameworks of rules.

Communists, too, regard the state as a capitalist invention used to exploit the working class. Marx predicted that, under a Communist system the state would 'wither away'. This approach has been modified somewhat by modern followers of Marx. They see a need to take into account a short period after the demise of capitalism during which the system rids itself of all other classes except the working class. This period would be used to accustom the workers to the system of private rules and equal treatment which would replace the old capitalist state. Lenin called this period the 'Dictatorship of the Proletariat'.

The Socialist attitude to the state has been coloured by national variations in response to events and to the writings of theorists.

Most Socialists, as opposed to Communists, regard the state and its institutions as virtually permanent. Some might agree that the state might, ultimately, wither away, but not for a long time to come.

One could argue that many Socialists should stand to the right of the Liberals on the diagram because they regard the role of the state as being central to the protection of specific groups of citizens, and, specifically, to ensuring fairness and economic equality. Socialists see the role of the state as being quite detailed: it should redistribute income through taxation, establish minimum wages, take major industries into public ownership (to ensure that the public as a whole get the benefit of any profits), and, of course, establish rules to ensure that all groups receive fair play (racial minorities, religious groups, women and children, one-parent families, etc.).

Liberals, on the other hand, have traditionally regarded the individual as the most important unit of society and have seen the role of the state as being, firstly, to provide **public goods**, and, secondly, to ensure that individuals are given the optimum opportunity to develop themselves. Usually these objectives have been expressed economically as the need to ensure efficient allocation of resources. Liberals believe that the greatest **utility** can be derived only by ensuring that resources are freely available to those who can use them and that they are not impeded by inefficiencies in distribution.

The state's role is to establish the conditions under which these 'free' markets in resources may exist. It may only become further involved if inefficiencies cannot be eradicated by the workings of the freemarket.

State intervention can be justified, therefore, only if required to take account of 'externalities', 'public goods' and 'public bads'.

Definition

Public Goods, Public Bads and Externalities

A **public good** *is a type of product or service which, once supplied in any quantity, can be utilised by everyone. It is not possible to exclude anyone from receiving the benefits of a public good – and similarly, neither is it possible to exclude oneself from experiencing the effects of a public bad.*

The law, defence and clean air are all examples of public goods. Polluted air or water are, of course, public bads.

Certain types of public good and bad are also **externalities** *– that is, economic factors which are external to a firm's normal accounting processes. For example, a chemical company is usually not required to take into account the pollution of the air which might be caused by its factory, and foundries do not usually have to put a price on the noise pollution they cause. The economic and social costs of these externalities are not being paid by the firm itself but by society at large.*

Consider what types of economic activity: transport (road, rail and air), nuclear power, etc., and what types of externality (both positive and negative) governments should have to take into account and in what way?

Another way of asking the same question is: to what extent should neutral states be responsible for intervening in the economic system to protect or help their citizens? How neutral does this leave them?

To most Liberals, therefore, (and this would include those who we, in Britain, call Conservatives) the object of the political system is to obtain the best possible allocation of resources. Economists call this optimum distribution of resources **pareto optimality** (note that it does *not* mean the *equal* distribution of resources. Pareto optimality exists where resources are so well distributed that no change can be made without making someone worse off.

Alternative Views of the State

(A) Linear View

PRO-STATE ←——→ **ANTI-STATE**

Nazi — Stalinist — Labour Centralist — One-Nation Conservative — New Right Conservative — Communist — Anarchist

(B) Linear with Left/Right Dimension

PRO-STATE ←——→ **ANTI-STATE**

Left: Stalinist — Centralist Labour — Communist — Anarchist

Right: Nazi — Fascist — One-Nation Conservative — New Right Conservative — Libertarian

(C) Two-Dimensional

Pro-state (↑) / **Anti-state** (↓); **Left** ← → **Right**

Communist (Stalinist)
Socialist
Labour (1950's)
Conservative (One-Nation)
Nazi
Fascist
Labour (1980's)
Liberal
Social Democrat
Communist (Trotskyist) (Maoist)
Conservative (New-Right)
Anarchist
Libertarian

The Public Choice School of Liberals

Whereas the above refers to traditional Liberal thought, there is a more modern group of Liberals who believe that the intervention of the state cannot be justified even to smooth out imperfections in the free market. This group regard *all* factors as being capable of being ironed out eventually through private or public rules without the need for the direct intervention of the state.

A company which pollutes a river was not, in the past, normally charged for cleaning it up. Traditional Liberal thought requires that the state intervene by taxing the company and by using the revenue to clean up the river. 'Property rights' theorists, on the other hand, would rely entirely upon the system of public and private law. These would allow individuals and groups to sue the company for damages and, thereby, place the onus upon the company to protect itself from the possibility of such suits by not polluting the river in the first place. (In the event that pollution does occur this system still places the burden on the company to clean up the river.)

The traditional Liberal approach to the state is, therefore, to see it as having a very minor role. The free market should be allowed to operate without interference. However, it has been recognised that the state *must*

Definition

Statism
. . . . The view that the state has a duty to intervene and to manage the economy with a particular set of social and economic objectives in mind. The state is seen in a paternal way and its role is to 'look after' its citizens' welfare. Statist views are generally associated with socialist thinking, although the brand of Conservatism developed by Harold Macmillan known as 'One Nation Toryism' is also statist.

Definition

Property rights
The 'property rights' or 'public choice' school of thought regards all inefficiencies in the economic system as being capable of being solved by negotiation and the process of law. Various types of law can be used to arrive at solutions without the need for taxation or subsidies to even-out the problems caused by externalities.

intervene to smooth out inefficiencies in the system. The property rights or public choice approach, by contrast sees the state as a passive institution which merely establishes the legal framework in which individuals can take action against others *if they so choose.*

The Nation

It is important to distinguish between the two concepts : **state** and **nation**. A state is a geographical organisation but it might comprise many nations – a nation, on the other hand, is a human group sharing common characteristics of culture, language, historical experience, customs, etc.

The boundaries of some states coincide with those of some nations but, more often than not, they do not. The United Kingdom is supposed to contain more than one single nation and the larger countries of the USA and the USSR both contain a large number of individual nationalities. From another point of view it is also true that for many countries in Africa, whose boundaries were drawn by the ex-colonial powers, the territorial limits took no account of deep divisions between tribal and ethnic groups. In Nigeria, for example, a bitter civil war was fought as a result. Similar problems, although for different reasons, can be seen in Europe with the Basques and even in Britain with the demands for nationhood from both Scotland and Wales.

Definition

Nation

. . . a group of people who share a common culture, language, customs and historical experience.

There need be no strong genetic link between the members of a nation but there is a distinct unwillingness to classify as a nation any group of people who do not have a significant degree of identity in common.

Consider the USA or the USSR as a nation and compare with the French or the Dutch.

The Nation and Nationalism

Rule Britannia, Britannia rules the waves,
Britons never, never, never shall be slaves.

These well known words from one of our most famous 'national' anthems illustrate both the strength and the fundamental ambivalence of the concept of Nationalism. They also happen to derive from the period when most historians agree that the concept of the Nation-State developed – the end of the eighteenth century and the beginning of the nineteenth.

Before that time the idea of a nation was usually limited to Biblical references. People owed allegiance to a person or to a religion, not to their 'nation'. Wars before about 1790 were fought between armies which, more often than not, had people from the same 'nations' fighting on opposite sides. English, Scots, Irish, French, 'Italian' and 'German' troops could be found on both sides of the same seventeenth- and eighteenth-century wars. Their loyalty was given to a person – usually a monarch – and to a religion. In 1688 it was not thought terribly strange for William of Orange, a 'Dutchman', to be asked to be King of England. In the early eighteenth century Britain began a line of 'German' kings and queens which still provides the basis for our monarchy. In those days it was considered far more important that the monarch be of the correct religion than that they be of the correct 'nation'.

The Origin of Nationalism

There is, of course, much controversy about the origin of the difficult concept of nationalism, but it seems likely that it arose at least partly as a result of the development of secular republics late in the eighteenth century (e.g. the

USA). The absence of a God-given monarch ruling by 'Divine Right' meant that the inhabitants of specific geographical areas had to acquire other reasons for being joined together – especially where they consisted of members of many, different religions. They did this, usually, by establishing a series of carefully argued reasons why they had come together in the first place and creating a set of rules (a **constitution**) by which they might be governed.

Example

The Rise of the Nation State

Nations can arise in many different ways. Amongst these are the following:

1 They can be created for specific, political reasons: e.g. Belgium, and East Germany.
2 They can be created especially to replace a set of older, similar states – usually on the basis of what is argued to be a common culture, heritage or language (e.g., Germany and Italy during the nineteenth century).
3 They can develop out of older monarchies or colonial possessions; again, generally on the basis of common heritage and language (e.g., France, the UK, Spain, and most of the old Imperial possessions of Britain, France, Holland, etc.).

Note that, where nation states arise out of older monarchies or colonial possessions, the 'glue' which bound them together as states under the old system is sometimes insufficient under the new. Many of the older colonies of Africa have suffered great stress from within because of the presence of two or more groups who perceive themselves as 'nations' within the old colony. The best examples of this were, perhaps, India and Pakistan in 1948, the nineteenth century 'nation-state' of Austria-Hungary, and French South-East Asia after 1945.

A nation-state is different from a nation in that, in the former, the borders of the nation and those of the state are co-terminous. There are, however, plenty of nations without states and states comprising either many nations or parts of many nations. One would, for example, find it difficult to speak of the American 'nation'; and the Soviet Union is made up of many republics not a few of which perceive themselves as separate nations (Russians, Ukrainians, Georgians, etc.). Even the UK could be seen as a collection of 'nations': the Welsh, Northern Irish, Scots and English.* In Britain, French (Norman) kings were replaced by Welsh (Tudor) monarchs who were, in their turn, followed by Scottish (Stuart) kings. When the Stuarts were eventually replaced it was by a Dutch king (with his English wife) who were themselves supplanted by a 'German' line of kings and queens!

Definition

Nationalism

The concept that one owes one's allegiance to a particular set of people who are regarded as a **nation**. *They might be members of a specific state or they might be scattered around various states but are still regarded as a single nation. The best current example of the latter are the modern-day Palestinians.*

Other 'nations' are regarded as 'external' to one's fellow countrymen regardless of historical, genetic or even linguistic ties.

A review of several good books on political history will demonstrate that there are many states which claim sovereignty over peoples which regard themselves as separate nations. Nationalism occurs in the following areas and it is an instructive exercise to ask oneself why:

South Tyrol — *Cyprus*
Gibraltar — *Falkland Islands*
Channel Isles — *Quebec*
Mellila and Ceuta in North Africa — *Alsace-Lorraine*

* The links between them are, of course, very close, as is indicated by the cosmopolitan mixture of monarchs.

Sovereignty

If the state and nation were difficult concepts to come to terms with then **sovereignty** is, perhaps, even worse. As we have seen, it appears to be fairly straightforward on the surface: it means complete and absolute power and authority to govern within a specific geographic area. The concept is so taken for granted that one hears of 'sovereign states' and 'Parliamentary sovereignty' almost in the same sentence. But what, exactly, do these terms mean?

How far is any state really sovereign? At one time there was no doubt that most states had complete power over what went on within their boundaries. Most monarchs were absolute and could order any and every aspect of the lives of their subjects and the destiny of their 'states'.

> *Definition*
>
> ***Sovereignty***
> *The concept developed with that of the nation state; its basic principles being that there are no limits on the state's powers within its boundaries and the state does not have to justify itself to any outside institution.*
>
> *This definition also refutes the claims of other associations within the state (such as the church) to share authority; for sovereignty cannot be divided.*

Today, however, even the most powerful countries can be constrained in their ability to order events within their borders. International bodies such as the United Nations have extended their influence over the internal affairs of most countries in such areas as human rights, education, aid and health. Similarly, many countries are members of collective security organisations such as NATO or the Warsaw Pact. These seek to coordinate their members' defence and thereby to reduce the freedom of action of individual states. More recently have come attempts to establish comprehensive economic cooperation (e.g. the European Community) which requires member countries to submit to collective decisions. Very few countries in today's world could claim to be truly sovereign; even fewer would be seen to actually possess it.

In Britain, the debate on sovereignty is usually conducted with reference to the centre of sovereignty and this is usually said to be **Parliament.**

Parliamentary sovereignty is customarily seen to be unlimited in that there is no rule placing restrictions on Parliament's actions. Parliament cannot therefore, by definition, pass an 'unconstitutional' act. The courts may interpret Acts but they are unable to place limits on legislation or to judge the 'constitutionality' of legislation. Under the current system, and by virtue of the fact that the House of Lords is seen as having less legitimacy because of its unelected nature, the basis for sovereignty lies, essentially, with the House of Commons.

> *Definition*
>
> ***Parliamentary sovereignty***
> *The idea that Parliament has absolute and ultimate power within the British system of government. To be completely accurate one must qualify the concept by saying that each Parliament is sovereign – for no Parliament may bind its successor.*

In other countries sovereignty is established in a written constitution and is protected by the courts.

Whatever the location of sovereignty, however, it is difficult, today, to accept that any nation is truly sovereign. International treaties and membership of supra-national organisations limit national sovereignty. When Britain signed the Treaty of Rome and joined the European Community it accepted that, for many areas, it would no longer have sovereign choice.

> **Example**
>
> ### Views of the State
>
> **Organic**
>
> Certain theorists, including Aristotle (384–322 BC), see the state as being superior to the people who live within it. Although Aristotle and many who followed him believed that the state's role was to make people 'good' – to improve them and to increase the public good – many later organic theorists developed the theory further.
>
> Hegel, for example, proposed in 1808 that the state was everything: it was the embodiment of the collection of people who lived within it and it carried their aspirations and their destiny. The fascist theorists took Hegel's view even further and gave the state a personality and a spirit:
>
> *The State is not only the present, it is also the past and – above all – the future.*
> Mussolini, 1936
>
> Mussolini invented Fascism and came very close to giving Italy a separate, mythical existence. He believed that he would recreate, in modern times, the greatness of the Roman Empire.
>
> Nazism, as developed by Hitler, took Fascism all the way into the final aspects of the organic state by endowing Germany with a complete spiritual character and a detailed mythology of its creation, growth and its role in a future world. Germans owed everything to their country and would receive glory and greatness in return for their devotion and sacrifice.

Example

Views of the State

Mechanistic

Other theorists regard the state as being created by people for specific purposes rather than people being there for the good of the state. Mechanistic theories see the state, by definition, as being subservient to its inhabitants.

Both Thomas Hobbes (1588–1679) and John Locke (1632–1704) were mechanistic theorists who originated the **Contract** school. Hobbes felt that people enter into society in order to obtain protection from internal or external violence, whereas Locke regarded the state as the result of a contract in which each individual agrees to undertake to observe the rules in return not only for security but also for prosperity, education and welfare. While the contract lasts, the individual must obey the state, but, Locke argues, everyone retains the right to resist the state if it becomes oppressive.

A sub-section of the mechanistic school are those who believe that the state was established not by everyone agreeing to some sort of unwritten contract, but by a single group or class. The **Coercive State** is usually seen as a class state set up by the upper class in order to subjugate the lower classes. Both Marxists and Anarchists see the state in this way but differ about how it should be replaced.

►►►►►►►►►►►►►►► CASE STUDY
A: Devolution of Government to Wales and Scotland

1 In the early 1970s the Scottish and Welsh 'nationalist' parties:
- SNP – Scottish Nationalist Party
- PC – Plaid Cymru ('Free Wales', the Welsh Independence Party)

began to succeed in winning seats in Parliament where they had been relatively unsuccessful over the previous decades:

Table 2.1 Nationalist Performance at General Elections 1970–1983

General Election	SNP		PC	
	% of Scots vote	Seats won	% of Welsh vote	Seats won
1970	11.4	1	11.5	0
1974 (Feb)	21.9	7	10.7	2
1974 (Oct)	30.0	11	10.0	3
1979	17.3	2	8.1	2
1983	11.8	2	7.8	2

Source: Pye and Collier *The Organisation in its Environment* Collins 1984

2 The two nationalist parties differed in their aims but at least part of both wanted control of affairs in each region passed over from Westminster to the respective 'national' parliaments (one in Cardiff and the other in Edinburgh).

3 The justification for these claims was centred on the contention that the Scottish and Welsh peoples were 'nations' in their own right and, therefore, had a right to decide their own affairs. The 'proof' of nationality lay in several factors:

a Both parties claimed that their countries had been independent for many years before coming under the domination of the English.

b They pointed to a large amount of common culture and a distinct heritage within each of their two 'nations'.

c Both argued that their countries had their own distinct histories.

d They pointed out that both countries had now, or had in the past, their own languages distinct from the Anglo-French spoken by the English. Each party could show a small number of Gaelic and Welsh speakers respectively in their 'countries'.

4 Much of the pressure for Scots independence came from those who argued that there was now a strong case for Scotland being able to manage its own affairs due to the revenue which could be earned from the new discoveries of oil in what they claimed were 'Scottish' waters.

5 That there was much popular support for the 'nationalist' cause – particularly in Scotland – is indisputable, but part of the success of the two parties lay in the failure of the two major parties of the time (Labour and Conservative) during the period in question (approximately 1971 to 1978). The Conservatives lost votes due to their apparent inability to control the unions in 1973–4; and the Labour Party was perceived by many to have shifted to the left and to have become, essentially, an English party.

6 As can be seen from Table 1.1, support for the two parties peaked during the October 1974 election. This peak coincided with a weak Labour Government first under Harold Wilson and then under James Callaghan. By 1976 that government was in a minority and required all the votes in Parliament which it could muster in order to remain in power. Consequently, that Labour government made agreements with the Liberal Party (the Lib-Lab Pact) and with the nationalist parties. The Liberals agreed to support the government for many reasons but the most important was the offer of a free-vote on proportional representation. The nationalist parties agreed in return for Acts of Devolution and the referendums which those acts entailed.

7 The issue was settled (at least for the time being) by the devolution referendums held in Scotland and Wales in 1979. In both regions the issue of devolution was defeated: in Wales by a large absolute majority and in Scotland by a weighted defeat.

Questions

1 To what extent, if any, were the SNP and PC justified in seeing their respective countries as separate 'nations'?

2 If devolved power had been won by the two countries, would they have been 'sovereign'? What limitations on their sovereignty would there have been?

3 What is the difference between the aspirations of the Scots and Welsh nationalists and those of other British regionalist parties such as Mebyon Kernow (Cornish Nationalists) and the Wessex Regionalist Party? You should note, also, that the Liberal Party always strongly supported the idea of devolved government to all British regions.

4 On the basis of this information how would you distinguish between 'nationalist' and 'regionalist'?

▸▸▸▸▸▸▸▸▸▸▸▸▸▸▸▸ CASE STUDY

B: Northern Ireland

Ever since 1969 the complex problem of Northern Ireland has been continually in the limelight. Placed in perspective, however, the last twenty years of troubles are merely a continuation of a bitter and bloody history which can be traced back to medieval times. At times the 'problem' has appeared to go away, while, at others, it has burst into violent life. Elizabeth I, Cromwell, and William of Orange all had their own problems with Ireland. In more modern times the 'Irish Problem' bedevilled Prime Ministers throughout the nineteenth and early twentieth centuries: Pitt, Peel, Gladstone, Salisbury and Lloyd George were particularly troubled.

Resistance to rule from Britain has been a constant factor throughout virtually a thousand years of Irish history. In 1798 the Irish Rebellion (by Protestants trying to seize Dublin) was mercilessly crushed by William Pitt: as was the 1916 Easter Rising (by Catholics trying to seize Dublin). In the midst of frequent riots throughout the nineteenth century there occurred acts of specific violence: against farmers by 'Moonlighters' and against diplomats. In 1882 a gang called the 'Invincibles' attacked Lord Cavendish and Thomas Burke in Phoenix Park, Dublin and stabbed them to death.

Following the First World War the Republican Movement led by Sinn Fein increased the level of violence against British troops. At the peak of this round of 'troubles' there were over 60,000 British troops in Ireland together with the notorious auxiliary police force known as the 'Black and Tans'.

Under the Irish Treaty of 1921, Southern Ireland was given Dominion status and British troops and police were withdrawn. The violence in the south did not end, however, as different groups began to fight each other over the terms of the Irish Treaty. Supporters of the treaty fought and eventually defeated those who wanted to break away from Britain altogether (Republicans led by Eamon de Valera). The violence in the south continued right up to 1932 when De Valera was elected President and Southern Ireland became an independent republic. Under the terms of the Treaty six counties in the north were to be left under the British Crown. In those 'Six Counties' lived the vast majority of the Protestants and they wished to remain 'British'.

In the north (the 'six counties' of Ulster) the violence erupted once more in the late 1960s as the Catholic minority grew frustrated at the limitations on their civil rights. The Irish Republican Army (IRA) had never given up the aim of eventually reuniting the north with the south and the upsurge of Catholic frustration presented them with a heaven-sent opportunity to recruit people to their own particular philosophy. They believed that (just as had happened in the south) the British government would never change the situation of its own volition or in response to civil protest. The IRA and its offshoot, the Provisional IRA argued that only violence could remove Britain from the north. The majority of the population of the north are, however, Protestant and wish to remain part of the United Kingdom. Consequently the British government was forced, as the violence increased to re-introduce troops to the province.

Since 1971, as the table below shows, the numbers of police and troops in Northern Ireland has increased tremendously.

Table 2.2 The Security Forces in Northern Ireland

Year	RUC	UDR	Army
1969	3,000	–	–
1971	5,400	4,100	7,600
1976	10,000	7,700	14,400
1981	12,200	7,400	11,200
1986	12,700	6,400	11,000

Note: British Army presence peaked at 17,000 in 1973.
RUC : Royal Ulster Constabulary
UDR : Ulster Defence Regiment (not to be confused with the para-military, unofficial, UDF and UDA (see below)

Source: *The Economist* – 12 April 1986; p28

While the peace-keeping forces have been enlarged, the politicians have tried two major solutions to the problem (the fact that only two have been tried in twenty years gives one some idea of the difficulty involved in establishing these 'solutions'):

1973 (Dec): The Sunningdale Agreement, between all parties, sought to introduce Protestant/Catholic power-sharing in a system of local, devolved government. Abandoned after a loyalist general strike in early 1974.

1985 (Dec): The Anglo-Irish Agreement, between the British and the Irish governments, sought to formalise cooperation between the two governments. An attempt was made to force the British government to abandon the agreement by the use of a general strike in March 1986. The strike failed in its primary aim but initiated a new form of violence not seen in Ulster to that date: by Loyalists against the predominantly Protestant RUC.

In addition, the Government has attempted to reach lasting agreements with all parties, north and south of the border, and has also felt it necessary to introduce one specific piece of legislation:

The Prevention of Terrorism Act, 1974. This Act allows thc police anywhere within the UK to hold a suspect without charge and without access to a legal representative for up to seven days.

Table 2.3 The Party and Paramilitary 'Line up' in Northern Ireland

Republican	Non-sectarian	Loyalist
Parties		
Sinn Fein	Social Democratic and Labour Party	Official Unionist Democratic Unionist
Paramilitary		
Provisional IRA	--	Ulster Volunteer Force Ulster Defence Association
Irish National Liberation Army INLA *	--	--

* INLA went through a period of vicious internal feuding in 1986–7 during which a large number of its gunmen were killed. The organisation split and is now thought to operate in two groups: the larger group keeping the original title, while a breakaway group now operates under the title of 'The Irish People's Liberation Army' (IPLA).

Questions

1 One part of the definition of a state is that it has the monopoly of the use of coercive force. Another aspect is that authority should be centralised.
How does the existence of secretive paramilitary groups like the Provisionals and the UVF, and the distribution of authority that these groups imply, therefore, affect the statehood of the United Kingdom?

2 The IRA seeks to remove Northern Ireland from the UK and combine it with Eire into a united Ireland. Given the fact that many Provisionals are citizens of the United Kingdom, does this not constitute a breach of the duty of a citizen to uphold and support the state to which they belong?

3 To what extent, if any, is a state justified in using violence to protect itself against its own citizens?

4 How tolerant should we be towards attempts to pursue group objectives through the use of violence?

5 To what extent is any state justified in instituting laws which, like the Prevention of Terrorism Act of 1974, limit the rights of its citizens in ways which contravene some of the oldest concepts of civil rights such as *Habeas Corpus*?

Note: Article 9; Universal Declaration of Human Rights: *No one shall be subjected to arbitrary arrest, detention, or exile.*
Article 5(2); European Convention on Human Rights: *Everyone who is arrested shall be informed promptly, in a language which he understands, of the reasons for his arrest and of any charge against him.*

▶▶▶▶▶▶▶▶▶▶▶▶▶▶▶ NOW READ ON . . .

Aristotle *The Politics*
An early 'handbook' for the practical politician. Aristotle studied at Plato's Academy for almost twenty years.

Plato *The Republic*
Born in Athens over 2,400 years ago, Plato's writing remains an essential and thoroughly 'modern' part of our political thinking. He was heavily influenced by Socrates. *The Republic* examines the nature of political organisations in general.

Jean Jacques Rousseau *The Social Contract*
The foundation of much in modern political ideologies. Rousseau abandoned the logic of the Enlightenment and gave the world a more emotive view of itself. Of his young life he wrote, '. . . I understood nothing . . . I felt everything'.

Benn, S.I. and Peters R.S. *Social Principles and the Democratic State* Unwin, 1966
Still one of the best analyses of the foundations of the modern 'state'.

Patrick Dunleavy and Brendan O'Leary *Theories of the State* Macmillan, 1986
A thorough examination of the modern 'liberal-democratic' state.

3 Power, Authority and Legitimacy

▶▶▶▶▶▶▶▶▶▶▶▶▶▶▶ BASIC PRINCIPLES

Power tends to corrupt and absolute power corrupts absolutely.
Lord Acton, Historian and MP (1834–1902)

Every Communist must grasp the truth that political power grows out of the barrel of a gun.
Mao Tse Tung, Chinese Communist Party Leader (1893–1976)

The political concepts of power, authority and legitimacy are central to an understanding of political activity and political systems, but it is often very difficult to distinguish between them. Authority is often only established because there is sufficient power to back up decisions, but the authority that is claimed to justify the exercise of power may not always be legitimate. It may all seem rather confusing!

Power in its simplest form is the ability to get someone to do something that they may not do voluntarily. The exercise of power will usually therefore require some form of sanction to ensure compliance, or it may be some form of inducement, or a combination of both.

Example

After General Pinochet seized power in Chile in 1973 his political regime was sustained by the continued support of the armed forces. The views of the Chilean people were not sought until 1988 when a referendum was held to decide whether he should be allowed to continue as President. Pinochet's request to stay in power was rejected in the referendum and demands were made for his immediate resignation. Whether the outcome of the referendum will be respected has been questioned because under the terms of the Chilean constitution, written by Pinochet himself, he is able to continue in office for two further years.

The quote from Mao Tse Tung, above, is a clear indication of one particular form of political power. Many political systems have been created as a result of the exercise of naked force and particularly through the intervention of military forces in political problems. Similarly many of these systems have survived through the effective and sometimes brutal use of physical violence to suppress opposition. The role of the military will often prove to be critical in this respect.

Most political systems, however, are not usually based solely upon the exercise of power in whatever form. It is much easier to run a political system if those who are subject to its decisions readily accept them and do not have to be coerced into compliance.

Most politicians, or political leaders, like to argue that they have **authority** to exercise power. The authority might, in effect, come from the barrel of a gun, but the justification for this will usually be based upon some other claim other than the ability to pull the trigger.

Authority may be based upon law, convention, tradition, social status, the personal qualities of the political leader, religious belief, hereditary principles, the powers attached to formal office, etc.

Whether such claims to authority are legitimate, or not, is another question. A dictator who has seized power through force of arms may claim to have done so in the 'name of the people', for example, but what is important is whether the people, subsequently, are willing to accept his political rule.

Authority is often associated with law but just acting in accordance with the law may not be enough. This is particularly so if the political leader has imprisoned all the judges and legislators from the previous political regime, and then rewritten the law for himself. Legal authority is therefore not always a sufficient justification for exercising power.

Legitimacy may be conferred by a variety of means, but will usually involve some form of popular endorsement of a political regime's actions. The most important indicator of legitimacy for most western liberal democracies is the holding of free and open elections (see Chapter 9).

In liberal democracies we feel that the periodic holding of elections is the best way to discover whether the people still approve of the government in power. Without such popular democratic devices as competition for office between various candidates, we feel the views of the people cannot be assessed accurately and legitimacy cannot be conferred upon the authority that is claimed for the exercise of power.

This does not necessarily mean that other forms of authority are not legitimate. As we have already seen it can be based upon many other factors, and the actions of political leaders may readily reflect the wishes of those affected by them.

DISCUSSING THE ARGUMENTS

Power

Politics is about power. It is the major concept in the study of politics and most political questions relate to:

- its distribution
- its management
- the legitimacy of exercising it
- the channels through which it is exercised
- the people who control or do not control it
- what is achieved with it.

As we have seen, power in its simplest form is the ability to get others to do what they otherwise would not do. Obedience may be achieved by positive or negative means, by the use of some form of inducement or some form of compulsion. The positive inducements could come in the form of special status, privilege, employment, food, money, etc. Many dictators, for example, are only able to maintain their position because they ensure special privileges for the armed forces. The negative inducements may be the threat of physical violence, imprisonment, or even death. Once again many military dictatorships have used violence as a very effective weapon. In the early 1980s the military ruling group that led Argentina were ruthless in their use of organised violence as a weapon of state power. Many hundreds of people 'disappeared', were imprisoned, and in many cases, tortured. The aim of such tactics is to generate a 'climate' of fear which will discourage opposition.

Sometimes positive and negative inducements will be used in combination with rewards for certain forms of behaviour, and punishment for others. The greater the range of positive or negative inducements available to those exercising power, then the greater the potential power. And all this may be backed up with the widespread, and often very effective, use of propaganda which can portray those who do not conform as 'enemies of the state', who, as a threat, must be dealt with 'firmly'.

Those who enjoy power are usually, although not exclusively, office holders and people with special resources. This provides the power. In most modern political systems the state will have set up particular channels for the implementation of decisions and any power that is exercised outside these channels will be frowned upon or even suppressed. So the ability to exercise power will generally be centred in established political offices and not given to office holders as individuals.

The powers and responsibilities of a British prime minister attach to the office itself and to individuals only for so long as they hold that office. This

Example

The former Conservative prime minister, Edward Heath, who held the office from 1970–4, has at times been a stern critic of Mrs Thatcher. His views are always widely reported and often, when critical, are seen as damaging to the Conservative government. At the 1988 Conservative Party Annual Conference, his speech on foreign policy was critical of government attitudes towards the European Community and he was urged not to make it as this would undermine the party's image. Mr Heath ignored these requests and his criticisms were widely reported.

is not to say, however, that former office holders do not continue to enjoy a considerable amount of **influence**.

The formal power of the office holder is not the only kind of power which may exist. If a group has sufficient resources it may become powerful enough to rival government. In the case of those operating outside the established channels the exercise of power is often determined by economic resources.

Political power is seen in the common phrase 'money is power'. Economic power is wielded not only by governments but by industry and by certain pressure groups. So far political power has appeared to be based primarily on force but economic power is often just as effective – if not more so.

Consider two companies which wish to prevent a new motorway being built through their grounds. One is a large multi-million pound firm; the other is a small company just starting out in business. The final result could never be certain, of course, but which company would be more likely to have the resources to advertise its case, to send letters to MPs, to arrange conducted tours for legislators, etc. and, therefore, would be more likely to get its own way?

One could replace the companies in this example with trade unions and the argument would remain the same; resources, in terms of money, people, etc., may not guarantee that political objectives are achieved, but they have a significant effect. (See Chapter 4.) It should be noted that these same resources also represent a type of negative power as well.

If some or all of the above types of power were concentrated into the hands of a few people then there would exist a 'sectional power base'. Some writers have identified this as an elite power: that is, political, economic, and bureaucratic power concentrated in the hands of an identifiable group of people.*

The British government has 'power' in that it can get things done. In England, Scotland and Wales, on the whole, the government has merely to order something to get it done. This is 'political' power: no force is needed or even threatened. One could argue that all political power is backed up with physical power (the implicit threat of police or armed force) but this is not the whole story.

If force was sufficient to gain 'political' power then groups like the IRA in Northern Ireland and ETA in Spain would be able to achieve their aims merely by ordering them. The fact that ETA cannot achieve an independent Basque nation and that the IRA cannot integrate Northern Ireland into Eire simply by ordering that it be done means that something else is required. 'Political' power may or may not rest ultimately on force but its every use relies on people regarding it as authorised and possibly, legitimate.

Example

In 1985, the US government accused the massive company, General Dyamics, of 'overcharging' on its work for the government. The administration said that GD had taken in excess of $100m over and above what was required by its defence contracts and asked the company to repay the money. General Dynamics denied that they had done anything wrong and said that all monies paid to them by the government had been clearly stated in the contracts. In April 1985, however, GD handed over a cheque for $120m to the US Treasury. The company did not regard itself as being at fault and the US government had not threatened GD in any way to regain the money or to withdraw all future defence contracts. In the event, of course, open threats were not necessary. The fact that the US government had the *potential* to withdraw billions of dollars worth of contracts was enough to ensure that GD had accepted the government's terms and handed back the money.

Consider two situations:

1. You are driving into Manchester when your car is stopped by an armed man who claims to be a member of the 'Manchester Liberation Army'. He says there is going to be a demonstration and tells you to turn your car around and to return the way you have come. You do so!
2. You are driving into Manchester and your car is stopped by an unarmed uniformed police officer. He explains that there is going to be a demonstration and orders you to turn your car around and to return the way you have come. You comply.

The end result is the same in both situations but why you have turned around in each case is different. In the first case you did so out of fear. You knew that the gunman had no authority and probably no legitimate reason for being there. He however had a gun which gave him power and consequently you did as you were told. In the second case you obeyed because the

*C Wright Mill's *The Power Elite* and W.L. Guttsman's *The British Political Elite* examine this aspect of power in the USA and UK respectively.

Example

Political power and physical power may well be linked but they are not the same thing. During the Vietnam war in the late 1960s and early 1970s the USA used tremendous physical force against the North Vietnamese and their allies in the South. At no time, however, did they recognise US political power and it was the absence of that political power which was eventually responsible for the defeat of the US.

policeman had the right to tell you to return. You may not have liked the order but you realised he had the authority and the power to make you obey. Note that although the policeman has immensly more potential power than a single gunman you would almost certainly not have obeyed him out of direct fear.

The government's power may be ultimately based on its control of the police and armed forces but it rarely has to rely on the exercise of crude force. As we shall see political power can be based on other factors, one of which may be an extension of charismatic authority. A leader such as Winston Churchill was often able to get people to do what he wanted even when he had no legal authority and where he could not threaten them with physical violence. His 'power' derived from his force of personality and from the special conditions of war. This is a clear example of 'authority' of a charismatic nature being transmuted into real political power.

Information as Power

Knowledge and communications are also sources of political power although they are often overlooked. The British government has a great deal of knowledge and significant control of what information is released or communicated and when. One should never underestimate the power inherent in the ability to retain or release information. It need not be positive power (in the sense of getting a specific thing done) but could be a 'negative' power (stopping something from happening).

Example

Consider what might have happened if the Republican President of the USA Richard Nixon had been successful in concealing his knowledge of a burglary at the Watergate building in Washington DC in June 1972. The Watergate was the headquarters of the Democratic Party's National Committee and 1972 was a presidential election year. The burglars, who attempted to install electronic surveillance equipment, were found to have close links with President Nixon's administration and he was forced to resign in August 1974. Had Richard Nixon, being at the centre of American government, been able to cover up his connections with the Watergate affair he would have been able to continue as President until 1976. This it can be argued could have had immense significance for the conduct of US foreign policy over the whole of the 1970s.

The measurement of political power is a very difficult task. The frequent use of sanctions, especially violence, by those holding power may not indicate the scope of their political power but the limitations of it. It may demonstrate the weakening of power in the face of growing opposition to it by rival forces. Few political systems are maintained solely by the exercise of power, in the form of force or coercion alone, for long periods. Political office holders, even if they have gained power through the use of force, for example, by a military coup, will usually attempt to give themselves legitimacy by some means or other. This now leads us to the concept of authority.

Authority

Authority is usually felt to be 'the right to do something'. But on what basis can those who exercise power claim to have the authority? One answer to this question can be seen in the work of the German sociologist Max Weber (1864–1920) who identified three ideal types of authority:

1. Traditional
2. Legal-rational
3. Charismatic.

Traditional Authority

This arises from the social status which is enjoyed by the person who is exercising power. A feudal baron or monarch, for example, had power which

Example

The authority of the religious leaders, the Mullahs, who head the political system in Iran is based upon their traditional social status and through their implementation of fundamental Islamic law.

stemmed from a well established social institution. In groups such as a tribe an ethnic or religious sect, the power exercised by the leaders is not based solely upon their personal abilities. It reflects their position in the social structure. This type of authority has suffered a gradual decline although it has not disappeared completely. Few modern political leaders will claim to owe all their authority to tradition, although the social status of political leaders may have some influence over those they lead. This holds true for some conservative political parties but less for socialist parties and it is most notably absent in Communist states.

Legal-Rational Authority

This is the most common form of authority. Unlike traditional authority, leadership is based upon the position held by the individual in a particular institution. Authority comes from the office and is not vested personally in the individual or because of social status. Individual skills will be important in gaining office, and by gaining higher and higher office the individual will gain more and more authority. The exercise of this type of authority however will usually be governed by an established set of rules. The personality of the individual office holder counts a good deal because political office will often require candidates for office to convince others that they are the right person for the job. This will of course be true if elections determine who gains office.

Whatever personal charm or skills the office holder possesses, the authority of the office is transferred when a change of personnel takes place. While one may be born to be a 'traditional' leader this type of authority could be transformed in a 'legal-rational' form perhaps through the holding of elections to confirm popular support. Legal-rational authority as well as being common in modern political systems exists in industry, commerce, trade unions, the civil service, schools, etc.

Charismatic Authority

This type of authority is based upon personality. The authority for the exercise of power rests upon the fact that there may exist widespread support amongst the people for a particular leader and he/she can command such support, not through traditional authority nor because of formal office, but merely by force of personality. The leader is able to convince others to follow freely. Such leaders often emerge at times of national crisis which affects a large proportion of the people. The leader may then become associated with attempts to solve the crisis and as the individual most likely to succeed.

The national struggle for independence from a colonial power gives us many examples of charismatic leadership developing in Third World countries. This type of authority is less evident in Western countries but may surface nonetheless when the political, social or economic structure faces a major crisis. As we have seen Winston Churchill came to power in 1940 on a personalised basis rather than as a result of being a loyal member of the Conservative Party.

An element of charisma is usually evident in most political leaders and it helps them to gain and retain office. Charismatic authority can be seen in communist states. Some of the communist states established at the end of World War II had leaders who had led groups of partisans who fought to end German occupation. An example of this was President Tito of Yugoslavia who was leader of his country after the war. Others who came to power after popular uprisings include Fidel Castro who became Cuba's leader in 1959 after a Communist takeover, and Mao Tse Tung who led the Communists to victory in China in the late 1940s.

In recent years some Communist states have begun to play down 'the cult of the personality' and to emphasise collective leadership.

Weber recognised that none of these three types of authority existed in a pure form. In Great Britain there is an essentially legal-rational form of political authority in government but the social background of politicians at least used to be given some importance.

Example

Mao is much less revered in Communist China today and a major reassessment of Joseph Stalin has taken place in the USSR. Stalin was portrayed as one of the primary figures in the establishment of the Soviet state but the true picture of his years in power in the 1930s, 1940s and 1950s is now being revealed to the Soviet people. In particular details of his 'purges' which led to the deaths of millions in the USSR are now being quite openly discussed.

Example

Conservative Prime Ministers Winston Churchill (1951–5), Anthony Eden (1955–7), Harold Macmillan (1957–63), and Alec Douglas-Home (1963–4) all came from aristocratic families. In fact it was thought by some that this added to their popularity with some sections of the electorate. This factor is probably less important today and the last two Conservative Prime Ministers Edward Heath (1970–4) and Margaret Thatcher (1979–90) come from relatively humble middle class backgrounds. However it must be remembered that the majority of the members of the House of the Lords enjoy authority based upon their social status.

Charisma is also an important ingredient in the image of a politician. No politician wants to appear to be dull and this is especially so during the conduct of election campaigns where so much attention is focused upon the personality of political leaders. This factor is emphasised strongly in the USA where presidential candidates in particular need to show a definite personal appeal in order to win. There is however much less evidence of traditional forms of authority in US politics.

President Ronald Reagan (1980–8) was described as the 'great communicator' and much emphasis was placed upon his personal appeal in winning votes. This factor also extended to his ability to maintain a high personal popularity even when his administration faced major political problems. Another President who exploited his personal qualities, especially on television, was John Kennedy (1960–3). Kennedy was seen as facing a difficult task in attempting to beat the Republican Vice President Richard Nixon in the presidential election of 1960. Kennedy managed to secure a narrow victory over the much less 'charismatic' Nixon whose TV performances were much less impressive. Charisma must not be overestimated however as Richard Nixon showed in his election victories of 1968 and 1972.

Richard Nixon enjoyed a clear victory in the 1972 US Presidential election, his Democratic opponent, George McGovern, won only 2 of the 50 states. Nixon, however, accepted that he had a lack of so called 'charisma' in an interview with CBS TV in January 1972. When asked by CBS reporter Dan Rather why many people thought he 'failed to inspire confidence and faith and lacked personal warmth and compassion', Nixon repled: 'My strong point is not rhetoric; it isn't showmanship; it isn't big promises – those things that create glamour and excitement that people call charisma and warmth'. (quoted in pp 86-7, *Why They Call it Politics*, Robert Sherill, Harcourt Brace Jovanovich Inc. 1974 (2nd Edition).

British political leaders have experienced defeat even when apparently more popular than rival party leaders. Harold Wilson the Labour prime minister was, according to opinion polls, more popular than Edward Heath the then Conservative Party leader during the 1970 general election but this did not stop the Conservatives winning. Many polls also placed James Callaghan ahead of Mrs Thatcher during the 1979 election in terms of personal qualities but once again the Conservatives won the election.

Many leaders who base their authority upon charisma nonetheless once they have gained power want to build up a legal-rational (or even a traditional) justification to sustain them in office. Charisma alone is a most unstable basis upon which to claim authority.

For example the popularity enjoyed by a political leader during a period of national enthusiasm aimed at securing independence may soon evaporate with the post-independence problems of economic management.

The process of transforming power into authority may not be a difficult task and can be attempted by giving a legal backing to the exercise of power. This may not automatically give legitimacy to the authority since law can be changed by government. What may be more important is that people willingly accept to be governed by the laws enacted by government. So law in itself need not give legitimacy to the authority claimed by those exercising power.

In some political systems authority may be established by a constitution (see Chapter 16) which recognises the sovereignty of the people. The writing of a new constitution in order to give legitimate authority to a new political regime may be of little use if the people generally prefer the previous constitutional arrangements. So the recognition of legitimacy of the exercise of authority from those affected by it and by other countries may take time to establish. Legitimacy may be conferred through a variety of ways. It may result from a political system's record on human rights, the holding of free and open elections, or merely by staying in power for a long time. Legitimacy may not be important in the short term but most politicians seek it in the long term.

Authority alone is not a sufficient basis for rule. Government will have enough power to take action to deal with those who for whatever reason question or refuse to accept its authority. Most citizens are likely to accept the authority of a policeman but a criminal will only be constrained by a policeman's power. When we talk of the power of a British prime minister we may argue about its extent and perhaps feel it to be great, but most would accept such power as legitimate.

We must conclude therefore that there is a very strong link between power and authority. Most people would feel happier when recognising the right of authority to compel them to act rather than to be coerced into doing so. This is true even when you respond to authority without your full consent, for at least your actions are partially voluntary. In responding to naked force you act against your will. People accept many forms of authority in their daily lives without question because they have been educated into accepting the legitimacy of government from an early age. To most citizens the power and authority of an institution or office holder are the same, for they know that it/he has prescribed and limited powers.

Consider how few people enjoy receiving a parking ticket but, in terms of power and authority, why is it that most people pay the fine rather than rip up the ticket?

Authority in Northern Ireland

The present problems of Northern Ireland which began in the late 1960s can serve as evidence of the difficulties that lie with the concept of authority. There are several levels involved in the breakdown of authority in the province. At the highest level a section of the community, who support the Republican cause and want a united Ireland, have ceased to regard the British government as having any 'authority'. At the everyday level those same people also do not acknowledge the authority of the police, the courts, the army, and any other representatives of government.

▼ *Sign in the Bogside area of Londonderry in Northern Ireland.*

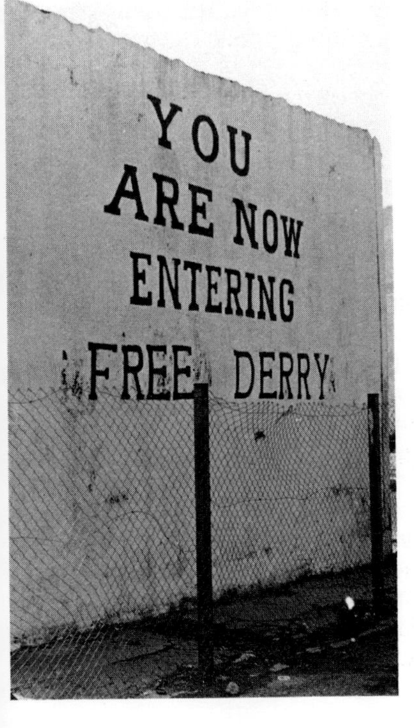

The important thing to note about what has been said in the last few sentences is that the words 'regard' and 'acknowledge' were used. It must be emphasised that the British government and the Royal Ulster Constabulary (RUC) do however still have 'authority'. This comes from the British Parliament and from the British Constitution. As such the British Government and the RUC have a 'right' to enforce their decisions upon the whole population of the United Kingdom including the section of the community in Northern Ireland who do not agree with or 'recognise' those facts.

The situation in Northern Ireland illustrates some further problems with the concept of authority in that it is possible for there to exist different types and degrees of authority within the same political unit. As well as the legal authority of the British state there is also the traditional authority of the churches and the charismatic authority of some sectarian leaders.

It is often the case that trouble can be averted more directly by the intervention of either the Catholic or Protestant churches than by that of the police or army. Similarly, individuals from both the communities carry great personal authority which does not stem solely from political office. Gerry Adams MP of Sinn Fein, the political arm of the Irish Republican Army, and the Unionist politician the Reverend Ian Paisley MP are two such individuals.

The authority of each of these sections of the political unit is not diminished by the presence of other forms of authority. Quite the contrary: the authority of each is probably supported and increased by the existence of the others.

Legitimacy

An important question to consider is at what point does the exercise of power become legitimate? As we have seen legitimacy implies that there is a willing acceptance by the people of authority that is exercised over them and this will involve them recognising that the authority has a quality of 'rightness'. It will also be coupled to an acceptance of the law-making processes and the law that is produced.

The difficulty is to identify whether such a willing acceptance of authority in fact exists. In most democratic countries, as we have seen, the existence of open and competitive elections involving rival groups of politicians offering alternative packages of policies is felt to be a primary test of legitimacy. In some political systems the ruling (and possibly the only) party may claim to have legitimacy in that they see themselves as the embodiment of the wishes and aspirations of the people. This perhaps is demonstrated by popular support for an independence movement led by the party, or in the overthrow of an unpopular regime. Such claims may be hard to sustain however if popular support was not evident.

The legitimacy which may be enjoyed by a political regime at one point will not necessarily remain for ever. For example, at one stage colonial rule was considered to be legitimate and this often included the people of the colony as well, who did not object to being ruled by a government possibly thousands of miles away. This was the case for the British Empire and many of its colonies. The legitimacy of this kind of authority was gradually eroded as indigenous nationalist groups demanded independence. Today colonialism is generally not accepted as a legitimate form of authority unless it can be shown that the majority of people in the colony wish to continue with it.

A group seizing power in the name of the people with promises of future elections once the political situation has been 'stabilised' may quickly be accepted as legitimate. If these aims take a long time to secure then this may result in its legitimacy being questioned. The introduction of Western style liberal democracy as 'proof' of legitimacy may however produce some difficulties for new political systems (see Chapter 9). Elections may be considered a luxury and a possible distraction from the need to tackle more immediate problems.

It is important to note that with the concept of legitimacy one finds an ethical aspect which is absent in power and authority. Legitimacy is the quality of 'rightness' or 'correctness' or even 'goodness' in an action. If students find the concept rather imprecise then they are not alone, for all such ethical concepts are essentially subjective and are based upon a specific set of cultural values.

Consider the example of an SS officer in a wartime concentration camp. He had the power to decide people's fate: to be sent to work parties or to their deaths.

He also, as an officer in the German Army, had the authority to take such decisions. The Nuremberg War Crimes Tribunal decided, however, that although in a strict sense SS officers had both the power and authority to carry out their concentration camp duties, they nevertheless were illegitimate because they did not conform to what the Tribunal saw as a higher authority than the German state. The SS officer had his power in the form of weapons and troops; he had his authority in the form of his commission from the German state and orders from superior officers, but his actions were not legitimate. They lacked the quality of 'rightness' or 'correctness' which come from a view of 'natural law' (see Chapter 5).

The prohibition of genocide is such a prescription of our own values that very few people would argue that the killing of millions was legitimate. At

Example

In the case of the Falkland Islands and Gibraltar the people have expressed a desire to remain British. Argentina claims the Falklands as part of its sovereign territory and invaded in 1982 to reclaim it. The subsequent military conflict with Britain resulted in defeat for Argentina, and any future negotiations will be difficult because the British government insists that the wishes of the islanders must come first.

In the case of Gibraltar, Spain has made claim to it and for many years closed its common border. Although the border is now open again there is little chance of Gibraltar returning to Spain if local opinion is against it.

this extreme, in other words, there is a wide consensus about what constitutes a legitimate act. But such consensus is not always indentifiable. Because legitimacy means more than just 'legal', there is no reliable means of measuring it. Just how subjective it is can be demonstrated by asking a group of people whether it is a legitimate right of government to execute wrongdoers.

Another problem is to establish who decides whether an act is legitimate or not and on what basis such decisions are made. In matters of life and death involving basic human rights your decisions would be relatively easy to justify. But what is to prevent each one of us identifying some aspect of our lives in which some decisions go against us and inventing a reason for ignoring the rulings of the authorities?

For instance, one person could say his (or her) basic right to privacy is going to be violated by a new housing estate which is planned to be built at the bottom of his garden. He could argue that the local council's decision to allow the development is therefore illegitimate. Another person could argue that our basic right to life is threatened by the government's policy of stationing nuclear weapons in the country. These people would then deny the legitimacy of the decision and use that denial to justify different sorts of action against the weapons, their bases and the people who operate them.

What arises from this is under what circumstances can an individual defy the acts of a legitimate government and at what point does any opposition to such a government become illegitimate and why? (See Chapter 1.)

CONCLUSIONS

We are left with a complex set of inter-relationships between the three concepts. Most people see the terms power and authority as the same, with authority needing some form of power to make the reluctant conform. The Inland Revenue may have the authority to assess our personal finances and demand an appropriate tax contribution but tax officers may have to use legal sanctions to make sure that we pay up! But why is it that we accept that the actions of the Inland Revenue are legitimate? Is it the appropriate taxation legislation, or the fact that the legislature that passed those laws was elected by the people? Not all political systems which are considered to exercise legitimate authority are elected. Their legitimacy may be based on other forms of clearly expressed popular opinion or simply because the regime has lasted for a long time without any serious domestic opposition. Simply passing a test of time may eventually prove legitimacy.

Example

Although there was a Communist seizure of power in mainland China in the late 1940s the Communist government failed for many years to be recognised as the legitimate voice of the Chinese people as far as some Western states were concerned, notably the USA. This led to China being excluded from the United Nations and such international events as the Olympic Games. Taiwan enjoyed the status of speaking for the Chinese for it was there the defeated leaders of the old regime fled and set up an alternative government. It was their government that was accepted by many Western powers even though in fact the vast majority of the Chinese people were governed by the Communist regime in Peking. It was not until its relations with the USA improved in the 1970s that the Communist government gained a seat in the United Nations and entrance to the Olympics.

Legitimacy, like beauty, is in the eye of the beholder.

Example

The South African government has attempted to create tribal homelands for sections of its black population and has given 'independence' to them. A major problem is that no other countries in the world accept them as independent states.

CASE STUDY

The United Kingdom and the 'Falklands Factor'

1. Prior to the invasion of the Falkland Islands in April 1982 the opinion polls showed that the Conservative Party was extremely unpopular. The Social Democratic Party had been formed during the previous year. Unemployment in the UK was increasing at a rapid rate.
2. Even at the beginning of the Falklands emergency, in April 1982, no less than 34 per cent of the voting public felt that Mrs Thatcher ought to resign.
3. But, by May of the same year, well over 80 per cent (84 per cent at its peak) were satisfied with Mrs Thatcher and the opinion polls showed her party well ahead of both opposition parties. A year later the Conservatives won a significant majority in an election which had been called almost a year earlier than it need have been.

Poll and Election Results (selected results July 1981–June 1983)

(%)	**Cons.**	**Lab.**	**Alliance***
July 1981	29	36	31
December 1981	27	29	42
February 1982	30	33	34
May 1982 (week 1)	44	30	24
May 1982 (week 3)	51	25	22
General Election: June 1983	42	28	25

* Combined vote of Liberals and SDP.

Questions

1 To what extent do opinion polls increase or decrease the power and/or authority of a government? Distinguish carefully between the two concepts.

2 How, if at all, does 'popularity' translate into legitimacy?

3 By late in the month of May 1982, Mrs Thatcher's personal 'satisfaction rating' was as high as 84 per cent. To what extent, in the context of British politics, does this represent, directly or indirectly, charismatic authority?

NOW READ ON . . .

Edward C. Page *Political Authority and Bureaucratic Power* Wheatsheaf Books, 1985

Machiavelli *The Prince*

4 Influence and Persuasion

Children, who have been taught, or conditioned, to listen passively most of the day to the warm verbal emotional appeal of the so-called TV personality, are often unable to respond to real persons because they arouse so much less feeling than the skilled actor.

Bruno Bettelheim, *The Informed Heart* 1968

BASIC PRINCIPLES

Influence and persuasion can mean many things. They are words which, like some other political concepts, are usually used very loosely in everyday life.

We speak of persuading a person to accept a particular line of argument and we talk of 'gangsters' who 'persuade' shopkeepers that paying protection money is in their own interest.

Television and newspapers are often held to be influencing people to vote in a particular way and, almost in the same breath, we speak of the influence of public opinion over government policy.

The number of different usages means that it is probably useful to look at their exact political meanings before examining the concepts in action.

In the political context both **influence** and **persuasion** relate to ways of exercising forms of political power. They are, in a sense, different orders of power.

Examples of the two concepts being used correctly are few and far between (for they tend to be used almost as interchangeable similes) but the following should illustrate the difference:

> *There is reason to believe that young people's perceptions of politics are greatly influenced by television programmes.*

This statement is arguing that, without them being aware of it, TV changes the way in which young people see politics. It is also implying, probably wrongly, that young people's perceptions can be altered by TV but those of older people cannot.

> *The Chairman of the party made a stirring speech in an attempt to persuade delegates to vote for the amendment.*

The chairman was not trying to 'influence' delegates in the strict sense of the word, but to persuade them openly through the use of logical arguments put in a persuasive (and, probably, emotive) manner.

It should be noted that neither influence nor persuasion is the same as 'power'. Even figures with great power such as the President of the United States have to persuade or to influence their legislatures. President Truman once said that Presidential power was 'the power to persuade' for the US President certainly cannot order Congress or the Supreme Court to do anything.

Definition

***Influence** is both a verb and a noun.*

The verb 'to influence' means to affect someone's thoughts or actions without, in theory, their being aware of the process.

The noun 'influence', as used in the declaration that 'Leaders of the British Trade Union Movement have great influence', *means the possession of faculties which allow one to affect the thoughts or actions of other people. These 'faculties' can range from other people simply being aware of the potential power of the person with 'influence' to a more subtle respect for the person's abilities, knowledge, or experience.*

Definition

***Persuasion** is the noun which relates to the verb 'to persuade'. It is much more direct and obvious than influence, meaning the act of trying to change someone's beliefs or actions in a more open fashion.*

DISCUSSING THE ARGUMENTS

How Does Influence Operate?

If the process of persuasion is an open one, while influence is exercised without the subject being aware of it – how does influence operate?

Probably the best way to approach this question is to consider how one would seek to influence people to feel better about your school or college. The objective would be to try to change their attitudes and preconceptions, their beliefs and prejudices without them really being aware of it. The Public Relations people would call this **image changing** and this is possibly the most important way in which influence is exercised in modern politics.

Influencing voters today is an extremely sophisticated affair involving the work of a variety of professional 'image changers' – press agents and spokesmen, public relations specialists, market research agencies, opinion pollsters, and advertising agencies.

When Mrs Thatcher became leader of the Conservative Party in 1975 the senior people of the party were not so much worried about her ability to do the job and, eventually, to win a General Election, but about the disturbing results which were coming in from the opinion polls and the market researchers.

All parties carry out regular market research to try to keep track of how the public are responding to their policies and to the performances of the leaders. In the case of Mrs Thatcher in the mid-1970s the research evidence was that people found her abrasive, old fashioned, hard and very forceful. A concerted attempt was made, therefore, to change Mrs Thatcher's image to one which, it was felt, the public would prefer. The visual effect of the changes can be seen from the photographs, but the change in her speaking style and even in the way she sat during TV interviews was just as revolutionary.

The attempt to influence voters is not something that is limited to the Conservative Party or to personalities. In 1986 the Labour Party, under Neil Kinnock, decided to drop the 'Red Flag' from the front of Labour Party manifestos. It was felt that the presence of the Red Flag might influence voters to believe that the party was Marxist or Trotskyist. The idea was that voters associated the Red Flag on previous manifestos with the party's ultra left wing elements in the Militant Tendency. In order to change the voters' perceptions of the political stance of the party the dropping of the Red Flag and its replacement with the Red Rose of European Socialists was felt to be important.

Parties are constantly aware of the importance of 'image' to their chances in elections so that, today, the 'media face' of all three major parties is of paramount importance.

▼ *Mrs Thatcher, Leader of the Conservative Party, in 1977.*

► *Mrs Thatcher, Leader of the Conservative Party and Prime Minister, 1985.*

► *One of the Labour Party's posters for the 1983 General Election .*

THE PACKAGING OF POLITICS

Every aspect of the party battle is now subject to the constraint of 'image'. At the lowest level constituency parties are aware of the need for a 'presentable' candidate, while, at the national level, the representatives who will appear on television are trained and groomed for their role.

Constituency candidates are expected, these days, to look presentable on TV. The implication of this is that the parties expect voters to be swayed by the way a candidate looks or talks rather than by what they actually believe or say.

National political parties take regular opinion polls of public opinion, they make use of advertising agencies to design their posters and their TV presentations. They also employ professional public relations experts to advise their national leaders so that they conform to what the polls show the public 'expect' their leaders to look and act like.

In this process the armoury of the modern political party is formidable: the dress, speaking style, stance, and even the hair style may be changed to appeal to prospective voters. The party 'advertisements', usually called 'Party Political Broadcasts', are slick and well presented. For all of the main parties, today, these broadcasts are put together by professional advertising agencies and have begun to rely less and less on detailed facts or arguments about the party's policies or record in government.

A review of the broadcasts of the 1983 and 1987 campaigns will show broadcasts by the Conservative Party which are amongst the most professional (in sheer advertising terms) ever mounted by a British political party. They rarely attempted to present detailed facts or to argue in a progressive and logical way that the Conservative Party was the best party to govern the country. Instead the broadcasts relied essentially on a series of very fast visual images: of Conservative successes and of what they claimed were past Labour failures. The images were delivered very quickly, almost subliminally, together with appropriate music.

The advertising agency which ran those advertisements for the Conservative Party in 1983 was one of the most successful agencies in the country, Saatchi & Saatchi, one of whose directors was alleged to have said during the campaign:

> . . . *what could be said well in ten minutes could be put across better in five.*

Example

The Rise and Rise of Saatchi & Saatchi

The advertising firm of Saatchi & Saatchi became the first major agency to be given control of a political promotional campaign in the UK. In early 1978, it was given the task of running the Conservative's campaign in the run-up to what was then thought to be an autumn 1978 General Election.

In the event, James Callaghan made what is generally believed to have been a major blunder in not calling the General Election in the autumn of 1978 but Saatchi & Saatchi organised the Conservative's campaign as though he would.

In the summer of 1978 the agency produced a campaign of TV advertisements, posters and newspaper advertisements which was designed to prepare the country for the coming election. Part of that campaign was what is still the most famous poster in modern British political campaigning – 'LABOUR ISN'T WORKING'.

This poster was revolutionary in that it gave prominence to the name of the 'other' party. It was, however, extremely successful. It provoked a furious response from the Labour Party and, thereby, gained considerable additional publicity in the national press and on TV and radio.

Saatchi & Saatchi revealed later that the poster only cost £50,000 and was only displayed on 20 sites throughout Britain. They estimated, however, that it received around £5 million of 'free' exposure through the press, radio and TV due to Dennis Healey's furious opposition to it and his claim that the 'dole queue' on the poster was really just Saatchi & Saatchi employees. It was actually Young Conservatives from South Hendon but the agency were able, honestly, to deny Healey's accusation.

The Saatchi & Saatchi approach

The agency spent a great deal of time and many hours of discussions on identifying exactly what constituted the reasons for success in elections and exactly what the Conservative Party's appeal to the people was.

They identified some very 'simple' rules which guided them throughout that and subsequent campaigns:

- whatever can be said well in ten minutes can be said better in five;
- governments lose elections, oppositions don't win them;
- oppositions win elections by ensuring that governments lose them.

They also discussed in detail what they felt was the real message of the Conservative Party in 1979. It was summed up as:

Freedom, choice, opportunity, small government, prosperity

For the first time in British politics an agency had identified not only the key rules but went further and stated the appeal of their 'product' in emotional terms. They were not interested in 'policies' but in emotions and the overall feeling of the public for their 'product'.

Saatchi & Saatchi's party political broadcasts on TV were like nothing the public had seen before. Instead of 'talking heads' (one or two senior party figures patiently explaining the party's policies on employment, on incomes policy, on the stability of sterling) they went for very fast moving and very visual 'ads'.

The 'ads' (for that is what they have now become) were designed to provoke emotive responses in the audience in favour of the 'product'. Instead of a patiently argued case for (say) laws which control the activities of trade unions, there were quick shots of pickets, of closed factories, of piles of refuse lying in the streets, of 'extreme' unionists like 'Red Robbo' from British Leyland, and of buses of workers being pelted by crowds of angry pickets. An emotive response against the unions was being orchestrated and the campaign did the same thing with virtually every other aspect of the Conservative Party's battle against the the Labour Government.

The 1979 campaign for the Conservative opposition was slick, clever, visually stimulating, even enjoyable but was it what elections ought to be like in a democracy?

Since 1979 all the political parties have taken on top-flight advertising agencies and subsequent campaigns have seen the development of similarly slick presentations by each of them.

In 1979 Britain took another major step away from the rational, boring, detailed, educated discussion of political issues and moved into an age when the issues are subsidiary. The parties are now 'marketed' in the same way as toothpaste, blue jeans and light beer. Elections are won, not by sensible policies, but by the public relations and advertising people: by the *look* of a leader and by the slickness of their 'party political broadcasts'.

Or are they?

► *Conservative poster in 1979 general election.*

In 1983 the Conservative Party spent more than £2 million on their advertising budget and, although the Labour and Alliance parties could not match this sum, they also used advertising agencies to get their 'message' across.

One view of this process might be that the result of this attempt to influence voters has been that:

- candidates and leaders have become standardised, 'presentable' and, even, plastic
- emotion has replaced logic and rationality
- visual response has replaced analysis of written arguments and programmes.

THE MEDIA AND POLITICAL INFLUENCE AND PERSUASION

While political parties try to ensure that their image is good enough to influence voters in their favour, the media are using their own special position to influence and persuade. Sometimes this is deliberate and sometimes unconscious or, perhaps, unintentional but, whichever it is, the newspapers, radio stations and television companies are seen by some as an almost sinister aspect of modern British politics.

Newspapers

If newspapers had been invented in the twentieth century they would probably be subject to the same sort of control as the television and radio stations. However, they were first published over two hundred years ago and were poorly named.

Newspapers have never been solely concerned with news. Indeed, some people would argue that even the news they carry has always been as biased as their editorials.

Each newspaper has usually promoted a clear set of political ideas (usually those of its owner) and has seen nothing wrong in trying to sway its readers towards a particular political ideology. To some extent this has been explained by the argument that people can always buy another newspaper if they don't like the political leaning of their current one. This argument was not one which could be used during the early years of broadcasting – there was only one national radio station (the BBC) and it was felt that it should not be partisan in the way that the newspapers were.

A comparison of the approach of a selection of national newspapers *on the same day* concerning the same political news item is sufficient to establish exactly how each paper gives the item a particular slant. It is important here to remember that bias is sometimes achieved by *leaving material out* and that the average reader who reads the same newspaper every day will not

▲ *Newspaper owner : A journalist is free to write whatever he wants and a newspaper owner is free to publish whatever he wants.*
Journalist : Can I quote that in your paper?
Newspaper owner : No!

necessarily be aware of the slant that this gives to the 'news' they are reading.

The problem is probably even deeper than is indicated by the apparent bias of our papers. The *way* in which the news is selected is a form of bias. The Glasgow Media Studies Group, for example, believe that the news which gets into British papers is 'selected according to unstated criteria'. In other words this means that the cultural or political bias of editors and journalists acts as a filter for 'news' which they think we wouldn't want to know about.

We should never forget that newspapers are, after all, in business to make profits. They have never been seen as 'public services' in the same way that the radio and television companies have.

Unlike the electronic media, newspaper owners and editors may take any 'line' they choose on an issue. Some papers are regarded as being 'right wing': *The Times, Daily Telegraph, Daily Express,* and the *Sun*; while others are either 'centre', or 'left of centre'. In the latter categories only one newspaper can really be reliably placed in the UK Labour Party camp, the *Daily Mirror.* Other 'centre' papers, such as *The Guardian* and *The Observer*, are, arguably, more Social Democrat or Social and Liberal Democrat than Labour. On the extreme left there is only one national newspaper, the old *Daily Worker*, now called the *Morning Star*, although there are many other nationally distributed newspapers and journals.

There are two quite different ways of looking at the influential power of the press:

1 They are powerful instruments of influence and persuasion used by the 'establishment' to maintain the capitalist system. The papers are owned by private groups or individuals and are free to 'push' whatever line they (or their advertisers) wish. While they do not necessarily support a Conservative government all the time, they do ensure that 'the system' survives.
2 Newspapers are businesses just like any other and will only survive as businesses if they provide what their customers want. They are also an entertainment medium – these days probably almost exclusively an entertainment medium – and need to attract audiences with spicy stories and exciting competitions rather than with boring discussions of the latest political blunders. According to this view of the newspaper industry the political stance of each paper is not a devious plot by the owners to try to influence the public but simply a reaction to people's already existing ideas and attitudes. A newspaper will only sell if its readers like what they find inside it and it will only become successful over the long term if it does not bore or annoy those readers.

There is evidence, naturally, for both viewpoints. On the one hand newspapers are *owned* by relatively small numbers of people and institutions. It is even possible to narrow this field down further by sifting out the overlapping share ownerships and the stakes held by 'nominee' companies for other, un-named, institutions. The press, in addition, does exhibit a distinct leaning to the political right.

However, there is also evidence of newspapers having to change their political stance in order to increase or maintain readership. One left wing newspaper, the *Daily Herald*, went out of business altogether due to decreasing readership and increasing losses. Owned, then, by the Mirror Group, the *Herald* was replaced by a new, left of centre title – the *Sun*. When this paper also failed to attract sufficient readers it was sold to News International. That group switched the political stance of the paper to the right, increased the entertainment content, and, thereby, have made the *Sun* the best selling daily paper in Britain today.

Radio and Television

Both of these media are supposed to be impartial in political terms. Both are restricted by the terms of the Royal Charters under which they were established:

- The BBC is required to broadcast an impartial account of the proceedings of Parliament every day and not to broadcast its own opinion on any matter of controversy.
- The Independent Broadcasting Authority (IBA) is likewise required to present news accurately and impartially. Even Channel Four, which was given some leeway for experiment when it was established is still required to meet the stipulation of 'due impartiality'.

The reason that these stipulations were made in the Charters of the BBC and the IBA was that Parliament judged radio and TV to be much too powerful as shapers of public opinion and influencers of people's views to be allowed the degree of bias to which newspapers had been accustomed to since they were first circulated.

POLITICIANS AS VICTIMS

So far the debate has centred around the way in which parties, politicians and the media attempt to influence the public.

However, politicians, and to a certain extent, parties, can also be victims of the media and the 'public opinion' which it may arouse.

Sometimes the media has acted as a provider of information and a source of influence for the public over a major issue. Perhaps the best example is that of the 'Watergate Affair' of 1972. Two Washington Post journalists investigated a strange burglary at the Democratic Party's offices in the Watergate Building and the result of months of research and publication of articles was the fall of an entire administration. In the UK the media were responsible for a great deal of the pressure and the information which exposed the espionage activities of Kim Philby and Anthony Blunt.

At other times the media has been instrumental in establishing an 'image' of a politician which *may* have been crucial to their performance in subsequent elections. President Ford of the USA was portrayed by the media as being accident prone and they managed to catch him (photographically) in some very embarrassing situations. This may well have had an influence on the voting public for Ford only lost the 1976 election by a very small margin. Before becoming President, Gerald Ford had been a Congressman, and a reasonably successful one, for many years.

In the early years of Richard Nixon, when he was first a Congressman and then the Vice-President under Eisenhower, the press were blamed for hounding him to a narrow defeat in the 1960 Presidential elections. It was after a further electoral defeat that Nixon 'retired for good' from politics and told the waiting press that they wouldn't have Nixon to kick around any more.

In the UK the influence of the media may not be quite as spectacular but there have certainly been occasions when the press had a devastating effect on a politician's career.

In the early 1960s a Conservative Minister's indiscretions with a prostitute were widely published in the national media. This resulted in John Profumo committing the unforgiveable sin of lying to the House of Commons and, ultimately, in his resignation from both the Government and the Commons, his career totally destroyed, although an official enquiry found no breach of national security had taken place.

More recently the wide publication of Mr Cecil Parkinson's affair with his secretary, Miss Sarah Keays, caused his resignation from the Cabinet. In this case, the view of political commentators was that, prior to the revelations, Parkinson was destined for high office in the government. The feeling in the government was, however, that the revelations about Mr Parkinson (particularly the allegation that he had discussed Cabinet proceedings with Miss Keays) were damaging the whole government. His resignation very quickly became 'necessary' after that. He was subsequently reinstated by Mrs Thatcher in 1987.

An attempt to use the media to discredit a fellow minister backfired on Mr Leon Brittan in 1986 and led to his having to resign his senior cabinet post (see Case Study B).

CASE STUDY A: THE INFLUENCE OF THE MONARCHY

In the nineteenth century, Walter Bagehot (editor of *The Economist* (1861–77) and author of the classic text *The English Constitution* (1867), described the role of the monarch as:

the right to be consulted, the right to encourage, and the right to warn

This was written at a time when it was felt necessary to clarify the position for Queen Victoria who, many felt, was attempting to reestablish many of the 'real' political powers of the monarchy. Since he wrote those words, Bagehot's view of the 'Constitutional Monarch' has been accepted as representing the 'correct' role for a British monarch.

Bagehot could not be expected, however, to predict and to take into account the major role which Queen Elizabeth II has taken on since her accession to the throne. As the individual elements of the British Empire became independent during the 1950s, 60s and 70s the 'Old Commonwealth' countries of Canada, Australia and New Zealand were joined by a large number of countries of the 'New Commonwealth': India together with newly independent states in Africa, the Caribbean and the Pacific.

'Empire Day' only became 'Commonwealth Day' in 1958 and, in the thirty or so years since then the Commonwealth has grown into a major international organisation of over 1,000 million people.

The Queen's role in the Commonwealth is that of Head and is one which is quite separate from her role as Queen of the United Kingdom and its remaining possessions.

1. The Role of the Queen

- In 1986 this convention was questioned closely when the Queen became involved in media speculation about her relationship with the Prime Minister, Mrs Margaret Thatcher, over the latter's attitude to the necessity for economic sanctions against South Africa.
- Mid-1986 saw the pressure for comprehensive sanctions against South Africa growing from almost every country in the world and from virtually every member of the Commonwealth. Mrs Thatcher held that, not only would economic sanctions be unlikely to succeed in their aim of forcing the South African government to begin the dismantling of their system of Apartheid but they would actually cause more damage to the poorer African states which depended on South Africa for their livelihood.
- Most of the members of the Commonwealth disagreed with this approach and were demanding that the UK apply some form of pressure to the South African regime. There were not a few calls for sanctions to be applied on the UK or for some members to leave the Commonwealth in protest at the UK Government's policy.
- The Queen, as Head of the Commonwealth, was said to have been extremely concerned at this situation and to have said as much to the Prime Minister.
- Several commentators have credited the Queen with some very subtle and discreet manipulation over the years which has averted crises within the Commonwealth, over both Rhodesia (now Zimbabwe) and over South Africa.

2. The role of the heir to the throne

The government was faced, in 1985, with a decision to approve or disapprove of a planning proposals for an extension to the National Gallery in Trafalgar Square.

- The design (by a very famous firm of architects) was the subject of much controversy.
- A speech by Prince Charles castigated the architectural style involved.
- There was a wave of public support for the Prince's speech and the design was subsequently not approved by the Government (who claimed that they were going to disallow planning permission anyway on appeal).

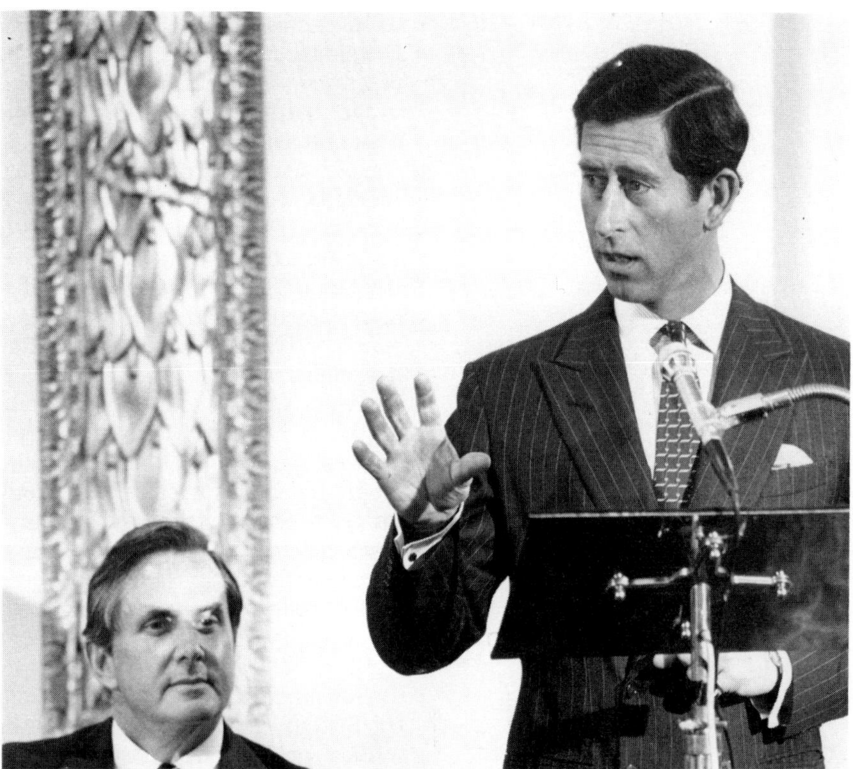

Prince Charles addresses the British-American conference on private sector initiatives in London in 1988.

Questions

1 As a monarch with more than 35 years of direct experience of British and Commonwealth political life, how much influence do you think the Queen ought to have over the policies and decisions of her Government?

2 What do you think the influence (such as it is) of the Queen is based on?
Consider any factors which you feel might cause people, not just politicians, to listen to her views and, perhaps, to have respect for them.

3 Consider this fictitious situation:
The Queen is advised to go on nationwide television to denounce a government plan to leave the Commonwealth.
Would such a broadcast increase or decrease the ability of the Queen to influence other events? Why?

4 Whether Prince Charles had any influence on public opinion over the planning proposals, or not, was he misusing his position as the heir to the throne in stating his own views so forcefully?

5 How much influence should the monarch have in modern Britain and how should the limits of such influence be defined?

►►►►►►►►►►►►►►►► CASE STUDY B: POLITICAL MANIPULATION OF THE MEDIA

- In late 1985 it became clear that the Westland Helicopter Company was going to go out of business if it did not find someone to 'rescue' it (by buying all or part of it in order to inject fresh capital).
- At first, the Secretary of Trade and Industry, Mr Leon Brittan, and the Secretary of Defence, Mr Michael Heseltine, agreed that the best solution to this problem would be if a consortium of European companies could be persuaded to buy Westland.
- At some point, however, Mr Brittan changed his mind towards this takeover in favour of an American company, Sikorski (owned by United Technologies Inc.).
- Whatever the merits of the two rivals for Westland, there followed a very public battle between Brittan and Heseltine in order to influence Westland shareholders to vote for one of the two takeover bidders.
- The Attorney-General, Sir Michael Havers, wrote to Mr Heseltine in the middle of this battle, on 6 January 1986, to inform him that, in his view, some of Mr Heseltine's statements in a letter to a Westland bidder were not completely accurate. (They were said to have contained 'material inaccuracies', but Mr Heseltine subsequently denied this). This letter was an extremely confidential one and was never intended by Sir Michael to be other than absolutely confidential between himself and the Secretary of Defence.
- The letter was 'leaked' to the press and its publication may have damaged Mr Heseltine's credibility at a crucial point in the battle. It was later revealed that the 'leak' had been authorised by Mr Brittan and carried out by his Director of Information (a civil servant). This, however, had not been the only 'leak' of the affair. A Cabinet minute of 4 October 1985, which criticised Mr Brittan, was published in the Observer on 22 December 1985.
- On 9 January 1986, following a disagreement in Cabinet over whether he was being given sufficient chance to put his case and over a Cabinet decision that all statements to the press would have to be cleared through 10 Downing Street, Mr Heseltine resigned from the Cabinet.
- Mr Brittan resigned later (on 24 January) following intense media and political pressure over his having 'leaked' a confidential document, over allegations that, at a meeting on 8 January, he had 'pressured' the Chief Executive of British Aerospace to withdraw from the European Consortium which had been set up to buy into Westland, and over an increasing lack of confidence in his judgement aggravated by the episode reported below.

NOTE: It was common practice, until the early 1980s, for government ministers to give what they called 'Press Briefings'. Each minister would call in a selection of favoured journalists at irregular intervals in order to 'brief' them about current developments. In theory the process was an exercise in better Government-Media communications. In practice it was more of an attempt by the government to give its own 'slant' to items concerning its affairs. It was common not only for journalists to be misled by these briefings but, also, for different government ministers to give totally different stories to their 'own' press.

In March 1989, Paul Channon, Secretary of State for Transport, ran into considerable controversy following the 'non-attributable briefing' to the press on the subject of the Lockerbie air disaster.

Questions

1 The use of 'Press Briefings' to give a particular slant to an issue has been a feature of most recent British governments – perhaps the best example was the way in which these briefings were used by the government to manipulate press accounts of the Falklands War.
Are governments justified in attempting to influence the general public in this way? What, if any, are the limits to such activity?

2 If a Minister, such as Mr Heseltine, is prevented from achieving a full hearing of his views in Cabinet, is he justified in using his power and position to ensure that his case is presented in the media? Or does this merely replace government by collective responsibility in the Cabinet Room with 'trial by media'?

CASE STUDY C: LOBBYING

1 It is the constitutional right of every Briton to lobby Parliament. Anyone who turns up at the House of Commons and who wishes to see their MP will be courteously shown to the lobby of the House and asked to wait while enquiries are made as to whether their MP is present.

2 This has always been the traditional view of lobbying in Britain. Even while the USA has built up a formidable professional, registered lobby system in Washington, British politics textbooks have tended to concentrate on the essentially amateur lobbyist.

3 Now, however, Britain has its own growing body of professional lobbyists. One writer has counted over 20 firms in the business. These firms 'lobby' in a variety of ways which only rarely include direct contact with individual MPs.

4 Modern, professional lobbying uses many methods within a variety of sophisticated strategies:

- Lunches and parties might be arranged so that a specific argument can be put to a large number of MPs;
- The case for or against a particular policy may be sent to every MP in the House;
- Lobby 'briefings' may be prepared which give the MP a great deal of accurate information about the subject;
- Contacts may be established with civil servants at senior levels.

Of these, two methods are particularly important. Briefings are extremely useful to British MPs who do not receive the research support of their American or West German counterparts. The contacts between professional lobbyists and senior civil servants ensure that views and arguments can be registered with the very people who actually filter the Ministers' papers and who construct most of their policies.

5 In 1988 some of the major professional lobbying organisations were:

- Public Policy Consultants (PPC)
- Sallingbury Casey
- Gifford, Jeger, Weeks (GJW)
- Hill & Knowlton
- Political Communication

These organisations represent individual businesses, trade associations, charities, consumer groups, overseas governments, local authorities, etc., in their attempts to convince the Government on specific policy issues.

6 Examples of their work were:

- the Westland Affair
- the 1988 Copyright Act

- the Nestlé takeover of Rowntree (without having to face an enquiry from the Monopolies and Mergers Commission)
- the British Aerospace takeover of the Rover Group.

7 It should also be noted that many MPs (estimated at around 100 at any one time) are now officially 'retained' by interest groups and lobbying organisations. The MPs receive an annual fee for being so retained and, in return, they represent the body in Parliament and keep it up-to-date with developments in Westminster.

8 To these 100 or so 'retained' MPs one should add the 150 or so Labour MPs who are 'sponsored' by specific Trade Unions. The MPs receive a small annual fee which goes to their constituency party and their election expenses are paid by the Trade Union concerned. In return they act in a similar fashion to the 'retained' MPs in (7) above.

Questions

1 How do you think the rise of the professional lobbying organisation affects the ordinary citizen's right to lobby their MP?

2 What do you think the effects of MPs representing and being retained by specific interest groups are on the business of Parliament?

3 What constitutional protection, if any, do we need from:
a professional lobbyists
b 'retained' or 'sponsored' MPs?

You should look at the situation in the USA before considering the answers to this case study.

Apart from the standard texts on US politics, which each have a chapter or section on the process of lobbying and the Federal controls upon it, you will also find the following useful and interesting:

K. L. Schlozman and J. T. Tierney *Organised Interests and American Democracy* Harper-Row, 1986

D. S. Painter *Private Power and Public Policy – multinational oil corporations and US foreign policy 1941–54* Tauris, 1986

EXAMINATION QUESTION

'Public opinion is so manipulated, to such an extent, by government and mass media that it has no independent influence on British politics'. Discuss. (Cambridge, Special Paper, 1987)

NOW READ ON . . .

Richard Neustadt *Presidential Power* Fontana, 1966
Probably the definitive work on Presidential politics. Several very good accounts of the ways in which candidates and Presidents seek to persuade and influence the public.

Kenneth Newton 'Mass Media' in Drucker *et al. Developments in British Politics 2* Macmillan, 1986
Partisanship and bias in the media.

B. Gunter *et al. Television Coverage of the 1983 Election* BBC/IBA, 1984
An all too rare account of the way in which an election was actually covered

Bob Woodward and Carl Bernstein *All the President's Men* Fontana, 1979
The famous account of a gripping piece of investigative journalism with the remaining mystery of who was 'Deep Throat'.

M. Cockerell *Sources Close to the Prime Minister* Macmillan, 1985
Journalists' eye view of how decisions are taken in Whitehall

Annabel May and Catherine Rowan *Inside Information: The British Government and the Media* Constable, 1983
An investigative account of relations between the two institutions

Dan Nimmo *The Political Persuaders* Prentice-Hall, 1970
One of the best original accounts of how political persuasion operates. The examples are very specific, though, and a little dated

Colin Seymour-Ure *The Political Impact of the Mass Media* Constable, 1974
A very worthy attempt to evaluate the impact of the British mass media. Again a little dated.

John Whale *The Politics of the Media* Fontana, 1977
An historical account from 1945 to 1976 which deals with the unions' influence over the media as well as industry's and government's.

Economist *The Queen's Power* *The Economist*, 12 December 1987
A brief assessment of the influence and power of the modern monarchy

Tyler, R. *The Selling of the Prime Minister* Grafton, 1987

Seaton, J. and Pimlott, B. *The Media in British Politics* Gower, 1987

Adams, V. *The Media and the Falklands Campaign* Macmillan, 1986

See *Anatomy of a Leak* in *The Economist* of 4 July 1981, pages 30–1

A serious indictment of the press and electronic media in the UK is contained in Curran and Seaton *Power Without Responsibility* Routledge, 1988

The early stages of the Westland Affair are summarised in *The Economist* of 11 January 1986 and the following weeks of that paper contain most of the important developments.

P. J. Madgwick *Introduction to British Politics* Hutchinson (latest edition)
The section on Political Communication is particularly good on the background to the debate on the role and legal obligations of the media in the UK

David Butler and Donald Stokes *Political Change in Britain*
Macmillan, 1988 Read the section on the press and partisanship

Henry Drucker *et al.* *Developments in British Politics 2* Macmillan, 1986
See, also, page 45 and Section 14, page 313

A discussion of the role of the Queen with respect to the Commonwealth can be found in Malcolm Rutherford's article for the *Financial Times*, 19 July 1986; 'The power to go on talking'.

The position of the monarchy and many other aspects of Bagehot's philosophy are briefly surveyed in an article by Bagehot's biographer, Norman St John Stevas, in *The Economist*, 12 April 1986.

See also, 'Politics and the Prince of Wales', *The Economist*, 19 July 1986.

5 Law and Justice

BASIC PRINCIPLES

Guilty, until proved innocent

Is there anything more that a government can usefully do to combat the vicious circle of drugs, unemployment and crime? Of course, if you are an ambitious minister eager for a story to tell to your annual party conference. This year Mr David Mellor, from the Home Office, seized his chance, and set out a wholly new government strategy for combating drug abuse.

Some parts of his plan were predictable: more customs officers, and £4m for drug advisers in schools. Others were not, like Mr Mellor's plans for the legal system. He has three proposals.

- A new offence of handling the proceeds of drug trafficking.
- A judicial power to freeze the assets of a suspected drug dealer even before arrest.
- A confiscatory fine after conviction for trafficking equal to the full extent of any illicit proceeds. When applying the fine, the judge will reverse the traditional burden of proof in criminal cases. All income and assets of a convicted trafficker will be assumed to come from drugs unless it can be proved otherwise.

The Tory faithful will not mind much if civil libertarians complain. But special exceptions to the fundamentals of English criminal procedure – even for something as heinous as drug dealing – rarely make good law.

Source: *The Economist*, 12 October 1986, p 33

The concepts of 'law' and 'justice' are well illustrated by this example. There is little doubt that the government had the power and the authority to pass such 'laws' but the article raises the question – were they 'fair' or 'just'?

At the simplest level the decision about what constitutes 'fairness' lies in the hands of each and every one of us. Only absolute monarchs can dispense justice according to their own definitions!

King Solomon is famous (and 'justly' so) for his decision in the case of the two mothers who claimed the same baby. He waited for both mothers to explain their claim to the child and then said that, as he had no real means of telling to which mother the baby truly belonged, it should be cut in two and half given to each woman. At that, the real mother is said to have screamed and broken down, saying something to the effect that the other woman was welcome to the baby as long as the King did not have it cut in two. Solomon, of course, then gave the baby to its real mother!

The fact that this story (real or not) has been passed down for thousands of years demonstrates that the quality of justice has not really changed. Thousands of years later, and in spite of technology, we still find it extremely difficult to know what true justice is.

The article above provides an excellent example of our problem. A fundamental principle of British law is that one is innocent until proven guilty and that, before the courts can confiscate one's property, they must first prove that it has been gained illegally.

One might ask, therefore, whether it is right or fair that we should have changed this ancient principle for one very specific class of wrongdoers. In the case of convicted drug traffickers *all* income and assets are held to have been gained illegally unless proven otherwise.

DISCUSSING THE ARGUMENTS

Definition

Laws *are simply rules which have been given some stamp of authority by the society in question and which are, thereafter, recognised as applying to that particular society (or, by agreement, to a group of countries).*

They may be written or unwritten and they may form a single body of law for the country in question or they may be subdivided into types of law such as a **Criminal Code,** *a* **Civil Code,** *an* **Administrative Code** *and so forth.*

It is difficult to think of a society which can do without laws but, over the years, there have been a few theorists who have proposed methods of arranging societies in order to do away with the need for them.

Plato is, perhaps, the best known of the earliest of these theorists. He believed that the 'just' society, ruled by leaders who were themselves 'just' (that is, they had an inbuilt sense of 'rightness') would not need sets of laws to govern the lives of its citizens.

Similarly, Karl Marx also envisaged a 'lawless' society. His classless, communist society would need no laws because their reason for being (the subjection of the working class) would have been removed along with the ruling class who used the law for that purpose. Instead, all would be equal and would cooperate together for the common good.

Every society, today, has a system of laws which guide and control the actions of the members of that society. The laws are usually written down in a 'statutory' form but might, in some countries, be unwritten.

Natural Law

The concept of 'natural law' is very important for the United Kingdom because a large part of the legal system is based on this foundation.

It requires that all laws should conform with 'universal moral standards' and it implies, therefore, that laws are never wholly made by humans alone but that some higher order (either of being or of moral law) has to be taken into account. The principles of natural law have been most clearly set out by the medieval philosopher St Thomas Aquinas. He believed that all laws were, ultimately, delivered to men from God and that any rule which did not conform with the Christian ethic could not be classed as a law. Any rule which merely possessed earthly authority or some kind of formal legitimacy had insufficient foundation of morality.

The concept of natural law went out of fashion for many centuries as theorists preferred to think of laws as being wholly man-made and wholly subject to rational construction without reference to external bodies of morality.

It is tempting to think that the 'rational' approach is more modern and, therefore, somehow, more suited to the twentieth century. However, the concepts of natural law have been dusted off since 1945 and are now very much a central part of most experts' thinking on the subject; even if those experts do not, sometimes, admit that this is the case!

Definition

Natural Law

Rules which have to accord with 'universal moral standards' before they acquire any real legitimacy. The tenets of natural law state that an immoral rule can never be made into a real law simply by being passed through a national legislature.

Note that it is on the ground of 'natural law' that officers and men in the armed forces, today, are expected to disobey any order which goes against accepted morality. The basis for this being the findings of the Military Tribunals in Nuremburg following World War II. Those tribunals did not accept the claim from German and other Axis soldiers that they were merely 'carrying out orders' when they committed what the Tribunals classified as 'war crimes'. It was not enough, in other words, that one had a legal order from a superior officer – it was also necessary for the act to be 'moral'.

The concept is central to the law of the UK, Australia, Canada, the USA and certain other countries whose legal systems have been influenced by links with the UK. Almost all of the system of 'Common Law' which exists in these countries today has evolved over the centuries from 'accepted' practices and implied morality. The concept is still extremely strong in Britain as can be seen from the example of the Chief Constable of Brighton (page 60).

Positive Law

The opposite approach to law is the attitude that laws are simply rules which are legally established by the authorised body. The content of these rules is largely irrelevant. Supporters of positive law argue that laws still exist and must be obeyed even though minorities may not be protected or specific groups may be exploited. Apartheid is still a legal requirement in South Africa in spite of the fact that most of the rest of the world and not a few white citizens of South Africa regard it as totally immoral.

Positive law theorists argue against natural law by saying that the idea of morality is too vague and that laws which claim to be 'natural' are, therefore, subject to much uncertainty.

Thomas Hobbes (1588–1679) (see page 9) was a firm supporter of this view of the law. He believed that the ruler (or 'sovereign') was the only source of law and that, in the interests of peace, harmony and security, citizens were obliged to obey even if they felt the laws to be wrong.

Positive law requires that all legal commands are backed by the threat of some kind of sanction. If the citizen disobeys a law then the courts have the power to punish by fine or by imprisonment.

But law is not, of course, as simple as this. Positive law is a form of *duty-imposing* rule which sets out what the citizen's duties are. There is a different form of law called a **power conferring law**, though, which enables the citizen to do certain things but does not, necessarily, impose any duties or sanctions.

These latter laws seem to imply that laws are not there merely to command, but that they also help to *structure* the way in which people in a society deal with each other and how they relate to the values of society. Laws on marriage, divorce, abortion, etc. are very much statements on morality. As the courts have had to try to deal with these types of law during the last half of the twentieth century so the concept of 'natural law' has, once more, become important. Many senior judges have argued, persuasively, that it is part of the duty of the courts to help to interpret the prevailing morality.

Definition

Positive Law
Positive Law is the idea that laws are, and mean, exactly what they say. The written word is to be taken 'literally' by the Courts and no attempt should be made either to imply *the intention of the law's writers or to* apply *over-riding ethical principles.*

Command Law

The views of Hobbes and others who followed him resulted in the establishment of a theory of 'Command Law' which has been widely used to describe the British system. Jeremy Bentham (1748–1832) and the school of **Utilitarians** who followed him during the early nineteenth century regarded rational laws made by the legally instituted ruler (Parliament) as the only true laws. They wanted, in fact, to remove all discretion from the judges about their interpretation of **Common Law.**

This approach (that Parliament passes laws and the courts are merely there to implement it, not to question it) has been central to British justice. Only in the last twenty years has there been any concerted attempt by theorists and by the judiciary to reinforce the claims of natural law and the place of the judges as the guardians and interpreters of that law.

Definition

Command Law
The concept of Command Law is the essentially British concept that Parliament passes laws which the Courts implement without discretion. *Similar to the more modern and international concept of 'Positive Law', Command Law differs in that it implicitly assumes that Parliament's laws will be both just and rational.*

Example

Comparative Law
One of the easiest ways to see the various philosophies of law in action is to look at the systems used by other countries and compare them with those of the UK.

France has a very rigid system of written law based on '**Codes**' which were established during the time of Napoleon I. The move to this wholly written system was partly due to an understandable desire to avoid the problems of the 'King-made' law which had preceded the French Revolution. Today the highest court is the *Conseil d'Etat* which is independent of the government and is extremely powerful.

West Germany created such a strong system of legal underpinning to the political system after 1945 that it is sometimes known as the *Rechtsstaat* (a 'Legal State'). The country's 'Basic Law' of 1949 requires that laws play an important role in all government decision making and the Federal nature of the country means that the courts have an important role to play in arbitrating between the *Länder* (States) and the Federal Government.

Justice

The term 'justice' is used in this chapter almost completely in its legal sense but it has important meanings within the concepts of **equality, freedom**, and **rights** (see the appropriate chapters).

As with the concept of **law**, there are really two quite different approaches to the definition of justice. On one hand stand those who believe that justice is the balancing of rights and wrongs against specified rules. The process is seen as a mechanical one in which the main requirement is to establish how closely one party's actions conform to the established law.

Legal or **Procedural Justice** is satisfied when the rules as laid down by society have been observed – whether those rules were 'right' or 'fair' or not. A swimming competition is won by the best athlete who conforms to the rules of the races not by the swimmer who is most socially deserving or morally upright.

The concept of procedural justice is parallel to those of positive law and the market economy. It relies, essentially upon the operation of set rules to resolve all problems. Considerations of inherent fairness are not entertained because, the supporters of procedural justice would claim, society operates on an unequal basis and the market system allocates resources according to the criteria of efficiency not fairness.

Procedural justice, argue many of its critics, can never be possible in the 'real' world. In any society, they would say, the justice which is meted out is a reflection not simply of the words written down in the legal statutes but of the prevailing culture and, more importantly, of the views of the dominant sections of that society. All justice is, to a greater or lesser extent, value-laden.

Definition

Justice
Justice is concerned with the 'fairness' of the application of laws and procedures and is, at least partly, derived from the statement by Aristotle that justice is the technique of:

> *'treating equals equally and unequals unequally'*

There was the assumption that any unequal treatment should always be in direct proportion to the inequality.

Definition

Procedural Justice
A view of the settlement of disputes within systems of rules as being merely the application of those rules without any further considerations. Procedural justice would be satisfied if a law was observed, whether the law was a 'good' law or not.

The rules governing the application of the laws concerning 'Unfair Dismissal' is an example of such justice in Britain. The Tribunals which hear claims for unfair dismissal are required to make decisions purely upon the actual facts of the case and upon the law as written down. They may not decide whether, for example, a specific case met the 'spirit of the law'.

Natural Justice

The ideas of 'natural law' led automatically to those of natural justice. That is, a form of justice which was more than merely conformity to the written words of the law. Natural justice assumes, as the concept of procedural justice does not, that a law may be passed which is **unjust.** The system of **English Common Law** has developed from widely accepted standards of what is fair and right in most circumstances and, to that extent, is a form of natural law. Natural justice flows from the universal standards of morality which underpin the systems of natural law.

Note carefully however: natural law and justice are *not* the same as social law and justice. They do not attempt to meet prescribed levels of societal fairness or equality, but simply reflect the prevailing moral views of the society in question.

A good example of what is meant here is provided by the slavery laws of the nineteenth century. Slavery was abolished in Britain earlier in the century than it was in the United States. This did not mean that either of those two countries were operating a system of social justice (in fact, neither were) merely that each country came to the decision that slavery was morally wrong at a different time.

Definition

Natural Justice
The view that justice can never simply be the application of rules to situations without further consideration. Laws can be unjust (i.e. unfair) and natural justice would require a judge to take this inherent unfairness into account when deciding a case.

Example

Natural justice is a development of the concept of natural law. It accepts that there is such a thing and demands that, where there are no other guidelines, legal decisions should conform to what the courts can deduce as natural law.

In 1964 the Chief Constable of Brighton was charged and tried on charges of conspiracy. He was subsequently acquitted by the court but was still dismissed by the Brighton Watch Committee (the old name for a Police Authority). In such cases the Police Act of 1919 laid down that there should be a formal enquiry, but the Brighton Watch Committee claimed that this was not required in this case as the Chief Constable was being dismissed for 'administrative' reasons.

The courts found not only that the requirements of the 1919 Act had to be applied but that the Watch Committee's refusal to allow the Chief Constable a formal hearing was a breach of the terms of natural justice.

Social Justice

Supporters of the concept of social justice argue that even natural justice does not go far enough towards what they would regard as the duty of the judges to make decisions which lead to socially desirable outcomes.

All justice, they would argue, assumes a set of moral and social values. **Social justice** merely requires a specific set of those values concentrating on the more equal distribution of resources.

Definition

Social Justice
Note that the concepts of procedural and natural justice do not require the state to take a hand. The legal system, in both cases, is quite able to dispense 'justice' without external aid. In the former the courts are merely disinterested arbiters applying the rules without fear nor favour. While in the latter, the judges are able to deduce the prevailing morality and use it to amend the rules or to assess when a law conflicts with the prevailing morality and is, therefore, unjust.

Social justice requires a more positive attitude by the state. The appropriate distribution of resources and the societal targets must be set by the central government so that the law can operate in such a way as to enhance the society's progress towards those goals.

Social justice requires that rules are applied with due consideration for their fairness not just in terms of the prevailing morality, but in terms of what the state feels the morality ought to be.

Whereas the main problem with procedural justice is that it results in inequality and unfairness, social justice has the result of increasing the state's activity. Someone has to set the social targets and to determine what the level of equality should be, and in what areas it should be sought.

Hayek argues that this has the result of involving the state deeper and deeper in value decisions. In order to enforce these decisions the State has to enmesh society in more and more rules and regulations. The inevitable progression, says Hayek, is towards a more and more Totalitarian system.

Friedrich August von Hayek (1899–)

Hayek was born in Austria but became a naturalised British citizen in 1938. He developed much of the thought which has, since, become known as the 'Chicago School' of economics. It is, essentially, a *laissez-faire* approach which emphasises individual responsibility above centralised systems of control and care. Hayek developed the concept of the 'minimalist' state and, in his book, *The Road to Serfdom* argued that government intervention in the economy reduces the amount of both economic and political freedom. By taking to itself the power and responsibility to take decisions on behalf of its citizens, the Government creates a 'feudal' relationship of dependency. Ordinary citizens become 'serfs' with little individual freedom to develop or to differ from the norm.

Hayek taught at the Universities of Vienna, London, Chicago and Freiburg, and received (jointly) the Nobel Prize for Economics in 1974.

See: *The Road to Serfdom*, 1944; *The Constitution of Liberty*, 1960; *Studies in Philosophy, Politics and Economics*, 1967; *Law, Legislation and Liberty* – Vols I-III, 1973-6.

The system of social justice requires judges to make decisions about whether a person *needs* or *deserves* a particular result. Areas such as health, education, employment, wealth, etc. have all been subject, in recent years, to the demands of the theories of social justice. Governments pass laws which seek to provide education for all and then leave it up to the courts to try to interpret those laws in individual cases as best they might. The problem for the courts, of course, has been to implement values which might not have been clearly set out in the legislation.

The question of school transport is a particularly thorny one for the courts. The Education Acts lay down specific requirements for children to attend school and local authorities make (or do not make) provision for their children to travel to school. Problems arise when parents feel that local authorities have, for example, abandoned school buses to rural areas unjustly.

CASE STUDY
A: THE LAW AND INDUSTRIAL RELATIONS

1 After Trade Unions were finally made legal in 1850 they 'naturally' became subject to the normal laws of the land. These led, however, to results which few people had foreseen or desired.

2 In 1901 a trade union involved in a dispute with a company went on strike and was sued by the company for the damages which the strike had caused. The result of the **Taff Vale Case** was that the union was fined well over £20,000 (equivalent to possibly £500,000 in today's money).

3 The public outcry against the unfairness of the Taff Vale decision was such that a new law was passed which effectively made the Trade Unions a different form of legal entity to any other. The **Trades Disputes Act, 1906** made unions immune from suit for what are called **torts** (negligence, slander, etc.) as long as they were acting 'in furtherance of a trade dispute'.

The lack of a specific definition of such a dispute gave trades unions almost complete immunity from legal action for their actions. Contracts were virtually unenforceable and industrial relations became extremely unpredictable.

4 Apart from slight changes during the 1920s, the Trades Disputes Act remained the basis of the treatment of trade unions in law up to the 1970s.

5 By then, however, the levels of industrial action caused many people to argue that the unions had to be given a new legal framework. The Labour government had proposed something of the kind during the late 1960s in its document 'In Place of Strife'. That document included provisions for a 28 day 'Conciliation Pause' which, if broken, could lead to financial penalties.

6 In 1971, the new Conservative government of Edward Heath introduced an even more comprehensive set of legal provisions for the unions: a completely separate legal system. The **Industrial Relations Act 1971** established a National Industrial Relations Court (NIRC) under a senior justice, Sir John Donaldson. The NIRC was abolished by the Labour government of 1974, but not before it had actually sent some dockers, briefly, to jail for contempt of court.

7 The 1974 Labour government not only abolished the NIRC but also passed the **Trade Union and Labour Relations Act** and the **Health and Safety at Work Act** – both of **1976**.
The first of these Acts brought together almost all previous legislation and made clear a number of aspects of the rights of trade unions:

- No collective agreement between unions and employers was to be enforceable at law. Even where the agreement was in writing it was only enforceable if *both* parties expressly wished it to be;
- No action was possible against a union in *tort* (i.e. for breach of a duty imposed by law other than a contractual duty – examples are trespass, nuisance, defamation, and negligence.) Only where it could be proved by an employer that the tort was committed where there was no contemplation or furtherance of a trade dispute could the union be sued successfully.

  During the 1979–80 Steel Strike, Lord Denning took the view that the steel unions were involved in secondary picketing and that this was *political* in nature. His judgement, later overturned by the House of Lords, was that this removed the union's protection under the 1976 Act and left it open to suit for damages by the employers. The House of Lords' rejection of Lord Denning's judgement led directly to the first of several later Conservative employment bills.
- Both 'Post-Entry' and 'Pre-Entry' closed shops were made legal and dismissal of an employee for refusal to belong to a trade union where a closed shop agreement operated was deemed to be 'fair' under the terms of the law's unfair dismissal provisions. By 1980 over 5 million employees worked in closed shops.

8 The Conservative governments of 1979, 1983, and 1987 followed a different route with respect to the position of the trade unions under the law. Instead of trying to set up a separate system of **Industrial Law**, they attempted to bring the unions back into the normal legal system while still maintaining some of the privileges which allow the unions to operate effectively.

Definition

Closed Shop
A 'closed shop' is an organisation or an occupation which requires that one be a member of a specified trade union as a condition of working in it. Some require trade union membership before *entering the job or the company (a 'Pre-entry closed shop') while others simply require that one join the trade union immediately upon taking up the job ('Post-entry closed shops'). Both are now illegal unless supported by votes of 80 per cent of the employees concerned in regular ballots.*

9 The Employment Acts of 1980 and 1982, and the Trade Union Act of 1984 created new sets of regulations for the unions by:

- restricting 'secondary' action against firms which are not directly involved in the dispute;
- narrowing the definition of a trade dispute thereby reducing the possibility of 'political strikes';
- requiring unions to hold secret ballots before industrial action and for the election of their officers;
- allowing unions to be sued for damages whenever industrial action is 'illegal'.

10 The Employment Act of 1988 continued this process by redefining the conditions under which union General Secretaries and Presidents need to be elected or re-elected by secret ballot.

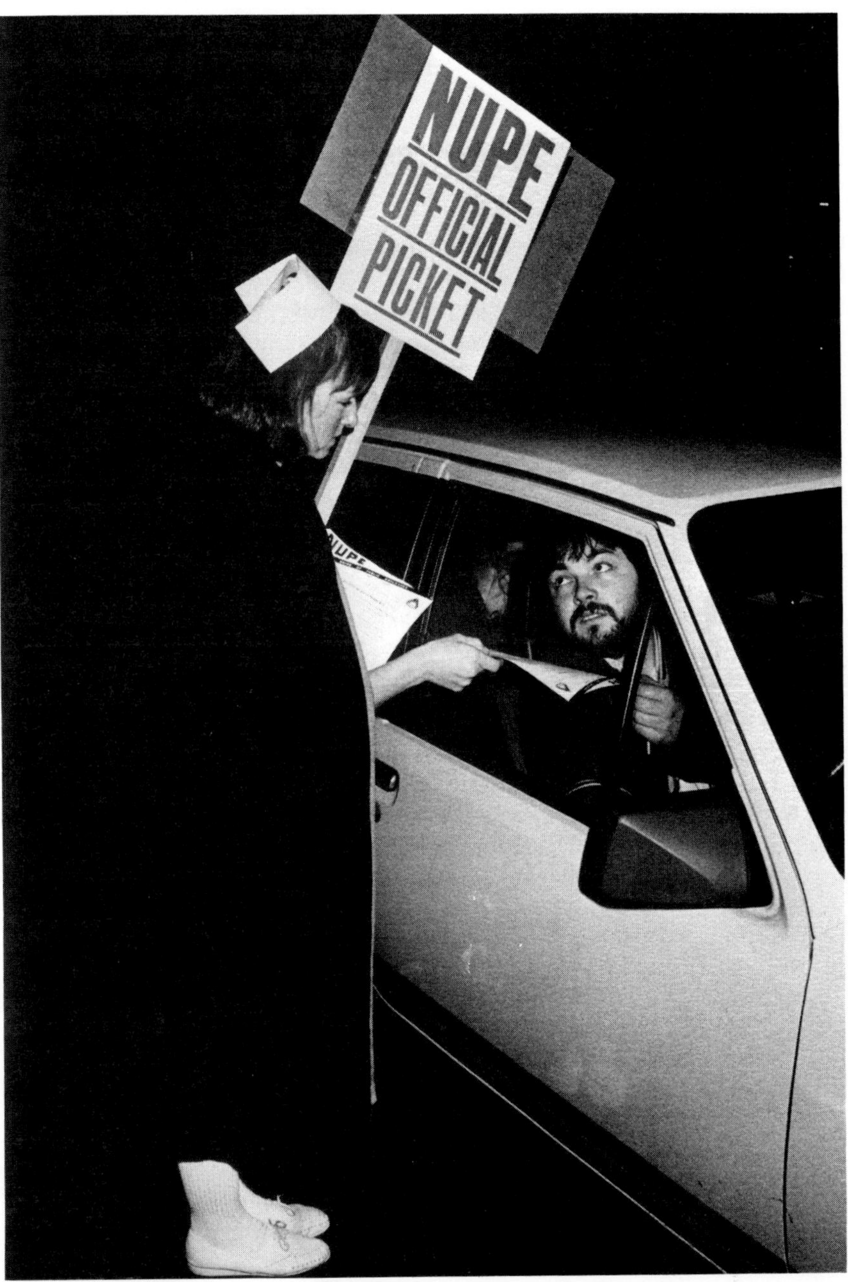

► *An official picket at North Manchester General Hospital in January 1988 – the first nurses' strike in Britain.*

Questions

1. What does the fact that there was a public outcry at the unfairness of the Taff Vale decision tell you about the type of law and the definition of justice which the courts understood at that time as compared to what the general public expected of them?
2. What are the limits to the use of industrial action? How far do you think that trade unions can legitimately go in the pursuit of their objectives? If a dependence on **Positive Law** is considered too crude for application to industrial relations should the courts rely on deduction of natural justice or should they be given laws which explicitly state the criteria of social justice?
3. To what extent are some people justified when they claim that the judges represent a different 'class' to the working population and that their decisions should therefore be ignored?

▶▶▶▶▶▶▶▶▶▶▶▶▶▶▶▶▶ CASE STUDY B: JUSTICE AND SOGAT

SOGAT'S assets STRIPPED

Britain's trade unions may yet thank Mr Rupert Murdoch: he has handed them an issue upon which they can agree. Since the Conservative government's first trade union reforms were introduced in 1980, unions have been tearing themselves apart over whether the new laws should be defied, tolerated or occasionally embraced. But all, from the loftiest idealist to the most hardened pragmatist, are agreed that the sequestration of the entire £17m-worth of assets of the largest print union, SOGAT'82, is unfair.

The union, 4,500 of whose members were sacked by Mr Murdoch's News International after they went on strike, has instructed members involved in wholesale distribution not to handle News International's four titles. Enough SOGAT members have followed this instruction to make annoying holes in the company's distribution network. Because the disruption constitutes unlawful secondary action under the 1980 Employment Act, the union was ordered to withdraw its instruction. It did not; this week's sequestration, on top of a £25,000 fine, was the result.

The sequestrators – from chartered accountants Ernst & Whinney – clearly intend to move more gently than did those from Price Waterhouse who seized Mr Arthur Scargill's mining union's assets in 1984. SOGAT leaders are also behaving much more circumspectly than Mr Scargill did. The sequestrators show no signs of turfing the union out of its office buildings, and will apply to the courts next week to make several payments on the union's behalf. If the court wants to make life as difficult as possible for the union until it has purged its contempt and called off the disruption, it may refuse. The National Graphical Association, the transport union, and the Union of Communication Workers (whose postmen have been blacking Mr Murdoch's bingo cards) have also been challenged in the courts; they may face sequestration too.

The most recent vote on the TUC's general council over whether to risk law-breaking – on a different issue – was won by the law-abiders by a mere 15 votes to 14. The strong support for SOGAT could swing the vote the other way this time. Short of law-breaking (which would mean, mainly, asking more unions to support SOGAT with unlawful secondary action), there is little the TUC feels it can do.

The News International dispute has shown that the law against secondary action is the most crippling of the trade-union reforms and, unlike others, will never be accepted by the unions. Employers can – and, like Mr Murdoch and fellow newspaper proprietor Mr Robert Maxwell, do – divide their companies into numerous smaller ones, so that action affecting anything outside one place of work loses immunity. British unions have the worst of both worlds: as Mr Murdoch's sacking of his strikers has shown, they do not have positive rights (to organise, to strike, and so on), and the News International dispute shows how far they have lost many of the compensating advantages of legal immunity.

An end of the law against secondary action would not mean a vast increase in disruption as long as the law enforcing pre-strike ballots stayed. Most workers, balloted on secondary action, would probably be more interested in preserving their own jobs than supporting the brethren.

Source: *The Economist*, 15 February 1986

Questions

1 Do you agree that the sequestration of the union's entire assets was 'unfair' (as appears to be the opinion of the writer of the article)?
2 Should the postal workers in this example be allowed to 'black' Mr Murdoch's publications in support of the printers? Does your own concept of justice include this type of action and, if, so, what are its limits?
3 In what way could the different types of law – positive, natural and social – be applied to this example?

4 Consider the system of rules and regulations which govern your life in school, college or at work. Draw up a brief list of:
a what the rules and regulations cover;
b who is responsible for enforcing them;
c what sanctions (both 'real' and moral) are available to use against those who transgress;
d what systems of appeal may be available.

What are the faults in the system? (For example: are the rules always applied? Are they applied in the same way for everyone – or is one section of the community excluded? Are the sanctions effective?)
What would happen if all of these rules and regulations were to be scrapped?
What elements of the rules would you like to see scrapped or amended in the interests of 'justice'?

EXAMINATION QUESTIONS

1 'From the police constable to the Lords of Appeal, from lowly official to the Minister, the exercise of discretion is an essential element in the Rule of Law.' Comment. (Cambridge, 1982)

2 'There is one law for the rich and one for the poor.' Discuss. (Cambridge, Special Paper, 1982)

3 To what extent are the activities of the State subject to the Rule of Law? (Cambridge, Special Paper, 1982)

NOW READ ON . . .

Thomas Hobbes *Leviathan*
One of the few books which ever deserves the appellation *tour de force*. A universal philosophy which attempts to merge physics with politics and ethics.

Montesquieu *L'esprit des Lois*
The Baron who was influenced by the English 'Glorious Revolution' and who was typical of the French 'Enlightened' School

Michael J. Elliott 'The Role of Law' in Drucker *et al. Developments in British Politics 2* Macmillan, 1986
The Drucker volumes are excellent updates in a variety of very pertinent fields.

F.A. von Hayek *Law, Legislation and Liberty* Routledge & Kegan Paul, 1973
Quite simply – a classic. The nearest one comes to essential reading.

John Rawl *A Theory of Justice* Oxford University Press, 1972
Takes many of the older legal theories apart and suggests many of the reforms which have been implemented since.

J.A.G. Griffith *The Politics of the Judiciary* Fontana, 1985
Controversial when it was first published and only slightly less so now.

Plato *The Last Days of Socrates*
Plato's defence of his friend and mentor after Socrates had been executed. The detailed logical argument is excellent.

Gerald J Postema *Bentham and the Common Law Tradition* Oxford University Press, 1986
A learned examination of the tradition of Common Law and the effect on that tradition of Jeremy Bentham.

6 Freedom, Equality and Rights

Free speech

Yes platform

Wiping the odd egg from his lapel is part of the politician's stock-in-trade; but there is worse than egg. On October 17th, the Ulster Unionist MP Mr Enoch Powell had to abandon a talk at Bristol University when it was hijacked by anarchists with stolen student cards. As well as yelling and spitting at him, they smashed the tables and chairs and made a charge for the platform on which he was standing. Luckily, the university rugby club was there to protect him.

The problem is not just with visiting speakers. Politically unpopular academics may also incur the wrath of mob. Mr John Vincent, a history professor at Bristol University, writes populist right-wing pieces for the *Sun*. Some of the students who dislike Mr Rupert Murdoch and his papers have boycotted Mr Vincent's lectures; life at the university has become so difficult for him that he has decided to take two terms' unpaid leave while tempers cool. And at Ruskin College, in Oxford, Mr David Selbourne, who wrote an article for *The Times* about the Labour party in Liverpool, annoyed the student union of his college so much that it wants him sacked. Ruskin College, say his critics, is a trade-union foundation, so he should not be "scabbing" for a boss the union movement dislikes.

Source: *The Economist*, 25 October 1986, pp 32–3

▸▸▸▸▸▸▸▸▸▸▸▸▸▸▸ BASIC PRINCIPLES

In the article above, certain groups (students and others) prevented people from speaking in public or from carrying on their work because the groups felt that those people were 'racist', 'fascist' or 'sexist'.

The problem the article poses is almost as old as time: which 'right' is the stronger:

the right of free speech; or

the right of racial and other minorities not to be 'attacked' in inflamatory speeches?

If one decides, as is usually the case, that the need for freedom of speech outweighs *most* considerations of what is actually said* it is usually because most of us would regard our **right** to hold an opinion as being one of our most important and basic rights. We would also regard as important our **right** to try to convince others of the value of our beliefs.

▸▸▸▸▸▸▸▸▸▸▸▸▸▸▸ DISCUSSING THE ARGUMENTS

Freedom and Rights

Already the two concepts of **freedom** and **rights** appear to be inextricably linked. However, there are really *two* meanings to the word **freedom** and they are linked to a peculiarity of the English language.

Note*: Do not forget, though, that there *are* constraints on freedom of speech associated with **duties and outlined later in this chapter.

In English we have two words meaning freedom: FREEDOM and LIBERTY. Other languages including French and German only have one word for this concept – in French it is *liberté*, in German it is *die Freiheit*. In the past the word liberty has generally meant physical freedom, while the word freedom has been reserved for the various rights which we hold dear.

It is probably better for the sanity of us all if we drop the use of the word liberty altogether (remembering only that it has traditionally been used for things like the liberty of the subject, liberation from a foreign invader, etc.).

Even after clearing the decks of the archaic use of 'liberty', however, we are still left with the two meanings of the word 'freedom'. Broadly, they are:

'Freedom *from*' and 'Freedom *to*'

Freedom From

This concept is essentially a negative one: freedom from unlawful arrest, freedom from tyranny, etc.

The crucial point is that the *law* does not get involved in this type of freedom except to constrain it in some way. In other words, these freedoms exist *unless* a law has been passed to restrict them.

'Freedom from' is a peculiarly English concept based upon our very individual culture. British society has always emphasised the individual as opposed to the family, clan or group (see Liberalism, Chapter 10).

Freedom To

'Freedom to' is a much clearer concept to grasp because it is a *positive* approach to the problem of freedom and requires some form of legal backing.

- **Freedom of Assembly** is the freedom to assemble wherever and with whomever one pleases.
- **Freedom of Speech** is the freedom to say whatever one likes (usually within the confines of certain constraints).

In most countries, these 'freedom to's' are simply listed as a set of **Rights** which the people are given by law. The usual form is to list them in the written constitution or in **Bills of Rights**.

The tendency in modern times has been to list more and more 'rights' in special sections of constitutions or in Bills of Rights:

- the Constitution of the Soviet Union has large sections which detail the rights of its citizens
- the first ten clauses of the United States' Constitution is known as the 'Bill of Rights'.

> *Definition*
>
> *The classic definition of* **freedom** *is that proposed by the great British philosopher John Stuart Mill (1806–74):*
>
> The individual is not accountable to society for his actions, in so far as these concern the interests of no-one but himself.
>
> *In other words one can only be free to do things which do not infringe the freedoms of others.*

Since 1945 quite extensive *international* Bills of Rights have been written and published in an attempt to ensure certain basic rights to all people throughout the world:

- the International Declaration of Human Rights
- the European Convention of Human Rights

One major international pressure group, Amnesty International, spends most of its time trying to defend people all over the world from violations of their 'human rights'.

Types of Rights

The word liberty has been dropped in favour of the concept of 'the freedom to' and now *that* concept has been effectively replaced by the universally used term **rights.**

There are, however, several different variants on the theme of rights: There are:

natural rights
civil rights
human rights

and each has a specific meaning and a distinct origin in political philosophy.

Example

The Development of Rights

It is important to understand that, even in countries which have a written and detailed 'Bill of Rights', the rights of citizens have to be constantly guarded.

By accident or design governments can misinterpret the meaning of the written word and then 'rights' have to reasserted.

In no country is this process clearer than in the United Kingdom where, contrary to accepted wisdom, many of the rights of its citizens are contained in written documents.

For seven hundred years certain fundamental rights have been asserted, accepted and written into fresh statutes later.

The 'Rights' Process in the UK

- Assertion
- Re-emphasis and Re-assertion
- Expansion
- Trend towards written rights.

The process has two other facets. As time has gone by so the list of established 'rights' has been steadily expanded; and, over the same period the tendency has been for 'rights' to be enshrined in statutes rather than being left to custom and common law.

It is also worth noting that, in the twentieth century, there has been a trend towards the assertion of 'international' rights common to all. The United Nations Declaration of Human Rights and the European Convention on Human Rights are the best known of the international codes.

It was in Europe, and particularly in Britain, that this process first began and the fight for the rights of citizens goes back long before the two revolutions of the eighteenth century in the United States and in France.

The Magna Carta, 1215

In 1215 King John was forced by his nobles to sign the 'Great Charter' at Runnymede. Today this document is known, and its importance is understood, more by the inhabitants of other countries than by the British.

The thousands of American, European and Japanese tourists who flock to Runnymede each year understand that they are visiting the place where, for the first time, the power of an absolute monarch was not simply overthrown to be replaced by another absolute ruler but was *limited by law.*

The Magna Carta established, primarily, that the rule of law should apply to the monarch as well as to his subjects. It also placed limits on the power of the King to raise certain kinds of taxes without the consent of the Common Council and stated the right of free men not to be arbitrarily deprived of freedom or property without the due course of justice.

Magna Carta:

- Rule of Law – all King's Acts had to conform with the Common Law.
- Consent of Common Council required for certain types of tax.
- No free man could be seized, imprisoned, dispossessed of land or outlawed unless through the lawful judgement of his peers.

Note: The Magna Carta was a Charter or Agreement between King John and certain subjects in 1215. It was only enacted as a Statute of Parliament during the reign of Edward I in 1297.

Statute the Fifth, 1351

During the reign of Edward III a Statute was passed which guaranteed and extended some of the rights given by the Magna Carta.

This Statute provided that no one could be arrested except by a warrant issued by 'good and lawful People of the same neighbourhood where such Deeds be done'.

In addition it guaranteed that no one could be disenfranchised or relieved of property except by course of law.

Statute the Fifth:

- Right to lawful arrest on warrant issued locally.
- Right to due process of law.

Statute of the Liberty of the Subject, 1354

The re-affirmation of the 'due process of law' right, this Statute stated that no one could be condemned without the due process of law.

Freedom from arbitrary arrest and the right to a fair trial are two of three most important rights and it is not surprising, therefore, that they were among the earliest to be set down in British Statutes. Today, when most people take these rights for granted, they have to be jealously guarded even in the world's most stable democracies. In the USA 'due process' is one of the most important clauses of the Bill of Rights (the Fifth Amendment to the Constitution).

Liberty of the Subject:

- None shall be condemned without due process of law.

The Petition of Right, 1627

One hundred and fifty years before the American Revolution one of the major complaints which led to that revolt was settled in Britain.

The Petition of Right complains of many of the problems which later beset the colonists in

America: the forced billeting of soldiers and sailors, forced lending to the Crown, arbitrary arrest and imprisonment, the levying of taxes by the King on the basis of a claimed 'prerogative' (in contravention of the Magna Carta).

Other problems during the reign of Charles I were the imposition by the King of special courts (those of the 'Star Chamber' and the 'High Commission') which came under the King's authority only. The 'Grand Remonstrance' of 1641, protested about these injustices and represented the opposition in the country to the monarchy taking upon itself 'prerogative' powers.

The petition of Right was not, in itself, very effective and did not constitute a 'law' but (together with other actions against Charles I) it caused the King to curb these practices.

The key elements of the Petition were that people had been:

> *required to lend certaine somes of mony unto your Majestie . . . others of them have been therefore imprisoned confined and sondry other waies molested and disquieted*

and that:

> *Whereas of late great Companies of Souldiers and Marriners have been dispersed into divers Counties of the Realme, and the inhabitants against their Wille have been compelled to receive them to sojourne against the Laws and Customers of this Realme and to the great grievance and vexacion of the people.*

It is instructive to compare this with the following:

> *He has kept among us, in times of peace, Standing Armies without the Consent of our legislative. . . .*
> *He has combined with others . . . For quartering large bodies of armed troops among us; For imposing Taxes on us without our Consent; For depriving us in many cases of Trial by Jury.*

(From the Declaration of Independence, adopted by the Continental Congress in Philadelphia, 4 July 1776.)

***The Petition of Right*:**
- No forced billeting of soldiers or sailors in peacetime.
- Attempted to restrict the King's ability to force people to lend him money and to impose taxes.
- Re-asserted the opposition to arbitrary arrest and imprisonment.

Habeas Corpus, 1679

The right to 'due process of law' includes the right to know the legal reason for your arrest and to a speedy trial at which you are present.

Habeas Corpus (or, literally, 'let us have the body/person') guarantees those rights by not only providing for a trial but laying down procedures to be followed (the 'body' was to be brought before the Court within three days except in the case of Treason or Felony).

***Habeas Corpus*:**
- Requires that the authorities show cause for any arrest.

Note: There have been a number of Habeas Corpus Acts since 1679 (notably in 1781, 1803, 1804, 1816, and 1862) each one of which has amended or extended the original rights.

The Bill of Rights, 1689

The horrors of the Civil War and the Interregnum* (1642–60) were followed by the experience of the attempts of James II to enhance the position of the Catholic Church and to reinstate what he regarded as the 'rightful' powers of the monarchy. The result was that Parliament 'invited' William of Orange and his wife Mary (the daughter of James II) to become King and Queen. James II was essentially, 'sacked' by Parliament and had to flee the country.

This episode is known by the slightly ironic title of the 'Glorious Revolution' of 1688. It was followed very quickly by an Act of Parliament designed to limit the power of the monarch for all time.

Strictly speaking, the Bill of Rights is concerned with the relationship between the Crown and Parliament, but several of its clauses also have the effect of guaranteeing the rights of the citizen.

The Bill abolishes the right of the monarch to suspend or dispense with laws thereby guaranteeing the citizen's right to freedom from arbitrary rule.

It abolishes the King's right to raise taxes without the consent of Parliament thereby – at least in theory – guaranteeing the fundamental right to representation before taxation.

The monarch's ability to raise or to keep an army in peacetime was also abolished.

The Bill also reasserted freedom of speech and debate in Parliament and the right of the citizen to petition the crown.

*The 'Interregnum', literally 'between reigns', was the period between the execution of Charles I in 1649 (up to then he had still been the rightful monarch), and the accession of Charles II in 1660. The period was known as the 'Commonwealth' under the 'Lord Protector', Oliver Cromwell. After Cromwell's death in 1658 his son Richard took over. Richard's control was not as firm as his father's, however, and the monarchy was restored in 1660.

Bill of Rights:
- effectively guarantees freedom of speech.
- ensures right to representation before taxation.
- abolishes monarch's ability to rule arbitrarily.

Slave Trade Abolition, 1807
This Act abolished slave trading but not slavery itself.

Slavery Abolition Act, 1883
After one of the earliest successful examples of 'pressure group' activity, the anti-slavers led by William Wilberforce succeeded in having the freedom of all citizens of the British Dominions guaranteed.

Slavery Abolition:
- Freedom of the person.

Sex Discrimination Acts, 1975–87
These acts make it an offence to discriminate between people on the grounds of sex with regard to recruitment, training, promotion and other aspects of employment. The 1987 Act extended equal treatment to the areas of retirement ages and pensions.

Sex Discrimination Act:
- Right to equal treatment on grounds of sex.

Race Relations Act, 1976
The protection of racial minorities was first entered into law in 1965 when the then Home Secretary, Roy Jenkins, guided the Race Relations Act of that year through Parliament.

The Act prohibited racial discrimination in public places, made incitement to racial hatred a criminal offence and established the Race Relations Board.

The 1976 Act extended the 1965 legislation to include recruitment, promotion, training, dismissal etc. and established the 'Commission on Racial Equality'.

Race Relations Act:
- Right to equal treatment for all regardless of colour, race, ethnic origin or nationality.

Data Protection Act, 1984
In the last quarter of the twentieth century one of the most important concerns for those interested in the liberty of the citizen has been the large amount of information about citizens which is contained on electronic databases and which can be bought, sold, transferred and updated without the individual's consent or knowledge.

The Act requires anyone who keeps information on electronic data bases to register and to provide that information if requested by the individual concerned.

Data Protection Act:
- Right to know of, have access to, and to be able to amend information on individuals kept on computer databases.

Religious Toleration
Freedom to worship whatever one wishes has been accepted for many years. The process of acceptance was long and very slow and involved many Acts in order to guarantee the rights of various groups not only to freedom of worship but also not be discriminated against on the grounds of their religion.

These Acts include:
Scottish Episcopalian Act, 1711
Roman Catholic Relief Act, 1829
Religious Disabilities Act, 1846
Jews Relief Act, 1858
Test Abolition Act, 1867
Roman Catholic Relief Act, 1926

Example

Japan
By way of contrast it is noteworthy that, in Japan, this relationship between lord and people and between lord and Emperor was not 'contractual' but 'absolute'. In the western European system the rights and duties were, at least in theory, two-way. In Japan the citizen owed total allegiance to the lord and the lord owed total allegiance to the Emperor (or, in reality, to the Emperor's Shogun, a military general-in-chief).

Before the seventeenth century there was no theory of 'rights' as such. Throughout the western world the relationship between people was regulated by the duty of a citizen to the 'lord'. The system was heavily influenced by the Christian church and resulted in a sort of 'contractual' relationship existing under which the 'lord' had a duty to take care of his people and, in return, the people owed a duty of obedience to their lord. The system was identical when it came to the relationship between a lord and the king. In return for protection from enemies the king could expect the loyalty and support of his lords.

One of the major 'rights' which could really be identified before the seventeenth century was the **Divine Right of Kings**. This asserted that, because God chose Kings, the right of those kings to rule was absolute. Many monarchs used this concept to support their absolute right to rule their lands in any way they wished. The ultimate examples of this type of rule were probably Louis XIV of France and the later Tsars of Russia.

NATURAL RIGHTS

In Britain the theory that people had rights which were theirs independently of the rule of the monarch developed gradually from about the thirteenth century. Probably the first written expression of these 'rights of the subject' was the **Magna Carta** which King John's lords forced him to sign at Runnymede in 1215.

In particular, the barons of Runnymede established what was probably the oldest of the **natural rights**: the right of **Habeas Corpus**, the right to a prompt trial.

The Magna Carta and the 'Rule of Law'

The northern and East Anglian Lords who rebelled against the luckless King John were not really concerned about the plight of the ordinary people or about enlarging their rights. However, due to the influence of the Church the document which John eventually signed was much wider in its political significance than the Barons had originally intended.

The Magna Carta mostly concerned the King's relationships with his Lords but, in Article 39, it stated the basis of what have evolved into some of our most important rights.

> *No free man shall be arrested or imprisoned or dispossessed or outlawed or harmed in any way save by the lawful judgement of his equals under the law of the land. Justice will not be sold to any man nor will it be refused or delayed.*

The Magna Carta, by its very nature, also established one other major element of our current political philosophy: that no one – *not even the monarch* – is above the law.

MAGNA CARTA (1297 c. 1)

Magna Carta de lib'tatib; Angl', et de lib'tatib; Foreste; co'firmata a R. Edwardo; Anno r' sui vicesimo q'nto. xxv°.

THE GREAT CHARTER OF THE LIBERTIES OF ENGLAND, AND OF THE LIBERTIES OF THE FOREST;

CONFIRMED BY KING EDWARD, IN THE TWENTY-FIFTH YEAR OF HIS REIGN.

EDWARD by the Grace of God King of England, Lord of Ireland, and Duke of Guyan, [*to all Archbishops, Bishops, &c.] We have seen the Great Charter of the Lord Henry sometimes King of England, our Father, of the Liberties of England in these words:

I.
Confirmation of Liberties.

In p'mis concessim deo, & hac psenti carta nra confirmavim' p nob & hered nris imppetuū, q'd eccl'ia Anglicana libera sit, & habeat omnia jura sua integra, & libtates suas illesas. Concessim' eciam & dedim' omib3 liberis hominib3 regni nri, p nob & heredib3 nris imppetuū, has libtates subscriptas, hendas & tenendas eis & hered suis, de nob & hered nris imppetuū.

FIRST, We have granted to God, and by this our present Charter have confirmed, for Us and our Heirs for ever, that the Church of England shall be free, and shall have all her whole Rights and Liberties inviolable. We have granted also, and given to all the Freemen of our Realm, for Us and our Heirs for ever, these Liberties under-written, to have and to hold to them and their Heirs, of Us and our Heirs for ever.

(MAGNA CARTA) (1297 c. 1)

X–XXVIII. . . . .

XXIX.
Imprisonment, &c. contrary to Law.
Administration of Justice..

Nullus liber homo capiatur vel imprisonet', aut disseisiatur de libo teñ suo, vel libertatib3, vt libis consuetudinib3 suis, aut utlaget' aut exulet aut aliquo modo destruatur, nec sup eum ibimus, nec sup eū mittem', nisi p legale judiciū piū suoz, vel p legem terre. Nulli vendem', nulli negabim', aut differem' rectum vel justiciam.

NO Freeman shall be taken or imprisoned, or be disseised of his Freehold, or Liberties, or free Customs, or be outlawed, or exiled, or any other wise destroyed; nor will We not pass upon him, nor [*condemn him,] but by lawful judgment of his Peers, or by the Law of the Land. We will sell to no man, we will not deny or defer to any man either Justice or Right.

THE PETITION OF RIGHT (1627 c. 1)

Reciting that by (25) 34 Ed. I. st. 4. c. 1, by Authority of Parliament holden 25 Ed. III. and by other Laws of this Realm, the King's Subjects should not be taxed but by Consent in Parliament;

HUMBLY shew unto our Soveraigne Lord the King the Lorde Spirituall and Temporall and Cōmons in Parliament assembled, That whereas it is declared and enacted by a Statute made in the tyme of the Raigne of King Edward the first cōmonly called Statutum de Tallagio non concedendo, That no Tallage or Ayde should be layd or levyed by the King or his Heires in this Realme without the good will and assent of the Archbishopps Bishopps Earles Barons Knighte Burgesses and other the Freemen of the Cōmonaltie of this Realme, And by Authoritie of Parliament holden in the five and twentith yeare of the raigne of King Edward the third, it is declared and enacted, That from thenceforth no pson should be compelled to make any Loanes to the King against his will because such Loanes were against reason and the franchise of the Land, And by other Lawes of this Realme it is pvided, that none should be charged by any charge or Imposicion called a Benevolence nor by such like Charge by which the Statutes before mencioned and other the good Lawes and Statutes of this Realme your Subjecte have inherited this Freedome That they should [*not] be compelled to contribute to any Taxe Tallage Ayde or other like Charge not sett by cōmon consent in Parliament.

Seven Hundred Years Later . . .

When one of Britain's greatest constitutional theorists wrote down what he considered to be **The Rule of Law** these were the things he felt were important:

1 No person is above the law; all are equal before the law; disputes are decided in ordinary courts.
2 No person is punishable except in the case of a distinct breach of the law.
3 The principles of the Constitution, especially the liberties of the individual, are the result of judicial decisions. The rights of the individual precede and do not derive from the Constitution.

A.V. Dicey *Introduction to the laws of the Constitution*
Macmillan, 1952

Throughout the centuries after Magna Carta people began to assert, mainly in Britain, that there were such things as **natural rights** and to try to draw up definitions of what they were.

One of the earliest expressions of these rights came from one of Britain's most famous judges. Sir Edward Coke (1552–1634) who was Chief Justice of the King's Bench identified *three* basic rights which he called **principles**:

- the right of Habeas Corpus;
- the right to trial by law;
- the right to be taxed only by consent.

(This last statement was to lead almost directly to the statements of rights by the American colonies before the War of Independence).

At a slightly later period John Locke proclaimed in his *Second Treatise on Government* (1690) that no legislative body may take away the fundamental rights because those rights were given to men by God and could not be taken away by men. Locke's rights are even more familiar to modern students:

- the right to life;
- the right to liberty;
- the right to property.

These theories were in wide circulation during the first half of the eighteenth century and resulted in their being used by British settlers in North America to justify their wish to be represented in the British Parliament. An early American scholar and businessman, James Otis (he of the modern lift fame), wrote a document called *The Rights of British Colonies asserted and proved* in which he propounded similar 'natural rights' to those put forward by John Locke, in defence of the American colonies.

Eventually, of course, an intransigent British government drove its subjects in North America to declare their independence and, in doing so, to put down on paper the first comprehensive account of 'natural rights'.

THE AMERICAN DECLARATION OF INDEPENDENCE – 1776
We hold these truths to be self-evident. That all men are created equal; that they are endowed by their Creator with inalienable rights; that among these rights are life, liberty and the pursuit of happiness . . .

Definition

Natural rights
Those 'rights' which are "natural" to man and which exist independently of any man-made rules and regulations. In other words, natural rights are those which belong to people irrespective of what governments say their rights are.

The reader will note that John Locke's third right – that of **property** has been omitted from the US Declaration. This is not because the colonies did not believe that people did not have such a right, but because they believed it to be so obvious as not to be worth restating.

During the war which followed the Americans' declaration of independence the colonists were aided in their battles against the British by French troops. Many of those soldiers returned to France convinced of the merits of the rights of men. They returned to a country in which the theories of rights had been well developed by such eminent theorists as Voltaire, Rousseau and Montesquieu.

The result, in France, was the **Declaration of the Rights of Man and the Citizen** (1789) which extended the rights of men into areas not considered by the earlier American document:

- the right to equality
- the right to liberty
- the right to security of person (ie freedom from arbitrary arrest)
- the right to property
- the right to seek happiness
- the right to be taxed only by consent

In the same year as the French declaration, the Americans enacted their second constitution which contained the famous **Bill of Rights** stating ten major rights. In this way, and for the first time, rights which had, up to then, been merely the moral assertions of theorists (**moral rights**), became **legal rights.**

HUMAN RIGHTS

The concept of rights was given great attention by the Socialist theorists of the nineteenth century, particularly by Karl Marx himself, but the next universal statements of rights had to wait until the middle of the twentieth century.

When World War II was still only a couple of years old and before the Americans had become fully involved the Prime Minister of Great Britain, Winston Churchill, and the President of the United States, Franklin Roosevelt, met, in secret, in mid-Atlantic on a British battleship. During that meeting they decided, between them, how they would like to see the world develop after the war had been won and the horror of Nazism had been erased.

The result was the famous **Atlantic Charter**: a statement not only of collective defence for the future against aggressors but of the rights which the two statesmen felt belonged to all human beings wherever they lived:

- the right to free speech;
- the right to freedom of belief;
- the right to be free from fear;
- the right to be free from want;

. . . and many others.

Their vision was brought to reality by the newly formed United Nations General Assembly which, on 10 December 1948, passed the **Universal Declaration of Human Rights**: a document which, to this day, is one of the most detailed, general and comprehensive statements of the rights of man.

► *Prime Minister Churchill hands President Roosevelt a letter from King George VI in mid-Atlantic. They signed the 'Atlantic Charter' on board the battleship* Prince of Wales, *in 1941.*

▼ *An extract from the Universal Declaration of Human Rights*

UNIVERSAL DECLARATION OF HUMAN RIGHTS

PREAMBLE

Whereas recognition of the inherent dignity and of the equal and inalienable rights of all members of the human family is the foundation of freedom, justice and peace in the world,

Whereas disregard and contempt for human rights have resulted in barbarous acts which have outraged the conscience of mankind, and the advent of a world in which human beings shall enjoy freedom of speech and belief and freedom from fear and want has been proclaimed as the highest aspiration of the common people,

Whereas it is essential, if man is not to be compelled to have recourse, as a last resort, to rebellion against tyranny and oppression, that human rights should be protected by the rule of law,

Whereas it is essential to promote the development of friendly relations between nations,

Whereas the peoples of the United Nations have in the Charter reaffirmed their faith in fundamental human rights, in the dignity and worth of the human person and in the equal rights of men and women and have determined to promote social progress and better standards of life in larger freedom,

Whereas Member States have pledged themselves to achieve, in co-operation with the United Nations, the promotion of universal respect for and observance of human rights and fundamental freedoms,

Whereas a common understanding of these rights and freedoms is of the greatest importance for the full realization of this pledge,

Now, Therefore,

THE GENERAL ASSEMBLY

proclaims

THIS UNIVERSAL DECLARATION OF HUMAN RIGHTS as a common standard of achievement for all peoples and all nations, to the end that every individual and every organ of society, keeping this Declaration constantly in mind, shall strive by teaching and education to promote respect for these rights and freedoms and by progressive measures, national and international, to secure their universal and effective recognition and observance, both among the peoples of Member States themselves and among the peoples of territories under their jurisdiction.

Article 1. All human beings are born free and equal in dignity and rights. They are endowed with reason and conscience and should act towards one another in a spirit of brotherhood.

Article 2. Everyone is entitled to all the rights and freedoms set forth in this Declaration, without distinction of any kind, such as race, colour, sex, language, religion, political or other opinion, national or social origin, property, birth or other status.

Furthermore, no distinction shall be made on the basis of the political, jurisdictional or international status of the country or territory to which a person belongs, whether it be independent, trust, non-self-governing or under any other limitation of sovereignty.

Article 3. Everyone has the right to life, liberty and security of person.

Article 4. No one shall be held in slavery or servitude; slavery and the slave trade shall be prohibited in all their forms.

Article 5. No one shall be subjected to torture or to cruel, inhuman or degrading treatment or punishment.

Article 9. No one shall be subjected to arbitary arrest, detention or exile.

Article 11. (1) Everyone charged with a penal offence has the right to be presumed innocent until proved guilty according to law in a public trial at which he has had all the guarantees necessary for his defence.

(2) No one shall be held guilty of any penal offence on account of any act or omission which did not constitute a penal offence, under national or international law, at the time when it was committed. Nor shall a heavier penalty be imposed than the one that was applicable at the time the penal offence was committed.

Article 13. (1) Everyone has the right to freedom of movement and residence within the border of each state.

(2) Everyone has the right to leave any country including his own, and to return to his country.

Article 16. (1) Men and women of full age without any limitation due to race, nationality or religion, have the right to marry and to found a family. They are entitled to equal rights at marriage, during marriage and at its dissolution.

(2) Marriage shall be entered into only with free and full consent of the intending spouse.

(3) The family is the natural and fundamental group unit of society and is entitled to protection by society and the State.

Article 18. Everyone has the right to freedom of thought, conscience and religion; this right includes freedom to change his religion or belief, and freedom, either alone or in community with others and in public or private, to manifest his religion or belief in teaching, practice, worship and observance.

Article 22. Everyone, as a member of society, has the right to social security and is entitled to realization, through national effort and international co-operation and in accordance with the organization and resources of each State, of the economic, social and cultural rights indispensable for his dignity and the free development of his personality.

Article 24. Everyone has the right to rest and leisure, including reasonable limitation of working hours and periodic holidays with pay.

Article 25. (1) Everyone has the right to a standard of living adequate for the health and well-being of himself and of his family, including food, clothing, housing and medical care and necessary social services, and the right to security in the event of unemployment, sickness, disability, widowhood, old age or other lack of livelihood in

circumstances beyond his control.
(2) Motherhood and childhood are entitled to special care and assistance. All children, whether born in or out of wedlock, shall enjoy the same social protection.

Article 26. (1) Everyone has the right to education. Education shall be free, at least in the elementary and fundamental stages. Elementary education shall be compulsory. Technical and professional education shall be made generally available and higher education shall be equally accessible to all on the basis of merit.
(2) Education shall be directed to the full development of the human personality and to the strengthening of respect for human rights and fundamental freedoms. It shall promote understanding, tolerance and friendship among all nations, racial or religious groups, and shall further the activities of the United Nations for the maintenance of peace.
(3) Parents have a prior right to choose the kind of education that shall be given to their children.

In 1950 an even greater step was taken when the nations of Europe agreed on the **European Convention on Human Rights** (4 November 1950). This is still a unique document in international law for it is the only statement of human rights to have a means of **enforcement** in the shape of the:
- **Commission on Human Rights** (one representative from each state elected for six years); and
- **European Court of Human Rights** (one judge from each state elected for nine years).

The Convention on Human Rights identifies many 'rights' but the major ones are such things as:
- equality
- liberty
- participation in government
- security of person
- free movement
- free choice of religion
- property
- equal pay
- freedom to join a trade union.

▼ *Trade unionists gather outside GCHQ in Cheltenham to show support for the sacked trade union members as they leave work for the last time. (See Case Study page 79.)*

Definition

Human rights
There is no absolute definition of human rights but the concept may be clarified by the following distinction.

Natural rights tend to be statements of respect for an **individual's** *rights. They require respect for such things as life, liberty, happiness, property, etc. More importantly, perhaps, is the distinction that there is no way of 'proving' natural rights because one either accepts that a God demands recognition of them or one does not.*

Human rights, on the other hand, tend to require restrictions on personal rights in order to protect the rights of others. They require positive action to protect the rights of others as in racial equality, equal opportunities, etc. Human rights do not require belief in some supernatural being in that they are statements of moral positions taken by human beings themselves (a human right exists because human beings *say it exists whereas a natural right can only exist if a* God *has sanctioned it).*

Civil Rights

Since World War II a narrower statement of rights has been developed: that of **civil rights.** In essence, civil rights are a specific variety of human rights which describe the rights of citizens vis-à-vis their own government.

The best known examples of civil rights being promoted are those of black people in the southern States of the USA in the 1950s and 60s and those of black people in South Africa in the 1970s and 80s. In both cases the 'minority' (although black people are certainly not a numerical minority in South Africa) were, and are, fighting for rights which they feel have been denied them by the national government. The United States' civil rights campaigns of the 1950s were led by Martin Luther King and resulted, eventually, in the legal emancipation of black people in the USA. In South Africa the battle has been going on much longer.

The Limits to Freedom

It is clear that our 'right' to travel wherever we wish without anyone asking us to obtain permission from the police and present internal passports (as is required in some countries) is not a *totally* unconstrained freedom. It cannot, for example, include the freedom to walk into anyone else's house without invitation or to walk across their flower beds. In most countries it is also accepted that properly constituted authorities shall have the ability to deny the people access to certain zones designated as dangerous areas (sewage farms, electricity sub-stations, waste disposal sites, etc.). The government may also place certain 'security' areas out of bounds.

Every freedom or right is limited to some extent and the best way to deal with this problem is to introduce the notion of **duties.**

It is an unfortunate characteristic of our modern world that, while most people are quick to claim that they 'know their rights', very few would admit to having *duties* associated with those rights. In fact, of course, every right which we acquire automatically brings with it a set of duties.

The famous American jurist Justice Oliver Wendell Holmes (1809–94) once said that a man is not 'free' to shout 'fire' in a crowded theatre. In other words he was saying that the 'right' to free speech was outweighed, in certain circumstances, by the **duty of care** for other people's safety.

The right of free speech is also restricted in other ways: there are laws on such things as slander, libel, sedition, blasphemy, incitement to disaffection, incitement to racial hatred, etc. Each implies an equivalent duty.

In Britain, today, the list of restrictions which surround our 'freedoms' is very long. The Official Secrets Act, 1911 and 1989, restricts our right to acquire information in many areas; the Public Order Act of 1936 prevents the wearing of uniforms at public political meetings; the Race Relations Act, 1976, prevents us from saying anything which might have the effect of stirring up racial hatred; the Employment Acts of the early 1980s have even made it illegal for a trade union to call a strike without first holding a secret ballot of its members; and, in the cinema, films are still censored for bad language or scenes which are considered to be inappropriate for specific age groups.

Freedom and Equality

Lord Acton (1834–1902) once said that:

. . the passion for equality makes vain the hope of freedom.

What he meant was that he felt that the two concepts of freedom and equality were not compatible. That it was impossible to have them both at the same time.*

In order to find out whether he was right one must examine the concept of **equality.**

Can one claim that 'All men are equal' (as the American Declaration of Independence appears to claim)? This certainly does not mean that we believe all people to be exactly equal in all respects for they patently are not. People are different physically and mentally and have different beliefs and aspirations.

Presumably what is really meant by the phrase is that all people are worthy of **equal consideration.**

There is a very strong case for believing that what we often refer to as 'equality' is really 'justice'. In other words, that what we mean by treating people equally is simply a call for them to be treated 'justly' (see Chapter 5).

The Equality Paradox

There is a further paradox associated with the concept of equality which is worthy of consideration.

Marx believed that true freedom was simply not possible in a system in which people acquired different amounts of economic wealth. He argued that wealth allowed rich people to do things denied to the poor (including having good medical care) and that only by equalising wealth would true freedom be possible.

Modern socialists go quite a long way down the same path and for some very good reasons. In our legal system justice may only be attainable by those who have the money to pay expensive lawyers and many of life's pleasures (at least the ones which do not come 'free') are denied to those who cannot afford them. Socialists believe, therefore, that a fundamental aim of government must be the equalisation of economic wealth in order that 'true' freedom be possible.

But:

If freedom is the right to do whatever one likes and equality is the right to be treated fairly and justly, what is to stop someone from treating another person unfairly (after all they are 'free' to do so)? By the same token, if we are all equal and must be treated equally (including, say, having our earnings taxed so that differences between us are smoothed out) how are we then 'free' to acquire possessions as we like?

It may be that there is a basic paradox about the two concepts of **freedom** and **equality** and that it is simply not possible to attain them simultaneously.

In order to at least partially get out of this paradox many philosophers have identified **property** as the main culprit. As long as we have a right to acquire property there can be no equality so, perhaps, the 'freedom' to own property must be restricted.

Jean Jacques Rousseau (1712–78) was one of the first political thinkers to identify and to wrestle with this problem. He decided that:

. . . the fruits of the earth belong to all and the earth itself belongs to none.

---

*It was also Lord Acton who said, 'Power tends to corrupt and absolute power corrupts absolutely.'

Example

Early socialism
The belief that it was the freedom to own property which caused all the problems led to some of the early attempts to suppress it.

In Britain and in France in the nineteenth century people like Robert Owen and François Fourrier established 'cooperatives' to try to eradicate property rights and to help people to co-operate together rather than to compete in the race to acquire possessions.

He also wrote one of the most famous political quotations about the concept of freedom:

> *Man is born free and everywhere he is in chains.*

The most important thing in trying to even out the distribution of wealth is to decide *how* the wealth should be doled out. George Bernard Shaw identified six different possibilities:

- give to each what he produces
- give to each what he deserves
- give to each what he can get and hold
- give to the masses enough to live and give the rest to the elite
- distribute wealth according to class
- carry on muddling along as we are

For himself, Shaw believed that there ought to be equal shares for all but he also left a warning about freedom:

> *For freedom, we know, is a thing that we have to conquer afresh for ourselves every day; like love . . . the battle for freedom is never done and the field never quiet.*

CASE STUDY
A: THE RIGHTS OF EMPLOYEES IN THE CIVIL SERVICE

1 Just after World War II the British Government established a communications centre near Cheltenham. It was called Government Communications Headquarters (GCHQ).

2 It became clear during the 1970s that GCHQ's role was not simply that of maintaining communications with the far flung reaches of British diplomacy and, by the early 1980s, government had admitted that GCHQ had a very important role in the gathering and processing of all types of intelligence data.

3 In 1981 civil service industrial action had led to a strike at GCHQ, and it appears that this led not only to unease in the British government but also to concern on the part of the American government (which made use of GCHQ facilities and was the recipient of much of its material).

4 In January 1985 the British government announced that membership of a trade union would not, in future, be allowed at GCHQ.
All those working at GCHQ were given two options: they could either maintain their trade union membership (in which case they would be transferred to less sensitive sites and offices in the civil service); or they could give up their trade union membership, remain in work at GCHQ, and receive an 'ex-gratia' payment of £1,000.

5 The unions protested about what they saw as the government's attempt to deny their members their rights as working people. A case was brought before the courts.

6 In the first instance the unions were granted an injunction by Mr Justice Glidewell. The reason for this was not that he felt the government was acting illegally in taking away the right to trade union membership, but that he felt that the government had not *consulted* the unions about the proposed action. Justice Glidewell said that this was a breach of *natural justice*.
Put another way he was claiming that there was a *natural right* of consultation.

7 The government took the case to the Appeal Court and, eventually, to the House of Lords. In both chambers the Glidewell decision was overturned and trade union members at GCHQ were, subsequently, forced to make the choice between membership of their trade union and continuing to work at GCHQ.

Questions

1 Do you think that there is a right to be consulted as implied by the Glidewell decision:
a for civil servants in general?
b for civil servants in security-sensitive jobs?

2 The right to belong to a trade union is an important right in most democratic countries. What do you think the criteria are for denying people that right?
Consider first the criteria associated with preventing members of the police and the armed forces from belonging to a trade union. Remember, also, that at least one country (the Netherlands) allows its armed forces personnel to belong to a trade union.

3 Is it possible to justify the removal of union rights by saying that it is for 'the greater good' of all citizens?

► *Oxford Pilgrimage of the National Union of Women's Suffrage Societies, 1913.*

CASE STUDY B: WOMEN'S RIGHTS

1 Women in Britain in the nineteenth century had very few rights. They could not, of course, vote and it was only by the Married Women's Property Act, 1882 that they became able to continue ownership of their own property after marraige.

2 After World War I women began to acquire rights, including the right to vote but they only won certain rights very slowly. The right to be paid the same as a man for the same work, for example, was only given to women by the Equal Pay Act, 1970.

3 Even then, of course, employers discriminated against female labour in many ways and the right to be treated equally was granted by the Sex Discrimination Act, 1975.

4 The interesting thing about women's rights is that they appear to disprove what was said above about the origins of British 'rights'. These, it was claimed, derived in a *negative* way from common law. One had a right to do anything which was not specifically forbidden or constrained by law. Other countries, it was said, took the path of prescribing *positive* rights.
However, women's rights have only been safeguarded in Britain by *positive* laws such as those mentioned above.

Questions

1 Why do you think that it has been necessary to prescribe women's rights in a positive legal form? Why does the system of negative rights appear to have broken down or failed us in this respect?
2 Are there any parallels with minority groups and are the reasons the same?
3 Does all this mean that Britain needs a Bill of Rights?
4 What sort of rights could be written into a Bill of Rights? Write them out in the form that they would be written into the constitution. How would it be possible to change these rights? Who would stand in judgement on them?

▸▸▸▸▸▸▸▸▸▸▸▸▸▸▸ EXAMINATION QUESTIONS

1 What political doctrines have been built on the idea of natural rights? (London, June 1982,3)

2 'Although there is no written constitution, the basic freedoms such as freedom of speech and association together with the right of organised opposition to the government are guaranteed'.
(a) How effectively are these rights guaranteed?
(b) Consider the case for reinforcing basic freedoms with a Bill of Rights. (AEB, 1984)

3 'The State is not an obstacle to freedom, it makes freedom impossible.' Discuss. (Cambridge, 1985)

4 What are the principle threats to citizens' rights in Britain today and how might such rights be protected? (Cambridge, 1984)

▸▸▸▸▸▸▸▸▸▸▸▸▸▸▸ NOW READ ON . . .

Thomas Paine *The Rights of Man*
In the footsteps of Rousseau rather than Locke. An eighteenth century angry-young man.

John Locke *Two Treatises on Government*
One of the foundations of the so-called 'liberal-democratic' tradition

George Bernard Shaw *The Intelligent Woman's Guide to Socialism and Capitalism* Constable, 1928
Sharp, incisive and witty. An amusing demonstration of Shaw's acute vision.

William Letwin (Ed.) *Against Equality* Macmillan, 1983
An interesting perspective on the concepts.

Robert A. Dahl *Democracy, Liberty and Equality* Oxford University Press, 1986
An advanced treatment by one of the most eminent professors in the field

7 Representation

Death penalty is rejected by majority of 123

By George Jones, Political Correspondent

THE CAMPAIGN to secure the return of the death penalty ended in failure last night as MPs voted by a larger than expected margin of 123 votes to reject the restoration of capital punishment for murder.

There were loud cheers from both sides of the Commons as the 14th attempt to secure the reintroduction of capital punishment since the abolition of hanging in 1965 was defeated. On a free vote, MPs decided by 341 to 218 to reject a proposal that juries in murder cases should be empowered to recommend the death penalty.

The 123 majority was 11 higher than when MPs last voted on restoration of capital punishment just over a year ago. It was the first vote on the issue since the General Election last June, and there were 160 new MPs voting on the death penalty for the first time.

There were some highly charged moments during the six-hour debate, as Tory supporters of capital punishment accused Parliament of flouting the wishes of the public.

Source: *The Daily Telegraph*, 8 June 1988

THE DEATH PENALTY ISSUE

The attempt to reintroduce the death penalty came in the form of a clause in the Criminal Justice Bill in 1988 and was supported by 80 Conservative MPs. The clause was tabled by Roger Gale MP who claimed during the debate that Parliament had ignored public opinion in rejecting previous attempts to restore capital punishment. Nonetheless he did add that:

> *Members of this honourable House are not mandated and should never be.*

This was not the view of some other MPs. Teddy Taylor, MP, a supporter of the clause felt that:

> *It is a bad day for democracy that Parliament is so far apart from the people. There will be an angry public response.*
>
> *Daily Telegraph*, 8 June 1988

As the article demonstrates there are several interpretations of the role of the representative in a political system. The evidence that can be drawn from public opinion polls suggests that a clear majority of people in Britain would favour the restoration of the death penalty for certain categories of murder. MPs have, nonetheless, rejected repeated attempts to reintroduce it.

The justification that is given for ignoring public opinion is that most MPs do not see themselves as delegates. They feel they have a duty, on occasions, to ignore the views of the majority of their constituents, and vote according to conscience or what they see as the public interest. The problem with this view is that it appears to conflict with the democratic principle of majority rule. In Britain, however, it can be argued that we enjoy 'responsible' as well as 'representative' government and this allows a degree of discretion in policy making to our politicians. The difficulty of responsible government however lies in how to place limitations on the exercise of discretion to ensure that the wishes of the majority are not ignored.

BASIC PRINCIPLES

- If your class were asked to elect a 'representative' to express its views in discussions with school or college authorities, what role should he/she play?
- How should the representative take decisions at meetings with the authorities?
- Should he/she return to class for periodic guidance when unsure of what action to take?
- Should the representative be allowed some discretion to use his/her good judgement rather than just constantly return for direction? If so how much, and for how long?

Definition

Representative or delegate

A **representative** *once elected will be allowed a degree of discretion in taking decisions on behalf of those he or she represents.*

A **delegate** *will be given precise instructions by his or her constituents and expected to follow them explicitly.*

If unable to do so he/she should report back for consultation and further instructions.

Example

In the 1987 General Election the Conservatives were returned to office for a third successive term with a majority over all other parties of 102 seats. This victory was achieved with the Conservative Party winning 42.3 per cent of the votes which gave them 375 MPs and this amounted to nearly 58 per cent of the seats in the House of Commons.

In an ideal world we would all wish to be involved directly in the decisions that affect our lives. Direct participation was perhaps possible in a classical Greek state or in a Swiss Canton, but in a modern mass society like Britain, with a population of 57 million, it is not practically possible, or perhaps desirable, for all to be directly involved in decision making. A constant series of referendums might make it possible, but would be extremely complex and time consuming with possible disruption of the governmental process.

One method for overcoming such problems is by the use of a system of **representative government.** In this way the citizen gives up responsibility for direct decision making and allows an elected representative to undertake this function. Almost everyone desires to be governed by such representatives, every political cause, or group, wants 'representation', and all governments claim, legitimately or not, to be representative.

In Great Britain if we look at what parliament does and then compare it to what the people want, can the British government be seen as representative? The case study on capital punishment (see page 82) appears to show that on some occasions there is a diversity of opinion between MP's and public opinion. A possible explanation of this may lie with a consideration of 'responsible' as well as representative government (see below). But, there is also the fact that if British governmental decisions are supposed to reflect the wishes of the majority of the people, how can this be so when all governments, since 1945, have been elected with less than 50 per cent of the vote?

▶ *Britain's black MPs elected in 1987: Paul Boateng, Bernie Grant, Keith Vaz and Diane Abbott.*

Example

The House of Commons contains only 32 women MPs (about 4 per cent) and only 4 black MPs. (who were elected in 1987) out of a total of 650.

The British House of Commons may also be seen to be unrepresentative in another sense because some major groups in society are grossly under represented, or totally unrepresented.

The problem of attempting to answer such a question lies in the considerable range of views that exist on the nature of representation. A fundamental assumption of a representative system of government is that the governors claim their decisions should be binding on the rest of the community. The vast majority are usually prepared to comply with the decisions reached because, hopefully, there is an acceptable degree of correspondence between what the governors decide and what the governed want.

DISCUSSING THE ARGUMENTS

In the British political system one crucial question concerns the nature of the relationship between MPs and the people they represent, the 'constituents'. Major questions arise from a discussion of this relationship and the range of answers that result varies considerably. At one extreme there is the view that it is the duty of the representative to reflect accurately the wishes and opinions of those he/she represents, but a totally contrary view sees the representative as being free to act in the best interest of his (or her) constituents as he interprets it. A variety of views exist between these two extremes.

A Highly Restrictive View

In this view it is argued that the representative should follow explicitly the expressed wishes of his constituents. Any deviation should not be tolerated and if the representative feels unable to follow the wishes of his constituents then he should resign and allow for the election of someone who will. The underlying assumption in this analysis is that the people know what is good for them and the job of the representative is therefore to identify what his constituents want, and act upon it.

This view is associated with the English political philosopher Jeremy Bentham (1748–1832). He rejected the notion of representation and argued that there is no one who knows what is in your best interests as well as yourself. This concept of representation is accepted by few MPs but can be found in the British trade union movement. Those chosen to speak for trade union branches or for the union as a whole, are **delegates** and have no authority to do anything other than that which has been endorsed by the membership.

The branch delegate, for example, when attending the annual conference is not expected to exercise any discretion, and, if unsure of any course of

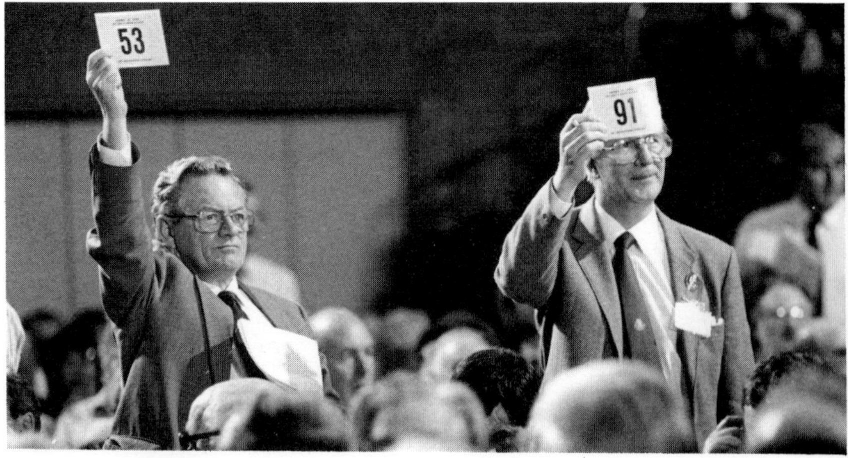

► *Union delegates in a card vote at the 120th TUC conference in Bournemouth in 1988.*

Example

In the USA delegates to the party conventions which choose presidential candidates may sometimes only be committed to supporting a preferred candidate on the first ballot. If the candidate fails they are then free to support one of the alternative candidates.

action, should report back for advice and direction. This is a way of ensuring that the delegate does not make decisions which are at odds with the wishes of his constituents.

A Less Restrictive View

Most political theorists and politicians would not accept such a highly restrictive role for the representative and feel that a degree of discretion has to be exercised because constituents cannot be consulted on all issues before a decision has to be made. A less restrictive view of the relationship would accept that discretion can be exercised by the representative providing that it does not involve anything new or controversial. If any such issue should arise then the constituents should be consulted before the representative makes any decision.

If the expressed views of the constituents prove unacceptable to the representative then he should resign. The difficulty here for the representative is to decide which issues are to be seen as 'new' or 'controversial', and also what methods should be used to consult his constituents. The relationship in this way is often seen as one of **principal and agent**.

In political terms some delegates when attending conferences may have precise instructions on some issues but yet still be allowed to choose from the best possible alternatives on others.

Definition

Principal and agent
The concept of principal and agent involves one individual, the principal, employing another, the agent, to act for him in some matter. The principal retains overall responsibility for what is transacted. Many people when selling a house employ an estate agent to undertake the negotiations of the sale. The person selling the house is, however, at all times, in charge of the sale, but the agent may be allowed some discretion in marketing the property.

An Even Less Restrictive View

This sees the relationship as one where the representative is free to exercise discretion in decision making unless specifically bound by election pledges or party manifesto. Providing the pledges are fulfilled or the manifesto is implemented, then the representative would be free to exercise discretion even though such discretion ought to take into account the general welfare of the constituents.

An Unrestricted, or 'Burkean' View

This viewpoint argues that, once elected, the representative should be given complete freedom in decision making and that the electorate cannot even demand the implementation of election promises. The representative is held to be free to exercise his judgement on whatever matters have to be dealt with. The views and wishes of the electorate are only one of a number of possible considerations that the representative will bear in mind in exercising his discretion.

The most articulate exponent of such a view of the role of the representative was Edmund Burke (1729–97) the Conservative political philosopher. Burke saw MPs as an elite group whose job was to consider, and implement, what was best for the nation. He felt that in all societies inequalities were natural and unavoidable, and that the mass of the people were incapable of ruling themselves, therefore an elite was necessary. Representatives had to be superior men in terms of practical reasoning but not necessarily popular men.

Burke felt that the representative need not consult the wishes of his constituents and government need not be carried on in relation to the wishes of the electorate. He argued that it would make little sense to consult the voters for they would not have been party to important parliamentary deliberations and therefore would be incapable of expressing an informed opinion.

Representation to Burke had nothing to do with enacting popular wishes but was essentially a process by which a select elite identifies the national good and acts accordingly. Burke also favoured a restricted mandate, for the process of selecting an elite group of MPs required an elite group of voters. His views were expressed in a famous speech to the electors of Bristol in November 1774 when he said:

> *Your representative owes you, not his industry only, but his judgement and he betrays, instead of serving you, if he sacrifices it to your opinion.*

Party Representation

A quite different view of representation has emerged in modern times where the representative is not seen as restricted by the views of constituents and therefore is not a delegate endorsed to express popular opinion. Nor is the representative free to choose, in the national interest, what is best for the public interest. In this analysis Parliament is seen as the central arena for the discussion of major public issues, but it is not the place to decide upon *policy*. For if it did it would put limitations on the role of the electorate who are seen to be responsible for such decisions.

This viewpoint does not, however, advocate a form of direct political participation because the role of policy making is assumed by the 'party'. The representative is therefore bound by the programme of the political party to which he belongs and is as such a **representative of the party.** The party produces a programme or **manifesto** on national issues and electors, by casting votes for a particular party's candidates, express opinion on the respective programmes. The successful candidate then has to support the programme because of his duty to the party.

A limitation of this argument is that it equates the party's interests with the national interest. Parties, obviously, often represent special interests and therefore it could be argued that the representative should still be allowed to identify national interests and put them above party considerations. Another consideration for a representative is whether, even if he desires to represent accurately the wishes of his constituents and advance them, should he respond quickly to every opinion that may be expressed. Perhaps it is more reasonable to expect that he should react only to those that will prove to be in the long term interests of his constituents. To decide in haste may be to regret at length! This viewpoint again makes the assumption that the representative is capable of knowing, better than his constituents, what is best for them in the long term.

One way of avoiding a difference of opinion between constituents and representatives is to ensure that the representative shares many of the characteristics of the constituents he serves. In this way the representative assembly will reflect broadly the social and economic structure of the electorate, and hopefully, thereby most groups will have their views expressed. No legislature can be a direct reflection of the electorate, but even if an attempt is made to make it so, many problems still arise.

- If all groups cannot be included who should be left out? What should count as more important: age, sex, religion, social class, occupation, race, nationality, membership of a particular group, etc?
- Should the electorate be viewed primarily as isolated individuals, or as members of groups?
- Should 'representativeness' extend beyond political representatives to include the police, judges, civil servants, the military, heads of nationalised industries, etc?

Constituencies

Definition

Virtual representation
Although not everyone has the right to vote and cannot therefore influence directly the choice of an MP, the role of the MP is to be the representative of the whole of the community so all interests are taken into account.

Another major consideration is what kind of constituency should be used to elect representatives? We normally expect a legislative assembly to represent everyone and therefore we talk of the 'people' or the 'electorate' or 'the nation' as being represented. In this way the whole body of the electors are seen as individuals who are equally entitled to representation. The medieval concept of representation, however, did not see the people as individuals but as members of groups. It was not individuals but social groups that needed representation and this led to the theory of **virtual representation.**

Example

In the eighteenth century many British politicians used the concept of virtual representation to defend the taxation of American colonists even though they had no MPs in the House of Commons. The colonists were far from satisfied with this argument and it was one of the major factors which led to the War of Independence.

To the problem of what forms a constituency can be added that of the best size for a constituency. One possible method of deciding on constituency size is to treat the whole country as a constituency for the purpose of electing representatives to Parliament. Some forms of **proportional representation** would adopt this approach: MPs would then be allocated to electoral districts by the political parties (see Chapter 22). The Netherlands, for example, uses the whole country as a single constituency in its system.

A more traditional approach is to divide the country into geographical districts. Territorial representation is administratively very convenient for the purposes of polling and electoral registration. Each constituency is considered to be equal but the basis of grouping electors together in this way is merely one of coincidence of residence, and not the need to represent a particular interest that dominates the district.

Some electoral constituencies may have an association with an ancient borough, or a district may be dominated by a particular industry or occupation (for example, coal mining). Overall, however, all electoral districts are seen to be equal as are the electors within them.

Liberal Theories of Representation

Example

In Britain there is an independent body called the Boundary Commission which has the job of reviewing, and recommending changes to, constituency boundaries in line with population movement.

The use of geographical demarcation for constituencies arose with liberal theories of representation. The emphasis, in particular, is placed upon the inviolability of an individual's property. Representation of individuals rather than groups based on status or occupation is the central consideration and in this way the geographical grouping of electors into roughly equal districts was a logical position.

If liberal theories of representation see society essentially as a body of individuals, then how is the representative to know what is in the public interest? How is the will of the people to be expressed? The usual answer to this question lies in discovering what the 'majority' want. The majority is seen as the only expression of opinion which can be trusted not to be influenced by self-seeking special interests.

Limits of the People's Rule?

The question that now arises is whether there is any limit to **popular sovereignty.** Some would argue that there are limits and therefore it should be possible on occasions for a government to do unpopular things. This is because representation is considered as only one, although important, factor in political life. **Responsible government** is also important.

Definition

Responsible Government
The assumption is that government in exercising power should be able to enjoy a degree of independence from the representative elements in the political system. This suggests that limits can be placed on popular sovereignty.

The problems that arise mean that it may be difficult to clarify on how many occasions, or in what circumstances, the government should be allowed to ignore the majority view. Another problem is the kind of limitations that can be placed on the exercise of such discretion by politicians, civil servants, etc.

In Britain it is assumed, constitutionally, that the government is not responsible solely to those who elected it for it is an independent body which, upon taking office, must have responsibility for governing in accordance with its own judgement. This then leads to a Burkean view of MPs as representatives not only of their own constituencies but of the nation as a whole. The result is felt to be that politicians, especially those holding formal office, should be allowed to act with a degree of independence and even on occasion depart from the wishes of the majority of the people. Limitations will be placed upon them, however, through their accountability to Parliament for the exercise of their duties. The whole concept of responsible government is a peculiarly British notion.

What justification can be used for giving a degree of independence to politicians?

- It reflects the need for efficiency in government. The claim is that if politicians had to refer constantly, and defer to, the wishes of the people, then the cost of governing would become intolerable.
- It helps avoid the 'tyranny of the majority'. In this way responsible government can protect minorities from the excesses of ill considered majority opinion.
- It derives from a particular view of the role of politicians, i.e. a kind of paternalism, whereby the mass of the people are considered not always to realise what is best for them. Politicians thereby take on an obligation to act responsibly for the good of the nation.

Responsible government must not be confused with 'responsiveness'. A government which responds quickly to public demands for some particular line of action may not be acting responsibly. The ill-considered and hasty demands of the people, may best be resisted by government in order to allow time for more sober consideration of the situation. Eventually, if the people maintain their original demands, then the government should respond.

Representation and Accountability

Arguments concerning responsible government have been used to resist demands for greater public accountability for the police, judiciary and civil service. In the case of the police they are seen as ultimately accountable to the courts for the exercise of their powers and greater public control would limit their ability to act independently. The police in Britain are not directly under the control of the Home Office, with the exception of the Metropolitan Force. Outside London the police force is maintained by local police authorities, but chief constables are able to enjoy considerable independence from local police committees. This has led to claims from some left wingers that there is a lack of democratic control over the actions of the police.

Example

The policing of mass picketing during the 1984 miners' strike led several local authority police committees to differ with their chief constables over police tactics.

Arguments also occurred in the Merseyside police committee after riots in Toxteth in Liverpool in 1981, when criticism was voiced of policing methods during the disturbances.

Proponents of **popular government** argue that there should be no limit to popular sovereignty and, if the British system of government is not sufficiently 'representative', then it should be changed so that it is. The views of the majority are to be followed and the only job of government is to identify accurately what the majority want and implement it. The idea of politicians or public officials knowing best what is in the public interest is rejected.

The question that arises from this view is how to avoid the 'tyranny of the majority'. The answer for the proponents of popular government is that majority opinion is not fixed, so minority opinion will not be the same on each issue. Simply (as a member of the majority on some issues) you win some, and (as a member of the minority on other issues) you lose some. This analysis is all very well providing that certain minorities are not always likely to lose out.

Participation

Proponents of popular government have come to feel that political activity which is limited to voting in elections is inadequate. This has led to calls for more **political participation.** The basis of these demands is a suspicion of representative government in which the governors appear to be drawn from a more or less permanent elite.

The process of government is seen to give the citizen very little opportunity to exercise any real control over the activities of government. And this is especially so when the range of activity of most governments has increased in recent times. The aim, therefore, is to provide citizens with ways of achieving direct control over the representatives elected to serve them.

One alternative to centralised representative government that generated some interest in British politics in the early part of the twentieth century, was **Guild Socialism.** With Guild Socialism, political power would be dispersed and the political system based on a form of direct worker control. Society was seen as made up of a collection of vocational groups where the essential factor for the worker was to have control over his workplace. Each trade or group of trades would be represented by a guild.

It would be the guilds that would undertake much of the running of society providing services to the public. The role of the state would be to act as a final arbiter in disputes between the guilds that represented various economic activities.

Participatory Democracy

In recent years in Britain calls for greater 'participatory democracy' and 'community involvement' have found many supporters. The assumption again is that the representative process has become unsympathetic to the 'true' wishes of the people. One method to ensure greater 'sympathy' could involve the use of **referendums** to decide issues between elections. The result of such referendums would then be binding upon the government. The 1975 example is, however, the only time that a national referendum has been held in Britain. Referendums did, however, take place in Scotland and Wales in 1979 on the question of devolving some political power to assemblies in Edinburgh and Cardiff (see page 132).

Example

In Britain in 1975 a referendum was held by the Labour government on the question of the renegotiated terms for Britain's continued membership of the European Economic Community. The outcome was a significant vote of support (66 per cent) for the government's proposals.

The use of referendums raises several further questions:

- Who should decide which issues go to a referendum?
- Should the result be binding on a government or merely advisory?
- What percentage for or against an issue is seen as representative of popular opinion? Is a simple majority on a low turnout enough?
- Can complex issues like membership of the EEC be reduced to a yes/no decision?
- Can the wording of the question be such as to lead the voter?

These questions were all raised during the 1975 and 1979 referendums. In the case of 1979 a majority voted in favour of the government's devolution proposals in Scotland, but an amendment to the government's bill meant that 40 per cent of the Scottish electorate had to vote 'Yes' for the proposal to be passed. The Scottish National Party felt cheated because they had 'won the day' in getting a majority but the 40 per cent requirement deprived them of victory.

Example

The leader of the Labour Party, since a change in the rules in 1981, is elected by an electoral college whereby votes are allocated 40 per cent to the trade unions, 30 per cent to constituency parties, and 30 per cent to the parliamentary party.

Representation within the Parties

Other calls for direct participation have surfaced in demands for giving the rank and file of political parties a greater say in the management of the party. This has been a particularly important debate in the Labour Party.

The constituency parties in the Labour Party have also been given greater control over the selection of candidates for parliamentary and local elections.* Problems have arisen, however, when some local parties have been accused of being 'unrepresentative' of opinion as a whole within the party.

Example

In 1986 the Knowsley North Labour Party chose Mr Lesley Huckfield, a left wing European Labour MP, as their candidate for a by-election. The National Executive rejected their choice and imposed a moderate candidate, George Howarth, against the wishes of the local party.

*Constituency parties are no longer 'required' to re-select sitting MPs, only to consider them among other possible candidates.

Group Representation

Demands for more participation have also developed in local politics where increased involvement by community groups in such things as planning decisions is now a common feature. Local authorities are now often required statutorily to consult with local groups and to elicit local opinion on a variety of matters before implementing policy. Whether this is direct participation in the decision making process or local authorities merely paying lip service to their obligations, is another question.

Consequences of Participation

Example

The public inquiry that was held to hear views on the proposed building of another nuclear reactor at Sizewell in Suffolk was the longest of its kind. It began in 1983, ran for three years, and cost the major contributor, the Central Electricity Generating Board, several millions of pounds.

The desirability of such extended participation has not gone unquestioned. Too much participation can be portrayed as an infringement of personal liberty rather than an extension of it, for the citizen should be free *not* to participate. Most people do not wish to spend a great deal of their time involved in political activity and the 'representativeness' of those who do is also often questioned. The most enthusiastic members of many organisations will tend to be the most committed and often the most radical or militant. Due to their dedication they will frequently attain a decision making position in the organisation even though their views may not be in line with the mass of the non-active membership.

Increased participation is also often seen as leading to increased cost and inefficiency. It may be desirable to give everyone a say, but this may not be the most efficient way of arriving at a decision and it could prove expensive.

The problem of cost, it could be argued, is a particular concern when the decisions are of technical nature requiring a rapid response and, therefore, need to be taken by those who possess appropriate skills. So, providing the decision makers are effectively accountable to the mass of the membership/electorate, and there is a clear mechanism to show approval/disapproval of their actions, then participation can perhaps be limited. To let the people loose upon the decision making process may result in all sorts of undesirable decisions being adopted!

Proponents of direct political participation argue that even if greater inefficiency results, then it does not matter, for participation is more important than efficiency.

Political participation can be seen as a way of stimulating politics by giving greater responsibility to citizens for decisions which directly affect their lives..

Example

Guild Socialists believed that direct involvement in the decision making process would improve efficiency. People would have a greater commitment to their work for they would be directly responsible for the goods produced.

Direct Participation in the USA

Several methods of direct political participation are to be found in the USA. Three of the most widely used tools being the '**initiative**', **referendum**, and the '**recall**'.

The **initiative** is a way of allowing an issue of public concern in a state to be decided by a vote at an election. Any citizen can ask for a question to be added to the election ballot paper providing enough prior public support for it is demonstrated by a petition. If the support is forthcoming, then the issue will be decided by the electors as they cast their votes in the election. This method has been used in many states to limit increases in local property taxes as well as to decide some social issues.

Example

In 1978 voters in California voted 60 per cent in favour of proposition 13, to freeze property assessments for three years and then limit rises to 2 per cent per annum. This was agreed even though much of the revenue from local taxes went on local services.

In 1988 Florida, Arizona and Colorado voters supported measures to make English the official language for state government business in spite of the fact that all of these states have large Hispanic populations.

Also in 1988 Maryland voted to ban the sale of inexpensive handguns and California voters agreed to cut the very high car insurance premiums in the state.

The **referendum** allows voters to review laws passed by state legislatures before the law comes into effect. The majority of states now allow such procedures which usually take the form of a series of extra questions on the ballot paper.

The **recall** allows for an elected official, such as a judge, to be recalled if enough voters sign a petition. If the electors decide in a ballot that the conduct of an official is in some way undesirable then he can be removed from office.

Example

In April 1988 Mr Evan Meacham, the governor of Arizona, was stripped of office after a campaign to recall him. Opposition to his Governorship grew when, after taking office in 1986, he made several controversal decisions and public statements. He alienated much black opinion by cancelling a state holiday on Martin Luther King day, and amongst other things described his critics as 'a bunch of homosexuals'. He also supported an education official who felt teachers should not correct children whose parents told them that the Earth was flat. The campaign ended short of his recall when Mr Meacham was investigated by the State Senate and impeachment proceedings begun. He was found guilty of an obstruction of justice charge and of directing public funds into his family's business. This was an unusual event, however, for he was the first state governor to be removed from office in this way since the Governor of Oklahoma in 1929.

These methods have been criticised in the USA for breaking up the work of representative government and bypassing legislative procedures. However, they are a very direct way of letting politicians know what people are thinking and their use has grown considerably in the last 20 years.

In Britain most of the demands for greater direct participation have centred on the working of local government. Much of the demand stems from a desire to ensure client/consumer satisfaction with services such as housing, education, and social services.

Example

In 1986 the Conservative government changed the law to allow parents, with the consent of the school governors, to withdraw children from sex education classes to which they objected. The government felt this was necessary as some local authorities allowed the use of material to which the government objected.

CONCLUSION

Given all the arguments over the nature of representation and how well the wishes of the people can be reflected in a system of representative government it would be reasonable to conclude that perhaps people need greater freedom from government.

This is a radical view expressed by those who can broadly be categorised as the '**new right**'. They feel that the best form of participation is exercised by the consumer in a free market. This is seen as the most effective method of ensuring that the individual citizen can control his or her own destiny. The establishment of market forces and the reduction of the scope of government is presented as a form of self-government for the individual. Representative government is portrayed as necessarily reducing the range of choice available to the political consumer. Competing parties can only offer packages of policies and therefore the consumer's choice is limited, for there is no option of choosing parts of each package.

The answer is therefore seen to be one of 'rolling back' the scope of government and extending choice through market forces. Government would provide less and leave many more services to be provided by the market. This they claim would ensure that services would be provided in a way that the consumer desired. There would be no question of the producer knowing better than the consumer what the consumer wants. Or of the producer knowing better than the consumer what is in his long term interests as opposed to his short term desires.

CASE STUDY A: REPRESENTATION, PARTICIPATION AND CITIZENSHIP

The Miners Strike 1984–5

In March 1984 a strike called by the National Union of Mineworkers (NUM) began in response to threatened pit closures and lasted for a year. The dispute became increasingly bitter and sharp confrontations developed in several parts of the country between striking miners and the police. In total something like 25,000,000 working days were lost with consequential damage to the mining industry and to the economy in general. The strike, however, was never the subject of a national ballot of the NUM membership. The main objection to a national ballot by the NUM leadership was that miners in relatively safe and prosperous coalfields should not decide the future of pits facing closure.

In February 1981, the (then) National Coal Board (NCB) announced a programme of pit closures involving 23 pits. In November 1982, Mr Arthur Scargill, the left-wing President of the NUM, claimed that, in fact, 75 pits were to close. The NCB's response was that over a period of 8 to 10 years up to 49 pits were to be closed.

In February 1983, in response to threatened pit closures in its area, the South Wales branch of the NUM came out on strike. However, in a national ballot the membership rejected a call from the NUM Executive for supportive industrial action by 118,954 votes to 76,540. This was the third time strike action had been rejected in a ballot since 1981. A strike over pay was rejected in January 1982 and it was also turned down over the issues of pay and pit closures in October 1982. Later in 1983, delegates to the annual conference of the NUM, authorised the Executive to call a ballot of the membership, when they felt it appropriate, if the NCB continued with its policies of closures and redundancies.

In February 1984, a strike began at Polmaise in Scotland, and in March the NUM in Yorkshire came out over the proposed closures of Cortonwood and Bullcliffe Wood pits. These actions won the support of the NUM Executive by a vote of 21 to 3 and they promised support for any other areas who came out. An alternative motion calling for a national ballot was effectively rejected and this enabled the Executive to apply union rules which empowered it to back strike decisions of individual area councils, without the need for a national ballot. A national ballot for strike action would have required the support of 55 per cent of the membership.

The NUM areas took up varying stances on the options over the strike action that now faced them. These were:

- holding area ballots
- calling for a national ballot
- calling for a special national executive meeting
- calling for a special delegate conference.

Some coalfields, in fact, voted against a stoppage of work, for example, Nottinghamshire in March 1984, voted 3 to 1 against a strike.

In April 1984 at a National Executive meeting, an attempt was made by Leicestershire miners to call an immediate national ballot, but this was unsuccessful and instead, by a vote of 21 to 3, it was decided to convene a special delegate conference.

At the delegate conference, later in April, four motions calling for a national ballot were rejected and by a vote of 69 to 54, a call was made to all coalfields to strike. The strike spread and by August over 70 per cent of miners were out. Opinion polls conducted between March and July among miners, appeared to show that the majority of them supported the strike. Over half of those still working, however, were in Nottinghamshire coalfields, despite the fact that their delegates had called on them to strike after the delegate conference. One outcome of the strike was the formation of a breakaway union, the Union of Democratic Mineworkers, based mainly in Nottinghamshire.

The dispute ended in March 1985, after a special delegate conference had voted by 98–91 to end the strike. By this time, the NCB claimed that under half of miners were on strike, although the NUM claimed a higher figure. Some areas did not participate fully in the strike which was conducted on an area basis rather than on a national one, as it would have been had a national ballot been called.

▲ *NUM President Arthur Scargill addressing a rally during the 1984–5 miners' strike.*

Questions

1 What different forms of representation can you identify in the case study?
2 What justification could be given for certain areas not striking given the decisions of the National Executive?
3 At what point, if at all, do you consider a national ballot should have been called?
4 Bearing in mind that going on strike costs an individual worker a lot of lost wages, what sorts of votes would you need before joining a strike? What proportion of votes would have to support the strike? What proportion of the members would have to vote?

EXAMINATION QUESTIONS

1 How far do you argue that 'the UK today has responsible, if not entirely representative, government'? (AEB Government and Politics, 1980)

2 Whom should an MP obey? His parliamentary whips? His constituents? His party conference? His conscience? (University of London, Government and Politics studies, A-level, 1981)

3 'Members of Parliament are accountable to the national interest and their conscience hence they are accountable to none'. Discuss. (University of Cambridge, Politics and Government, Special paper, 1984)

NOW READ ON

A. H. Birch *Representative and Responsible Government* G. Allen and Unwin, 1964
A major text for the subject

H. Pitkin *The Concept of Representation* University of California Press, 1972
A comprehensive analysis

Dr F. O'Gorman *Edmund Burke: His Political Philosophy* G. Allen and Unwin, 1973
See the chapter on the British constitution.

8 Welfare

Tory emphasis shifts to social responsibility

By Colin Hughes
Political Correspondent

THE PRIME Minister's speech to the Church of Scotland was yesterday confirmed by the Home Secretary, Douglas Hurd, as a determined Tory attempt to switch the political battlefront from economic freedom and selfishness to a new emphasis on social and individual responsibility.

The shift is partly a response to the dissent and unpopularity which have descended on Margaret Thatcher's third term social reforms – health, social security, the poll tax, and to some extent education and housing.

Both the Prime Minister and the Home Secretary insisted that the essentials of the welfare state should remain intact. "In our generation, the only way we can ensure that no one is left without sustenance, help or opportunity, is to have laws to provide for health and education, pensions for the elderly, succour for the sick and disabled," Mrs Thatcher said.

Mr Hurd said: "You are going to go on having a health system, an education system and a social security system, which are overwhelmingly funded out of the taxpayer's pocket." But he added that the state's systems could not produce "all the answers that people now require". The recent Tory emphasis on voluntary service, neighbourhood and parental involvement, and on charitable giving was intended to reach the parts the state could not reach.

The Government could extend its statutory schemes, but that would mean "the fountain plays over everything . . . a very inflexible and wasteful way of doing it". It was better to choose voluntary people and groups, "and encourage them to find places, not reached by the schemes, where there is need".

Source: *The Times*, 23 May 1988

The ability of the state to provide an adequate level of welfare services has come into question in recent years and also whether individuals have a 'right' to state welfare. Some argue that it may be more desirable for people, where possible, to provide for their own needs. Others would argue that the right to an adequate level of health provision, educational opportunities, good housing and a reasonable income should be *guaranteed* by the state. One of the major difficulties for any government however is to decide what constitutes a 'reasonable level of provision' and which of the many competing claims for assistance should be given priority. All British governments since 1945 have accepted the need to maintain the welfare state but arguments over the most efficient way to administer state provision and the ways it could be, or should be, extended separates the major political parties.

BASIC PRINCIPLES

A dictionary definition of 'welfare' would include such statements as 'well being', 'good fortune', 'prosperity', 'good health', 'happiness', or maybe even 'affluence'. If the term 'welfare state' is used then we think of social security provision, health schemes, education, social services, etc. In Britain we pride ourselves on an extensive range of state services and feel we have created a welfare state.

> **Definition**
>
> ***Welfare State***
> *A welfare state is one where the government takes responsibility for the provision of services for enhancement of the well being of its citizens.*

The term 'welfare', however, should not be limited to certain state-run activities. The idea of the state promoting the welfare of its citizens is closely associated with concepts such as equality, freedom, social justice, rights and duties. In Britain as in many other countries, state provision came after the provision of welfare by private citizens.

The major difficulty for any state in the provision of welfare is to decide on the limits of what can be identified as 'welfare'. If the definition is limited to mean just the physical well being of all members of the community, then many countries would claim to be a welfare state. If the definition is extended to include equality of opportunity in most areas of social and economic activity, then the role of the state would have to be extended considerably. Welfare could also be seen to include recreation, cultural activities, sport and entertainment. In this sense the state can be seen to be attempting to extend the 'happiness' of its citizens through a variety of measures including financial subsidies to approved organisations.

The concept of welfare is therefore open to a wide range of interpretation but is often limited to state provision which can be categorised broadly as 'social services'.

In Britain the major services provided directly by government or through various government agencies are mainly:

- local authority social services
- housing provision
- the National Health Service
- education
- social security.

In addition a welfare state would include the need for government to pursue economic policies that will help avoid problems such as poverty and unemployment.

It should be realised that when government attempts to tackle social problems and improve welfare it has to recognise the inter-relation of many problems.

The difficulty is to decide at what point the responsibility of the state ends once it enters into various forms of welfare commitment. For example, what is the responsibility of the state, if any, in respect of marital breakdown?

There is no single universal welfare responsibility that is accepted by all countries. The United Nations Declaration of Human Rights of 1948 does however include the right to education and medical care. Only the provision of education is near to universal. Yet in many countries even basic educational provision is either not widely available, or non-existent.

In Western industrialised countries it is the normal practice to provide free primary and secondary education but higher education will often be determined by a student's ability to pay, and there may be no automatic right to education after the minimum school leaving age.

> **Example**
>
> The problem of poverty is, to a large extent, tackled through the financial provisions made available by the Department of Health and Social Security. However, the problem of poverty in some circumstances may originate with unemployment. This can in turn cause housing difficulties which might lead to low achievement in school by children of families with poor accommodation and so on.

DISCUSSING THE ARGUMENTS

Early Welfare Provision

In Britain the blueprint for the modern welfare state was laid down in the **Beveridge Report 1942.** The report aimed to stimulate the development of a range of social services in the post-war period so as to provide protection from the 'cradle to the grave'. Few countries would accept such an extensive role for the state in welfare provision. The reasons for the advancement of the state provision in Britain come from a variety of influences.

Example

In the late eighteenth century workers began to establish saving schemes for themselves so that, if any members were sick or injured, the fund could provide some relief from their hardship. These became known as 'Friendly Societies' and were the model for later state run sickness insurance schemes.

Victorian Welfare

The impetus behind early Victorian measures was quite different from today. The legislation passed by Parliament was generally regulatory and did not form the basis of a statutory social service. The individual was expected to look after himself and his family with some help being available through charities and voluntary organisations.

Nineteenth century services were established mainly through local authorities, under powers granted by Parliament to tackle particular problems or 'public nuisances'. The problems considered worthy of attention related mainly to 'pauperism', urban public health, some exploitive employment practices, and poor educational standards.

Today we see welfare as embracing far more than just the spread of disease, establishment of basic standards of literacy, the removal of insanitary housing, and preventing the exploitation of some groups of workers, especially children.

► *Child labourers carrying clay in brickyard in 1871.*

Early Twentieth Century Welfare

The change in attitude to state welfare provision can be seen by the start of the twentieth century in the writings of social reformers such as **Sidney** and **Beatrice Webb.**

The Webbs belonged to the Fabians, a socialist group whose other members included George Bernard Shaw and H.G. Wells. For the Webbs, the best way to achieve socialism and social reform was through the extension of state activity and by the efficient management of the machinery of government. Once properly organised, the state could be directed to produce economic strategies which would in turn generate an array of social reforms. For the Webbs it was State Socialism that was the practical way forward, not any idea of a proletarian revolution, which would lead to the establishment of an idealised form of Socialism. The Webbs, however, were concerned about the possibility of an overpowerful state bureaucracy developing, for they stressed constantly the importance of using local authorities to achieve their ends.

The Webbs set out their ideas in the **Minority Report of the Poor Law Commission** in 1905. Beatrice Webb and others on the Commission argued that social conditions were such that large sections of the community could hardly avoid poverty. The state therefore had a responsibility to prevent poverty and not merely provide very limited poor relief. They argued for the establishment of a **national minimum** standard of living for everyone. In addition education had to be extended, workers protected against sickness and unemployment, and the elderly given a small income.

The foundations of the modern welfare system were laid shortly afterwards by the 1906 Liberal government. Old age pensions, unemployment insurance and health insurance were introduced and Labour Exchanges were created to help the unemployed find work.

The provision of these benefits marked the start of a movement towards the modern welfare state but were still quite limited in their scope. It was still felt to be the responsibility of the individual to make provision for himself and his family. The limited help provided by the state was to assist in times of difficulty.

For example, the financial help available under the national insurance scheme was intended to act as a supplement to the savings of unemployed workers and lasted for only a fairly short period. The reasoning behind this was that if the government provided extended help then the cost would be very high and the contributions to the scheme paid by workers would also have to be high, thereby limiting the workers ability to save or invest in private insurance.

Liberal principles of self help still dominated: it was not a kind of socialism which would lead to greater equality. Also there was no question of the Liberal government creating a national minimum. Even the administration of some of the national insurance scheme was left to private enterprise with 'Friendly Societies' organising the distribution of benefits.

Beveridge Report

The idea of a national minimum was raised again with the publication of the Beveridge Report in 1942. The impact of the report was quite dramatic for it was the first ever comprehensive survey of the British system of social insurance.

It dealt with the problem of abolishing 'want' or as we would call it today, poverty. The report recognised that poverty did not have a single cause and called for reforms to tackle unemployment, poor housing, poor health standards, and low educational achievement. The report came to be regarded as the blueprint for the modern welfare state.

Beveridge saw his proposals as assuring welfare from the 'cradle to the grave' with no one in the future being allowed to fall below an established national minimum. The state would take on the overall responsibility for the welfare of all citizens. Many dismissed the report as impracticable but nonetheless its principles were largely incorporated by the Labour Government (1945–51) into its welfare programme.

The idea of a national minimum has never been fully adopted, for the needs of individuals have been recognised to be so diverse that a universal financial limit would be inappropriate. Also, the needs of some groups may not be easily measured in financial terms. The problem, increasingly for government, has become one of identifying various kinds of need and social problems, and distributing necessarily scarce resources in the face of competing claims for help.

Defining Welfare

It may be difficult for government to decide exactly what constitutes a social problem which requires the provision of *state* welfare. At the beginning of the nineteenth century poverty was not seen necessarily as something to concern the state. It was considered to be a fact of life. Some in society would be unfortunate and others would not, but overall there was nothing the state could do about it anyway.

The relief of poverty was seen as the responsibility of charitable organisations and they would rely upon the generosity of the wealthy to fund them. In fact it was considered that if too much were done, the incentive for people to look after themselves would be diminished. In this way increased reliance upon public provision would lead to moral and social decline. The 'benefits' made available to those who suffered poverty were therefore very penal.

The aim was to *deter* people from applying for help and so those who did apply would have to be in grave need or they certainly would not do so. This was a central feature of the 1834 Poor Law Amendment Act. The central benefits made available to those applying for help was the 'workhouse'. The conditions that prevailed inside were often so harsh that people would do anything to avoid entering. Limitations were placed upon personal freedom, including the loss of the right to vote, and although originally never intended, often no distinction was made between the 'deserving' and 'undeserving' poor in the general workhouse. The philosophy was that no worker, however lowly paid, would enjoy a standard of living as bad as that in the workhouse: the principle of 'less eligibility'.

► *Inmates of the Marylebone workhouse at the turn of the century.*

Today we feel such principles to be inhuman and degrading. The state is felt to be responsible for those who are unable to look after themselves and recipients of welfare should not be stigmatised as second class citizens. Whether this is achieved in the modern welfare state is a matter of great debate.

Example

In December 1986, a Church of England report argued that despite welfare benefits, Britain was still a society which divides off the less fortunate and treats them differently, and attaches to them an inferior status.

Avoidance and Relief of Poverty

One solution to the problem of stigmatising those who apply for welfare benefits is to introduce the concept of **universality.** In this way benefits are available to all, irrespective of the personal circumstances of the claimant. This avoids the problem of **means testing** whereby a declaration of personal circumstances has to be made in order to decide eligibility for the benefits available.

Means testing of welfare benefits has unpleasant connotations for many older people who can recall the 'household' means test of the 1930s. This involved the income of the whole family being considered before any benefit was granted. The means test officials became particularly hated in many areas which suffered high unemployment and resultant poverty.

The problem in extending universality is that by treating everyone the same, those who need help most receive the same benefits as those whose needs are far less. Means testing does have advantages, for, by introducing a degree of **selectivity** in the provision of state benefits, the authorities can identify those who need the most help and direct resources towards them, rather than spreading resources thinly across the whole of society. Conversely those who do not need help do not get it.

Example

When Family Allowances (later called Child Benefit) were introduced in 1945, no means test was attached. The benefit was paid through the post office to women for their second and subsequent children. The scheme has been extended since to include all children, but the principle of no means test remains.

Problems of Selectivity

- The process of form filling, interviews, etc. required in means testing can act as a deterrent by creating an atmosphere that appears to stigmatise those who apply.
- The reluctance of many to claim benefits is often attributed to a wish not to be classified as a second class citizen. Old people often do not wish to admit they are poor, especially those who have had good jobs during their working lives, but never had the opportunity to save for an occupational pension scheme.
- The complicated nature of some of the administrative procedures can also act as a deterrent, as can ignorance of the existence of benefits, and who is entitled to them. This is particularly true when the benefits might apply to only a small section of the community.
- Reluctance to apply is often very apparent amongst those people who have low educational standards and who avoid form filling whenever possible.

The outcome is that each year in Britain millions of pounds of welfare benefit goes unclaimed by those entitled to it. The government often has had to mount advertising campaigns to explain entitlement and to encourage people to apply. This shows that the concept of welfare provision is now completely different from that of the nineteenth century when the aim was to deter demand. We now see governments often actually stimulating demand in some areas.

Another method of avoiding the problem of 'stigma' is to make the receipt of benefit dependent upon the payment of a contribution. In this way the recipient can be seen to have a 'right' to welfare benefit through a form of **insurance.**

The state can impose a compulsory scheme of insurance for all workers to cover specific risks like sickness, unemployment, disability, etc. This can also be extended to provide benefits for workers' families, and the range of benefits can also be varied according to the type and size of contribution paid into the scheme.

There is also the possibility of the state imposing a scheme but leaving its administration to private insurance companies. The main advantage is that insurance establishes a right to benefit and it is not a free handout, or 'dole', from the state.

Problems of Insurance Schemes

- Administrative costs of a state run scheme can be very high for contributions have to be registered in order to establish the validity of claims.

- The state has to be careful not to make the level of contributions so high that the worker is deterred from looking after his own interests by taking out additional private insurance.
- This type of welfare covers only those in work and paying contributions.
- Insurance schemes are unsuited to help those who are unable to work or have an interrupted work record. The handicapped are particularly affected in this way.

Example

The average cost of educating a child at secondary level would certainly be far more than most families could afford. In 1989 the cost was estimated by the Department of Education and Science to be around £3800 per year per child.

There is an element of 'insurance' in all welfare provision however in that the state takes from all to give to the few in need. Private insurance schemes work in exactly the same way. The company will hope to take in enough money through insurance premiums in order to more than cover the claims made by policy holders. State provision differs from private provision in that it adds **redistribution** to the insurance principle. When the state provides 'free' health care or education, it is actually applying not only the insurance principle (i.e. everyone pays but only a few receive) but as those who earn more, pay more, it is also redistributing income.

NEEDS

A major question for state welfare is what types of social need should attract help and even if it is possible to identify them, is it not inevitable that the problems will change? Public expectations will also grow so what may have been seen as adequate provision 20 or 30 years ago perhaps will no longer be acceptable. Methods for tackling the problems will also change and government will have to decide which of the new ideas will be value for money. Many of these difficulties occur in welfare provision generally but they are especially evident with health care.

Health

Example

In the USA most health care is privately funded with patients paying medical bills mainly by taking out appropriate health insurance.

In many countries the physical well being of the population is not seen to be the responsibility of the state, beyond public health measures to prevent the outbreak and spread of disease.

In Britain since 1948 we have had the **National Health Service.** At its foundation there was a commitment to provide a comprehensive range of health care, free of charge, to all. Since then some charges have been introduced, notably prescription charges for drugs, spectacles, etc, but all governments have continued to spend large sums of money to provide state health care. The difficulty for British governments has been the apparently limitless demands that health care can make on the national exchequer.

Example

In December 1986 the government announced it would spend £20 million on an advertising campaign to help stop the spread of the AIDS virus. By comparison, expenditure of this size would have a dramatic effect, for example, on the availability of kidney machines which are in very short supply.

Back in the 1940s it was assumed that health care was a finite problem. It was felt that government investment would improve the health of the nation which in consequence would lead to less days lost at work and as health standards rose, a fall in demand on the NHS would occur.

In fact demand has grown every year. As the nation's health has improved and new medical techniques have prolonged life expectancy and cured many diseases, new medical problems have arisen. The NHS has had to adapt to changes in the pattern of illness away from infectious disease to things such as cancer and heart disease.

The population has also changed. There are not only far more old people to be cared for, but the elderly are disproportionately high consumers of health care and governments therefore often have to make difficult choices in funding. The range of services required also has expanded and medical technology has become increasingly expensive.

Example

Family planning clinics are now a well established part of the NHS but such provision was not anticipated in 1946. At that time ultrasound machines, brain scanners, and lasers were no more than science fiction.

In order to provide adequate care the government also has to see that the education system provides sufficient opportunities to train doctors, nurses, laboratory technicians, radiographers, etc.

Housing

Similar problems of growing demand and public expectation have also affected state housing provision. Housing need may not be considered a welfare problem at all but merely a financial arrangement between landlord and tenant, or as a sale price between buyer and seller. The welfare commitment was firmly established after World War II with a massive housing programme. It involved the building of several hundreds of thousands of houses mainly by local authorities and virtually exclusively for rent, with a subsidy to keep rents low. The demand for council rented accommodation has always outstripped supply and has led to long waiting lists in many parts of the country.

Here again can be seen the problem of increasing expectation. In the late 1940s it was expected that a young married couple would live with one of their parents for quite some time after the marriage. Apparent 'demand' for rented housing was therefore quite low and governments of the day believed that about 1.25 million new houses would solve the post war shortage. In fact over 1.25 million houses were built by 1952 (both council and private) but demand grew as household size fell.

Total house building averaged around 300,000 per year during the 1950s and 1960s. In 1967 the figure reached over 400,000 and by 1963, a total of 4.5 million houses had been built since the war. As the years have gone by, so our definition of the 'problem' has changed. In 1945, the problem was to replace war damage and house families with children: in the 1950s slum clearance was the priority. Today one of the problems is to create enough housing for single people.

Attempts to make up the housing shortfall in the 1950s led many authorities to build high rise blocks of flats. Today it's widely felt that this was a mistake and created as many problems as were solved. Now many 'tower' blocks are being demolished. The extension of home ownership is now considered a more desirable housing policy and since 1979, particularly, public sector housing provision, has been reduced and emphasis placed on giving financial incentives to those wishing to buy their council houses.

▲ *Kelvin Flats, Sheffield.*
▶ *On the left is a Sheffield council house; beside it an ex-council house bought by the tenant.*

Education

All British governments, since the passing of the 1944 Education Act, have accepted the need to provide free education up to the age of 15 and, in 1971, 16 years of age for all. This is not to say that this welfare provision has not generated many problems and arguments. There have been sharp policy differences between the political parties over secondary education in particular.

Changes in population growth and especially the post war 'baby boom' put tremendous pressure on the education system and educational expenditure. There was also subsequent pressure for places in higher and further education brought about by both population growth and the increased opportunities provided by the 1944 Act.

Comprehensive Schools

A major debate took place over the form of secondary education between those who wished to retain the selective grammar school system, who were mainly Conservatives, and those, largely Labour supporters, who wished to see the introduction of comprehensive education. The outcome overall was a victory for comprehensive schooling but was often a protracted wrangle. The whole debate raised many questions over concepts such as equality of opportunity, freedom, and the right to a fulfilling life.

Questions

1. Should a section of the community be able to opt out of participating in general welfare provision, such as education, having already paid for it, by sending their children to private schools?
2. Does welfare in education mean identical education for all, as we hoped for in comprehensive schools, or for a talented few as in grammar schools and the city technology colleges created by the Conservative government in the late 1980s?
3. At what age should education cease to be free, bearing in mind that not all will necessarily have had equal access to education up to school leaving age?

ALTERNATIVES TO THE WELFARE STATE

In recent years the whole concept of state provided social services has come into question. Several reports on the working of the welfare system in Britain have concluded that the real beneficaries of welfare provision are the middle classes and that the major objective of tackling the problems of the lower paid and the poor is not being addressed. It has been claimed that the middle classes are the greatest consumers of health and education services in particular.

One answer to this apparent phenomenon is to reduce drastically the state's involvement in welfare and to allow greater freedom of choice for the consumer of such services, by returning them to the 'market'. The job of the government would then be to equip the individual with the means to purchase welfare services. The state would then only be left to provide help to those who cannot fend for themselves.

The majority of people would be able to look after their own interests because the reductions in taxation that would be possible together with reduced welfare expenditure, would allow them to make their own arrangements.

The **National Health Service** would be financed by payment for receipt of service, with tax concessions for those with private health care and compulsory medical insurance for everyone else. The insurance scheme need not necessarily be run by the state.

Education would be paid for by low interest repayable students loans, tax concessions for private schooling and higher fees for higher education. The bulk of schooling would be provided by a system of education vouchers, whereby the parent would be free to purchase education up to the value of a government funded voucher. If local authority schools did not provide the kind of education demanded by parents then the voucher could be 'cashed' in the private sector. Any additional cost, not covered by the voucher, would then be met by the parent.

Housing would cease virtually to be a welfare service at all. Emphasis would be on owner occupation, the sale of council housing and help to private landlords. The work of local authorities would be limited to slum clearance and to questions of 'greenbelt' planning.

A package of measures of this kind would clearly change the concept of welfare, but the equalising effect of market forces are disputed.

Opposing Views

Opposition to this kind of criticism of the welfare state, and arguments for greater emphasis on free market forces, centre on the argument that it would result only in the rich getting good services. Quite simply those able to pay the most would get the best doctors, nurses, teachers, etc. looking after their interests. In the health service for example, it is argued that free market forces would divert the best doctors, etc. into the most expensive and exclusive clinics. Those least able to pay would get a second class service as in the past.

This criticism occurs again with the question of whether all citizens have a 'right' to social services and, if they do, then social services should be equally available to all. It is also argued that if the better off in society are fully committed to state provision then their influence would be felt as a force for improvements in standards. To remove the better off through the operation of the market would damage overall standards. These arguments are also used to support the idea of comprehensive schools as opposed to grammar schools, better council house provision and greater health service spending.

CONCLUSIONS

There are a wide variety of interpretations that can be attached to the term 'welfare', but, as we have tried to establish, it is most frequently associated with the provision of certain services by the state. The idea of a 'welfare state' in Britain was a new concept and it meant that the state moved beyond the limited nineteenth century responsibility of ensuring law and order, securing British territory from foreign aggression, and 'relieving' only the worst cases of need.

The state came to take on a positive responsibility to work for the welfare of its citizens and in some cases to discriminate in favour of some groups in society so as to reduce inequality.

The provision of welfare has come to be regarded by some as a vital function of the state where citizens gain the 'right' to various forms of social services, and the extension of these services a primary function of the tax system by taking from the 'wealthy' and giving to the 'poor'.

Critics of such a view see the extension of state provision as a symptom of the growth of 'moral decline'. The state is seen as providing for the individual, more and more, of what should be the responsibility of the individual to provide for himself. This is argued to be a threat to self-reliance and individual initiative. The answer is therefore to stimulate the economy so that the overall wealth of the community can be increased and people can then provide for themselves.

The idea of a welfare state as a positive provider of services for the community contrasts sharply with the nineteenth century view of limiting state activity to the physical protection of the community by a law and order function.

Example

In the 1960s attempts were made to discriminate positively in some areas of education so that schools in poorer areas gained a proportionately larger share of resources than the school size would have otherwise commanded.

Today it is not seen to be enough for the state to be a provider of remedial services to treat social problems. Government is expected to have a responsibility to direct the economy in a way which is socially desirable and that avoids conditions which may affect the general well being of the community.

This view has led governments to create a wide variety of schemes both to avoid unemployment, and where it does occur, to generate new industry to lessen its affect.

There are a wide range of regional development schemes which offer incentives to employers who are prepared to move to areas of high unemployment. Whole sections of the education system are also geared to provide alternatives for young people who face 'the dole' upon leaving school, and the government has used the Training Agency to direct many of these schemes in colleges.

Environmental Welfare

Example

After the Toxteth riots in Liverpool, the government announced and implemented urban renewal programmes in many inner city areas over and above the provision that was already available.

The concept of state welfare responsibility has been broadened further in recent years through growing interest in Britain's physical environment. The arrest and removal of urban decay has been given special attention by governments. It is recognised that many social problems are associated with environmental problems such as those which have been experienced in inner city areas.

So despite the usual association of welfare with the provision of social services in various forms, the concept can be seen to be far more wide ranging.

▲ *The site of the International Garden Festival in Liverpool, 1984.*

CASE STUDY
HEALTH CARE IN BRITAIN AND THE USA

Britain

Out of the total that was spent on welfare by government, the National Health Service in 1988 cost £22 billion and in real terms health expenditure has risen three fold since 1948. The NHS is the biggest single individual employer in Western Europe, employing a total of 1.3 million people, of which 28,000 are doctors, and its expenditure amounts to roughly 6 per cent of the British Gross Domestic Product. But, despite rapidly growing costs, neither of the main political parties has been prepared to cut health expenditure when in office.

- The vast majority of the money required is raised by taxation and only 5 per cent comes from charges to patients, although prescription charges have risen sharply since 1979.
- Two-thirds of the NHS expenditure goes on the elderly and they proportionately are the fastest growing group in the community. On average in 1988, the NHS spent £190 per year on each of those aged 16–64; £570 on those 65–75; and £1475 on those 75 and over.
- Despite these figures Britain spends proportionately less on health care than most industrialised countries and has relatively fewer doctors, hospital beds, and nursing staff. However, Britain does lead its European neighbours in the amount of publicly funded health care that is available to its citizens.
- As questions have been raised about the standard of health care in Britain in recent years, the private sector of health care has grown. In 1971, there were 25,300 private nursing homes and hospitals but by 1982, the figure had risen to 36,000.
- Private health care still however covers only 1 in 9 people in Britain, but health insurers are optimistic that if the financial problems of the NHS continue and long waiting lists exist for some medical treatment more people will turn to the private sector. By 1988 one in four non urgent operations were undertaken in private hospitals.

Doctors per 1,000 population in 1983	
United Kingdom	0.5
France	2.1
West Germany	2.4
United States	1.8
Japan	1.3
Spain	3.0
Italy	3.6

(OECD Country Reports 1986–87)

United States

- The USA spends three times as much as Britain on health care and expenditure accounts for 11 per cent of GDP which is the equivalent of $1 billion each day.
- However approximately 90 per cent of medical bills are not paid for directly by individuals although health insurance schemes are not always comprehensive. For example, a kidney transplant could cost $30,000 but would most likely not be covered by a private insurance scheme. In some cases hospital bills can literally bankrupt a family. Even the government funded Medicare System does not cover the full cost of treatment with perhaps 20 per cent of a doctor's bill having to be met by the patient.
- The cost of health insurance in the USA has risen rapidly in recent years, but private health care is big business. The medical health care companies that own hospitals, nursing homes, and clinics, have now gained 20 per cent of the health market, and these companies have 'chains' of establishments across the country.
- Their critics claim that they cream off the wealthiest patients and best qualified medical staff, thereby leaving the poor to be treated in community hospitals run by public funds.
- The health care programmes of these organisations are advertised, packaged and sold just like any other commercial product. The aim, of course, is to make a profit.

Question

1 What methods for providing welfare can be identified in the case study?

2 Can or should limits be placed on the state's responsibility to provide health care? What would they be?

3 Does the individual citizen have a 'right' to adequate health care whether privately or publicly funded?

4 In welfare terms 'health' has usually been seen as curing diseases, etc. Today many health professionals see it as more important to prevent disease, etc. Does the state have a duty to prevent illness and disability?

5 Many health problems could be prevented or reduced by government regulation such as forcing workers to wear protective clothing, making employers install expensive safety equipment, the compulsory wearing of seat belts, or even outlawing the consumption of cigarettes and alcohol. What political issues are raised through such regulation in terms of welfare and freedom and how should they be resolved?

EXAMINATION QUESTIONS

1 Has the liberty of the individual been affected by the growth of the welfare state? (University of Cambridge, Public Affairs, 1980)

2 To what extent have the original spirit and the purpose of the welfare state been fulfilled? (University of London, Government and Political Studies, A-Level, 1986)

3 Is it still appropriate to call Great Britain a welfare state? (University of London, Government and Political Studies, 1987)

NOW READ ON . . .

J. Le Grand and R. Robinson *Privatisation and the Welfare State* G Allen and Unwin, 1984
A clear analysis of recent developments.

R. Robinson *The Welfare State Under the Thatcher Government* Wheatsheaf, 1986
An examination of recent trends in Conservative welfare policy.

H. Drucker (ed.) *Developments in British Politics 2* Macmillan, 1986
See the chapter on social policy by N. Bosanquet.

9 Democracy

BASIC PRINCIPLES

Democracy is the recurrent suspicion that more than half the people are right more than half the time.
E.B. White, Notes and comments from 'Talk of the Town',
'The New Yorker', 3 February 1943

Example

In 1949 UNESCO set up an inquiry into the ideas associated with democracy and sent a questionnaire to over 100 scholars in many countries. The result was that it received no replies hostile to democracy. A subsequent report argued that for the first time in history 'democracy' was seen to be the ideal description for all political systems. However, the report also pointed out that most of those who replied considered the idea of democracy to be ambiguous.

One of the most difficult concepts in the study of politics is that of democracy. Yet few concepts are viewed so favourably and universally used, but mean so many different things to so many. Most people in Britain, without giving the matter much consideration, would assume that not only do they live under a democratic government, but also in a democratic society. Further, democratic practices would generally be felt to be morally desirable.

The concept has a long history and is generally applied to political systems where power is held to rest with 'the people'. The term democracy in fact, comes from the Greek words *demos* and *kratos*, i.e. 'people' and 'government'. The concept of democracy developed between 450 BC and 350 BC in small Greek city states, and since then it has been used to describe political circumstances where power is not allocated to the few, but distributed to the many. By the twentieth century 'democracy' had come to be viewed with almost universal acceptance and virtually all political systems claim to be 'democratic'.

If democracy is 'rule by the people' it is often still difficult to decide who constitutes 'the people' and what is meant by 'rule'. Does 'the people' imply everyone? Does 'rule' imply the right of the majority to command others?

The concept of **citizenship** may help to decide who the 'people' are but citizenship has always been subject to widespread variations in interpretation. Citizenship has been denied to various groups on the basis of religion, sex, race, property ownership, etc.

The methods by which, and the extent to which, people can govern actively will vary considerably. Compare, for example, a small rural Swiss canton to contemporary Britain. In such a canton there will be the opportunity for town meetings where the local population can gather together and discuss directly, and decide, local political issues. In a modern mass industrial society such opportunities are not realistically possible. But, nonetheless, for government to be described as 'democratic' there must exist a high degree of correspondence between the actions of the governors and the desires of the governed. Further the position of the governors will be based upon the consent of the governed.

Example

In Britain women did not gain full political suffrage until 1929, and in parts of the USA blacks were often effectively barred from voting until the 1960s. But would Britain in the 1920s and the USA up until the 1960s not have been classified as democracies?

What we mean by democracy in western liberal countries is considered as the antithesis of democracy by countries of the Soviet bloc. In the West we pride ourselves on having created a system of democracy that places a high value on 'liberty' and majoritarian rule. As such we tend to equate democracy with western liberal forms and deny the right of non-liberal systems to use the sacred term democracy.

Other political systems may see our system of democracy as synonymous with capitalism and its associated market forces and competition. In communist countries it is argued that it was precisely the overthrow of capitalism that allowed the development of democracy to take place.

Marxists believe that the replacement of capitalism by the 'dictatorship of the proletariat' will create a society without conflict for the exploiters of the people will have been removed and the collective will of the people established.

► *The* Landesgemeinde *or open air parliament of a group of Swiss cantons which takes place every April.*

We now use terms such as:
- Industrial democracy
- Direct democracy
- Liberal democracy
- Pluralist democracy
- Participatory democracy
- Representative democracy
- Proletarian democracy
- Corporatist democracy etc.

There seems no end to the different interpretations that can be applied to the term democracy and this has been exaggerated in recent years by using 'democracy' in conjunction with a variety of other concepts.

Perhaps the one common feature is that everyone seems to want more of it and denies the claims of enemies to be practising it.

DISCUSSING THE ARGUMENTS

The Development of Democracy

Democracy, as we have tried to establish, is viewed universally to be the most desirable political system for any country. Attitudes towards democracy have, however, changed over time for 'rule by the many' has not always been seen to be desirable. For a long time until this century, rule by the mass of the people was considered a threat to individual freedom and a danger to cultured living.

Although the Greeks were first to organise a democratic political system, and the Athenian example is held to be the most notable, the political philosophers, Plato and Artistotle, were critics.

Athenian Democracy

From the fifth century BC to the middle of the fourth century BC, the government of the small city-state of Athens was based upon the idea that all power rested with the people who exercised it by direct participation in public affairs. The citizens of Athens in return had a duty to the state to undertake military service, attend festivals, and act as jurors in the courts.

The concept of citizenship was quite different to that of today, for it was not extended to resident foreigners, women, children or slaves. Citizenship was traditional and not something that could be generally established by residence. However, Athenian citizenship did imply political equality for those who possessed it.

The Assembly, which met once a month, allowed citizens to help form laws and decrees, authorise expenditure, and generally settle policy matters. It also elected officials and boards of citizens to run the city's agencies. This, Athenians considered, would enhance public awareness of political problems. Offices were allocated by lot from the elected candidates in order to allow all citizens an opportunity to enjoy office.

Most of the offices were paid so that poorer citizens would not be deterred and payments for attendance at the Assembly also became established. The possible abuse of power by officials was curbed by regular reviews of their work and through the need for them to submit to popular reapproval or censure. Each office was held for a year and not normally more than once by the same person. At the end of the period, the office holder had to account for the monies for which he had been responsible. These practices, Athenians felt, made officials truly accountable to the people, prevented them becoming insensitive to popular demands, and removed the need for a permanent bureaucracy.

Decisions in the Assembly were reached by a majority vote after free and open debate. Motions for discussion could be raised by any citizen, not just the officials. The proposer of any decree or law, could be challenged in the courts and charged with acting unconstitutionally. In this way, it was hoped that rash or hasty decisions generated by inspirational orators could be checked.

There was a notably high degree of political freedom in Athens and discussion in the Assembly could be very wide ranging. Even those like Plato who attacked the Athenian democratic system were tolerated. The Athenian system of democracy has come to be regarded as somewhat of a 'model' against which modern systems should be compared. The Athenian model, however, did have its contemporary critics, particularly Plato.

Mob Rule

Plato was sceptical of the value of mass meetings for he felt they were liable to exploitation by passionate orators who would be able to appeal to the self interests of 'the mob'. The result he considered would be notable unpredictability in decision making which could only damage the governing process.

Plato also argued that because decisions were made by a mass meeting no one individual citizen would feel directly responsible for any decision. Again Plato felt this would be damaging for the state. If the state was to be run by 'the mob' how could rational decisions be arrived at? And also what future could such a state hope for?

Plato argued that government required skills that the ordinary citizen did not possess. Those who undertook the task needed special training and would perform their duties on a full-time basis. So the offices of state should be open only to those with great talent because to entrust government to those without it would only result in poor decisions. He believed that only those with the appropriate talents would be able to realise what was in the best overall interests of the state.

▼ *Greek philosopher Plato (427–347 BC).*

The critical views of democracy as expressed by philosophers like Plato and Artistotle were considered valid for 2000 years thereafter. The word 'democracy' was generally used unfavourably and even the American Founding Fathers referred to 'republicanism' as the basis for their constitution. Democracy in the form of rule by the common people was generally seen as rule by the largest group in society, i.e. the plebians. Rule by such an 'undesirable' group could only lead to a destruction of the values that 'men of substance and learning' held dear. So democracy had to be avoided; to let the common people take the major role in the governmental process could only result in disaster.

Even in the nineteenth century Liberals like John Stuart Mill were keen to avoid an electoral system which would give the working class the greatest voice in politics. Mill felt that the people could simply not rule themselves, so one part must rule another part.

Other nineteenth century liberals were also concerned about the potential problems of 'mob rule'.

> *No people of a magnitude to be called a nation has ever, in strictness, governed itself; the utmost which appears to be obtainable under conditions of human life, is that it should choose its governors and that it should on select occasions bear directly on their action.*
>
> Gladstone *The Nineteenth Century*, July 1878

The transformation in the reputation of 'democracy' as a political theory and aspiration took place during World War I. The famous war effort slogan of the Woodrow Wilson administration in the USA was 'Make the World Safe for Democracy'. This may have been an effective rallying cry but it could have hardly applied to all the Allies, especially Tsarist Russia.

There was some questioning of democracy with the rise of fascism during the 1930s. Yet even Mussolini and Hitler felt it desirable to emphasise their popular base and claim to be the embodiment of the hopes of the people. Both, in fact, claimed that their systems were 'socialist' and only differed from traditional socialism in that instead of being internationalist, their systems were 'National' socialist.

Direct Democracy

The nature of direct/indirect democracy is closely bound up with theories of **representation** and **participation** as well as the differences between **delegates** and **representatives** (see Chapter 7). Direct democracy, similar to the 'Athenian model' where citizens are directly and immediately involved in discussions and decision making, does have some advantages but also some drawbacks, when compared to forms of representative democracy where the responsibility for decision making is entrusted to a group of representatives who are subject to periodic popular election.

Advantages

- It ensures that the wishes of the people will be implemented, for representatives cannot always be trusted not to substitute their own ideas of what would best serve the public interest. The assumption is that only the people *know* what is in their best interests.
- It educates the people in the problems of running the state and demonstrates the difficulties politicians and public officials face. This, therefore, will lead to sound decision making by the people.
- It enhances the concept of citizenship by generating a sense of achievement in the people by them taking responsibility for decisions which affect their lives.

Disadvantages

- It is costly in terms of time for it is difficult to arrange meetings, referendums, etc.
- Inconsistency and bad decisions may result from people directly deciding issues they cannot fully understand because they possess insufficient specialist knowledge.
- Orators may sway the crowd with an inspirational performance not sound argument and logic.
- Large meetings can develop a psychology of their own which can result in intolerance towards minority viewpoints and subsequent threats to liberty.

TYPES OF DEMOCRACY

Western Liberal Democracy

Democracy need not be equated solely with the particular form that exists in western liberal countries for other political systems claim to be democratic. In the west, however, there are several features which are considered necessary for a country to legitimately claim to be 'democratic'.

Liberal democracy is associated with capitalism, for this particular type of democracy is almost wholly to be seen in countries with a capitalist economic system. This is not to say, however, that countries with a capitalist economic system will necessarily be democratic.

The 'democracy' of liberal democratic states tended to develop after the growth of the **liberal state** (see Chapter 10). The dominance of liberal ideas led to the establishment of the principle of free choice in politics as well as in economics. Each individual was seen to be the best judge of what is in his own interests and therefore should be allowed the maximum opportunity to exercise that judgement. This view connects with *laissez-faire* notions and liberal economists' views about the desirability of a non-interventionist state.

The liberal democratic view is that the political system is **individualistic**, or **pluralistic**, with society made up of a mass of autonomous individuals or groups. The role of government is to act in accordance with the expressed wishes of the people.

So if society is made up of the total of all these individuals or groups the major function of government is to identify their wishes and act accordingly. The principle mechanism to achieve this is that of 'elections' where individual views can be identified by the unrestricted expression of opinion.

Overall, the liberal view was that the individuals should be able to arrange their lives as they see fit in terms of religion, occupation, lifestyle, etc. This choice was then extended to politics. It was the market that was felt to determine economic relationships and provide the rewards. The rewards of labour, investment, etc, could then be spent freely in whatever way the individual desired.

The freedom of choice afforded to any individual would be determined by the level of rewards gained, but for the mass of people the only thing they had to offer in the market was their labour.

The establishment of a capitalist market economy occurred in many western countries during the eighteenth and nineteenth centuries. As market forces came to dominate peoples' lives, increasingly this meant that social status became less important and one's ability to compete in the market increasingly more important. The liberal society may have provided a greater freedom of choice, but it also produced a society with great inequality. The rewards of the capitalist system may have been theoretically open to all, but few were able to compete sufficiently well to gain rewards.

The system of government that developed in many liberal states reflected these principles. The government supplied certain services which were vital to the running of the capitalist economic system. These would include law and order, defence, taxation and some public expenditure on projects to develop the economy, education, public health, etc.

The question of whether the government was supplying the right 'political goods' to its consumers (i.e. the electorate) was settled by periodic elections. The elections again reflected market principles, with the electorate allowed a free choice between the candidates running for office.

In order to make this an effective choice, other 'freedoms' were established. There had to be **freedom of association** to allow electors to meet together to discuss the abilities of candidates or rival political parties and this implied a need for **freedom of speech**, which was in turn accompanied by **freedom of publication.**

This is not to say that all these 'freedoms' were given to all, for as we have seen, the idea of democracy as rule by the common people was a very unpopular idea amongst men of substance, i.e. those who could vote.

The problem which arose was that many individuals did not have the means to influence the supply of political goods (i.e. the ability to vote) and therefore were excluded from the political 'market place'. The political goods that were subsequently supplied by government reflected only the wishes of those who were enfranchised.

Enfranchisement and Choice

Democracy came about through the demands and political agitation of those excluded from the process. The process of enfranchisement was a long one in many countries and was not fully achieved until often well into the twentieth century. The history of many working class movements, therefore, was one of demanding a place in the competitive political market place and not one of wishing to overthrow it and substitute a socialist alternative.

As new 'consumers' won a right to take part in political market activity, the kind of political goods that were 'on offer' from political parties changed in order to meet the new demands. In many countries considerable extensions of state welfare provision took place, together with measures to limit some of the undesirable consequences of the competitive market system for those least able to compete.

The essence, therefore, of what is seen as democracy in the West centres on the freedom of the individual to choose between competing parties and candidates in elections where there is freedom of association and freedom of speech. With this analysis of democracy in mind certain principles can be seen to be important.

Principles of Liberal Democracy

Popular Control of the Governors

A primary concern of liberal democracy is the choosing of governors at periodic elections. This is not to say that the policies which are offered as election packages by political parties will be decided directly by those voting upon them. The concept of **responsible government** (see Chapter 7) further argues that the governors need not always respond directly to the wishes of the people on every occasion.

Nonetheless, although direct popular control may not be evident, the principle still remains that at regular intervals the elected representative should be judged upon his or her performance in office by having to win popular approval in order to continue.

The concept of **popular sovereignty** is central to the need to control those in power. The ultimate right to exercise political power is vested in 'the people'. Even though it may prove impossible for everyone to be directly involved, the rulers should at least have to justify their actions and be removable.

Equality

The American Declaration of Independence claims that all men are created equal but the equality assumed by the Founding Fathers was political equality.

People will naturally have differing abilities, so, in a democratic sense, equality implies establishing equal political rights, equal voting rights, equality of opportunity, and equality before the law. What this means is that all those eligible to vote should be able to exercise this right freely at appropriate elections.

It is also usually seen to involve '*one person one vote*', so that all votes therefore should carry equal political weight in influencing the policy makers.

This idea of political equality has been taken up by proponents of **proportional representation** in Great Britain, who argue that the present relative majority system prevents votes in effect being equal (see Chapter 22). They claim that those who vote for minority or third parties under the British system are discriminated against in that governmental majorities in the House of Commons are secured with less than 50 per cent of the votes cast.

Example

In 1987 the National Party of the South African Prime Minister, Mr P.W. Botha, won a clear victory in a general election where the voters had a choice in a secret ballot of 5 parties representing 471 candidates and 8 independent candidates. However, although all votes presumably were 'equal' and all the electorate given the opportunity to vote, only the minority white population are included in the electorate.

The 'equality' created by universal adult suffrage is also questioned in other ways. Formal equality of the franchise may mean little if power really is exercised by a small group who own the means of production in a capitalist system.

So many Marxists argue that, until economic inequality is removed, the political equality of liberal democracy is only a sham. 'True' democracy for a Marxist can only be established when the state is reorganised to look after the interests of 'the people' and not just a small exploitive economic elite.

Another problem may arise if equality, in terms of the ability to vote, is only extended to citizens of the state and citizenship is restricted.

Most concepts of citizenship which lead to the granting of political equality, however, are drawn fairly widely with only specific exclusions such as age, criminal conviction, insanity, a period of residence, and, in Britain in national elections, being a member of the House of Lords.

Political Freedom

For votes to count equally and for there to be popular control of governors the voters must be able to freely express their opinions and be given a choice of candidates and parties. They should also be free to, if they desire, form alternative or new parties.

Free expression of choice can only be secured through methods to ensure that voters are not coerced in any way. This in western liberal democracies has led to many electoral safeguards such as the secret ballot and limitations on the spending and conduct of candidates.

The choice of candidates offered to the voter may also not be sufficient if all the candidates belong to the same party. So political freedom also implies the right of nearly everyone to offer themselves as candidates with alternative sets of policies and party organisation.

The ability to do so effectively also implies a need for adequate opportunities to publicly criticise the policies of other parties and to enjoy freedom of association without fear of harassment.

Without the existence of these freedoms it is difficult to see how the governors can be held to account for their actions at periodic elections.

Majority Decision Making

Once free elections have taken place, issues have been discussed and representatives elected, the problem then emerges of *how* decisions should be reached.

In a modern representative parliamentary system unanimity cannot be expected from a group of politicians who, at an election, presented a range of policies and ideas, even if linked to the manifestos of political parties.

The solution of the problem rests with a **majoritarian principle.** Policies are decided by a majority of representatives voting for them.

This principle again offends supporters of proportional representation in Britain, for they argue that it is unreasonable for government to implement policy on the basis of a majority vote in the House of Commons, no matter how large the margin. All governments that have enjoyed a majority in the House of Commons since 1945 have secured less than 50 per cent of the vote in the general election which produced the majority.

The difficulty of a majoritarian principle lies with the position of those groups who form a permanent minority, whose views may be permanently ignored. The temptation for such minorities will be to employ non-democratic means to achieve their objectives. (See Chapter 4.)

The majoritarian principle assumes that all groups can seek majority support and if successful replace the government by a victory at the polls.

This can work well if all competitors for office accept the principles and abide by them. A major problem arises when a group uses a majoritarian position to remove the democratic rights of others.

If democracy in the western-liberal meaning of the word is held to include the vital component of 'rule by the majority', then, if the majority is happy to see an end to democracy, should the will of the majority not prevail?

Example

The Supreme Court in the USA ruled that a group called Students for a Democratic Society should not be banned for advocating violent political change providing they did not actually engage in such activity.

Definition

Democracy:
is a system of government where decisions are arrived at by majoritarian' principles with representatives elected at periodic elections where political equality and political freedom allow the voter an effective choice between competing candidates in a secret ballot.

Democracy may therefore mean that democratic rights and political freedoms are extended to a group which has the expressed intention of building up a majority in order to end democracy itself.

It can be argued therefore that a majoritarian rule implies more than just a group having the support of 51 per cent.

Democracy is argued to include the necessity of minorities to enjoy rights and freedoms which the majority cannot remove. The majority principle assumes more than just the sheer power of numbers.

Nonetheless liberal democracies have often had to tackle the problem of whether anti-democratic groups should be allowed the same political rights and freedoms as everyone else. For to deny them such rights would in itself be a denial of the democratic principles of freedom of speech, freedom of association, etc. The problem, of course, remains largely academic as long as anti-democratic groups gain little popular support.

The rise of the Nazi party in Germany in the 1920s does however highlight the problems that democratic political systems can encounter when dealing with anti-democratic groups.

At what point should democrats act to protect democracy? Self-proclaimed defenders of democracy are often happy to justify widespread attacks on groups loosely categorised as 'anti-democratic' or 'subversive' in this way. The record of several South American regimes on human rights serve as notable examples.

If we accept these four general principles as central to a liberal western criteria of democracy it may be possible to arrive at a definition for this form of democracy.

PLURALISM AND DEMOCRACY

The growing complexity of industrial societies in the twentieth century led some political thinkers to doubt whether individuals could have any real influence in a democratic political system. It was discovered in several studies that, except for voting in elections, few people ever participated in the political process.

Pluralism developed as a way of explaining that liberal democracies were basically organised around the activities of organised groups and not individuals. The major principle in pluralism is that political power is dispersed amongst many groups and that political decisions are reached as a result of bargaining and interaction between the groups.

Such a system is seen to safeguard the individual, for the individual alone can hope to have little impact on government. As part of a group the individual is strengthened politically and the need for government to consider his or her wishes, when making policy, is enhanced.

Pluralism considers that organised groups are legitimate channels of communication between individuals and politicians. Modern mass industrial societies make it impossible for individuals to play a direct political role, so pluralism, it could be argued, is the only practical democratic alternative.

For the groups to act effectively people had to have complete freedom of access to them and other basic freedoms become necessary. People must be able to freely express themselves and organise with others. The necessity for freedom of speech, freedom of assembly, and freedom of association thereby is a central feature of pluralist thinking.

The range of interests represented and the number of groups that exist reflect the economic, social, cultural, ethnic, religious, components that make up society. Anyone who belongs to a group is therefore represented in the political system. Individuals may not generally consider themselves as belonging to only one group, and may have several interests covered by several groups. A solicitor may have his professional interests represented by the Law Society, his interest in animal welfare promoted by the Royal Society for the Prevention of Cruelty to Animals, and as a car owner, his interests advanced by the Automobile Association.

The result of group activity is that political decisions will be arrived at through a process of bargaining and compromise between government and various competing interests. All will have the opportunity to gain from the system and it will be in everyone's interest to see that the system works well.

All interested groups will have to accept that they will not be able to have their own way on every issue, so a sense of compromise and willingness to work towards consensus will be necessary. The established political system will need to be accepted and, if this is done, a political balance between the groups can be established with political stability ensured. Political activity can then be reduced to a process of limited adjustments between the position of the groups in order to protect the established balance between them.

Pluralism for many political socialists became the central feature of western liberal democracy where political power was dispersed and no one elite group could possess a monopoly. The opportunity for groups to compete for political power came to be seen as a safeguard against the control of political power passing to any group.

Pluralism came to be viewed as a way of securing an open political system which would tolerate competing viewpoints and produce guarantees for basic political freedoms. The benefits of a pluralist system are seen to be that it is comprehensive, in that all interests are considered and everyone operates on the basis of establishing a consensus.

Criticisms of Pluralist theory

The assumptions that lie behind pluralism have not gone unchallenged. It can be argued that, although many groups may compete for political power, nonetheless the major interests in a capitalist society, particularly those of big business, always have the resources to win. Whilst everyone may be able to take part in the competition the winner is nearly always the same competitor, or group of competitors.

▼ An anti-squatter door in London displays posters about issues of concern to the community.

The role of government in a pluralist system has also been questioned. A pluralist view is that government remains neutral in the competition between groups. It is seen to act as a kind of referee or umpire, independent of the groups. The competition is supposed to ensure this. Some pluralists, however, argue that the government cannot be totally passive in the sense of waiting for the outcome of the competition and then awarding the 'prizes'.

Governmental interests may also be pitched against the competing groups. An example can be said to be seen in Britain where government departments attempt to head off challenges that might injure their established positions. Critics, however, see it as inevitable that government will always side with the most powerful interests in a capitalist society. This has led some political writers to the conclusion that the close relationships between government and powerful interests has developed into a form of **corporatism** in many western liberal democracies. In this sense the groups become almost an institution of state which affords them privileged access to the policy-making machinery of government. (See Chapter 14.)

Pluralist arguments have also been used to justify the growth of **pressure group** influence in government policy-making. Group activity can be argued to be an essential feature of liberal democracy in that it ensures governments have to be responsive to the wishes of the people as communicated through organised interests. Without their active participation, government would be far less effective. (See Chapter 21.)

Another challenge to pluralist thinking concerns the degree of competition between groups. Power may be spread across a large number of groups, but this it is argued, gives no guarantee that the groups will actually compete with each other. In fact quite the opposite situation might develop with groups coming to recognise each other's areas of interest and thereby accepting the mutual benefit of avoiding 'trespass' and resultant competition.

In this way it may be that no one group comes to dominate the control of political power, but, nonetheless, many groups will control their particular area of interest. The consensus reached by the groups through compromise might not be the 'best' policy but merely the one that will be most easily accceptable to all.

ONE PARTY DEMOCRACY

In a liberal democracy the people, who are seen to be a mass of individuals, are expected to be able to make a choice between alternative policies and sets of governors. If the governors fail to convince sufficient numbers of the people of their suitability for office and their capacity to reflect and implement the wishes of the people, they can be removed at periodic elections.

An alternative view to this involves a concept where the wishes of the people are seen to be identified in one **popular will**. This popular will can then be represented in a single party and implemented by a government made up of such party members. The role and scope of government will be determined by the process of implementing the will of the people.

Communist One-Party States

This form of 'democracy' can be seen in the writings of Marx and Lenin and in the beliefs of many modern African leaders. For Marx 'real' democracy was created with the dictatorship of the proletariat following a revolutionary overthrow of the bourgeoisie.

Marx argued that capitalism was certain to be destroyed. The state, he said, was merely an instrument for the repression of the working class and as such denied the possibility of the development of democracy. Only with the removal of the capitalist system could democracy be established. Throughout history, Marx argued, man had been unable to fulfill the potential of human nature because the mass of mankind had little option but to labour in order to survive. The organisation of labour required, as such, a ruling class.

For Marx the advent of capitalism provided for the first time the opportunity and technical productive capacity to 'release mankind' from continued toil. Nonetheless, capitalism was oppressive and, for Marx, it had to be destroyed, although its productive capacity could be harnessed for the achievements of socialist objectives.

Democracy was to be a class state but would comprise only the first step, for the overall objective was to establish a 'classless' society. The dictatorship of the proletariat was democracy because it would involve the majority of the people. When the process of transforming economic relationships was complete and everyone benefited, the need for such a form of class rule would disappear.

The history of many working class movements, as we have established, did not follow the path predicted by Marx. Instead of rejecting capitalism and liberal democracy, working class movements often attempted to use their emerging political power to win concessions and gain more influence over the working of the capitalist system both in economic and political terms.

Democracy after the Russian Revolution

The first real opportunity to test Marxist theories came, however, not in an industrially developed state like Britain, or Germany, as Marx had anticipated, but in Russia. In Russia the industrial proletariat, so vital to Marxist analysis, made up only a small minority of workers and were vastly outnumbered by peasants.

Lenin, the leader of the 1917 Bolshevik revolution, believed Marxist analysis to be true and felt that to apply it in Russia required a 'vanguard' to achieve the revolution on behalf of the mass of the Russian people.

The vanguard for Lenin was to be made up of the Communist Party who would have the difficult task of transforming Russia from peasant to industrial economy. By creating an industrial base, Lenin hoped to achieve the conditions necessary for a transformation to the stateless society predicted by Marx. The vanguard was therefore to create a democratic state for the

► *Painting of Lenin addressing a revolutionary meeting. Stalin and Trotsky stand behind him (as they probably never did in real life).*

people even though the people had no choice in the personnel of the vanguard.

The mass of the Russian people were viewed by Lenin to be unready to achieve 'true' democracy because they were still committed to old values and beliefs. Only when the old system had finally been overcome could the people be entrusted with the responsibility of creating a new society.

If there is only one party, can a government be considered 'democratic'?
If we apply liberal-democratic principles then the answer would be 'no', but, given the application of other criteria, then the answer may not be so conclusive. In a series of lectures given in 1965 on the nature of democracy Professor C.B. MacPherson argued that democracy could be possible in a one party state if three conditions were evident:

- the existence of mechanisms for effective control of party leaders by rank and file members
- open party membership
- party membership should not place upon the individual an unreasonable burden of work.

The difficulty for many political observers in the West is that they are not convinced that such conditions exist in most communist states, even if they accept that the three conditions above lend credibility to the claims of such regimes to be democratic.

In the West it is often argued that average rank and file members are unable to exercise any real control in many centralised communist states which are controlled by a single party.

Party membership is often severely restricted and subject to 'ideological orthoxody' as a prerequisite to membership. The threat of expulsion and consequent loss of privileges and rights acts as deterrent to any party member who may be accused of 'dissidence' by not following official party doctrine.

The level of activism required of party members, although not exceptionally demanding in many communist states, would, nonetheless, be considered greater than that expected of party members in the West as a price for party membership.

Overall there are few contemporary communist one-party states that would meet Professor MacPherson's criteria and none that would meet western-liberal standards.

Non-communist One Party Systems

Other non-communist one party states have claimed to be democratic although they possess few western-liberal features. With the granting of independence to many former colonies frequently western states hoped to leave behind replicas of the representative parliamentary systems they held to be the essence of democracy. To the dismay of many colonial powers the newly independent nations quickly abandoned such arrangements and established one party states. This happened, for example, in Kenya and Tanzania.

This should not be surprising, for the basis of liberal democracy, as we have identified it, was not readily transferable to countries with very different social and economic structures.

Nor can the Marxist analysis of class struggle be easily applicable. The struggle for most new nations was not to overthrow a repressive capitalist class but to expell a foreign power.

The result has often been that the political movements which fought for independence in many African and Asian countries carried over into the post-independence period with a dominant single party claiming to be the only legitimate vehicle for the realisation of the aspirations of the people. In many states a single, dominant tribe also formed the 'natural' basis for single party government.

The overriding need to create a national identity for a country, where in many cases individuals saw their immediate loyalty as belonging to a tribal or ethnic group, led to the suspension of what in the West are seen as political rights and political freedoms. Freedom of speech, assembly, etc. were argued to be merely providing opportunities for enemies of the new regime and therefore had to be carefully managed.

The claim for the label of 'democracy' for this type of one party state rests on the argument that the wishes and aspirations of the people are effectively incorporated in, and expressed by, the single national political party. The support for the party, it may be claimed, was shown during the independence struggle. Without doubt many independence movements enjoyed mass support often resulting in widespread acclamation for the leader of the single dominant party.

The primary question, however, is for how long after the period of struggle to win independence can a single party continue to claim the support of the people without a means to test the solidarity of that support?

If no elections are held and if only candidates from the ruling parties are offered as a choice, then how is it possible for the leaders to ensure a correspondence between their actions and the will of the people?

The daunting economic problems which have faced many emergent nations have placed a premium upon the need for economic development and national solidarity in order for survival. The result has been that often the features of choice, competition, freedom of speech, rights of the individual generally, all of which are so central to western-liberal democracy, not only are seen as inappropriate, but also as an imported 'luxury' for which these nations have little use.

THE 'INEFFICIENCY' OF DEMOCRACY

Democracy in the western-liberal sense has attracted criticism from those who consider it as an inefficient way of organising political activity. It is portrayed as slow because, before a party programme can be implemented, there has to be a process of electioneering, elections, and then parliamentary debate. This leads to the accusation that democracy comes under threat at times of crisis when a swift response from government is needed.

It is also argued to be inefficient in the sense that such decision making procedures may be suitable for a small political system such as a Greek city state but not for handling the problems of a modern complex society.

Democracy can further be attacked, on the basis of the leaders that get elected, for an ability to 'please the crowd', and so attain office, may not be the same as those which are required to reach sound judgements in government. All kinds of strategies may be employed to win votes, but sound policies are not always the most attractive options offered to the electorate. Rash promises may be far more marketable!

The democratic decision making processes of government may also lead to gross inefficiency because political institutions are empowered to cancel each other out. The situation in the USA where each branch of government is potentially capable of holding up the work of the others, has been described as the 'deadlock of democracy' and a 'veto system'.

To break such a 'deadlock', compromise has to be reached and this in itself has been claimed to be inefficient. Compromise can mean that everyone loses and that the decision which is finally arrived at will not be the best but merely the one that is most widely acceptable to those involved.

This process may also encourage selfish interests to bargain for advantage knowing that their power will have to be acknowledged and their views taken into account.

Bargaining and compromise could also be argued to create a situation where no 'principles' can be guaranteed thus for the mass of the people this process can only lead to cynicism and distrust.

These criticisms can of course be challenged.

Challenging the Criticisms

Despite the 'inefficiencies' of politicians and the necessity of striking bargains on some occasions, at least the *process* is conducted publicly, and decisions reached are subject to the periodic assessment of the people. The result is that the 'rascals can be thrown out'. No such opportunity would be available to the people living under a despotic or totalitarian regime, however efficiently administered.

The mass of the people may well be 'ignorant' and government would perhaps be managed more efficiently by a superior elite, as Plato or George Bernard Shaw would have wished, for example. There is no guarantee, however, that such a group would not be corrupted by the possession of such power and simply govern in their own interests.

Government by a superior elite also produces the problem of how its membership should be identified and recruited. Can we be sure that a particular level of intellectual capacity, for example, will necessarily lead to wise decision making?

Further questions also arise with such an elite for, without some mechanism to give approval to the decisions reached, how will they know the wishes of the people are being observed, therefore making decisions legitimate?

A more fundamental factor about the 'inefficiency' of democracy occurs when you consider what the ends of politics are about.

It may be very plausible to argue a superior elite would govern efficiently and impartially.

It may also be true of democracy that decisions can take a long time to emerge and yet still be bad ones. The people may also be taken in by sophisticated rhetoric and as a result elect dishonest or incompetent rulers.

Ultimately however democracy places the responsibility for decision making into the hands of the people so that, if necessary, they will make mistakes but, it is hoped, learn from them.

For a democrat this must be a better politically educative process than having all matters decided by a group always supposed to know better than the people what is in their own interests.

EXAMINATION QUESTIONS

1 How accurate is it to describe the United Kingdom as a liberal democracy? (AEB Government and Politics, A-Level, 1985)

2 In what ways, if any, could Britain be a more democratic country? (University of Cambridge, Government and Politics A-level, 1980)

3 What arguments have been advanced by political theorists against democracy? (University of London, Government and Political Studies, A-Level 1982)

NOW READ ON . . .

R. Eccleshall *et al* *Political Ideologies* Hutchinson, 1984
See the chapter on democracy by Richard Jay.

C. B. McPherson *The Real World of Democracy* OUP, 1972
A central text.

B. Holden *The Nature of Democracy* Nelson, 1974
A good analysis of the problems of democratic theory.

10 Liberalism

▶▶▶▶▶▶▶▶▶▶▶▶▶▶▶ BASIC PRINCIPLES

The Liberal Party existed as a separate entity in Britain for over a hundred years: from the mid-1800s to 1988 when it merged with the larger part of the Social Democrat Party to form the Social and Liberal Democrats (SLD).

For much of its early history the Liberal Party (the 'Whigs') alternated in power with the Conservatives under such Prime Ministers as Palmerston, Gladstone and Lloyd George. However, its failure to attract and to hold the growing working class vote during the late nineteenth and early twentieth centuries began the process of decline and fission.

By the 1930s the Party was a mere shadow of its former self and, following World War II, its main problem was survival.

The fact that there is no longer a Liberal Party, as such, in Britain does not release students from the need to study the idea of Liberalism. It returns them to a period in which the names of the political parties did not contain the word 'Liberal' but in which the ideas of Liberalism were paramount. During much of the nineteenth century the Tory and Whig parties battled for supremacy using ideas which were almost wholly **Liberal**.

Today, in the last years of the twentieth century, the ideas of traditional Liberalism are not only alive but form the very cornerstone of much of Government policy. The radical liberalism of the SLD is but one road down which liberal thought has been travelling for around three hundred years.

It is particularly ironic that even the problems of the 1980s have been those with which the Victorians fought:

- Free trade
- Ireland
- Social welfare
- Government power.

The Liberal approach

Each political party is built upon a particular approach to politics and on its own view of people and society. The Liberal approach stems from our central commitment to liberty, to the development of human potential in its full range and diversity and to the importance of the community. We seek economic prosperity not as an end in itself but as part of the necessary foundation for a free and open society. We recognise the inter-dependence of human life and liberty in different communities, not only in Britain but throughout the world. Above all, we seek to spread wealth and power, believing that liberty is best promoted through the responsible actions of men and women working together within diverse communities. We therefore see equality, or rather a diminution of gross inequalities, as a consequence of such a liberal society rather than an end in itself. We judge state intervention, not as in itself good or bad, but by its contribution to the development of a liberal society.

People are more likely to behave responsibly if they are tested as responsible citizens. Our political institutions fail to do this and our electoral system reinforces the deep divisions in society. Political reform must therefore play a central part in the Liberal Programme.

The rebuilding of public confidence requires that central government must also be made open and accountable. Cynicism about Britain's political institutions is reflected in declining turn-out at local and parliamentary elections. Conservative and Labour politicians wax eloquent in defence of citizens' rights and democracy abroad whilst resisting their extension in Britain. The Liberal concept of democracy – and of efficient government – involves effective mechanisms of accountability, open and informed debate, wider representation of the diversity of views through a more democratic voting system, and greater protection for the individual citizen against the state.

Source: *These are Liberal Policies*, Peter Knowlson, published by the Liberal Party, 1986

Like the word 'conservative' the concept 'liberal' has two similar but quite separate meanings. We usually distinguish between them by actually saying in everyday speech things like 'he is conservative with a small "c"', or 'She's Liberal with a capital "L"'.

'Liberal' and 'liberal' are closely connected words but it is important to distinguish between them. Using a small 'l' means that the person you are describing is tolerant of the beliefs and actions of others, that they are fair minded and open to many different ideas, and that they will usually weigh up those ideas in a rational manner. Most members of the Social and Liberal Democrats would like to think of themselves as 'liberal minded' and many undoubtedly are, but this is not necessarily the case.

The Liberal Party in Britain is sometimes seen as being 'centre of the road' and as having 'no real policies except those which fall between the two other parties'. Needless to say this view is not very accurate. Liberalism is a distinct set of political ideas and has resulted in very clear differences of approach between it and the two largest parties. It may well be that the British Liberals have not presented themselves clearly enough to the electorate or that Liberalism is not very clearly understood. Some would argue, also, that the other two parties have consistently 'stolen the Liberals' clothes' – that is, they have taken the Liberals' policies for their own. Whatever the reasons, however, one must understand where Liberalism has come from in order to recognise the main elements of the modern creed.

DISCUSSING THE ARGUMENTS

Conservative Liberalism

The origins of liberalism lie far back in the eighteenth century; indeed, some would argue that they lie in the period when the Barons were forcing the King to guarantee certain rights to both themselves and to the people (the Magna Carta). Liberal ideas were first written down in a comprehensive form by John Locke who established the concept of **Natural Law** and, through that, the idea that there were such things as **Natural Rights** (see Chapters 5 and 6).

John Locke (1632–1704)

John Locke's family came from the English West Country which was largely Royalist during the Civil War. As Locke's father was a staunch supporter of the Parliamentary cause the family suffered much hardship during the upheavals. He is said to have had great respect for his father and it is often said that Locke acquired his essentially decent and humanitarian view of life from his father's attitudes.

Locke is known for two great works of British political philosophy both of which were published in the same year:

Two Treatises on Government (1689) of which the second is the most important.

A Letter Concerning Toleration (1689)

Locke's writings influenced liberal thinkers throughout the western world. In the American colonies the settlers began to wonder why, if they had a right to representation, they were not allowed to have their own MPs at Westminster. In France many people used Locke's concept of 'rights' to criticise a monarch who considered himself absolute and unquestionable.

In Britain, Locke's ideas were given concrete form when the last Stuart monarch (James II (1633–1701) who reigned 1685–8) was dismissed. In 1688 the 'Glorious Revolution' created a unique institution in the world – a king and queen who did not claim a God-given right to rule a country but who had been *invited* to reign under quite strict conditions. The idea of a **constitutional monarch** had been born.

The liberal ideas which grew throughout the eighteenth century resulted in an ideology which was at once liberal and conservative. It was best illustrated by a politician who is, today, considered more one of the founders of the Conservative ideology than a founder Liberal. Edmund Burke was one of the most famous MPs of the late eighteenth century, but his views on government have become a standard against which developments may be measured.

▲ *Edmund Burke (1729–97).*

Edmund Burke (1729–97)

Burke was born in Dublin and, after a short career as a lawyer and slightly more success as a writer, he entered Parliament as a Whig MP for Bristol. He gained the nickname 'Dinner Bell Burke' because other MPs would leave to dine when he rose to speak.

He believed that Parliament should rule Britain for the benefit of its people, but did not believe the people were necessarily the best judges of what should be done. Although he objected to the policies towards the American colonists, he attacked the French Revolution. His defence of English institutions led him to be considered by many as the 'founding father' of conservatism.

Reflections on the Revolution in France 1791

The Liberalism which Burke represented became the basis of the beliefs of the **Whig Party** and constituted what has since become known as **Conservative Liberalism** or **Victorian Liberalism** or, even, **Classical Liberalism**. Whatever the creed is called, it stood for certain well defined things:

- for limited government (for governments to be involved in the affairs of its citizens as little as possible);
- for religious freedom (at a time when Catholics and those who did not agree with the Church of England, the Non-Conformists, were regarded as little better than second class citizens);
- for the right of individuals to acquire wealth;
- for free-markets, unfettered by government restrictions;
- for private enterprise.

The early Whigs were definitely not, however, in favour of such things as democracy and the rights of the masses. Burke believed that only those who had property had the necessary motivation to govern the country well (for they had a stake in its future). Consequently, only people with a reasonable amount of property could be allowed the vote.

These views are very little different from those held today by the right wing of the modern Conservative Party.

Radical Liberalism

In the American colonies before, and shortly after, the War of Independence (1775–8) an Englishman by the name of Thomas Paine developed a more radical brand of Liberalism. He believed in democracy and in the rights of the disadvantaged (slaves and women) as well as the traditional values of Classical Liberalism. His views were developed during the French Revolution towards the more extreme end of the spectrum and were taken up in Britain by radical thinkers like Jeremy Bentham, James Mill, John Stuart Mill and Charles James Fox.

Thomas Paine (1737–1809).

Thomas Paine (1737–1809)

Born British, Paine became an American after the Revolution and eventually took part in the French Revolution too. He believed that Locke's ideas on rights did not go deeply enough into the basic rights which all people were born with. Tom Paine believed that the basic rights were liberty, security, the possession of property, and resistance to oppression. He believed in open government and in full participation by the people.

At one point he was the representative to the French National Convention for the town of Calais.

Common Sense (1776); **The Rights of Man** (1791/1792)

James Mill argued for votes for all adult males and his better known son, John Stuart Mill took that idea a step further and pressed for full adult suffrage (votes for adult men and women). Bentham wanted governments to realise that their first duty was to the happiness of the population. He argued that all government policies should be measured against a single criterion only: do they result in the *'greatest happiness of the greatest number'*?

Charles James Fox (1749–1806), one of the earliest radical reformers, was a lifelong enemy of George III and supporter of the House of Commons against the Monarchy. Fox and Rockingham called themselves 'Whigs' but were not part of the mainstream 'Whig' tradition. Their support for the concept of liberty and 'the people' and their opposition to the Crown and its advisers made them suspect as 'revolutionaries'. (A suspicion which was further enhanced when the French Revolution occurred and Fox openly acclaimed it as a victory for 'the people' against the established monarchy and entrenched privilege.) Fox took such an 'extreme' line in favour of reform in Parliament and in the franchise that he and his followers formed an almost permanent opposition in Parliament during the years of the Revolutionary and Napoleonic Wars from 1789 to 1815.

Charles James Fox (1749–1806)

An aristocratic politician who was a brilliant orator and who espoused radical reform in the constitution – particularly where it concerned the powers of the House of Commons versus the Monarchy. He became a lifelong enemy of George III and, consequently, spent much of his political career on the opposition benches.

Fox entered Parliament in 1780 on the back of the unrest which followed the disastrous end to the American War of Independence. At the age of 19 he led the calls for economic and political reform and promoted himself as a man-of-the-people. As the troubles at home and abroad grew during 1792, Fox supported limited constitutional reform with the object of forestalling revolution. His followers established a 'Society of the Friends of the People' in the same year. Edmund Burke, who had been an associate of Fox's in the years preceding the French Revolution, publicly distanced himself from Fox in 1791.

Fox's fear of the overwhelming power of the monarchy earned him George III's enmity and, in 1804, the King placed an absolute veto on Fox ever becoming part of a serving British Government. The veto lasted only as long as the life of the then Prime Minister, Pitt. In 1806, when Pitt died, the King was faced with an extremely difficult decision on the choice of the next government. Fox and his followers became essential to a firm government in those times of continued war and the King was forced to accept both Fox and some of his followers into the 'Ministry of all the Talents'. In return for this brief Ministry (Fox died at the end of the same year), Fox dropped his calls for constitutional reform.

▲ *Jeremy Bentham (1748–1832).*

It is often said that Fox was about a hundred years ahead of his time and given the nature of his calls for greater power for the Commons, a more closely restricted Royal Prerogative, and an extended franchise, this is probably true. What is clear is that Fox can be placed firmly in the rank of the radical liberals of the age.

Jeremy Bentham (1748–1832)

Bentham was a radical thinker who believed that it was possible to govern 'scientifically' by applying certain basic principles and by the use of what he called 'Hedonistic Calculus'.* In this Bentham identified 14 different categories of pleasure, 12 categories of pain (meaning, really, displeasure), and 7 standards of measurement for governments which wished to assure the greatest happiness of the greatest number.

He was a strong supporter of extremely advanced ideas such as the reform of the prison system, extension of the suffrage, and secret ballots in general elections. He provided many of the ideas for the Chartist Movement, calling in 1809 for annual elections for Parliament.

An Introduction to the Principles of Morals and Legislation (1798)
A Fragment on Government

Of these four thinkers the most famous was undoubtedly John Stuart Mill whose genius in politics, philosophy, logic, and economics had no rival at the time and few since.

Mill warned about the dangers of democracy and, particularly, those of allowing 'ignorant' people to vote. In this, however, he was not arguing for limits on democracy but for better education so that people might be able to cast their votes more rationally and with greater understanding. He argued for state education and taxes on the wealthy.

John Stuart Mill (1806–73)

Mill grew up in an intensely academic environment, being rigorously taught by his famous father, James Mill. J.S. Mill was three when his father began teaching him Greek and he was proficient in Latin, Greek and differential calculus before he was ten. He wanted a society which was tolerant of all of the beliefs held by its citizens, which was open, and which allowed its citizens to develop as human beings (in other words, to be educated and to have opportunities to expand their awareness through literature and public lectures).
Political Economy (1844); **Principles of Economy** (1848); **On Liberty** (1859); **Utilitarianism** (1861).

The Radical Liberals could be summed up, therefore, in the following way they were for:

- limited government;
- religious freedom and toleration;
- the rights of the individual (Tom Paine's 'Rights of Man');
- the government's duty to help its citizens to a better life;
- democracy and a full adult franchise (as long as education allows people to use their votes properly – until then, most of the Radicals supported the idea of weighted voting systems in which professionals, graduates and commercial people received multiple votes).

*Hedonism was the theory that the ultimate end of all action was pleasure.

Victorian Liberalism

Liberalism in the nineteenth century derived from the philosophy of Locke, Burke, Bentham and Mill and influenced both the Tory and Whig parties.

In 1832 the 'Great Reform Act' represented one of the most significant steps towards liberal ideals in that it began the process of extending the franchise beyond the wealthy and privileged circles to which it had, hitherto, been confined.

Example

THE GREAT REFORM ACT, 1832 – One of Fox's young followers, Earl Grey, was leader of the Whigs in 1831 when Lord John Russell proposed a Reform Bill to initiate Parliamentary reform. After two attempts to pass the Bill, Grey had to ask the King (William II) to threaten to create Peers in order to force it through the House of Lords. The compromises necessary to secure its eventual passage in 1832 made it but a mere shadow of the 1831 original but it began the process of nineteenth century constitutional reform by:

- allowing all householders rated at £10 per year – in boroughs – to vote;
- extending the vote in the countryside (the counties) to copyholders of £10 and leaseholders of £50 per year.

Even the Whigs, however, were not ready for such revolutionary steps as the secret ballot. Many of these traditional, 'conservative' liberals regarded secret ballots as 'unmanly' and cowardly. They did not wish the franchise to be extended beyond what they considered to be the educated middle classes.

Definition

Whig and Tory:
'Whig' and 'Tory' were originally terms of abuse. Each party – the Court (Tory) and Country (Whig) – chose an insulting name for the other based upon different bands of outlaws or protestors. The 'Tories' were Irish Papist outlaws (the word comes from the Gaelic Toraidhe *meaning a pursuer or robber) and the 'Whiggamores' were Scots (the term was given to a group of Scots who marched on Edinburgh in 1648 to oppose the King's supporters).*

The transition from 'Whig' party to 'Liberal' party was centred, essentially, upon attitudes to the franchise and towards the rights of the Irish. The Whigs were content with a broad form of 'pluralist' representation, that is, with groups and interests being represented in Parliament rather than each citizen having direct representation through their own vote. The more radical 'Liberals' were, however, anxious to emphasise individual rights and the concept of 'one man, one vote'.

The older Tories and Whigs were relatively content to allow a very gradual widening of the franchise to the middle classes, but held that the working classes should not receive the vote for a very long time, if at all.

By the time of Disraeli's 'Representation of the People Act' of 1867 the franchise stood at approximately 16 per cent of adults. Gladstone's Governments from 1868 through to 1892 widened that base considerably. By the 1890s over 50 per cent of adults were entitled to vote in General Elections and a whole series of 'liberal' policies had been implemented:

- corrupt practices had been almost stamped out with the Acts of 1868 and 1883;
- the secret ballot had become a reality with the Secret Ballot Act of 1882;
- many of the grounds by which people had been disqualified from sitting as MPs had been abolished. Among these were religious and property disqualifications;
- social reforms continued in the form of a series of Factory Acts and Public Health Acts;
- even as Chancellor of the Exchequer in 1853, William Gladstone began the process of abolishing duties on imports and, thereby, encouraging free trade;
- the early Liberal Party took the first steps towards trying to give Parliamentary representation to the working people. In 1874 the Liberal Party sponsored and had elected the first 'working class' MPs: A. McDonald and T. Burt.

The nineteenth century Liberals were split by the issue which, even today, forms one of our most intractable problems: Ireland. Gladstone tried on many occasions to get an Irish Home Rule Bill through Parliament. In 1886 he resigned when it was defeated and the Liberal Party split into the majorit of the Party, which kept the 'Liberal' name, and a group of 'Unionists' Gladstone's fourth government also foundered upon the rock of Irish Hom Rule. The second Home Rule Bill was rejected by the House of Lords.

Twenty-four years later the Irish, tired of waiting for the Britis Parliament to make up its mind, revolted. The 1916 Uprising was put dow by British troops, but Home Rule was granted shortly after the end of Worl War I. Our own Irish problem stems directly from the partition decisio which was taken in 1932.

Twentieth Century Liberalism

The late nineteenth and early twentieth centuries saw Liberalism develo further from its classical and radical roots. Many of the reforms which th early radicals wanted had been achieved, at least in part, and many other were high on the agenda.

One of the greatest influences on Liberal thinking in this period wa Thomas H. Green, the Oxford professor of moral philosophy. He restate the radicals' ideas of the duties of government in the late nineteenth century and influenced many of the Liberal politicians who held office in the earl part of the twentieth century, such as Herbert Asquith.

Green's writings restated much of what had already been said by Benthar and Mill but he added a more 'active' element. The Liberal suspicion o government activity which is seen in their desire for 'limited governmen came under great pressure during the latter part of the nineteenth century As the century progressed it became apparent that, if governments were t achieve the desires of the radicals and improve the lives of the people, the they would have to take a much more active and direct role in nationa affairs. If the cities were to be cleaned up, if the children were to be educated and if the sick, the old, the crippled, and the unemployed were to be care for, then governments had to raise taxes and to redistribute the money t those who needed it. All this could not be achieved with limited governmen and thinkers like Green encouraged Liberal politicans to place greate priority on **Utilitarianism** (see Bentham) and on the happiness and welfar of the people than on the ideal of limited government.

Alfred Marshall, one of the best known economists of his day, added t this ideology from an economic standpoint. He argued that one of the mos important duties of government is to try to ensure that the old economic an social differences are removed, not by revolution and violence, but b government action to help those in need and to create a better society. H wanted to see progress:

> *'till the official distinction between working man and gentleman has passe away; 'til, by occupation at least, every man is a gentleman.*

Varieties of Liberalism

Conservative	**Radical**	**Utilitarians**
Limited government Free Markets Private enterprise	Individual Rights Free Trade	Social Justice Welfare
Locke Burke	Paine Bentham	Green Marshall Keynes Beveridge

The Liberal Government of 1906

Perhaps the best way of seeing twentieth century Liberalism in action is to look at the record of what was probably the greatest Liberal government.

Sir Henry Campbell-Bannerman came to office in 1906 with a Cabinet which included Herbert Asquith and David Lloyd George and which had one Winston Churchill as a junior Minister. Bannerman was a sick man and resigned and died in 1908 to be replaced by Asquith who led the government through one of the most decisive sets of changes which this country has ever seen.

1906: The Trades Disputes Act gave trade unions immunity from all legal action where the trade union could claim that what they had done was 'in furtherance of a trade dispute'.
The Education Act took all elementary schooling out of the direct control of the Church and gave it to local authorities.

1907: Women were allowed to sit on borough and county councils for the first time.

1908: The Children Act reformed the treatment of children (for example, it prevented anyone under 14 from being sent to jail).
Pensions were introduced for old people and miners were given an eight hour working day.

1909: The first Labour Exchanges (Job Centres) were opened and boards were set up to regulate fair wages for certain industries.
Schoolchildren could be given free school meals and medical inspections for the first time.

1911: The Parliament Act restricted the power of the House of Lords to block legislation and introduced salaries for MPs (£400 per year).
Probably the most famous piece of this government's legislation and certainly comparable with the great Welfare Acts of 1945–9: of the National Insurance Act which allowed people in Britain to be insured under a national scheme for the first time. It provided for treatment from doctors, sickness benefits, disability benefits, benefits after childbirth, and basic unemployment benefits.

1912: A national minimum wage for coal miners.

▼ *David Lloyd George (1863–1945) in 1924.*

As far as taxation was concerned, the 1906 Liberal government really introduced the concept of redistributive budgets. Asquith, when he was Chancellor under Bannerman, had introduced a distinction between earned and unearned income; while Lloyd George, who was Chancellor under Asquith, introduced higher death duties (on estates valued at over £5,000); increased income tax to one shilling and twopence in the pound (about 6p in the pound); and introduced the first 'Super-Tax' (a higher level of income tax on earnings exceeding £5,000 per year).

The principles of a more active government while still retaining the Liberals' basic respect for individual rights were carried on into the later twentieth century and, in fact, still form the basis of the liberal element of the modern SLD party.

In the 1920s John Maynard Keynes developed his great theories of economic management which he regarded as central to the Liberal ideal. He proposed a 'mixed economy' of publicly owned enterprises working alongside a thriving private sector in which the government would carry the responsibility for economic management. This management would, he believed, enable governments to achieve the **Utilitarian** goals of full employment, stable prices, economic growth, and state welfare systems.

Alongside Keynes, another great Liberal, Sir William Beveridge worked on the detail of state welfare and led the Committee which produced the basis for the post-war welfare systems: the National Health Service, the comprehensive National Insurance system and the full state education system.

In the years which have followed World War II, Liberals have supported many policies which have later been implemented by governments of other

▲ *David Steel, last leader of the Liberal Party.*

political parties. In the 1950s the Liberals called for Britain to join the European Economic Community, for council houses to be sold to their tenants, and for equal pay for women. In the late 1950s they also pressed for devolved Parliaments for Scotland and Wales and argued the case for comprehensive education.

Modern Liberalism in Britain

Liberals in the Britain of the 1980s are interested in many of the same things that have exercised the minds of Liberals since the eighteenth century. The fight for the rights of the individual has not, they would claim, been won; the balance between the state and the individual has to be constantly monitored; and toleration remains one of the most treasured concepts.

Modern Liberalism is:

1 **Suspicious of the State** Centralised political and economic power is regarded with considerable distrust and modern Liberalism would much rather see individuals or groups of individuals helping themselves and each other rather than the state having to provide benefits or facilities. Liberals would rather support Housing Associations in which groups arrange, design, and build their own houses, than support mass council estates built by governments and their officials.

2 **For Decentralisation** At a local level Liberalism supports the transfer of as much power and authority as possible to local governments. In many areas Liberals support what is called **Community Politics** in which decision making is brought as close to the people as possible. At a national level, Liberals support the devolution of power to regional parliaments.

Example

Devolution

In 1976, when James Callaghan became Prime Minister, the Labour Party was a minority government and had to negotiate support from other parties in order to stay in office. As part of this arrangement between the Labour Party and the Nationalist parties, the Labour Government agreed to sponsor acts which would devolve power to new assemblies in the two regions of Scotland and Wales. In return, the two nationalist parties – the SNP (Scottish Nationalist Party) and Plaid Cymru (Welsh Nationalists) – agreed to support the Labour government with its legislative programme.

The result of this arrangement was a lengthy and extremely difficult process which involved the government launching two complex constitutional Bills each of which had slightly different conditions written into them.

The 1978 **Devolution Acts** for Scotland and Wales allowed the Scottish Assembly to have some legislative powers but not the Welsh one. Neither Assembly had the right to raise its own revenue by tax and all finance was to be decided upon in the form of a 'Block Grant' from the British Parliament at Westminster.

A referendum was required under both Bills and a proviso was written into them to require at least 40 per cent of the **electorate** in each of the two regions to vote in favour of devolution before it could be passed into law. The object of this proviso was to try to ensure that the important constitutional issue of devolution could not be implemented by a small minority of Scottish and Welsh voters.

The Referendums of 1979 produced a small majority of **voters** in Scotland who were in favour of devolved power. However, this majority represented only 33 per cent of the Scottish **electorate** so the Bill failed.

In Wales there was no majority even amongst those who turned out to vote and only 12 per cent of the electorate supported devolution.

Devolution of power to the regions of Great Britain remained a central feature of Liberal Party policy right up to the Party's amalgamation with the Social Democrats. It remains to be seen what the new Party's policy over an extended period will be.

3 **For Industrial Democracy** For councils of workers in every workplace which would help to take decisions on the future of their firms and businesses. As part of this process, Liberals would encourage workers to take shares in, or to participate in the profits of, their firms (co-ownership and profit-sharing).

▲ *Paddy Ashdown, elected leader of the Social and Liberal Democrats in 1988.*

4 **Convinced of the value of a new form of electoral system** Liberals believe that the current electoral system merely emphasises the class divisions of the nineteenth century, the **us** and **them** mentality. They also believe that it is unfair in that it acts against minor parties, over-emphasises voting figures, and disenfranchises voters.

If the social and political structure of modern Britain is more complex than merely a battle between owners and workers then, they argue, there must be a more representative electoral system: one which recognises the balance of forces not only between the various shades of economic right and left but between the many shades of social and environmental policy.

5 **For the rights of the individual** Modern Liberalism places great importance on individual rights: in the workplace, for tenants of both public and private housing, and for all citizens. Most would argue for a full, written Bill of Rights in which freedom of information was given great prominence.

6 **International** Liberalism is still an international creed which regards nationalism as a slightly outdated concept. This suspicion of nationalism stems from the nineteenth century and from Liberals suspicion of the establishment which they saw as operating almost entirely for its own benefit. Today, Liberals are keen supporters of the EEC and are enthusiastic members of other international organisations.

▶▶▶▶▶▶▶▶▶▶▶▶▶▶▶ EXAMINATION QUESTIONS

1 Is anarchism simply liberal individualism pushed to a logical conclusion? (London, June 1983,3)

2 What concepts do Liberals use to curb the power of the State? (London, June 1982,3)

3 'Liberalism is as much an economic doctrine as a political doctrine.' Discuss. (London, June 1980,3)

4 'The only consistent liberals in Britain are those found on the right wing of the Conservative Party.' Discuss. (London, Jan 1979,3)

5 If liberalism is a dominant belief of Western society, why are Liberal Parties not more successful? (London, Jan 1983,3)

▶▶▶▶▶▶▶▶▶▶▶▶▶▶▶ NOW READ ON . . .

John Locke *Two Treatises on Government* See Chapter 6

Edmund Burke *Reflections on the Revolution in France*
Burke's antipathy to the French Revolution was well founded and sets out, clearly, the Classical Liberal defence of individual rights against those of whole sectors of society

Thomas Paine *The Rights of Man, Common Sense*
Paine despised the British and admired the French. He fully supported their view of Liberty

John Stuart Mill *On Liberty Utilitarianism* and *Principles of Political Economy* Penguin, 1985
Mill's genius lay in his strict adherence to logical principles. A skill which is practised all too seldom today

Jeremy Bentham *A Fragment on Government*
Bentham was convinced that government could be structured and run in a completely logical and scientific manner

Chris Cook *A Short History of the Liberal Party 1900–1984* Macmillan, 1984
A history of what was the strongest Liberal Party in Europe before merger with the major part of the SDP.

Norman S. Barry *On Classical Liberalism and Libertarianism* Macmillan, 1986
An excellent essay on the distinctions between the two traditions.

11 Conservatism

BASIC PRINCIPLES

Conservatism is a particularly difficult concept to deal with because many writers (including some Conservatives) do not accept that Conservatism is an ideology. Liberalism, Communism, Socialism, Anarchism, for example, all attempt to produce a picture, albeit often not a very clear one, of the type of society that would be created by the implementation of certain ideas. They attempt to answer questions about the role of state, the system of government, and the economic, political and social relations that should develop in a particular form of political community.

It is, however, far more difficult to identify and describe the features of an 'ideal' conservative society. In conservatism it is hard to isolate a basically consistent set of permanent ideas which are followed by conservative writers. Conservatives often claim that it is this very lack of 'ideological' approach to politics which separates Conservatism from other 'isms'. Conservative thought has often been notable for demonstrating considerable doctrinal 'flexibility'.

Conservatism is often argued to be less an ideology or set of doctrines and more an attitude, or a way of looking at life and social order. In some respects for a conservative to take an ideological stand means that he ceases to be a conservative.

Conservatism unlike other 'isms' produces no universal cure all for political ills. Practical solutions to practical problems, for a Conservative, necessarily must vary from one country to another. Successful solutions will have to take into account the unique combination of political, social, economic, cultural and historical circumstances that exist in any particular society.

> *Definition*
>
> ***Conservatism***
> *Despite the lack of an ideological basis, conservatism still displays several principle features which can be grouped into four broad areas:*
> - *a view of human nature where man is seen as imperfect;*
> - *an organic view of society;*
> - *a respect for tradition and opposition to change;*
> - *a dislike of abstract theory.*

The word 'conservatism' itself produces problems, for the process of 'conserving' an ancient building is not the same as conserving political values in a society. Dominant values change from generation to generation, whereas the aim of preserving a Tudor manor house is to preserve it in its original condition. This often leads to Conservatism being criticised as 'reactionary' or 'obstructionist': 'reactionary' in the sense of a wish to return to the past and reaffirm outdated beliefs and practices.

This is not the view that most Conservatives have of themselves for, despite being opposed to radical ideologically based solutions for political problems, they will usually be prepared to accept moderate, pragmatic, and gradual reform. Their view of the kind of change that is needed nonetheless will be firmly rooted in what they see as sound historical experience.

DISCUSSING THE ARGUMENTS

Conservative View of Human Nature

Conservatism believes that human nature is imperfect and that man is not naturally good and not even naturally sociable. This view has led many conservative writers to conclude that great schemes for radical social restructuring, as advocated by socialism or communism, for example, must fail. If man cannot be perfect then an ideal form of society cannot be constructed.

Utopian solutions will not work because man cannot be trusted to act rationally and live in harmony with his fellows. This philosophical view contrasts sharply with the view of human nature expressed by Anarchists and Utopian Socialists (see Chapters 12 and 13), who believe man to be naturally sociable and that, if the repressive power of the state is removed, he can have the opportunity to demonstrate it. Human nature, for the conservative, is weak, selfish, and aggressive. Man needs external constraints to ensure an ordered and free society. This view often leads conservatives to a liking for authoritarian political systems.

Conservatism questions the capability of man to organise in accordance with the ideals of Utopian schemes. The first objective of the state, therefore, will be to maintain law and order and to guard against unsocial behaviour. Disruption must be avoided for, only then, can careful reform be attempted in order to bring about an improvement in the human condition. Conservatism, unlike Socialism for example, seriously questions the ability of government to improve the human condition and therefore the importance of politics overall is questioned.

An Organic View of Society

Conservatism sees society as a very complex organism. It denies the possibility of mechanical solutions to the problems of society. Society is not seen to be a machine that can be tampered with, because each component of society is vital to the survival of the others, as in a living and growing organism.

This leads to the view that the interests of the community must always come before the desires of the individual. It is an idea of an essential 'oneness' in society. It presents a picture of society which is composed of a hierarchy of groups and classes. For each class to prosper, it is vital that cooperation exists between them, and this will in turn ensure the well-being of the community as a whole.

Society is not seen as the construction of various units, each of which can be removed or altered. It is a living thing with connections that reach back into the past and to interfere with one element will upset the delicate balance of society and threaten its very existence. Each group or class is felt to perform a function that is essential to the healthy existence of the rest. Society is a fine combination of these inter-dependent parts which, unlike a machine, will develop and grow. Each part performs its own function, but the individual functions can only be understood in relation to the whole.

This does not mean that each of the functions is equally important and, therefore, Conservatism believes in a natural inequality that cannot be removed by a form of social engineering such as Socialism. Equality as an abstract political concept cannot be part of Conservative thinking. Everyone cannot share equally in the benefits and products of society because not everyone can equally contribute to their production.

The organic society, therefore, is seen as a set of integrated and inter-dependent components. Each is important, but some are more important than others to the functioning of society as a whole.

A Respect for Tradition and Opposition to Change

Conservatism does not like change; it wishes to preserve the status quo (i.e. keep things in their present order). The difficulty with change for Conservatism is that it leads society into unknown regions, and the results of man-made change through social and political reform cannot be accurately predicted. Certainly no universal principle for change can be applied because the unique characterstics of each political community would prevent it. This opposition to change is linked to a great respect for established customs, traditions, practices, habits, etc., and tradition has to be protected against the 'excesses' of radicals and socialists.

Without question the worst form of change for Conservatism is **revolution** (see Chapter 1). Revolution is seen to be most dangerous because it implies that the slate can be wiped clean so as to start again. A complete break with the past and creation of something new for the Conservative is viewed as quite impossible. Additionally the outcome of a revolution cannot be predicted in advance, so such a step is extremely risky. Conservatives value social continuity for it is better to 'live with the devil you know than the one you do not'. Continuity is seen to be the element that binds society together; to break it threatens social and political stability.

What we have today, a Conservative might argue, although not perfect, is the result of the accumulated experience and knowledge of our ancestors and therefore should not be abandoned lightly. By following precedent and past practice we cannot go too far wrong. Those who wish to change and innovate can never know if they are undermining the very foundations on which contemporary political society stands. Any change, therefore, must be carefully considered in relation to its long term consequences, as opposed to any short term advantage.

Conservatives as a result consider Liberalism, Socialism, and any other form of radicalism as potentially dangerous. Their apparently 'simple' solutions must be suspect because society is far too complex to be subject to 'simple' solutions. Conservatism is therefore concerned to emphasise that sober and thoughtful consideration precede any action for change. Tradition is not seen as inflexible, for small changes can take place providing essential traditional values are maintained. Amendments can be made to existing arrangements providing they occur within established frameworks.

A Dislike of Abstract Theory

Conservative opposition to forms of radical change is strengthened by the fact that such ideas are based on abstract theories and are not rooted in historical experience. Conservatism should not, however, be seen to be acting as a complete brake on change, for change can be accomplished but it must be by way of cautious, or evolutionary, reform.

The Conservative view of the organic nature of society accepts that the 'organism' will not remain static, it will grow and possibly change, but this will occur 'naturally'. Social progress can be achieved by an extension of existing social values rather than aiming to recall some distant and idealised goal. Change should reflect new social and political circumstances and yet be the result of careful adjustment based upon past experience.

This is often referred to as **empiricism**. Empiricism implies that the facts about the political world are all that a Conservative needs to know, any untried theory about how the world 'ought' to be will be of no practical use. An ideological approach to politics is seen as unsatisfactory because it is dreamed up by intellectuals and philosophers who search for a rational model for the world.

For Conservatism this is a mistake. Political society cannot be run on abstract theories for, to do so, would result in the disruption of 'natural', social and political conditions. With empiricism, situations are dealt with as they arise for the facts of the situation will show the Conservative how to act. Each problem may well have to have a different solution. Intellectual thought may be logical and interesting but it is of little use to practical politics.

BRITISH CONSERVATISM

Given the nature of Conservative thought as set out above, it is difficult to reach firm conclusions as to it having any universally applicable features. Conservatism as it has emerged in different countries has taken on quite individual characterstics. In examining British Conservatism we must see that Conservative 'ideology' as propounded by various writers does not always directly equate with the doctrines of the Conservative Party as set out in party manifestos and as implemented by Conservative governments.

European or American Conservatism by comparison may appear extremely illiberal and conversely many British Conservatives would appear by European or American standards to be quite left wing.

If we wish to identify the origins of British Conservative thought we do well to begin with **Edmund Burke** (1729–97). (See page 126.)

Ideas about British Conservatism may have expanded since Burke, but he nonetheless laid their foundations. Burke was opposed to abstract political theory and in particular to the results of their application during the French Revolution of 1789. He argued that the constitutional arrangements in Britain were a major guarantee to stability and that the application of radical solutions to the established order should be strongly opposed.

In *Reflections on the Revolution in France*, Burke argued that society was an organic entity and that sustained continuity was essential. He accepted that change could be accommodated on occasions and, in the most extreme circumstances, a major reconstruction could be conceivable. But even so the objective of such change would be to guarantee continuity.

Change, for Burke, would best be achieved slowly and undertaken for the purpose of conserving existing society. The only possible justification for revolution was the immediate likelihood of a collapse of the existing order. In this way Burke justified the English Revolution of 1688 but not the French Revolution.

Burke argued that the revolution in France was actually a threat to the interests of the French people. It was based on philosophical presuppositions which were claimed to be universally applicable, and this made it even worse for Burke. He believed the French Revolution was certain to fail because it attempted a complete break with the past and the establishment of a new social and political order based on a philosophical argument which emphasised the 'rights of man'. (See Chapters 6 and 10.)

Those who supported the revolution, Burke thought, had been misled by the concept of 'natural rights'. He said 'rights' depended upon the constitution of the state in which people lived and not upon any universal moral right. He was more concerned to emphasise the duty of the citizen to the state. Burke like many subsequent conservatives felt human nature to be imperfect and that the state of nature was a violent struggle of each man with his fellows. The state therefore gave the individual protection and produced a civilised society.

Burke did not reject change because of a dislike for it, but he was unconvinced, unlike many radicals, that established practices of government were wrong. He felt radical thinkers deluded themselves by an over-confidence in the efficiency of the solutions they had reached through abstract reasoning and predetermined principles. Burke argued that society could not be run on abstract principles for it would destroy the inherited wisdom of the past. Society, he believed, could only be changed by building upon such inherited wisdom. Contemporary abstract blueprints were not a match for the accumulated experience as embodied in existing contemporary political institutions.

These views were coupled with a belief in the imperfectibility of man. Man, for Burke, should attempt to come to terms with existing society and hope for limited improvements. There could be no ideal society. Burke's rejection of abstract theories, such as **natural rights**, together with his empirical approach to politics, his organic conception of society and adherence to the importance of tradition and accepted practice, have endeared him to many subsequent Conservatives. Although his speeches did not endear him to his contemporaries.

MODERN BRITISH CONSERVATISM

An examination of modern Conservatism will lead to the identification of two broad 'schools' of Conservative thought:

- Organic Conservatism
- Neo-liberal Conservatism

Neither of the 'schools' is exclusive and few Conservatives could be exclusively located in one or other of them. Both have a long history in Conservative thinking and to some extent compete with each other to determine the kind of practical policies that emerge from the Conservative Party. It is difficult, however, to consistently equate the actions of any Conservative administration with the philosophy of one of the schools of thought.

The major difference between the two schools lies in their attitude towards the role of the state. The 'Neo-Liberal' view argues that state activity in all areas of life should be kept to a minimum. 'Organic' conservatism argues that the state will always have a significant role to play, although state intervention will not be based upon abstract ideological assumptions, but upon the need to solve specific problems for the national good. This emphasis on **pragmatism** is central to Conservative thinking.

Organic Conservatism

Organic Conservatism is often referred to as **One Nation Conservatism**. The idea of an organic society means this type of Conservatism considers that all members have a contribution to make to the overall well being of society. This implies that those who enjoy wealth and power in society also have a responsibility towards the less fortunate. The contribution of some classes may not be so important, but still are vital to the continued existence of society and, therefore, the interests of all classes and groups must be protected. 'Rank' as well as bestowing 'privilege' and 'status' also bestows a duty on those in positions of power to ensure the general welfare of the whole community.

This idea when translated into political terms leads to the notion of a Conservative government having the responsibility to look after all groups and not just those who own and contribute most to the means of production. It implies that a kind of 'benevolent paternalism' should be exercised in order to ensure that the conditions of all classes should not become so bad as to encourage them to challenge the existing order and possibly overthrow it. For, if you have nothing, you have nothing to lose!

In practical terms this style of thinking had led Conservative governments over the years to press for, and to introduce, many schemes of social reform to ameliorate unfavourable social conditions. This is not to say that Organic Conservatism does not endorse the market system or capitalism in general. There is a firm commitment but also a major concern to ensure that the results of the market do not lead to some groups being severely disadvantaged and exploited. This kind of thinking is closely associated with Benjamin Disraeli.

Disraeli felt that if no social reform were undertaken to alleviate the condition of the working classes in the nineteenth century, then revolution

▼ *Benjamin Disraeli (1804–81) with Queen Victoria.*

Benjamin Disraeli (1804–81)

Disraeli entered the Commons in 1837 and was prime minister from 1874–80. He made a major contribution to the passage of the 1867 Reform Act, and believed that enfranchisement would lead the working classes to vote Conservative. He was very interested in the condition of working people and this is evident in his novel *Sybil* (1845) where he presented a picture of Britain as 'two nations', i.e. rich and poor, a phrase which has been used in conservative thinking many times since.

could well be the result. He argued that the 'palace would not be safe unless the cottages were happy'. National unity could be protected by limited social reforms.

This Disraelian view has been present in British Conservatism ever since and is evident in contemporary Conservatism. In particular it can be seen in those elements of the Conservative Party that oppose the monetarist policies of Mrs Thatcher and claim that high unemployment is in effect creating 'two nations'.

A number of Conservatives who expressed these views have become known somewhat derogatorily as 'wets'. The 'wets' are concerned that the party is developing an uncaring and unsympathetic attitude towards the problems of the unemployed. They place particular emphasis on what they felt to be the truly 'national' essence of Conservative thinking which was concerned for the welfare of all classes in society. On this basis they reject Socialism as socially divisive and likely to generate class antagonisms rather than national harmony.

Organic Conservatives have argued that one of the main methods of ensuring the development and protection of the national community is by extending the welfare state, and additionally if necessary using the power of the state to limit the 'undesirable effects' of market activity.

This approach emphasises that Conservatism should adopt a very pragmatic approach to the solution of economic and social problems. Responses therefore should vary to meet changing circumstances, rather than being determined by the application of theory, the results of which cannot be known in advance. Conservatism in practice, they argue, should not be concerned to direct Britain towards an ideal society but to emphasise the remedial responsibility of the state to tackle particular social and economic problems.

Example

A major debate took place during the second Thatcher administration over an apparent North-South divide in Britain. The picture painted by some interpretations of official statistics was that Britain had developed into two nations with the prosperous 'south' having low unemployment and attracting new industry, whilst the north took the brunt of the economic recession. Much of the criticism of Mrs Thatcher's economic strategy came from those who felt that her approach was too 'ideological' and incompatible with traditional Conservative values of the Disraelian kind.

Neo-liberal Conservatism

Neo-Liberal Conservatism has been evident in the Conservative Party since the nineteenth century, but has gained considerable influence since Mrs Thatcher became leader in 1975. It contrasts with 'Organic' Conservatism in many areas of social and economic thought. This new liberalism is associated with nineteenth century *laissez faire* liberalism with its emphasis on market forces and individualism. (See Chapter 10.) Modern Neo-liberal Conservatism draws heavily on the ideas of such writers as Adam Smith, Alexis de Tocqueville, Schumpeter, Hayek, and Milton Friedman.

Several Conservative groups have argued for Neo-liberalism during this century:

- Economic League (established in 1919)
- Aims of Industry (established in 1942)
- Institute of Economic Affairs (established in 1957)
- Centre for Policy Studies (established in 1974)
- National Association for Freedom (established in 1975)
- Adam Smith Institute (established in 1979)

Neo-liberalism places much less emphasis on the role of the state as a provider of services and wishes to see the state 'rolled back', allowing market forces to be freed. The role of the state, it is argued, should be minimal in terms of economic policy. Society is viewed as a collection of individuals and, because they are seen to be motivated by self-interest, the state therefore should interfere as little as possible.

The only responsibility of the state is to provide the circumstances under which individuals can work and prosper because market forces are seen to be the 'natural' forces which generate wealth. Attempts by the state to plan economic activity are therefore bound to fail. The whole process of economic activity is considered to be far too complex for effective government intervention and more likely it will be positively harmful in disrupting 'normal' economic relationships.

Government, by providing for the less fortunate through public expenditure, have to raise money in the form of taxation and this is argued reduces the incentive for those who create wealth. The more the government provides, the greater the slice of profits and wages that will have to be taken as taxes.

The Neo-liberal school of Conservatives also accepts the 'monetarist' economic view that government spending not only fails when applied to increasing demand (it is seen merely as inflationary), but it also has the effect of 'crowding out' private sector borrowing.

The argument is that high public sector borrowing leads to high interest rates for private borrowers. Neo-liberalism argues that it is much better for the state to limit its activities, thereby allowing people to develop the financial capacity to provide for themselves. Inequality is seen to be an inevitable consequence of individual freedom, but, overall, the efficient performance of the market will benefit rich and poor alike (see Chapter 8 on Welfare).

The arguments of Neo-liberalism are not solely economic ones; they also have 'moral' overtones. The assumption is that it is morally more desirable for people to take responsibility for their own affairs because it is dispiriting for the individual to have to rely upon various forms of the state 'handouts'. A major problem for Britain, modern Neo-liberals feel, has been that governments since 1945 have accepted an open-ended responsibility for the welfare state and economic management. The result of which is seen to be that people have developed unrealistic expectations of what government can provide and have ceased to have the motivation to create economic growth for themselves.

The answer to the problem is to reverse this trend and revive Britain by the stimulation of market forces and the increase of services available to the consumer. This can be done by allowing the market and not the government to dictate the range of services available. It is argued that this is just as applicable to services provided at present by the state as it is for services provided by the private sector. In practical terms this style of Conservatism led to a major change in both Conservative ideology and policies after a conference that took place at the Selsdon Park Hotel in 1968.

It marked the beginning of the change towards a Neo-liberal approach. Attempts to implement such an approach began with, but were largely abandoned by, the Heath government of 1970–4. Even after Mrs Thatcher became leader in 1975, it took her some time to restructure the party to support her views. By 1979, when she formed her first government, only five members of her cabinet had voted for her in the leadership ballot.

The influence of Neo-liberal thinking, however, has grown since 1979 and can be seen in the implementation of a policy of 'privatisation' in many parts of public services.

Example

Privatisation of public services

Cleaning and laundry services for the National Health Service have been offered to private contractors. This involves a method of competitive tendering where cooks, cleaners etc are no longer employed directly by health authorities but private firms are invited to offer tenders to run the service for a hospital. The most competitive tender will win the contract for the company concerned.

Further evidence of Neo-liberalism can also be seen in the sale of state owned assets such as British Airways, British Gas and British Telecom. The argument has been that consumers of these services will benefit because market forces will 'naturally' improve efficiency due to increased competition and lower prices. In the case of the privatisation of British Telecom in 1985, the government was concerned to break its monopoly of business telecommunications and encourage the creation of a rival company,

Mercury. Additionally, the equipment aspect of British Telecom's market was opened up to competition.

The **minimal state** of Neo-liberalism is not however a weak state, and indeed it is thought to be vital for the state to take a strong line on such issues as social 'indiscipline'. The calls for firm governmental responses to issues of **law** and **order** are felt to be necessary for political stability and as a guarantee for conditions favourable to the development of market forces. A harmonious society requires effective and strong laws.

The state has to be on its guard against social indiscipline in the form of crime, permissiveness, and a general reduction in respect for the forces of law and order. National defence is seen as a sound investment against internal disorder and external aggression. Challenges from 'disruptive' social forces must be met by strong measures to ensure the continuity of the 'British way of life'.

The 'Liberalism' of economic Neo-liberalism is replaced by a significantly authoritarian attitude to matters of social indiscipline. 'Short, sharp shocks' in the treatment of young offenders and football hooligans, together with calls for longer prison sentences for many other offences reflect this approach.

The **trade unions** have been a particular cause for concern to Neo-liberal Conservatives.

> *We say that union power should be reduced, not because we are 'anti union' nor because we think it is the sole cause of our problems, but because the present imbalance of power bars our way to national recovery.*
>
> Sir Keith Joseph *Solving the Union Problem is the Key to Britain's Recovery*, Centre for Policy Studies pamphlet, February 1979

The violence that occurred during the 1984 miner's strike and the dispute in 1986 and 1987 between sacked print workers from News International and the police, which led to almost pitched battles outside its Wapping plant in London, are examples of the kind of actions that concerned the government.

Trade union activity, for Neo-liberalism, is yet another barrier to economic recovery because it restricts the free operation of the labour market and the determination of wage levels. For the Neo-liberal these are matters which should be settled by the operation of demand for and supply of labour. These views can be seen as reflected in the trade unions legislation by the Conservative government after 1979.

▲ *Police in riot gear use truncheon charges to clear demonstrators at the* Times' *offices in London's Wapping, January 1987.*

Example

Employment Act 1980

- Public money made available for secret ballots on strike calls.
- Protection against dismissal for workers not wishing to join a 'closed shop' arrangement.
- Unions made liable for civil damages for picketing anywhere except the place of the dispute.
- Definition of lawful secondary picketing greatly limited.

Employment Act 1982

- Increased protection for workers not wishing to join a 'closed shop'.
- Employers able to end closed shop arrangements unless 80 per cent of the workforce support it in secret ballot.
- Legal protection for secondary picketing ended.

Employment Act 1984

- Requirement for secret ballots extended to elections for the membership of union national executives.
- Secret ballots made necessary to protect unions against damages brought for breaches of contract.
- Secret ballots introduced for the retention of creation of a union political fund, the bulk of which goes to the Labour Party.

Impact of Mrs Thatcher

The impact of Mrs Thatcher's leadership upon the Conservative Party and Conservative thinking has been considerable. The post World War II consensus which dominated the relationships between the major political parties on most major questions has disappeared. From the late 1940s up until the 1970s there was broad agreement between the parties on major issues of economic and social policy.

The economic philosophy of John Maynard Keynes and the social policies of William Beveridge seemed to provide the answer to the problems that had confronted inter-war governments. The policies followed by successive post-war governments seemed to secure full employment, low inflation, continued economic growth and an expanding welfare state. Political differences were still apparent, but they tended to be about *priorities* and not *principles.*

The first signs of disillusion with this consensus appeared during Edward Heath's government of 1970–4, but a movement towards market solutions for Britain's economic problems was not carried through. The following Labour Governments of Harold Wilson (1974–6) and James Callaghan (1976–9) experienced difficulty in maintaining the post-war 'settlement'. Public expenditure was restrained and unemployment rose, but it was the election of Mrs Thatcher's first government that ended the consensus. Since 1979, the Conservative Party has moved in a different direction and there has been a major shift in emphasis in economic and social policy.

The 'Thatcherite' view of the post-war mixed economy is that it had tilted the balance between the private and public sector. Too much state intervention in economy had limited the scope for private enterprise to flourish and Britain's problems would only be solved by correcting the balance.

The answer for Mrs Thatcher's supporters was the stimulation of economic activity by 'rolling back' the state and allowing free market forces to flourish. Nationalised industries were to be sold off, financial assistance by government to 'inefficient' British industry was to be ended, taxation was to be reduced so as to stimulate individual enterprise, the trade unions were to be weakened so as to remove restrictions in the labour market, and public expenditure on welfare was to be reduced.

This thinking contrasts sharply with the policies of previous post-war Conservative Governments. Their confidence in the working of the mixed economy, the benefits of the welfare state, the state's assumption of the responsibility for the overall direction of the economy, and the advantages of a close relationship between government, unions, and employers in the formulation of economic policy, came into question.

▼ *Margaret Thatcher MP, Leader of the Conservative Party 1975–1990*

A major objective for Mrs Thatcher's governments was the creation of a 'property and share-owning democracy' where a greater opportunity is available for individual initiative and reward. Whether or not these objectives have been achieved and with what cost is a matter for party political debate, but the impact of such thinking on the Conservative Party since 1979 has been very significant.

This change in Conservative thinking however has not gone unopposed and Mrs Thatcher faced criticism from within her own party. In 1985, for example, former cabinet ministers Francis Pym and Ian Gilmour together with 30 other critics of Mrs Thatcher's economic policies formed a group, the Conservative Centre Forward. This group of 'wets' aimed to campaign for the reinstatement of what they felt to be more traditional values in Conservative policy.

The group, however, brought down upon itself the criticism that they were merely an unrepresentative faction whose disloyalty could only damage the Conservative cause. As such these 'one-nation' Tories were unable to pose any real threat to Mrs Thatcher.

Further criticism of some Thatcherite policies came from a former Conservative Prime Minister, Harold Macmillan (the Earl of Stockton). Mr Macmillan was closely associated with consensus politics and 'one-nation' Toryism when in office from 1959–63. He was particularly critical of the policy of selling public assets and likened it to 'selling the family silver'.

Other critics were concerned over the level of unemployment in Britain and the impact this has had upon the image of Conservatism. Some argued that Conservatism had come to be seen as uncaring and insensitive to those in need, with economic policy favouring the rich at the expense of the poor. Some critics saw Mrs Thatcher's policies as amounting to an abandonment of the traditional Conservative values of social responsibility for all members of the community. These, they said, have been replaced by a dogmatic and ideological belief in the efficiency of market forces.

Conservative ministers have denied these charges and point to the large sums of public expenditure that have been directed into schemes to help the unemployed and revitalise industry in depressed areas. Rather than abandoning traditional Conservative values, Mrs Thatcher claimed that her governments expanded state welfare provision. The major objectives, she claimed to have pursued, in welfare provision, increased consumer choice, and increased efficiency through the application of private enterprise methods.

Despite the criticisms of Mrs Thatcher's brand of Conservatism, even after three election victories, there appears to be no reason to assume that there will be a major shift back to the old style 'one-nation' Conservatism that influenced Conservative Party thinking prior to her leadership.

Her most enthusiastic supporters claim that since she became Conservative Party leader there has been a profound change in the ideological 'landscape' of British politics. They argue that the shift in Conservative thinking has meant that Conservatism has now displaced Socialism as the most logical radical alternative to post-war consensus politics. This of course is not a view that would find much support in the Labour Party – nor, indeed, in the SLD or SDP.

CONCLUSIONS

Given the apparent lack of a universal set of ideas, or a central and undisputed 'founding father' of Conservatism, it could be argued that Conservatism does not form a coherent ideology. It does have, however, all the recognisable features of a set of coherent beliefs of which the two 'schools' are merely differing aspects. Other 'accepted' ideologies also have many variants and this is especially so of Socialism (see Chapter 12).

Even though traces, or may be large doses, of 'Organic' or 'Neo-liberal' Conservatism can be identified in various Conservative governments over the years it would be hard to classify any one administration as exclusively located in one camp or the other. Most Conservative governments (like most Socialist ones) have displayed a notable degree of pragmatism and a generally non-ideological approach to the problems of governing.

The significantly Neo-liberal policies of the governments since 1979 have led critics, within the Conservative Party, to claim that a too ideological approach has been adopted. Yet Britain still has almost half of the national income spent by the government, a welfare state, and widespread governmental regulation of economic activity, even in those industries sold off by the government to the private sector.

This does not match up to the view of the 'New Right' who believe state direction of the activity to be redundant and counter-productive. Even on the question of unemployment, where the government has attracted a good deal of criticism, large sums of public money have been spent on retraining schemes and in programmes to keep young people out of the 'dole' queue.

So, perhaps, analysing the pronouncements of Conservative politicians and the policies of Conservative governments will not provide the answer to discovering the 'essence' of Conservatism. Conservative traditions in Europe and the USA also provide limited help because British Conservatism differs quite considerably, as a Conservative would expect, given their dislike for universally applicable theories.

Beyond the four broad characteristics examined at the start of the chapter Conservatism is perhaps best described in the following two quotations:

> *If any fellow were to ask me what the Conservative cause is I am sure I should not know what to say.*
>
> (Lord Buckhurst in Disraeli's novel *Coningsby*)

> *Conservatism is not so much a philosophy as an attitude.*
>
> (Viscount Hailsham, *The Conservative Case* Penguin, 1959)

▶▶▶▶▶▶▶▶▶▶▶▶▶▶▶ EXAMINATION QUESTIONS

1 To what extent does the Conservative Party derive its character from the past? (University of London, Government and Political Studies, A-Level, 1980)

2 Outline and comment on the Conservative defence of traditional institutions. (University of London, Government and Political studies, A-Level, 1981)

3 Has Conservatism had a consistent philosophy? (University of London, Government and political Studies, A-Level, 1982)

12 Socialism

BASIC PRINCIPLES

Socialism is probably one of the most complex of the political concepts with which this book deals. It stretches over a wide area of both ideology and time and it has given birth to a large and confusing number of different varieties.

The idea of people helping each other and cooperating in a communal society rather than 'oppressing' each other in a society in which one 'class' dominates and exploits another is not new. There were elements which can only be called 'communist' in many ancient civilisations including that of the Incas, Maya and Aztecs in South America. In Europe these ideas were mirrored by thinkers like Plato with his ideas of perfect societies and Sir Thomas More who wrote the book *Utopia*.

The most important stimulant to socialist ideas came, however, from the effects of industrialisation. As British and, later, French society became more urbanised and industrialised and as the relationships between those who employed people and those who were employed became more formalised, so thinkers began to develop different ways of structuring society.

The fact about early industrialised society which most offended those with any sensibilities was its overt inequalities: the wide gulf between those who owned the mills and factories and those who merely worked in them. The differences were based upon wealth but involved obvious consequences for their standard of living, their level of education and the social and cultural experiences which were available to them. Both Liberal and Socialist theorists developed ways of easing or erasing these inequalities – the Liberals wanted:

- a fairer system of justice, and
- more help for people to be able to develop themselves.

The Socialists wanted the means of making people more equal.

Socialism can best be described by tracing its development. In the eighteenth century there arose two different visions of a Socialist future and they have continued to underlie different types of Socialist thought to this day. On the one hand there were the **Utopian Socialists** who believed that a fair, equal and just society could be created by creating ideal small societies to show people how the future would work. On the other hand there were the **Revolutionary Socialists** who were convinced that an egalitarian Socialist society could only be created by destroying the existing order – that is, by overthrowing, by violence, those who dominated the old society.

Definition

Socialism and Liberalism

Liberals begin with the basic premise that it is the individual who is important. Introducing fairness into the social system must begin with helping individuals to educate themselves and giving them equal opportunities.

The Socialists, however, begin with the idea that a fair society can never be achieved as long as people are unequal, by which they usually mean economically *unequal. Socialism's central objective is, therefore, to create a more equal distribution of wealth and property – even where that may entail constraints and restrictions on individuals acquiring property and wealth.*

DISCUSSING THE ARGUMENTS

Utopian Socialism

Utopian Socialists are characterised by their adherence to the view that it would be possible to convince people of the merits of a new Socialist order simply by *proving* to them that it would work and by *showing* them it in action. Almost all of the Utopian Socialists developed ideal new societies most of which were based on some form of **communal** living.

The idea that people can live in small societies, in complete harmony with each doing what they want to do, each contributing what they can to the communal production, and each receiving what they need from that same production is a vision that has convinced many people from the 18th century right through to our own times.

▲ *French philosopher, Claude Henri, Comte de Saint-Simon (1760–1825).*

The Frenchman Count Saint-Simon developed not only a vision of an ideal society but also constructed a new, 'ideal' system of government consisting of three separate chambers of legislature:

- the Chamber of Invention: in which policies would be thought up and developed;
- the Chamber of Examination: in which social scientists would check whether the policies were viable;
- the Chamber of Deputies: in which elected deputies would decide whether to put the policies into effect and would oversee their implementation.

In Britain the most famous of the Utopian Socialists was Robert Owen. He was a factory owner who decided that treating his workers properly (giving them reasonable wages, some holidays, and building decent houses for them to live in) was not only a humanitarian gesture but was also good for both them and him. Owen attracted much attention for his humanitarian treatment at the New Lanark Mill (just south of Glasgow) and developed his ideas on an ideal society during his lifetime. He eventually attempted to use his wealth to help to set up **communes**: that is, small towns in which all wealth and all material possessions were held in common by the people. Everyone worked at what they did best, and, in theory, what they enjoyed most, and they received from the commune enough to give them all a comfortable life.

Utopian Socialists begin from the view that all human beings are basically friendly and cooperative and that the aggressive, competitive world in which we live is the result of centuries of being forced into this lifestyle by those who dominate society. Given the chance to live in friendly, cooperative communes people will, the Utopians argue, enjoy a fairer and more fulfilling life.

Another theorist who developed the utopian idea was François Fourier who believed that many of our social customs were part of the means by which those who gained most from our current social structure maintained the competitive system. Fourier believed, therefore, that not only did we have to begin to live in small, cooperative units (towns, villages and social groups which he called **phalanxes**) but that many of our traditional forms of social organisation should also be abolished. Among these he listed: marriage, the family unit and religion.

Although the communes which were established by Owen and Fourier in Britain, France and America all failed, the idea has maintained its attraction to our own times. In the 1960s many young people believed that a new society could be established in which people would live together in happy, cooperative groups. There would be no need for material wealth, for they felt that the pursuit of more and more material possessions was empty of any real meaning, and so the 'communes' could simply be 'self-sufficient'. Most of these failed, too, but in modern Israel the idea of the **kibbutz** (an agricultural commune in which all work for all and the concept of the family as a single, isolated group was virtually abolished) is still being developed.

Revolutionary Socialism

Revolutionary Socialists saw the Utopians as fools and dreamers who expected the world to be changed by example and the ruling classes to sit back and watch their dominant position be eroded without lifting a finger. Revolutionary Socialists believed that a fairer, egalitarian society could only be achieved if the existing rulers were physically removed from positions of power and if their wealth was physically redistributed.

One of the very earliest Revolutionary Socialists, and one who developed many of the central ideas of the ideology, was François Babeuf. Babeuf established a society of egalitarian socialists called the Société des Egaux, the 'Society of Equals', who called for a radical form of social system which would be achieved through violent revolution. Those who have studied Marx will find many of Babeuf's ideas familiar: except that they were developed more than half a century before those of Karl Marx. Babeuf wanted the revolution to be led by an elite who understood what was required and had the commitment to do whatever was necessary. This elite would rule 'for the people' for a short time after the revolution until the people could be taught how the new system would operate and until they could be disabused of the ideas they had learned under the old system.

The new system, according to Babeuf would involve:

- the *equal* division of all land;
- the banning of all inheritance of money or property except for very small, sentimental objects;
- the complete and *equal* redistribution of wealth;
- the provision of a full welfare system by the state;
- the implementation of a system of direct democracy using frequent referendums.

Babeuf and his followers developed these ideas during the 1770s and 1780s and were a little disappointed by what they saw as the half-hearted attempts at revolution of the people who led the French Revolution. The Societé des Egaux began to plot a further revolution to overthrow the Directory but were betrayed and 'dealt with' (this latter euphemism included the guillotining, in 1797, of most of its members, including the leader Babeuf).

As the nineteenth century progressed so did the ideas of Revolutionary Socialism, mostly based in France. Alongside the socialists, and sharing many of their views and objectives, were the **anarchists** (see Chapter 13). The alliance between the two creeds continued right up until the 1870s and, indeed, was still quite strong at the time of the Russian Revolution. One of the greatest Anarchist thinkers, Peter Kropotkin, was allowed to return to communist Russia after the Revolution and was given a massive state funeral when he died in 1921 (but this was the last time that the black flag of anarchism was seen in the USSR until the anarchist symbol was paraded amongst those defending the Russian Parliament building during the failed coup of 1991).

The Anarchists and the Revolutionary Socialists fought side by side at the barricades in many of the century's bitterest battles including the 1848 Paris Commune and the Dresden Revolt of 1849. When Marx set up his First International in 1864 it contained Anarchists like Bakunin as well as Communists.

Marxism

Workers of the world unite – you have nothing to lose but your chains.

The most important form of Revolutionary Socialism to develop during the nineteenth century was that of Karl Marx. Many of its ideas were not new but Marxism remains one of the most important developments in political philosophy in the past two hundred years.

As an ideology **Marxism** calls for the establishment of a **socialist** state as a first step towards the ideal **communist** state. The revolution, which would herald the onset of Socialism would, said Marx, almost certainly have to be violent.

The major contribution of Marx was not that he called for a revolution to introduce Socialism (many thinkers had done this), but that he constructed a rationale for Socialism which based itself upon 'scientific' method. In constructing this model Marx introduced several concepts which are of great importance to the understanding of Socialist thought today.

Economic determinism

Many political philosophers in the past had seen different objectives in peoples' lives: Hobbes felt that security was the main objective, Bentham

thought it was happiness, John Stuart Mill believed that people sought individual fulfilment. Marx believed that all of these objectives were secondary to the basic goal – **economic wellbeing**. Marx's lifelong friend Friedrich Engels had conducted a deep study of the conditions in which working people lived and worked and Marx had seen these conditions for himself.

It did not require a great deal of insight to realise that the ordinary working people of the mid-nineteenth century found it very difficult to fulfill themselves. The daily grind of twelve or fourteen hour days five and a half or six days a week in factories and mills did not allow much opportunity for the better things in life. To Marx it seemed silly to educate the workers for a better life and then deprive them of that life by keeping them extremely poor.

One's economic position determined not only one's class in a hierarchical society but also one's ability to have a reasonable life in that society.

▲ *Karl Marx, German Socialist, at about the age of 50.*

▲ *Friedrich Engels (1820–95) political theorist.*

Karl Marx (1818–83)

A middle class German Jew, Karl Marx went to the University of Bonn when he was 17 to study law. He did not take to the subject and was described by one of his teachers as 'idle'. In 1836 he transferred to the University of Berlin and, eventually, achieved a Doctorate in Philosophy.

He edited the radical newspaper, *Rheinische Zeitung* in 1842 and, after it had been closed down by the German government in 1843, he went to live in Paris.

There Marx met most of the famous (or, infamous) revolutionaries of his time: Pierre Joseph Proudhon and Michael Bakunin being the best known today. During this period he also renewed his friendship with Friedrich Engels, another German, who ran his family's mill in Manchester, England, and who Marx had met in Berlin.

Marx wrote *The Communist Manifesto* (1848) while in Paris. He moved to England following the failure of the French and German revolts in 1848. He lived in England for 34 years and was almost totally supported during that period by his friend Engels. Most of his research and writing was done in the famous Reading Room of the British Museum. It was during his years in England that he compiled and wrote his best known work. The first volume of *Das Kapital* (Capital) was published in 1867 and he spent many years supervising the work of the first international grouping of socialists (called the First International).

He died in 1883, before the other two volumes of *Das Kapital* could be published and he is buried in Highgate Cemetery in London.

The Communist Manifesto
Das Kapital

NOTE: **Friedrich Engels**, himself, is one of the relatively unsung heroes of the Communist cause. Before meeting Marx he had already produced one of the century's most damning indictments of capitalism: *The Condition of the Working Classes*, a detailed study of the social conditions in which the British working class lived during the early Victorian years. Engels supported Marx and his wife both financially and administratively and, after the death of his friend, it was Engels who continued the work of organising the Communist Internationals and who also published volumes two and three of *Das Kapital* in 1885 and 1894.

The Condition of the Working Classes

The Dialectic

Until the time of Karl Marx Socialism was a creed which required 'belief'. That is, it required one to have a basic empathy with the concepts of social justice, fairness and equality. The arguments for Socialism were moral rather than political. Marx changed all that by giving Socialism a basis in 'scientific' argument. To all intents and purposes, and within the context of nineteenth century understanding, he *proved* that Socialism was the *inevitable* next step in the development of modern society.

He did this through a monumental analysis of the history of man in society through which he deduced what he saw as one of the basic laws of the universe: the dialectic applied to history and society. The concept is better known today as **Dialectical Materialism.**

A **dialectic** is an argument between two diametrically opposed positions (the concept was orginated by Hegel who argued that all history was a conflict of ideas in his *Philosophy of Right*, 1821) and Marx's analysis of the history of man led him to the identification of six distinct periods in human history each of which was characterised by a specific dialectic (usually known as Marx's 'Stage Theory)':

1 **Primitive communism** In which human society was disorganised and in which each individual carried out all types of work: every man was a hunter, builder, farmer, potter, etc. In modern economic terms there was no **division of labour** and no **specialisation.**

   Gradually, people began to specialise in certain tasks, for example, building, baking or farming, and the old communal form of society began to disappear to be replaced by societies in which specialisation was carried to extremes.

2 **Empire** The second stage of Marx's history saw specialisation result in some people having power over others due to the fact that they had acquired wealth. At the lower end of society were slaves who had no rights at all. Human beings became as specialised as domestic animals and were treated as such.

   Marx argued, however, that, outside the Imperial system, another form of society was developing which had every incentive to destroy it. Most of the Empire period's slaves came from the ranks of the 'barbarian' tribes and Marx argued that this was why, in the end, they had to destroy the Imperial system.

3 **Feudalism** The end of the Imperial system resulted in the establishment of a new system in which aristocrats protected the peasant farmers in return for military service. This was called the feudal system and was overturned, said Marx, by the rise of a commercial class in the growing cities. This commercial class – or **bourgeoisie** – was more successful and adaptable than the old feudal lords and triumphed over them.

4 **Capitalism** The bourgeoisie developed systems of fake democracies which gave the people the impression that they were involved in decision making. Marx felt that the owners of capital, the bourgeoisie, were really in full control because they controlled the economic wealth. However, Marx believed that this system also contained the seeds of its own inevitable destruction. The demands of 'modern' industry, he argued, required a level of education which gave the workers an insight into the system which oppressed them. This urban **proletariat** would, therefore, eventually rise and destroy the **capitalist** system.

5 **Socialism** The inherent contradictions in the capitalist system would lead to its downfall but there would still remain one further stage on the road to the true 'Communist' society. The need to rid society of its bourgeois elements and to 're-educate' and resocialise workers, meant that, for a short period, a **dictatorship of the proletariat** would be required. The full panoply of State institutions would be retained and used to restructure society. Only when this process was complete could the final stage be entered.

6 **Communism** When each individual citizen understood his or her equality with all others and when there were no remaining 'bourgeois' elements, there would be no further need for the coercive institutions of the State. Furthermore, other countries would also have passed through the socialist stage and true harmony between the workers of *all* nations would result.

Hence, there would also be no need for the defensive capabilities of the State. The State would 'wither away' and laws would be developed, not by central institutions but, by groups of cooperative workers and by the communities in which they lived.

There would be no dialectic at this stage of history, said Marx, because there would be no group in society who did not agree with and benefit from the communist system.

It is important to appreciate the importance of this analysis. Marx had done what no one had done before him. He had constructed a 'scientific' argument for Socialism which presented the communist system as *inevitable*. The dialectic was a *law* of history and therefore everything that Marx had written would come about. There was really no need for a violent revolution (even Marx admitted this) but sheer humanitarianism required that Socialists do all they could to speed on the day. If that meant violent revolution then it was all in a good, and inevitable, cause.

Surplus Value

Part of Marx's argument concerning the evils of the capitalist system relies on his concept of 'surplus value' and on the conclusion that such value really belongs to the workers. Marx argued that, in the production of any goods, the workers who actually produce the goods get only a fraction of what they are worth on the market. The worker merely sells his labour. All production actually belongs to the capitalist who gives the worker a wage in return for his labour. The difference between the value of the product and the value of the labour is what Marx called 'surplus value' and, in the capitalist system, goes to the capitalist. This surplus value was, to Marx, part of the work put in to the goods by the worker and, by rights, belongs to the worker. The capitalist, in taking this surplus value without having done any 'work' for it, was really stealing it from the worker.

Marxism and the State

To traditional Marxists, the state is merely the instrument by which the ruling class ensures its continued control of the political process. Religion is seen as an additional means of control in the sense that most established religions reinforce the hierarchical structure of society. The liberal view of society, as a complex web of interlocking, competitive interest groups, is, to Marxists, just a sham. It hides the fundamental conflict between the two classes: the capitalists and the proletariat.

Marxists believe that this also extends to the way in which 'Parliamentary Democracy' operates. An impression is given of the people having 'power' by means of the ballot box. In reality, a Marxist would argue, this is merely a 'front' covering up the real source of power: capital.

Marx believed that there would be two stages to the introduction of true Communism: immediately after the revolution the Marxists would need to take control of the State. Although they despised the State and what it stood for there would be a period during which the last elements of the capitalists and their bourgeois middle-class allies would need to be cleansed from the system. Marx did not under-estimate the ability of the ruling class to overturn the revolution and regain power. It would be necessary, therefore, for the workers to actually take over the State and to use its power to guarantee their own supremacy. Only when the last vestiges of the other classes had either been eliminated or re-educated would the need for the mechanisms of the State disappear. Only after the State, with all its institutions of repression (the police, the courts, Parliaments, armed forces, etc.) had 'withered away' could the revolution be called complete and true Communism be attained.

It is within this concept of the role of the State that the major problems between Marx and the Anarchists were to be found. To Marx it was essential for the State to be taken over and used by the workers so that the revolution could be made to work. When the true Communist society had been attained, said Marx, that society would also be truly 'anarchist'. Bakunin and the Anarchists believed, on the other hand, that the State could not be allowed to survive: only by destroying the State and its institutions completely could true freedom and equality be attained (see Chapter 13 – Anarchism).

Revolutionary Socialism after Marx

The writings of Karl Marx have had an immense effect on political thinking. They were taken up by British, French and German Socialists and became the required reading of revolutionaries everywhere. Marx predicted, of course, that the dialectic demanded that revolution should take place first in the society which had gone the furthest through the capitalist system and he fully expected Britain or Germany to have the first Communist revolution. In reality we know that this did not occur. Instead, the first communist revolution took place in Russia in 1917.

The man who translated Marx from his western European setting into the feudal, peasant system of Tsarist Russia was **Lenin**. He believed that an elite of professional revolutionaries could create and lead a revolution in a society which had not even properly entered the capitalist phase. These people of the elite, constituted effectively by the Party, he called the **vanguard of the proletariat.** They would create a socialist state and, during the period of the Dictatorship of the Proletariat, would enable the peasants to learn how to live in a communist one. Lenin's revolution, led by his Bolsheviks*, was – in the end – successful and led to further development of the Revolutionary Socialist creed.

Nicholai Lenin (1870–1924)

Lenin's real name was Vladimir Ilyich Ulyanov was born into what was almost the nobility in the town of Simbirsk (now known as Ulyanovsk). He was only 17 when his older brother, Alexander, was executed for revolutionary activities.

He was expelled from the University of Kazan and was forced to teach himself law and to take the law exams at the University of St Petersburg (Leningrad) as a private candidate in 1892. He was sent to prison in 1895 for 14 months for his radical activities and, as was normally the case in Russia, was then sent into 'internal exile' in Siberia. He spent about three years in exile in a small village near the River Lena (from which he took his alias 'Nicholai Lenin'). While in exile he wrote his first book, *The Development of Capitalism in Russia*.

He was allowed to leave Russia in 1900 and travelled to Switzerland where, with a fellow revolutionary, Plekhanov, he wrote articles for the underground, revolutionary news-sheet *Iskra* (The spark).

Lenin's contribution to Marxism was extensive. He organised and led the Bolshevik Revolution of 1917 which heralded the advent of the world's first 'communist' state and he re-thought the Marxist doctrine that the revolution would occur in a developed, capitalist society. Lenin argued that, although Russia could not be said to be fully into the 'capitalist' stage of history, it could still experience a revolution against the ruling classes. The 'proletariat' would not be the source of the revolt, rather it would be created by an elite. The elite of intellectuals, workers and students would form the 'Vanguard of the Proletariat'.

Lenin argued that the period of 'socialism' during which the State would be controlled by the workers would be longer than Marx had foreseen but,

*'Bolshevik' was the name given to the Marxist followers of Lenin. It means in a literal sense 'majority-man' because Lenin's group was in the majority at the Socialist Conference of 1903.

Another term 'Menshevik' ('minority man') was given to the other, more moderate, grouping at that conference. The Mensheviks held power briefly in Russia after the Revolution of 1917 but were soon overthrown by Lenin's Bolsheviks.

eventually, the State would wither away as Marx had predicted and the true Communist society would arrive.

He also realised that capitalist states might not merely sit back and watch the birth of communism without doing something. The ultimate success of the revolution would depend on the creation of revolution worldwide and, of course, the defence of the Russian revolution against capitalist states.

Lenin was successful in creating the Russian revolution and in beginning the creation of a socialist society. He established, through Trotsky, both the Red Army which eventually defeated all attempts by Russians and the western powers to reverse the revolution, and the web of international support for revolutionaries through which world-wide revolution was to be attained.

The Development of Capitalism in Russia; The State and Revolution

Trotsky was, arguably, more important than Lenin in that it was he who fully developed Marx's original theory into one which could be applied to the least developed countries. Trotsky was War Commissar during the civil war which followed the revolution and he disagreed with Lenin's attempts to stabilise the Soviet Union during the 1920s. He saw this as a trend which would result in a party bureaucracy simply replacing, and becoming almost as bad as, the old Tsarist state which they had fought to overthrow and to change.

Trotsky believed in **permanent revolution**: in a society being constantly in political upheaval. Leaders must be changed frequently, no groups of senior people should be allowed to entrench themselves in positions of power and influence, teachers and educators must themselves be constantly re-educated in the problems of the real people (the farmers and the factory workers).

He was eventually driven out of the Soviet Union and murdered but his ideas have had, if anything, more sustained influence than those of Lenin. Mao Tse Tung developed most of his own ideas from those of Trotsky and 'Che' Guevara combined Trotsky's ideas of a peasant led, agrarian revolution with Mao's teachings on guerrilla warfare (see page 154).

Leon Trotsky (1879–1940)

Born Lev Davidovitch Bronstein, Trotsky led the 'traditional' revolutionary's life, with spells of prison alternating with periods of exile. He worked with Lenin from the very early years and took part in the unsuccessful revolution of 1905.

With Lenin, Trotsky was one of the most important organisers and thinkers behind the Bolshevik cause. After the revolution he was given the supremely important task of organising the Red Army.

When Lenin died in 1924 it was widely expected that Trotsky would take up the leadership. However, Stalin, who was believed to be less dangerous than Trotsky, was able to combine with others at the top of the party to take power. Eventually Stalin took sole power and began the process of discrediting Trotsky who was deported in 1929. Trotsky was murdered by a Soviet agent in Mexico City in 1940.

His contribution to Marxism is seen by many to have been greater than Lenin's. Trotsky wrote *The History of the Russian Revolution* in which he correctly prophesised the eventual result of the centralist policies which had been pursued first by Lenin and then by Stalin:

> *Lenin's methods lead to this: the Party organisation at first substitutes itself for the Party as a whole; the Central Committee substitutes itself for the organisation; and, finally, a single 'dictator' substitutes himself for the Central Committee.*

Trotsky believed that only by maintaining the revolution (by continual radical change) could the ideals of a truly communist society be attained. One of his most fundamental disagreements with Stalin concerned the latter's doctrine of 'Socialism in One Country'. Trotsky believed that it was the Soviet Union's sacred duty to spread revolution around the world and not simply sit back and try to establish the Russian State.

Joseph Stalin (1879–1953)

Unlike the other Russian revolutionary leaders, whose real names were reasonably easy to pronounce, most students are only too pleased that Stalin (born Joseph Vissarionovitch Dzugashvili) took an alias. He was born in Georgia in the south of Tsarist Russia and studied theology until he was expelled in 1899. As an early revolutionary he worked underground in the Caucasus under the alias of Korba until he was exiled in 1913.

He was a senior Party member during the revolution and the Civil War which followed and he became General Secretary of the Communist Party in 1922.

Lenin wrote a political 'will' just before his death in which he recommended that Stalin be sacked. Stalin overcame both this, and the opposition of Trotsky, however, to become one of Russia's leaders and in 1927 *the* pre-eminent leader.

Stalin's contribution to communism was not as great as his contribution to the survival of the Soviet Union. He believed in 'Socialism in One Country' and he set about ensuring the survival of the communist society in Russia through a series of bloody 'purges' during which he liquidated anyone who he felt might pose a threat either to himself or the State. Soldiers, party workers, factory managers and independent farmers (known as *Kulaks* were executed in large numbers. Stalin is thought to have had between 15 and 20 million people killed in the 1930s and 1940s.

Through the use of secret police (NKVD) and informers Stalin created a totalitarian state with himself as 'Vozhd' (Supreme Leader). He instituted a rapid industrialisation of the country by means of 'Five Year Plans' and, whether by luck or by judgement, it was this which gave Russia the military power to withstand the German invasion of 1941. It is interesting to theorise that, if Trotsky, with his emphasis on the peasants and on devoting resources to world revolution, had been successful in the battle for the leadership, Germany might well have won its war with Russia.

Leninism

▲ *Joseph Stalin in the late 1940s.*

▲ *Mao Tse-Tung*

Mao Tse-Tung (1893–1976)

Mao was the son of a peasant farmer in the Chinese province of Hunan. He was an early activist and took part in the overthrow of the Imperial (Manchu) dynasty in 1912.

He became a librarian at Peking University and it was there that he became a Marxist. He was one of the founder members of the Chinese Communist Party in 1921. In 1927 he led an unsuccessful revolt against the government of Chiang Kai-shek and, after a retreat, he proclaimed the 'Chinese Soviet Republic' in Kiangsi Province in 1931.

The civil war between Mao's communists and Chiang's Nationalists lasted from 1931 until 1949 with an intermission between 1941 and 1945 during which both parties fought the Japanese.

Once Chiang had been defeated, in 1949, Mao proclaimed the People's Republic of China.

Mao was an influential thinker far beyond the borders of his own, massive, country. He has had an influence in both the political and the military arenas.

In the military sphere Mao was the first modern leader to compile a comprehensive guide to guerrilla warfare. A great many of the ideas were not new (having been written down by the philosopher Sun Tzu in 500 BC) but, in modern times the writings of Mao form the basic rules of guerrilla war and are studied in every military academy in the world, for example:

- there is no such thing as a defensive battle; because no territory is ever worth holding for itself;
- guerrilla war must be highly mobile;
- one should never fight where the enemy wants to fight, but only where he does *not* want to fight; etc.

Although Mao accepted Lenin's call for an elite-led revolution he believed that revolutions should be led not by the industrial proletariat (who, he argued, had been tainted by their closeness to the capitalists) but by the peasants (whose strength lay in their 'pureness and simplicity').

He also accepted Trotsky's arguments that world revolution was a sacred duty and should be fiercely promoted. Mao also believed in 'continual revolution': that the original spirit of the revolution should not be allowed to die. It was this idea which led Mao to start the '**Cultural Revolution**' in 1964.

The watchwords of that revolution were: '*Let 1,000 flowers bloom*'; and '*Learn from the people*'.

It resulted in a comprehensive reorganisation of Chinese society. Teachers, professors and business leaders were instructed to go to work in the countryside and were not allowed back into the cities. Conversely, peasants and factory workers came into the cities to proclaim their revolutionary zeal and to take posts as teachers and professors.

The full dislocation of the Cultural Revolution, with its phalanxes of young, zealous Red Guards, only lasted until 1969 but its effects were still being felt long after Mao's death. Even as late as 1980 city dwellers were expected to return to the countryside once every four years to help with the planting or the harvesting.

▼ *Che Guevara poster at Cuba's Ministry of the Interior*

Ernesto 'Che' Guevara (1928–67)

Guevara was a close friend and associate of Fidel Castro. They fought together during the Cuban Insurrection in the late 1950s and Che (pronounced 'Chay') was one of Castro's most trusted ministers during the early years of establishing Communist Cuba. The two men disagreed fundamentally, however, about the course of the revolution. Castro tended to favour the 'Soviet' approach which emphasised strong central control directed to economic and social development. Guevara, on the other hand, favoured the Trotskyist/Maoist theories of 'continual revolution' and, in particular, continual social upheaval in order to prevent the emergence of new 'elites'.

In the end Guevara left Cuba in 1965 for Bolivia, a country which, he argued, was ripe for a 'Maoist' peasant-led revolution. Che Guevara was betrayed by the very peasants he was trying to 'set free' and was killed in a police ambush in 1967.

SOCIALISM IN BRITAIN

The Methodist Difference

British Socialists have always had an approach to the ideology which was virtually unique. It was not simply that there were Utopians among the early Socialists in Britain, it was that much of the ideology was of an entirely different variety to that which arose on the continent under the influence of men such as Rousseau and, later, Babeuf.

The credit for this 'difference' must go, at least in part, to the Methodist religion. **Methodism** was, itself, an attempt at egalitarianism. It was a form of belief which placed all men as equal before God. In Methodist services no one was given precedence. In the eighteenth century a Church of England service was a ceremonial enactment of the social relationships of the community. The clergy were highly educated sons of gentlemen and were, of course, gentlemen themselves, the services were well organised ceremonials full of tradition and music which the common people found it difficult to identify with, and even the seating arrangements mirrored the social status of the worshippers (the more wealthy or titled members of the congregation sat at the front, the middle classes sat behind, and those who were least well off sat or stood at the back of the grand church).

In rural communities this social division could never be effectively challenged. Populations were sparse and one's whole livelihood depended on having a good relationship with the landowners, those who sat at the front of the church! You 'knew your place' and you kept to it.

However, when people in the north of England began to gather together in large industrial towns they found hundreds and thousands of similar working class people who did not like the Church of England system and they quickly took to the system of belief preached by John Wesley in the late eighteenth century.

Methodism held that all people were equal and its religious services were held anywhere people wanted them – in barns, in people's kitchens, even in the open. The services were conducted in ordinary, everyday English which everyone could understand, by preachers who came from the same background that they did and who understood their working class problems. The music, too, was different: not the traditional, classical music of the Church of England but modern music which everyone enjoyed singing (Methodist hymns were, in their day, as enjoyable as the pop music of today).

Socialism in Britain did not spring ready formed one bright day from the pen of a brilliant political theorist. Like Liberalism and Conservatism, it is the result of a complex intermixing of beliefs, culture and ideologies. In the early nineteenth century the **Chartists** with their demands for fairer systems also added their weight and it must be remembered that much of the ideology of Chartism came from radical Liberals like Jeremy Bentham and James Mill. Utopian Socialists, Methodists, Chartists and early trade unionists (the founders of the first 'combinations') all contributed to the development of the unique form of Socialism which is specifically British.

The practical centre for much of the Socialist activity in Britain during most of the nineteenth century was, of course, the trade union movement. It is noteworthy that, when trade unions were legalised in 1850, the first major unions were the so-called 'Model Unions' which attempted to become part of the established political process (even to the extent of banning strike action) rather than taking up either the language or the activity of the revolutionary wing of the Socialist movement.

The Influence of Marx

By 1848 Marx had published the 'Communist Manifesto' in England and it created, for the first time, two distinct types of Socialist and trade unionist in Britain. On the one hand were the original 'model' unions of the skilled working class (such as the Engineers and the Teachers) which advocated a law-abiding, strike-free approach. On the other hand, and heavily influenced by the writings of Marx, were the unions of the unskilled workers (the transport workers and other general workers) which were far more militant in their attitudes.

These divisions in the trade union movement were also reflected in the Socialist movement itself. The revolutionary supporters of Karl Marx formed their own groups and looked forward to a time when 'the revolution' could be begun in Britain. There were also groups who believed that it would be possible to develop Socialism gradually and without violence. Neither group had much time for the other – the revolutionaries despised the 'gradualists' as middle-class intellectuals while the gradualists disliked the revolutionaries as misguided, over-reacting workers.

The Fabians

The strongest element in British Socialism was the non-violent variety which was heavily influenced by the Fabians – a group of middle class intellectuals who believed that Socialism could be achieved through the ballot box and the established political institutions.

Support for this viewpoint came not only from the middle classes but from a good proportion of the working people themselves. It cannot be emphasised too much that the political culture which resulted from the mixture of Utopian Socialism and Methodism was strictly non-violent. Even today the argument continues about who was right: were the Fabians correct (as demonstrated by the fact that the Labour Party got into power twice before 1939) or were the revolutionaries correct (in that neither Labour government could do anything of note)?

The Fabians were led by Sidney and Beatrice Webb, and included such eminent writers as George Bernard Shaw and H.G. Wells.

The Fabians, together with an extreme left wing group known as the Social Democratic Federation and the trade unions helped to set up and fund the early Labour Party (in the form of the Labour Representation Committee in 1900).

Guild Socialism

At about the same time as the LRC became the Labour Party, the ideas of 'Guild Socialism' were being developed. Instead of attempting to set up a Socialist state by using the institutions and mechanisms of the pre-existing capitalist one, Guild Socialists believed that a whole new system of government had to be established. In this sense they were a distant echo of the old Utopian Socialists such as Saint-Simon who had also recommended such measures. The central tenet of the Guild Socialists was that Britain's government would be conducted by two chambers:

- a chamber called a 'Congress for the Producers' (i.e. the workers and their managers)
- a chamber called the 'Parliament for the Consumers' which would be elected in the normal territorial way.

BRITISH SOCIALISM

Early Emphasis

The years immediately before, during and after World War I were heady ones for British Socialism. Every year brought successes and increased strength, 1917 brought the first Marxist revolution in Russia, in 1920 the British Communist Party was founded, and 1924 brought the first Labour Government.

Public Ownership

The emphasis of those early years was on public ownership. One of the first few clauses of the Labour Party Constitution was *Clause Four* which promised that the party would strive for the public ownership of the means of *production, distribution* and *exchange.* Among the first targets for such ownership were the coal mines, the railways and the steel works (in those days these three industries were the life blood of all economies, what the Labour Party called the 'Commanding Heights'). Unfortunately the first Labour Government of 1923–4 had neither the majority nor the time to initiate such changes and the second, again under Ramsay MacDonald, of 1929–31 did not begin to institute what many in the Party felt was its solemn duty. Why the second MacDonald government did not begin the process of introducing true Socialism is still a matter of not a little controversy, but it had at least something to do with the parlous state of the economy at the time. The end result of those two governments was that almost nothing had been done to progress the cause of Socialism and Ramsay MacDonald went down in Socialist history as a traitor to the movement.

Centralisation

Most of the early statements of Labour leaders and theorists during the years before 1939 show that they were wedded to the idea that a true Socialist state would need to have strong central control of all production and planning. In this they were no different to Socialists all over the world and took heart from what they regarded as the early successes of centralised planning in the Soviet Union.

Example

Labour Governments and Prime Ministers

Date	Seats by Party		Prime Minister
1924	LAB	192	Ramsay MacDonald
	LIB	157	
	CON	258	
(Labour governed with Liberal support. Lasted only 9 months)			
1929–35	LAB	287	Ramsay MacDonald
	LIB	59	
	CON	260	
1945–51	LAB	393	Clement Attlee
	LIB	12 + 11 NL*	
	CON	197 + 2 NC*	
1964–70	LAB	317	Harold Wilson
	LIB	9	
	CON	304	
1974–9	LAB	319	Harold Wilson (1974–6)
	LIB	13	James Callaghan
	CON	277	(from 1976)

*NL = National Liberals
*NL = National Conservatives

Equality

This, the linch-pin of Socialism was much in evidence during these early years. The issue which brought down the MacDonald government of 1931 was that of cuts in salaries and social insurance benefits. Most Socialists found it impossible to believe that a Labour government could even contemplate such moves, never mind actually implement them.

Post-war Socialism

The third Labour Government, that under Clement Attlee from 1945 to 1951 was the first to begin to implement a 'Socialist' programme; although ther were, and are, many critics who say that it did not do nearly enough. It ha to be remembered, however, that much of the social legislation had bee drawn up by an all-party committee chaired by the Liberal Sir Williar Beveridge.

Nationalisation

Almost as soon as it took office the Attlee government began an ambitiou programme of taking large sections of British industry into public ownershir The coal mines, the railways, the gas and electricity industries, and the iro and steel industries were all nationalised.

Central Planning

A new Ministry was established (the Ministry of Economic Affairs) to ensur that the growth and development of the British economy should be properl planned and, what is more important, in an environment which was nc dominated by the Treasury. The conversion of virtually all politica persuasions to the principles of Keynesian economic management helped t ensure that the ideas of central control of the economy outlasted the Attle government.

Equality

The years between 1945 and 1950 saw a stunning series of changes in th social fabric of Britain. Most of the changes were the result of cross-part agreement, but they were no less radical for that:

- The National Health Service established free medical care at all level for all; for the first time things like dental treatment and optician services were included.
- A full system of state education had begun to be established in 1944 whic allowed for free education of a very high standard for every child up t and beyond secondary school.
- The most far reaching development, in years when all changes were on monumental scale, was the introduction of a comprehensive system o social insurance which provided for such things as sickness benefits maternity allowances, unemployment benefit and old age pensions.

There have been three Labour governments since that first post-war one those of Harold Wilson between 1964 and 1970 and again between 1974 an 1976; and that of James Callaghan between 1976 and 1979 – but none ha had the impact of the Attlee government. Indeed, many people would argu that the radical nature of Socialism had left the party of the 1960s and 1970s

Socialism in the Early 1980s

The Labour Party

The events of the 1970s and the disappointment which many supporters fel at the lack of real progress towards Socialism made by the Labou governments of those years led to a significant re-appraisal of the meaning of Socialism.

This reappraisal led not only to the development of left-wing alternative to the traditional labour policies of the 1960s and 1970s, but to the willingnes of many in the main stream of the Socialist movement to consider new ideas These can be summarised under the following headings and illustrate th changes which have taken place in Socialist ideology since the 'Butskellite policies of the 1960s (so-called because their critics felt that the policies o the Labour Party under the leadership Hugh Gaitskell (1906–63) were hardl distinguishable from those of the Conservative Chancellor, R.A. Butle (1902–82).

1 **Local Politics** In a way which mirrors the policies of the Liberals, many Socialists have been experimenting with local Socialism. The supporters of these policies are usually known as the 'urban left'.

The central idea of local Socialism is exactly the same as that behind local Liberalism: if people can be shown that Socialism works on a local level then it can be built up into a successful national movement. The leaders of this ideology were men like Derek Hatton in Liverpool, Ken Livingstone in London and David Blunkett in Sheffield.

It should be understood that, in a similar way to the Liberal idea, local Socialism is not merely a political policy (it is not simply the local Labour council taking decisions in the traditional fashion); Socialism at a local level means bringing the ideas of cooperation, democracy and joint decision making down to the levels of education, welfare services, and the health services.

2 **Nationalisation** Socialists in the early 1980s were disappointed with the obvious inefficiencies of the old-style nationalised industries and developed new ways of running these industries. Specifically, they looked at methods of spreading share ownership in them much wider and giving the management more day-to-day power. The wider share ownership would not be the same as that envisaged by the Liberals or the Social Democrats, instead it would involve 'shares' which could not be traded on the Stock Exchange but which would participate to a certain extent in the 'profits' of the industries.

3 **Central planning** The Labour Party still seems to be convinced of the value of central planning and envisages a full set of new institutions which would manage the infusion of capital into British industry and commerce as well as planning the directions of growth. The Labour Party of the early 1980s would like to see such things as a new central planning ministry, a British Enterprise Bank and a National Investment Bank.

At the fringes of this development are the radicals of the party who would like to see more of the type of local development board (like the Greater London Enterprise Board, established by the now defunct Greater London Council) which could channel funds into deserving enterprises. The GLEB came under strong criticism, however, for some of its decisions and the types of enterprise which it decided to support with the ratepayers' money.

4 **Equality** The emphasis on equality is unchanged and uncompromised among Socialists. It remains effectively the central tenet of Socialism and one which requires strong legislation to redistribute income and wealth, to control public schools, to restrict overseas investment, and to control the inheritance of wealth and property. In all of these areas the Labour Party has maintained its faith to the original Socialist ideology – that one's economic position determines one's social position and one's ability to lead a fulfilled and decent life.

Social Democracy

In the past there has been much debate within the Labour Party about what type of Socialist party it is. Is it a **Social Democratic** party or what it calls a 'broad church', that is, a party which covers the whole spectrum of the left? Whether one believes in Fabianism or whether one believes in more radical or militant ways of achieving the Socialist future, there has always been an ideological home in the Labour Party.

If, however, one examines the policies of the Labour Party since 1918 one can see that, by and large, they have been the policies of a social democratic party. It was the belief among some senior Labour MPs and ex-MPs that the modern Labour Party was becoming a Democratic Socialist party which led them to establish the **Social Democratic Party** as a separate entity in 1981.

The difference between the two ideologies could be seen in the policies the SDP today:

- They were far more willing to accept the value of the free market tha most members of the Labour Party and wished to see a strong free-mark sector to allow for freedom of consumer choice and greater econom efficiency.
- They placed the same emphasis on welfare and care, but allowed th some of the services (such as pensions) could be provided privately.
- They placed great emphasis on institutional means of protecting people rights and pressed for a Bill of Rights.
- They had a commitment to devolved power: to the transfer of quite larg amounts of decision-making power from the central government Westminster to regional governments.
- They had a clear commitment to electoral reform in the form of som sensible system of proportional representation.

It is, perhaps, in this latter proposal that the basic difference between th Labour Party and the new Social and Liberal Democrats and the SDP ca be seen. The SLD believe that the British political system over-states th importance of just two ways of looking at each issue; that it creates th impression that the only way to solve any single problem is to use a aggressive, adversarial approach between the two 'great' political and soci forces – those of **capital** and **labour**. Social and Liberal Democrats believ that this view of British society is outdated and that it is dangerous simplistic. The electoral system allows either of the two major parties controlled by their extreme wings, to acquire almost total political pow without hindrance. Mrs Thatcher, they argue, gained a massive and al powerful majority in the House of Commons with only 43 per cent of the vo in 1987. What would happen to British economic and social life if an extrem left-wing Labour Government were to acquire similar amounts of power i the same way?

SOCIAL DEMOCRACY AND DEMOCRATIC SOCIALISM

Broadly defined, Social Democratic parties are those which wish to achiev a fairer, more equal society by the use of constitutional means: through th ballot box and existing political institutions. They would accept the need fo a democratic system in which the voters have a real choice between parties.

A Democratic Socialist party, on the other hand, is one which believes th true Socialism can only be achieved by the single minded application Socialist principles. This can only be achieved by clearing the state of th distraction and sham of capitalist 'liberal democracy', in other words establishing a single party state. Democratic Socialists argue that our curren system of democracy is but a sham: the image of democratic choice throug parties that really believe in the same thing and are subject to the control the capitalist elite. Instead, they argue, a single Socialist party can be bot more efficient at creating a Socialist state and more democratic.

By this definition it is clear that both the Labour Party and the SD (although perhaps not the SLD) are Social Democratic parties but there ar many who regard the presence of Trotskyists and other extreme left winger within the Labour Party as cause for concern.

These terms have not always taken the somewhat different meaning which have been ascribed to them above. Up to the mid-1970s they wer almost interchangeable. Today, however, the term 'Social Democrat' ha been appropriated for use by parties (mostly in the non-communist world which seek power within the liberal-democratic system of competing parties The term 'Democratic Socialist' seems to have become closely associated wit those Socialist parties of the Communist Bloc which rule within a 'single party' framework. The reason why the British Labour Party calls its policies 'Democratic Socialist' is somewhat unclear.

SOCIALISM IN THE LATE 1980s AND EARLY 1990s

In Britain

The loss of three General Elections in a row between 1979 and 1987 provided ample material for thought within the Labour Party. The drift towards the left in the early 1980s created the conditions in which the split between the main party and the 'Social Democrats' became virtually inevitable. The dominance of the left within the union movement and the Party during those years also ensured a relative consistency of left wing policy which alienated a large number of traditional Labour voters. The Trotskyist 'Militant Tendency' merely added fuel to these fires.

Following the loss of their third General Election in a row, however, even the most die-hard trade unionists came to realise that the electors were registering decidedly anti-Labour votes as well as a few pro-Conservative ones. Neil Kinnock began, in 1987, to change the Party's direction and this process was aided by the collapse of the Alliance between the Liberals and the Social Democrats. Much of the support for the Alliance drained away when the two parties decided to merge under the title 'Social and Liberal Democrats'. By 1990 the party balance in Great Britain was much as it had been in the mid-1970s, Labour about three points ahead of the Conservatives (44 to 41) with the now 'Liberal Democrats' having about 7 per cent and the Owenite Social Democrats having about 4 per cent. The old Liberal vote had returned to the former and a small group of dissident Labour voters had remained loyal to David Owen.

From a Socialist viewpoint the Labour Party had returned, by 1990, to a range of policies which were similar, in many respects, to those which they had espoused during the late 1960s. The emphasis on nationalisation had been removed and the party was supporting the idea of a social partnership between the private and the public sectors. Similarly, the party had, again, dropped its 'unilateral disarmament' stance and was concentrating upon the new Strategic Arms Reduction Talks (START) as a way of eventually eliminating nuclear weapons from Europe.

In early 1990 the party released a further document resulting from its extensive 'policy review' process which had gone through three separate phases since 1987. The document was called 'Face the Future: Make the Change' and it outlined broad policies on issues such as Europe, defence, social services, privatisation, the national health service and the environment.

Perhaps the greatest blow to the left wing of the British Labour Party came not from Mrs Thatcher or from the anti-Militants in its own ranks but from the massive changes which occurred in Eastern Europe during the last months of 1989 and the first of 1990. Those changes undermined many of the arguments which had been used by the Labour left over the years. People in Eastern Europe may not be rich, they had argued, but at least they have a fairer society and one in which they are protected and happy. The toppling of the Communist Party and its replacement in most Eastern European countries by a multi-party democratic system and a mixed economy based upon the free-market ended those arguments forever.

Socialism in Britain has taken note of these changes and has changed itself in the 1980s and early 1990s. It remains to be seen how it will adjust to the removal of an overt Marxist orthodoxy. With the rejection of Marxism in the East the dialectic is, once again, in question. Clearly, the philosophy of social democracy has taken precedence over that of so-called 'democratic socialism' but the contibution of Marx, Engels, Methodism and the Webbs to British Socialism will remian a viable and potent mixture.

In Europe – The fall of Communism and the Democratic Revolution

Definition

Glasnost
Glasnost is the Soviet policy which introduced political *reform on a limited scale into the Soviet Union and, by example, into countires in the Soviet Bloc.*

Definition

Perestroika
Perestroika is the Soviet policy of economic *reform which did not have as great an influence as* Glasnost *and was, perhaps, an attempt to copy some, but not all, of the economic relaxation and reform which had already taken place in countries like Hungary during the 1980s.*

Very few people could have foreseen the events of 1989 and 1990 in Easter Europe. The gradual relaxation of Soviet influence and control durin Mikhail Gorbachev's policy of *Glasnost* did not provide the ideas but provided an environment in which the individual countries could experimer without too much fear of immediate Soviet invasion as had happened i Hungary in 1957 and in Czechoslovakia in 1968.

Within a few short months between the summer of 1989 and the spring c 1990 the political map of Europe was changed forever. This, largely peacefu set of changes, was the most far-reaching political revolution in Europe sinc 1945 and rivalled the massive changes which had occurred as a result of th Napoleonic and Great Wars.

When this book went to print it was still too early to be able to commen reliably, on the implications of the changes for Socialism as a whole. I Poland, East Germany, Czechoslovakia and Hungary the moves towarc multi-party democracy were extremely strong and almost immediat assistance from the European Community and the United States meant th economic changes were initiated at an early point. In countries lik Yugoslavia, Bulgaria and Rumania the transformation from single to mult party state were slower and less certain. In Albania the Communist monopol of power looked almost unshakeable even as late as the summer of 1989.

There was a tendency in Britain for the changes in Eastern Europe to b seen almost as a simple change of government. In fact, the events were a extensive conceptual and government revolution which, virtually overnigh destroyed most of the foundations of Communism. The concept of a state i which there was only *one class* which wielded power through its ow representatives was finally destroyed by the almost spontaneous calls fc multi-party representation and free elections. The concept of the 'comman economy' with its reliance upon massive structures of state control over a aspects of production was utterly destroyed by the collapse of many of thes economies which had relied upon state control. The idea of a single harmonious people planning their own lives without the oppression of th 'ruling class' and the 'bourgeoisie' was clearly shown up as a sham by th revelations of privilege among the top Communist Party bosses in Ea Germany, Czechoslovakia and Rumania, and by the sheer scale of th internal security services in those same countries.

In a peaceful revolution unknown in the world's history the peoples of som five or six countries overthrew their leaders and the systems they represente and changed direction almost overnight.

This is not to say, however, that all these countries have someho returmed to 'capitalism'. Most have embraced some kind of multi-part system with a degree of free-market economic arrangement but the degree c each will remain to be seen over the next few years.

It is worth noting that the Communist Party in Britian – down to just 750 members by early 1990 – chose the period of the peaceful revolutions i Eastern Europe to elect not only their youngest ever General Secretary bu also their first woman leader. Nina Temple took the opportunity provide by her election to outline a provisional new programme for Communists. Sh spoke of the need to change the image of Communism away from the ol bureaucratic, centralist, authoritarian image of Stalinist Russia. The ne Communism, she felt, would be much closer to the socialism of Willia Morris than to the dialectic of Karl Marx and would embrace such issues a feminism, environmental concern and social inequalities. They woul support proportional representation and coalition government.

The forces of change which were working on Socialism at the start of th 1990s promised to make for exciting and radicial developements in socialis thinking and practice.

EXAMINATION QUESTIONS

1 Why do some British left wing thinkers believe that there can be no parliamentary road to socialism? (London, June 1979,1)

2 Marxists claim that the institutions of the State can never be politically neutral. Discuss this contention. (London, Jan 1983,1)

3 Social Democracy today is more committed to democracy than to socialism. Discuss. (London, June 1983,3)

4 Is Marxism a method or a prophecy? (London, June 1982,3)

5 Has the Labour Party deliberately rejected the liberal theory of Parliamentary Representation? (London, June 1982,1)

6 On what grounds have Euro-Communists asserted that pluralism and parliamentarianism can be reconciled with Marxism? (London, June 1980,3)

7 How many distinct political doctrines can you identify and characterise within the British Labour Party? (London, Jan 1979,3)

NOW READ ON . . .

R. N. Carew-Hunt *The Theory and Practice of Communism*
One of the classic essays on the subject.

Karl Marx *Communist Manifesto*, 1848 and *Das Kapital* (Capital), 1867
Difficult to read but essential if the complexity and depth of Marxism is to be fully understood.

Friedrich Engels *The Condition of the Working Classes*
Another piece of essential reading. Not only does it give a view of the thinking behind the 'Communist Manifesto' but it places many other British political traditions in their historical context.

Nicholai Lenin *The Development of Capitalism in Russia and The State and Revolution*
Heavy going; demonstrates, however, the pressures which led to the peculiar form of Marxism practised by the Soviet Union.

Leon Trotsky *Stalin*
An excellent critique of the leader. The book criticises not only Stalin's methods but also sets out Trotsky's approach to the problem of 'permanent revolution'.

Tony Benn *Out of the Wilderness* Hutchinson, 1987
The peak of the left wing attempts to swing the Labour Party away from Kinnock's centrist policies in the late 1980s.

Michael Leapman *Kinnock* Unwin Hyman, 1987
Useful background to the development of the leader as well as of the Labour Party itself in the 1970s and 1980s.

Stuart Schram *The Political Thought of Mao-Tse Tung*
A dated but extremely thorough account of Mao's thoughts.

Evan Luard *Socialism without the State* Macmillan, 1979
Classic material.

Anthony Wright *Socialisms* Oxford University Press, 1986
Academic examination of the varieties.

13 Anarchism

BASIC PRINCIPLES: A LIFE WITHOUT 'ORDER'

Some questions to consider:

1 Do you think it would be possible to run your school or college without an organised system of authority to ensure that order is maintained?

2 Is it necessary for teachers, lecturers, and administrators to have the greatest say in the way the school or college is run?

3 Would it be feasible and more desirable to have most decisions affecting school or college life arrived at by communal agreement with any decisions being voluntarily enforced by those affected?

An Anarchist would probably answer 'yes' to questions 1 and 3 and 'no' to question 2.

Chapter 1 on 'Order and Disorder' attempts to show that one of the primary concerns of the state is to secure and maintain 'order'. Thomas Hobbes, the seventeenth century English political philosopher, felt that without the state to guarantee stability the result would be chaos. Every individual would be plunged into a mortal struggle with his fellows.

It is such pictures of disorder and chaos that are frequently referred to as 'anarchy' in popular usage.

Newspapers, for example, often talk of 'industrial anarchy' to describe a series of strikes that have a significant impact on the functioning of industry and commerce. This is particularly so if they involve a breakdown in vital services such as buses, trains, electricity supply, etc.

So the opposite of 'order' and an ordered set of relationships between groups of people in society is commonly called 'anarchy'.

Anarchists are also often portrayed as those who have no principles, or **nihilists** having no constructive ideas, wishing only to destroy and offering no alternatives to the 'order' destroyed.

Anarchism is associated in many peoples' minds with violence and terrorism. There persists a picture of anarchists as the bomb throwing assassins of the late nineteenth century. Between 1893 and 1901 Anarchists assassinated President Cornot of France, President Canovos of Spain, President McKinley of the USA, Empress Elizabeth of Austria and King Umberto of Italy.

This image is reinforced through the association of Anarchism with terrorist groups such as the Red Army Faction in West Germany and the Red Brigade in Italy. In Britain the anarchist 'Angry Brigade' in 1971 planted a bomb at the house of Robert Carr, the Secretary of State for Employment.

Yet despite this association many Anarchist writers have rejected the use of violence as a means to achieve their ends.

The Nature of Anarchism

Anarchism is not a purely negative concept as Nihilism is. It is a belief in the need for no government. A society without government, however, may not mean chaos and confusion, but it is these elements that are often expressed and misrepresented in common usage.

Anarchists differ profoundly in their view of the nature of man from, say, Thomas Hobbes. Anarchism is a belief in a society free from domination. It sees government and, more particularly the state, as the primary source of repression. The removal of the state would allow for the development of a

Definition

Anarchism
Anarchism is a belief that rejects the need for the externally enforced order of the state to prevent society disintergrating into chaos and confusion. Freed of such constraints, man would develop his natural social tendencies and live in peace with his fellow man.

more harmonious society. Simply society would function 'naturally' and better without enforced order.

This is not to say that all Anarchists are anti-social thinkers, or extreme individualists. On the contrary, they feel that social relations would be considerably enhanced by the lack of an hierarchically organised pyramid of state power. They feel that, without the state, self-discipline and voluntary cooperation would result and replace artificially imposed order.

External restraints upon people will not be necessary, for they will voluntarily discipline themselves and realise the necessity for socially responsible behaviour towards others.

DISCUSSING THE ARGUMENTS

Anarchism and Authority

Anarchism is not just anti-government or anti-state. For the anarchist all forms of authority are seen to be repressive. This would include anyone, or any institution, that possesses the power to control the actions of another, and would include the law, education, religion, politics, police, armed forces, the penal system, etc.

Anarchism sees it as contrary to human nature for man to be either master or servant. As soon as power is given to one individual to control the actions of another that power will be used oppressively and thereby undermine **equality** and **freedom**. The greatest opportunity for oppression rests with the state through its possession of a monopoly of coercive power. (See Chapter 2.)

For Anarchism **freedom** is a central consideration, and, like **Liberalism** (see Chapter 10), it has a great belief in individualism, so anything a government attempts to impose upon the individual has got to be 'bad'. Any form of government has by its nature to be a restriction on personal freedom.

Any government has to be the government of the few over the many even in a **democracy**. The reason is that democratic theory places major emphasis on the sovereignty of the people whereas the Anarchist is concerned with the individual. Representative democracy involves the individual giving up his right to make decisions to a representative. Decisions are made on behalf of the individual, yet he will have no control over the decision. (See Chapters 7 and 9.)

There is also often an assumption in liberal democracy that it is the will of the majority that must prevail, and this can result in decisions being inflicted upon a minority of dissenting individuals. For an Anarchist the weight of numbers does not necessarily equate with 'right'. This reasoning has also led modern Anarchists to argue against class and economic domination, thereby taking Anarchism in a Socialist direction.

Anarchism and the Law

In rejecting the authority of the state, Anarchism also rejects law as produced by legislators and enforced by judges and the police. The only law man should obey is a 'natural' law, which can only develop once the individual is freed from the 'unnatural' laws imposed by legislatures and courts. Law is seen to be inevitably biased in favour of those who control institutions of the state and, therefore, is yet another instrument of oppression. The legal system is created for this purpose, not to protect individuals or ensure freedom or equality.

Crime, the Anarchist would argue, is generated by society and, by removing the oppression of the state, man can develop his natural social behaviour with the result that crime will disappear. The need for a legal system and a police force would cease. The police are a particular target in Anarchist thinking because, rather than being arbiters in disputes and protectors of life and property, they are seen as acting merely as an instrument for the enforcement of oppressive state power.

Anarchism and Property

Law is seen by the Anarchist as created and enforced for the protection of the ownership of property which in itself is another means for the few to exploit the many.

Probably the first person to call himself an Anarchist was Joseph Proudhon.

Pierre-Joseph Proudhon (1809–65)

Pierre-Joseph Proudhon was the son of French tavern keeper who rose to fame for his theories of a society without a governmental system. He served as Deputy in the National Assembly during the 1848–9 revolution and founded a People's Bank. Proudhon edited a number of radical journals but the views he expressed resulted in him serving a long prison sentence. Possible further prosecution after his release led him into exile in Belgium although he eventually returned to Paris and became active in the founding of the First International.

▲ *Pierre-Joseph Proudhon (1809–65)*

Proudhon's most notable work was called *What is Property* and he answered the question himself in a famous declaration that 'Property is theft'. He opposed the ownership of property on the grounds that it was used by its owners to exploit the labour of others. He was not, however, opposed to all property ownership for he felt it reasonable for a workman to own his own domestic home and any tools, and even possibly land, that were required for his own sustenance.

Proudhon, in claiming to be an Anarchist, felt that the only just society was the one in which the worker was not exploited through the ownership of property. Justice and equality had to go hand in hand. Property could not exist in a society that was 'just'.

Proudhon's society was to be almost totally agrarian and based upon a network of small-holders linked together by naturally advantageous contracts. Manufacturing was not to be achieved through mass production but by craftsmen and artisans in small workshops.

He did not, however, advocate violent revolution, and he believed mankind could be educated to bring about the necessary reforms. This separates Proudhon from subsequent Anarchists who believed that those who held power would not give it up without a struggle. Proudhon's work had a significant impact upon the Anarchist literature that flourished at the end of the nineteenth century.

Proudhon was not the first political theorist to envisage a society based upon cooperation for William Godwin set out similar ideas 50 years before him.

William Godwin (1756–1836)

Godwin trained as a pastor but abandoned his faith and became a professional writer. His writing did not provide a good income and he often relied upon help from his son-in-law, the poet, Shelley. It was the conservative reaction in England that led him to write his greatest work *Enquiry Concerning Political Justice* in 1793.

The *Enquiry Concerning Political Justice* was the first major exposition of Anarchist beliefs. It contained a rejection of governmental authority, ownership of property, the law, and penal system. Godwin wished to see the creation of small communities which would allow for the development of a much more simple lifestyle.

Anarchist Society

For the Anarchist it is natural that people should live in 'society' and man is seen as naturally capable of living in peace with his neighbours. It is the introduction of man-made laws and institutions that destroy his ability to live in harmony with his fellows. In Anarchism there can be no overall fixed plan for **Utopia**; it must develop in the way best suited to those who live in that society.

Definition

Utopia
Utopia is an ideal form of society where a transformation of existing society has occurred and a peaceful and harmonious environment has been created for all.

In common usage, however, 'Utopian' is often associated with hopelessly unrealisable or idealised concepts. **Utopian Socialists** (see Chapter 12), for example, rejected the usage and argued that their ideas could be achieved during their own life times.

Unlike **Marxists**, Anarchists do not wish to seize the power of the state and redirect it to Socialist ends, they simply want to abolish the state. The likelihood of a seizure of state power being followed by the creation of another oppressive regime is regarded, by the Anarchist, as very high.

Example

The type of centralised state system created in the USSR after the Bolshevik revolution in 1917 serves as a good illustration to an anarchist of the need to sweep away the state completely rather than simply replacing one set of rulers with another. It does not matter who runs the state, for the state by definition must be oppressive.

A variety of views exist about the nature of Anarchist society. These range from extreme 'individualism', which rejects all but the most limited cooperation, to others which envisage a complex system of interrelated groups. Most Anarchists, however, have a view of society which is not a Hobbesian chaos but a society based on human cooperation, organised in small communes each in free association with each other.

One Anarchist who quite clearly set out his ideas on the form of society he felt desirable was Peter Kropotkin.

Peter Kropotkin (1842–1921)

Kropotkin was a Russian nobleman of the highest standing and was at one time an aide to Tsar Alexander II. He was a highly educated geographer who was well respected in the academic world. He became a revolutionary around 1872 and after imprisonment in Russia and France, escaped to England in 1886. He lived in England for 30 years returning to Russia after the revolution. Kropotkin was disappointed by the results of the Bolshevik revolution but was highly regarded by the Soviets who gave him a 'state' funeral at his death in 1921. This was the last time the black anarchist flag was openly flown in the USSR until the failed coup of 1991.

Peter Kropotkin's funeral in the Soviet Union.

Kropotkin, as a scientist and geographer, drew upon his studies of birds and animals in arriving at the conclusion that the continued existence of many species did not depend upon the survival of the fittest in a combative evolutionary process but upon the degree of cooperation achieved by a species.

He felt there was no need to assume that the conclusions he had drawn from observations of the animal and insect world could not be applied to human social organisations. Humans, he considered, were just as sociable and this could be witnessed in the organisation of man in tribal societies.

Kropotkin argued the common ownership of the means of production (i.e. the ownership of all industries and services by all) to be a rational and practical proposition, and that it was the existence of the state that had reduced the opportunity of people to act in such a social manner. Kropotkin envisaged the possibility of a society where the state law and all forms of centralised authority would be abolished.

The basic component of society, the **commune**, would be a self-regulating productive unit combining both industrial and agricultural activities in a given area. Each individual would undertake a productive task and the commune would supply all the goods required. However, the performance of tasks would be freely chosen and not allocated authoritatively by any council or committee.

Kropotkin argued that people would be prepared to undertake tasks as long as they were able to direct their own work and were not simply ordered to do it or forced to do it by economic circumstances. The mutual sharing of tasks would in turn bring people closely together and lead to the development of a sense of community. Individuals would be free to leave the commune if they so desired and seek another commune, if they considered it to be more closely in tune with their needs.

Crime in an Anarchist Society

How would criminal and anti-social behaviour be dealt with in an Anarchist society?

The difficulty of answering this question is often raised as an objection to Anarchist visions of society. Many people regard the control of criminal or anti-social activities as being impossible without a 'police' force and various forms of punishment to deter potential wrongdoers.

Most Anarchists reject any form of punishment because they see punishment as having no positive purpose: in the sense of it resulting in an improvement in behaviour. And, anyway, once freed of state oppression Anarchists argue that most crime simply would disappear. They see crime as the result of state organisation and the repression of various groups in society.

The most extreme form of sanction Kropotkin would accept was expulsion from the commune. He anticipated that very little anti-social behaviour would occur, for the weight of group solidarity generated by the commune's lifestyle and established modes of behaviour would simply result in any such problems disappearing.

The rules of behaviour he felt would become established and so widely and enthusiastically accepted that no commune member would consider breaching them. Kropotkin saw that on occasions the use of an arbiter may be needed, but even this form of authority would only exist because the parties to the dispute voluntarily accept it. A breach of accepted modes of behaviour would be a threat to the very existence of the group and therefore would be unlikely to occur.

Lifestyle in an Anarchist Society

Kropotkin did not, like some Anarchists, argue for a form of communal living with shared meals in communal dining halls etc. He felt that this would place a strain on relationships, and so, argued that the basic unit would still need to be the family. This kind of society would end the need for wages because all products would be free to all.

Kropotkin did not accept that an Anarchist society should necessarily involve a return to a rural and pastoral existence as some Anarchists like Proudhon did. Machinery could still be employed but only to undertake labour saving and boring routine tasks so as to free the individual to pursue more creative activities.

Kropotkin welcomed technological advance in the home as well so as to reduce the burden of tedious housework. He would no doubt have been happy to see the development of vacuum cleaners, washing machines and microwave ovens! Nonetheless most Anarchists wish for a society where the features of modern industrial society have vanished and have been replaced with a far more simple lifestyle.

William Morris (1834–96), although hard to categorise as an Anarchist in his writings, rejected what he felt to be ugly Victorian commercialism in favour of a society based upon the revival of the arts and crafts. The best example of his ideal society was drawn up in *News from Nowhere*. (See Chapter 1.)

Anarchism and Utopian Socialism

Anarchism is not the same as Utopian Socialism (see Chapter 12). The essential difference lies in the rejection by Anarchists of any form of externally imposed authority upon the individual.

Anarchism and Nationalism

Anarchism in emphasising the commune as the basic form of social organisation, also rejects the concept of the **nation**. Nations, and, in particular, **nationalism** are seen as a threat due to the propensity of governments to conduct a policy aggression towards other nations they judge to be rivals. The removal of artificial territorial boundaries and divisions by the creation of small communal units is seen as vital to ensure freedom from external aggression.

THE 'FAILURE' OF ANARCHISM

Anarchists of various types are agreed overall that in an Anarchist society, people will enjoy an essentially simple style of life. They generally reject methods of modern economic organisation whether Socialist or Capitalist, and wish for their complete destruction before a new society is created. This rejection of modern mass production in industrial society has led to the criticism that Anarchists are, at best, hopeless romantic dreamers wishing to create a society that can never practically be established.

Attempts by various political movements to alleviate the worst aspects of industrialisation and reform contemporary society have been rejected by Anarchists as palliatives providing only limited relief to the symptoms of the 'disease' without tackling its 'cause'.

The practical applications of Anarchist principles have largely been ineffective. As a political movement Anarchism has failed. Most industrialised countries have experienced an extension and consolidation of centralised state power together with the increase, rather than a decrease, in nationalism.

Anarchism had its greatest influence in countries such as Russia in the late nineteenth century and Spain in the 1930s. Both had little industrialisation and a large poor peasant population. Anarchism was generally unable to win significant support amongst large groups of workers in industrialised societies. In principle Anarchism is opposed to traditional forms of politica organisation and its lack of organisation inhibited its impact upon industria societies. This was especially true in states in which the groups who felt the were being oppressed needed to be organised in order to achieve reforms.

The overthrow of the existing economic order would require organised an sustained effort. It seems hard to see how 'enslaved' industrial workers coul come to throw off their 'chains' and create a new alternative society base upon communal cooperation, by a spontaneous uprising. The trade unions for example, required organisational structure to achieve their objectives and 'revolution', if it was ever to occur, needed leaders.

Anarchism also had to compete with the counter-claims of Socialism whic presented an alternative economic and social system together with th apparently practical means to achieve it. Anarchism therefore came to b viewed by many as only a set of theoretical ideals.

By the early years of this century, Socialism also had an example of successful Socialist regime which had been established (in the USSR) an there were extremely efficient Socialist parties beginning to challenge fo government in several countries.

EXPERIMENTS WITH ANARCHISM AND 'ALTERNATIVE' SOCIETIES

A totally Anarchist society has never been created and there has never bee a fully recognisable Anarchist revolution. There have been revolutions however, in which Anarchists took part. For example, a small number wer active supporters of the Bolshevik revolution in Russia in 1917. Despite th apparent failure of Anarchism as a political movement there have bee attempts to create communities run on Anarchist principles.

Anarchism in Spain

Perhaps the most notable example of attempts to establish an Anarchis society took place in some parts of Spain prior to the outbreak of civil wa in 1936. The largest organisation in Spain, with over one million member was the Confederation Nacional del Trabajo (a national labour federation and it was strongly influenced by Anarchist ideas. In Barcelona, for example most industries were run by CNT on collective lines and were administere by workers' committees and trade unions. The police force was made up o a part-time militia of workers and justice was dispensed not through courts but by revolutionary tribunals. Anarchist influence also extended to part of Catalonia, Aragon, and Andalusia where CNT-controlled industr developed in many industrial cities and smaller towns.

In rural areas large numbers of villages were organised upon Anarchis principles as communes. In some instances village communes abolishe money, established communal means of production, and undertook decisio making by local assemblies and direct democracy. The Anarchist movemen in Spain did not survive the civil war. It was crushed by the Fascist repressio of General Franco who led the Nationalist forces to victory in 1940.

Anarchism in France

The black anarchist flag has been seen several times since the Spanish civi war. It reappeared in the 1960s and was evident during the 1968 riots i Paris. Anarchists played a part in the civil disturbances that led trad unionists, students and left wing organisations to clash violently with rio police. The anarchist flag was flown, with the red flag, over the universit of Sorbonne. The 'revolution' was a major challenge to the Presidency of th 79 year old Charles de Gaulle and he resigned after a referendum defeat i the following year.

Example

George Bernard Shaw, the Fabian socialist, rejected anarchism in *The Impossibilities of Anarchism* (1893) not on the grounds that it was undesirable, in fact he was attracted to its ideas, but on the basis that it was impractical.

Cooperative Communities

The philosophical impact of Anarchism can also be identified in the ideas of some political thinkers and activists who would not readily be identified as Anarchists.

There is also a history of groups attempting to create cooperative communities in the USA. Many were based upon a rejection of contemporary social values expressing a desire to return to a less complex style of life and work. Some of these movements were also reinforced by shared religious beliefs.

Example

A group which came to be known as the Shakers was formed by a Baptist minister Joseph Meacham in 1787. The community was influenced by the teaching of Ann Lee, a factory worker from Manchester who went to the USA in 1774 and established a commune in New York State.

At the height of the movement in the middle of the nineteenth century the Shakers had over 6000 members living in communes across the USA. The members of the sect shared most things and took communal meals but celibacy was a major principle. Today only one Shaker community still exists, in Maine, but many former ones have become museums which arouse considerable interest as examples of attempts to create alternative lifestyles to those offered by American society.

Example

There is a long history of self-governing cooperative communities in India and the leader of the Indian Independence Movement, Gandhi, placed great emphasis on these traditions in his teachings.

Beatniks and Hippies

The influence of Anarchist values can be discerned in some movements since the 1950s which sought to create an alternative society to replace what they felt to be the increasingly centralised authority and bureaucracy of the modern state.

Beatniks first appeared in the USA during the late 1950s and were influenced by the 'alternative society' theories of writers such as Allen Ginsberg. Beatniks had some impact in Britain and other parts of Europe. They generally rejected and 'dropped out' of society. They were heavily influenced by Eastern religions, especially Zen Buddism. They also shared an enthusiasm for music, primarily modern jazz, but overall Beatniks were only a fringe group and had little lasting impact.

Hippies/Flower People as a 'movement' of the late 1960s had a much greater impact than the Beatniks of the 1950s. It attracted large numbers of mainly young people in the USA, Britain, and many parts of Europe. They rejected much of modern commercialism and associated social values.

Again like Beatniks they believed in 'dropping out' and wished to produce a new alternative culture. The movement was spurred by opposition to American involvement in the Vietnam war, a 'revolution' in pop music, and increasingly liberal attitudes towards such matters as sexual morality and the use of drugs. The hippies favoured communal living and a commitment to 'love and peace' which would be achieved by non violent action.

▶ *'Flower children' in London's Hyde Park.*

In 1968 in Chicago, hippies organised an 'alternative' convention to the one being held by the Democratic Party and nominated a pig as presidential candidate. They also threatened to put the hallucinatory drug 'LSD' in Chicago's water supply and 'turn-on' the city. It led to the National Guard being called out to guard the supplies. Despite the peaceful intentions of the hippies the reaction of the authorities was generally very violent.

FINAL THOUGHTS

Anarchism may not have succeeded as a formal political movement in the sense of establishing an Anarchist society or fermenting an anarchist revolution, but it has had an impact. Its ideas have provided a critique and continuing criticism of existing society, its political institutions, politicians, as well as social and political values.

▶▶▶▶▶▶▶▶▶▶▶▶▶▶▶▶ EXAMINATION QUESTIONS

1 Is anarchism of any relevance to advanced industrial societies? (University of London, Government and Political Studies, A-Level, 1980)

2 On what grounds do anarchists criticise the state? (University of London, Government and Political Studies, A-Level, 1985)

3 'There is no single theory of anarchism only a variety of tendencies'. Discuss. (University of London, Government and Politics, A-Level, 1981)

▶▶▶▶▶▶▶▶▶▶▶▶▶▶▶▶ NOW READ ON . . .

R. Hiskes *Community without coercion* Associated University Presses, 1982
A clear examination of anarchist alternative society.

G. Woodcock *Anarchism* Penguin, 1963
A central text for the subject.

Colin Ward (ed.) *Kropotkin's Fields Factories and Workshops Tomorrow* G. Allen and Unwin, 1974
A major work on the Russian anarchist.

14 Corporatism

BASIC PRINCIPLES

The most important first step when trying to understand Corporatism is to clearly distinguish it from government involvement in the economy and state planning and from pluralism. But it is also important to understand that there are many different types of corporatism.

In order to begin to pick one's way through this theoretical minefield a few initial distinctions might be helpful.

Definitions

- **The managed economy**: This is generally taken to mean the State playing a role in directing economic activity. There can be a variety of different levels of involvement.
- **The Corporate State**: A state in which decision-making is formally shared between functional interest groups. The system is, essentially, co-operative.
- **The Pluralist State**: A state in which the government has the main policy-making power but in which a plurality of interest groups compete with each other to be able to influence that process.
- **Tripartism**: A system, usually Liberal-Democratic, in which the Government has formal links with both the owners of industry and commerce and with the trade unions. The 'Tripartite' bodies which are established then assist the Government in policy-making.

Corporatism is a distinct political theory and is, in its most original form, clearly different from Liberal, Conservative and Socialist approaches. One variant of the theory was developed, partly pragmatically and partly by design, by Mussolini.

There are two distinct types of Corporatism and perhaps the best way of distinguishing them is to misuse, slightly, the terminology of Philippe Schmitter who identified **State Corporatism** and **Societal Corporatism**:

1 **State Corporatism** developed from Mussolini's ideas on a new 'national' form of Socialism (see Chapter 15). It emphasises class cooperation rather than the class conflict of Socialism. The important features are its emphasis on decision making by cooperating groups; State control of most aspects of the productive process, and the establishment of a totally new structure of representation.

2 **Societal Corporatism** In Britain this actually developed from Conservatives such as Harold Macmillan who regarded Socialism as a counter-productive method of achieving soceity's goals. It is characterised by the retention of the same governmental structure, little or no additional State control, and cooperation between two identifiable groups and the government. The fact that this type of corporatism emphasises cooperation between Government, Industry (or Capital) and Unions (or Labour) has led to it being called '**tripartism**'.

State and Societal Corporatism

State Corporatism	**Societal Corporatism**
Cooperation between formally established groups.	Cooperation between already existing groups in a formal structure, usually tripartite.
New structure of government – based on occupational and industrial representation.	No new structure – geographical representation remains.
State control; private ownership	Little state control; mixed economy

State Corporatism

Much has been said about Mussolini's development of Italian Fascism in Chapter 15 and it will not be repeated here. It is, however, important to highlight some of the main corporatist features of his regime.

Corporatism in Italy required that the entire country be governed by what were, effectively, twenty 'Corporations'. Trade unions had been effectively abolished and the Corporations became the focus for representation. Each of the twenty Corporations included not only workers but also the owners of the businesses in that sector of the economy. Italy was governed by a '**Council of Fasces**' consisting of the heads of each of the Corporations. *Il Duce*, Mussolini, was, of course, the Leader of the Council.

State Corporatism requires, therefore, not only cooperation between the State and the most powerful interest groups, but also the restructuring of the entire representative process.

(It is to be noted that some of the proposals for the reform of the House of Lords would wish to see a second chamber consisting of 'groups' rather than individuals representing geographical areas. That is, functional rather than geographical representation.)

Societal Corporatism

In Britain there have been few people, except those on the extreme right (notably Oswald Mosley in the 1930s) who have promoted the idea of State Corporatism.

It became clear, during the depression of the 1930s, however, that there were interests which were not being taken into account by the traditional representative process. On the right of the political spectrum some of the more moderate and broader thinking Conservatives began to consider ways in which the decision-making process could be made less one of conflict and more of one of cooperation.

Perhaps foremost among these thinkers was the young Conservative MP, Harold Macmillan. Macmillan, regarded as dangerously intellectual by some of his fellow Conservative MPs at the time (he was once warned not to be seen reading *The Times* in the Members' Reading Room), was seeking some way of avoiding both the evils of totally free enterprise and those of socialist centralisation. He began to develop his ideas with a group of like-minded Conservatives and published, in 1927, *Industry and the State* (Macmillan, 1927; with Robert Boothby, Oliver Stanley and J. Loder).

The introduction to that book stated that it was:

> *. . . a first essay in devising some coherent system . . . between . . . private enterprise and collectivism.*

A few years later, Macmillan published his work *The Middle Way* (Macmillan, 1938) in which he called for much greater State involvement in the control of the economy. Macmillan wanted to see the Bank of England nationalised (that did not occur until after World War II), State subsidies for industry, and State control of investment.

Keynsian economic policies and the 'demand management', which it was widely believed that they encouraged, became bipartisan policy after 1945. Both main parties accepted the pledge given in the 1944 Employment White Paper that governments would accept the role of maintaining 'full employment'. The story since 1945, and certainly up to the 1970s, was of a continual struggle to make the Government's 'control' of the economy effective. The most usual method was by some form of planning.

By the end of the 1950s it became clear, however, that Government planning alone could never 'manage' the economy effectively. There were two major groups in society whose cooperation was essential if economic management was to work. The Macmillan government of 1959–64, therefore, introduced a body called the **National Economic Development Council** (NEDC) together with a system of administrative support in the form of the National Economic Development Office (NEDO). The NEDC was the beginning of **tripartism** in Britain: an attempt to allow the leaders of business, unions and government to settle their differences around a single table.

The NEDC was a form of corporatism: an attempt to introduce cooperative, functional systems which would achieve harmony in a society in which the traditional representative system (Parliament) had patently failed.

The reasons for its failure are too varied to be dealt with here, but part of the problem was, undoubtedly, the fundamental one of getting the union rank and file to accept and obey decisions which their leaders may have taken in the NEDC. A similar lack of linkages operated within the business fraternity.

DISCUSSING THE ARGUMENTS

Corporatism and Pluralism

The concept of Corporatism is concerned with the role and influence of organised groups, particularly economic interests. It deals with the relationships of these interests with the state and each other; in fact the political community in a Corporatist state is seen to be the sum total of these groups.

The relationships between the interests is often described as 'organic', that is: each element relies for its continued existence upon the others that constitute the 'organ'. Each element cannot exist without the others.

In a Corporatist society decisions are made by a process of consultation and negotiation between the major organised interests, with the government being only one of these elements.

A truly Corporatist state would not require the institutions of a representative system, but at least in Britain Corporatism is held to mean that the negotiations are conducted separately from the usual legislative and executive institutions. This has led to the fear that, with the development of a corporatist state, institutions such as Parliament will be bypassed by the decision makers.

Definition

Pluralism
Pluralism is a system in which political power is diffused amongst many groups and there is continued competition between them to gain influence in the political system.

Definition

Corporatism
Corporatism is an economic and political system in which organised interests enjoy a mutually beneficial, institutionalised, and cooperative relationship with the state policy making processes.

In liberal democracies it is assumed that the views of individuals are communicated to policy makers through the electoral system, political parties and pressure groups. The policy makers then respond to the demands of the electorate by producing popular policies.

A **pluralistic** view of liberal democracy sees no problem because it assumes that society is made up of a large number of groups that compete with each other to gain a favourable response from government to their demands. This competition is seen to be an extension of the type of competition that occurs at periodic elections and therefore can only enhance the democratic process. In all this competition of the pluralistic political society the government remains the final arbiter between the groups.

The balance of power between the groups constantly changes and new groups emerge to ensure no one group comes to gain undue influence.

A movement towards Corporatism, in the British sense, means, however, that these groups become an almost institutionalised and integrated part of the political system. The groups are allowed special privileged access to the governmental policy making process.

So the result is, instead of competition between groups, which a pluralist would see as enhancing the democratic process, the groups build up a formal relationship with the government with both sides expecting to benefit.

With a pluralistic relationship, power is dispersed amongst a number of competing groups, whereas with Corporatism, power is concentrated into a relatively small number of groups which work closely with governmental policy makers.

Many political scientists have argued that Britain, over the past 25 years, has begun to develop into a corporate state with functional interests becoming incorporated into the governmental machinery.

Developments in Corporatist Theory

Group Theorists

The ideas of group theorists developed by the late nineteenth century as an alternative view of society to those held by Victorian Liberals. Society was seen to be made up not of a mass of individuals, but of a number of groups with whom people often identified. It was felt that the claims of these groups should be recognised by government. This had implications for the concept of **Parliamentary sovereignty** because it was argued that, not only did groups have rights in the same way as individuals, but that government could never win in a struggle against determined opposition by determined groups.

G.D.H. Cole, for example, argued that the concept of **representative government** was impossible because society was made up of a complex of functional groups. Representative government, Cole felt, should be reconsidered for people could not be represented as individuals and should be recognised as belonging to groups.

The **Guild Socialism** of Cole reflected this view. Guild Socialism was based on the organisation of society around functional groups (see Chapter 12). Cole argued that the arbitary division of people into geographical constituencies merely led to misrepresentation.

Corporatism and Liberal Democracy

The increasing concern of many liberal democracies has been the growth of corporatist political structures and the bypassing of parliamentary government and the party system in public policy making. Corporatism is more than just the articulation of interests associated with established patterns of pressure group activity.

The theory, as understood in Britain, is difficult to accommodate in traditional patterns of representation and could be seen as a serious challenge to the established constitutional framework. The interests involved in a Corporatist model appear to have an intrinsic power that cannot be challenged by government.

A distinguishing feature of Corporatist theory is the development of a pattern of collaboration and consultation between groups in shaping social and economic policy. The bargaining that occurs between them generally takes an informal pattern with compromise having to be reached. Any lobbying that takes place is not conducted from outside institutions through established channels, for the groups become an integral part of the political system.

The deals that are struck usually do not have any legal status and therefore cannot be questioned in the courts. The Corporatist view of policy making would argue that there is no 'common good' which government should attempt to identify and impose. Any government decision is seen necessarily to be the result of bargains worked out between the interests involved.

Corporatism is the bargaining process. The importance of groups and the need for them to be involved in discussions over proposed policy and legislation is widely accepted in liberal democracies, but ultimately the job of government is seen to be to identify the public interest and not be directed by influential group interests.

Example

Government Involvement in the Economy and Planning in the UK

The involvement of the government in the 'progress of the economy is not something which began with the twentieth century or with Socialist theory.

In the seventeenth century the government, in the form of the Monarchy and the Parliament, were closely involved in protection of trade and in promoting British interests in the rest of the world. The eighteenth century saw the development of theories of 'free trade' and of *laissez-faire* doctrines; consequently the period of the Industrial Revolution saw little 'interference' from the government in commercial affairs.

The Nineteenth Century

The excesses of the Industrial Revolution brought increasing government involvement towards the middle of the nineteenth century.

Unfettered growth of urban areas and uncontrolled exploitation of workers had created truly terrible conditions and the governments of the day found themselves increasingly involved in legislation controlling such things as:

- the powers of local authorities to levy taxes to build public facilities (the Municipal Corporations Act, 1835)
- the conditions and hours of work in factories and mines (the various Factories and Mines Acts)
- the rapid expansion of the railways. The problems of uncontrolled building of railway lines had to be met by a long series of special 'Railway Acts' for individual lines.

As the responsibilities of government increased so it found that the need for finance grew. Income Tax, which had first been imposed by Pitt in 1802, was reintroduced in 1842. The growth of banks and the need to protect the investor meant a string of banking legislation beginning with the Acts of 1833 and 1844.

As the century progressed so the original involvement in commercial and economic affairs spilled over into the need for a government role in social matters. The 'free market' was not responding to the need for higher standards of education so the government had to legislate for more schools and for an increased supply of better qualified teachers. Local governments demanded, and were given, powers to extend the social facilities available to their citizens. Free libraries, public baths and washing facilities, higher quality housing and better sanitation were just a few of the benefits which resulted.

The Twentieth Century

The twentieth century saw a massive expansion of the involvement of the government in both economic and social affairs until it is difficult to imagine, today, a society which did not have its government involved in almost every single aspect of its affairs. It has reached the stage, in the 1980s where many people believe that the government should be responsible for everything.

The 1906 Liberal Government began the process of government responsibility for large areas of welfare: old age pensions, health provision, unemployment pay, employment exchanges, etc., and World War I created the need for the government to become directly involved in business for the first time.

During World War I the government took a leading role in many areas: agriculture (with the creation of marketing boards and the control of agricultural labour); industry (many factories were taken over and were known as 'National' factories (there were 240 of them by 1918); control of the railways; control of coal mining.

By 1945 no one really questioned the right of the government to be involved in all these ways. Indeed, many regarded it as a sacred **duty** of government to take responsibility for all aspects of its people's lives. The 1944 White Paper on Employment pledged that, in future, government would take responsibility for ensuring that there was 'full' employment. This pledge, which was agreed by all the main parties (Conservative, Labour and Liberal) meant that, from 1945 onwards, British governments would have to 'manage' the economy in order to ensure that economic adjustment (to any changes in circumstances) occurred in ways other than an increase in unemployment.

Planning

If governments were to have this depth of responsibility, the Labour Party argued, a degree of forward planning would be necessary. When that party formed the first post-war government in 1945, Attlee decided that a framework for forward planning would be established.

The new Ministry of Economic Affairs was set up in 1948 together with a specially constituted 'Central Economic Planning Staff'. Neither operated very well against the entrenched power of the Treasury and they were abolished by the Conservative government when the latter came to power in 1951.

The Conservatives attempted to manage the economy without any formal planning structure between 1951 and 1964, but they found, by 1961, that they needed some sort of new structure to ensure that the system worked properly. In 1961,

Macmillan set up the NEDC (see p. 173) in the hope that collaboration between the three main actors in the economy (Government, Unions and Business) would result in less conflict and smoother growth.

Harold Wilson became Prime Minister in 1964 and was determined to reinstate a formal planning process. He set up a new Department of Economic Affairs under the then Deputy Leader of the Labour Party, George Brown, with the object of writing a five-year forward plan for the entire economy. A combination of the need for haste in the preparation of the plan, the opposition of the Treasury, difficult economic circumstances and a less than ideal relationship between Brown and the then Chancellor, James Callaghan, meant that the DEA and the National Plan were not successes.

The 1974 Labour Government, again under Harold Wilson, decided not to attempt the same sort of structure. Instead they opted for an agreement with the Unions known as the **Social Contract** (see below).

In addition to the Social Contract, which was made to appear to be 'tripartite' after the event by getting the agreement of the CBI to its public terms, the Labour government introduced the idea of 'Planning Agreements'. In theory these would allow businesses to plan their future development with the government and, perhaps, to gain government help thereby.

Only two of these 'voluntary' agreements were ever signed (one by the National Coal Board and one by Chrysler (UK) Ltd). Neither firm was in good economic shape, both received large amounts of government financial backing and it would not be stretching the imagination too far to suspect that both agreements were something less than voluntary.

Planning, in the sense of the government attempting to plan for and influence the output and direction of the entire economy, is not, needless to say, something which the Conservative governments of 1979, 1983, 1987 felt to be of the greatest import. Indicative planning of the 1967 'National Plan' variety has been somewhat discredited and planning under the Conservative governments has been limited to the traditional planning of government spending, borrowing and taxation. Fiscal planning of this sort works on a five-year 'rolling plan' and does not attempt to control or influence the detailed operation of industrial or commercial sectors.

The Social Contract

The apparent trend towards Corporatism in British politics seemed to some to take a major step forward during the period of Labour Government 1974–9.

The establishment of the 'social contract' between government, the Confederation of British Industry and the Trades Union Congress seemed to imply that these major interests were becoming firmly incorporated in the economic policy making process. It also provided evidence for those who felt that government was becoming increasingly reliant upon major economic interests to secure the successful implementation of its economic strategy.

During its period in opposition, between 1970 and 1974, the Labour Party held a series of talks with the trade unions with the intention of improving relations. To this end a new body was created in January 1972: the Labour Party-TUC Liaison Committee, which brought together leading members of the TUC General Council, the Shadow Cabinet, and the National Executive Committee of the Labour Party. It was the work of the Liaison Committee that produced the agreement which came to be called the 'Social Contract'.

The Labour leaders promised to repeal the 1971 Industrial Relations Act if they won the next election, together with the statutory incomes policy of the Conservative Government.

Other discussions included measures to make trade union membership easier, the establishment of a conciliation and arbitration service, and greater protection for workers against unfair dismissal. In return the TUC undertook to seriously consider the overall position of the economy when formulating wage claims.

The Labour Party was returned to power with the General Election of February 1974, albeit as a minority government. The party's position was improved slightly by the election of October 1974.

The Prime Minister, Harold Wilson, was determined to continue the good working relationship that had been established with the TUC. The Confederation of British Industry was also called upon to support the 'Social Contract' for it was seen to be in the national interest to tackle the problem of rising inflation.

During 1974–5 the Social Contract appeared not to be working as wage rises went up sharply. The rate of inflation by the Spring of 1975 stood at nearly 25 per cent (the highest rate of any country in the western industrial world).

The government did however manage to secure the support of the TUC in an agreement to limit pay demands. A voluntary ceiling of £6 per week for pay claims was endorsed and this began a process of nationally negotiated pay bargaining between TUC, CBI and government, which lasted until 1978.

The period of the 'Social Contract' was not without its problems, with some trade union leaders expressing doubts over the government's overall economic strategies as early as 1976. The TUC was disturbed by the government's deflationary measures and the increase in unemployment which rose to one million by October 1975.

When James Callaghan became Prime Minister in April 1976, the situation was no better, but the TUC, under the auspices of the Social Contract, did accept a 10 per cent limit on pay rises for 1977–8.

The TUC was now talking of an 'orderly' return to collective bargaining. Industrial conflict increased with major strikes by bakery workers, air traffic controllers and firemen.

The government attempted to strengthen their position by threatening sanctions against employers who broke the Social Contract by offering more than the agreed level of 10 per cent. The sanctions were mainly the withholding of government contracts.

In 1978 the government attempted to win support for a new negotiated pay round with a limit of only 5 per cent, even though inflation was now down to 8 per cent. This policy failed to win the support of the unions and what followed has been called the 'winter of discontent'. The winter of 1978–9 saw a wave of strikes, many in the public sector, where unions attempted to breech the 5 per cent limit.

Strikes affected hospital manual and ancillary workers, and action by local authority workers amongst other things, led to piles of rubbish in the streets. Action was also taken by Ford car workers and lorry drivers belonging to the Transport and General Workers Union.

▼ *A London street during the rubbish collection strike in 1979.*

The effect of the strikes was very damaging to the credibility of the Labour Government who wished to show that they could engage the unions and employers' organisations in national pay bargaining without recourse to legislation.

In March 1979, the Labour Government which was by this time in a minority, was narrowly defeated in the House of Commons on a vote of no confidence and resigned. Attempts to patch up relations between the TUC and the Labour Government were made but the real beneficiary of the 'winter of discontent' was Mrs Thatcher, for the election of May 1979 showed considerable support for Conservative policies amongst rank and file union members. The Conservatives were returned to power, with 33 per cent of trade union members in some areas voting Conservative.

Was the Social Contract a Pinnacle of Corporatism?

One interpretation of the period of Labour Government (1974–9) is that an apparent trend in British politics towards Corporatism was clearly identified and firmly established.

It was the collaboration on the establishment of national limits to pay awards that took place which could be taken as evidence to confirm such an analysis. The significance of the Social Contract, as evidence of a Corporatist trend, can be exaggerated for it was fairly short lived and viewed by many trade unionists and employers with suspicion. The TUC entered into the agreement with notable reluctance.

Almost from its beginnings the unions were keen to emphasise their desire to return to the established pattern of collective bargaining with the employers. This feeling was reinforced by a significant expression of 'shopfloor' opinion in many trade unions where local officials felt their major bargaining power had been taken away.

Many trade unions, especially in those industries which had enjoyed high wage levels, considered that collaboration with the government had proved 'costly', for they could have expected higher wage awards than the nationally agreed levels.

Employers in some industries were also happy to abandon the Social Contract when faced with the possibility of damaging industrial action by groups of workers wishing to gain pay awards above the levels set in the Social Contract.

CORPORATISM IN THE 1980s

The critics of the apparent trend towards Corporatism as evidenced by the Social Contract, argue that important decisions were increasingly being taken without reference to the representative institutions of the political and parliamentary system.

Not only did it appear to its critics to be politically and democratically undesirable, but economically undesirable as well. The 'Corporatist' decision making process was apparently not acting in the long term economic interests of the nation because the short term self-interest of a few influential groups had become dominant.

Critics of the Social Contract in particular claimed that the government had given away a great deal in concessions to the trade unions by repealing industrial relations legislation, but had received little in return in terms of improvement in wage demands and industrial relations.

Since the 1979 General Election the 'trend' towards corporatism (if it indeed ever existed) has been reversed with group theory in general going out of fashion.

The arguments of the New Right (see Chapter 11) have played a significant part in 'reversing the trend'. Corporatism is seen by the 'new right' as mistaken in assuming that governments should attempt to bring about a consensus between major interests. Economic planning is seen as impossible, given the complexity of the process by which economic decisions are made in the market place and the factors which have to be taken into account.

Planning, it is felt, will necessarily be inefficient; free markets can be the only answer for the stimulation and growth of the British economy.

In practical terms this style of thinking has led the Conservative Government under Mrs Thatcher to largely ignore the NEDC, and to minimise contact with the CBI and TUC, where consultations on new policy may have taken place in the past.

The NEDC still exists but it has ceased to play the important role it did in the 1970s. Its role today tends to be that of a forum for general discussion of policies which have already been decided by the government. Its ability to form or influence that policy has been greatly reduced.

► *Mrs Thatcher made one of her rare visits to the NEDC in March 1987 to celebrate its 25th birthday.*

CONCLUSIONS

Many traditional elements of British political and constitutional models are challenged by Corporatism.

Example

Parliamentary government is challenged because Parliament is not seen as the focus for the bargaining process that is central to Corporatism. A two chamber Parliament is seen as an over-simplification of the policy forming process which ignores the important interests which have little or no direct presence.

Representative government is challenged because Corporatism is concerned to represent group interests and not individuals. The assumption is that individual interests can be represented through the individual's membership of a group; and that the total membership of all groups is equivalent to the sum of individual interests.

Rule of Law is challenged because the results of the bargaining procedures of Corporatism cannot be subject to any judicial review because generally they have no legal status. Also legislation that arises will be the outcome of some groups gaining access to, and influencing, government, not through everyone's interests being equally considered.

Responsible government is challenged because the groups can in no way be regarded as responsible and the doctrine of ministerial responsibility in decision making is unclear for the influence of group pressure may be hard to estimate.

Popular government is challenged because the wishes of the people may become less important to government than winning the support of influential groups. The wishes of the majority may be ignored in favour of the opinions of specific groups.

A defence of Corporatism

The major defence of Corporatism against its critics is that the representation of important functional groups is inevitable and that the representation of a mass of individuals is unrealistic.

It is regarded as being fairer than a **pluralist** system, because groups have a formal position and all members of society are represented through these groups.

Despite a good deal of Conservative opposition to Corporatism and an emphasis on free market forces, Edmund Burke (see Chapter 11) who was an influential source on British Conservative thinking, would not necessarily have opposed Corporatism. Corporatism's emphasis on interests rather than numbers would have appealed to Burke. He would not have been pleased however with the emphasis on striking bargins by negotiation, an essential element in Corporatism.

Burke's probable displeasure would have stemmed from the fact that he would have preferred informed debate in Parliament on the merits of the case, leading to genuine agreement on what is best for the long term interests of the nation. Closed negotiation with each side making concessions would be no substitute for open debate for Burke.

Corporatism is also claimed to make government more 'responsive' to the wishes of the electorate between elections. Even at elections it could be claimed the electorate are offered only rival 'packages' of policies in the form of manifestos, with no opportunity provided for a choice of items from each.

The process of Corporatism is seen as a way of keeping the government informed and aware of what the electorate wants.

Is group politics inevitable?

Despite the apparent opposition of the Conservative government since 1979 towards group politics, it can be argued, that, given the complexity of modern government and the problems that it faces, there is no choice but to include major interests in the process of policy making. Any government which attempts to exclude them can only do so temporarily.

For Corporatism to become established, as we understand the concept in Britain, there should exist a limited number of major non-competitive economic groups in regular contact with government, sharing the responsibility for the development and implementation of policy, for most other groups would be excluded.

In Britain the government may prefer to deal with some organisations more than others and some groups may be more readily admitted to the consultative process but these groups, nonetheless, remain independent of government.

When strong links between major groups and government have been established, the result has been 'tripartism' and not corporatism. Also the establishment of such links between government and major groups has not necessarily been accompanied by similar links between the groups themselves.

A developed pluralistic set of relationships has been more evident with a large number of competitive groups being offered a range of opportunities to consult and pressurise government.

EXAMINATION QUESTIONS

1 Should the big economic interest groups be given representation in a second chamber of Parliament? (University of London, Government and Political Studies, A-Level, 1981)

2 Is the Government of Britain a tripartite relationship between industry, the unions, and Whitehall? (University of London, Government and Political Studies, A-Level, 1982)

3 Do private individuals or groups of individuals have any chance of influencing projected legislation in Great Britain? (University of Cambridge, Public Affairs, 1985)

▸▸▸▸▸▸▸▸▸▸▸▸▸▸▸ NOW READ ON . . .

S. Beer *Modern British Politics* Faber and Faber, 1969
A hymn of praise to the growing relationship between government and major economic interests.

S. Beer *Britain against Itself* Faber and Faber, 1982
A reversal of Beer's conclusions in *Modern British Politics.*

W. Grant *Business and Politics in Britain* Macmillan, 1987
An assessment of the relationships between government and industry.

15 Totalitarianism

▸▸▸▸▸▸▸▸▸▸▸▸▸▸▸ TOTALITARIANISM: FACT AND FICTION

Extracts from *Nineteen Eighty-four* by George Orwell

The aim of the Party was not merely to prevent men and women from forming loyalties which it might not be able to control. Its real, undeclared purpose was to remove all pleasure from the sexual act.

. . . All marriages between Party members had to be approved by a Committee appointed for the purpose.

. . . The only recognised purpose of marriage was to beget children for the service of the Party.

* * *

The three slogans on the front of the Ministry of Truth read:

'WAR IS PEACE'
'FREEDOM IS SLAVERY'
'IGNORANCE IS STRENGTH'

'BIG BROTHER IS WATCHING YOU' the caption said . . . In the far distance a helicopter skimmed down between the roofs, hovered for an instant like a bluebottle, and darted away again with a curving flight. It was the police patrol snooping into peoples' windows.

* * *

The television received and transmitted simultaneously. Any sound that Winston made, above the level of a very low whisper, would be picked up by it; moreover . . . he could be seen as well as heard . . . How often, or on what system the Thought Police plugged in on any individual wire was guesswork.

* * *

He was back in the Ministry of Love with everything forgiven, his soul as white as snow. He was in the public dock, confessing everything, implicating everybody . . . He gazed up at the enormous face . . . But it was all right, everything was all right, the struggle was finished . . . He loved Big Brother.

1934: Extracts on Nazi Germany from Frederic V. Grunfeld's *The Hitler File*, 1934

In the 1930s an actor named Wolfgang Langhoff managed to leave Hitler's Germany and told the story of a fellow prisoner at Dachau Concentration Camp named Frank or Franke who belonged to a fundamentalist Protestant sect which believed that God had forbidden them to honour Hitler.

When the SS guards discovered that he never raised his arm and that he refused to say 'Heil Hitler' they gave him a week of solitary confinement in the 'dark cell'. When he returned his eyes were blood shot. "Be sensible," his comrades told him. "What does this bit of 'Heil Hitler' matter? Do as we do, with your tongue in your cheek!"

He shook his head. The next day he was found out again. This time he spent a fortnight in the dark cell. We could scarcely recognise him when he came out. But he did not raise his arm to salute.

Now fat Zimmerman took it upon himself to teach him. Accompanied by five SS guards Franke was led down to the little courtyard.

"Up with your arm. Up with your arm" . . .

They fell on him . . . He rolled down into the ice covered pools. "Arm up; Heil Hitler! Get a move on."

This went on until he lay there unconscious. His blood froze on the ground.

We implored him. In vain. His face became set . . . he would not salute. We felt desperate.

Now he was separated from us and put into the cells with the habitual criminals . . . Day after day he had to run along with the latrine boxes. His hands were bloody from the strain. He spent his life between arrest, blows and latrine duty.

. . . After many weeks he joined us again. On entering the corridor, he met an SS man. His right arm rose awkwardly. His hand, crusted with blood, stretched out. He whispered . . . "Heil Hitler."

The Disciplinary Regulations for the Concentration Camp at Dachau were drawn up in 1933 by Heinrich Himmler and prescribed shooting or hanging for such things as talking politics or refusing an order. Many prisoners were hung by the arms from a post until their arms became dislocated.

BASIC PRINCIPLES

For anyone who has lived in a society which is even moderately democractic, life under a truly Totalitarian regime is almost impossible to imagine.

One can imagine living in a Communist society or under an absolute monarch but the total subjugation of the individual which is demanded by a totalitarian system defies the imagination. At school in such a system the subjects are chosen by the State and the actual content of the textbooks is vetted by and has to be approved by the State. At work the only unions are those established by the State and in order to get and keep a job one has to have a work permit which it is in the State's power to refuse. One's children belong to State organisations which encourage them to spy on and report about their parents. The films one sees, the radio programmes one listens to, the plays at the theatre and the books and papers one reads – everything lies in the control of the State.

Just as Jesus saved people from sin and from Hell, Hitler saves the German 'Volk' (*) from ruin. Jesus and Hitler were persecuted; but while Jesus was crucified, Hitler was raised to the Chancellorship. While the disciples of Jesus denied their master and deserted him, the sixteen comrades of Hitler died for their leader. The apostles completed the work of their lord. We hope that Hitler will be able to complete his work himself. Jesus built for heaven; Hitler for the German earth.

A piece of dictation for Munich Primary school pupils in 1934, quoted in Grunfeld's *The Hitler File*

The indoctrination of children in a Totalitarian system cannot begin too soon. They must understand the myths and the legends which the leaders of the State build around themselves.

---

*'Volk' is the German word for a 'People' – i.e. much stronger than simply 'citizens' and probably stronger than 'nation' for it implies heritage, culture, and continuity.

▲ *Suitable subject for 'art' in Nazi Germany.*

In order to maintain these myths and to ensure that no other impressions could intrude into the trained minds of its populace, the Nazi hierarchy determined that all works of art and literature should be purged and vetted.

The Nazi government of Germany first began the burning of books in 1933 but the destruction of literature and art treasures continued throughout the period of the so-called Third Reich. Anything which the leadership called 'degenerate art' was destroyed. The barbaric destruction reached a peak in 1940 with the fall of France: several hundred paintings by Miro, Picasso Ernst, Klee, Leger, etc. were burned in a garden next door to the Louvre gallery. Perhaps more importantly, books were graded according to the danger which their contents represented for a system which demanded absolute belief and obedience from its citizens:

> *Prohibited books are best divided into three groups. Group 1 is destined for destruction such as Remarque*. Group 2, such as Lenin, goes into the 'poison cabinet'. Group 3 contains doubtful cases such as B. Traven which must be carefully studied to determine whether they are afterwards to belong to Group 1 or 2.*
>
> Grunfeld, op.cit., page 249

▸▸▸▸▸▸▸▸▸▸▸▸▸▸▸ DISCUSSING THE ARGUMENTS

Definition

Totalitarianism

. . . is a system in which the State controls all aspects of its citizens' lives. The individual citizen has no 'rights' and only the State can allocate and remove 'privileges'. In a Totalitarian state everything and everyone is subservient to the wishes of the State.

Unlike the other 'isms' in this section of the book 'Totalitarianism' is not a philosophy which was ever written up as a single idea. Rather, it has emerged from a progression of political and philosophical writings and has really only been recognised as a form of political system since World War II.

To make life even more confusing it is the case that many political scientists would argue that there has *never* been a Totalitarian state. However, as there are others who argue that there has never been a true Communist state either, we are probably on firm ground in identifying and discussing a number of states which appear to have got *close* to being Totalitarian.

It must be recognised that there are Totalitarian states of both the left and of the right. Both stress 'order' and social discipline and it is a matter of continuing controversy as to whether right wing regimes have achieved a purer form of Totalitarianism than left wing ones.

On both sides of the political continuum there is a case for arguing that Authoritarian or Totalitarian regimes (see below) can develop more easily from specific social and political conditions.

Erich Fromm's classic book *Fear of Freedom* argues that the German people were especially vulnerable to Nazism because they had always been governed under an Authoritarian regime. Their 'culture', in other words, was Authoritarian. Up to 1918 the Emperor was the head of a society which, although it had all the trappings of a liberal-democracy, was still very much elitist, aristocratic and militaristic. Fromm argues that the abolition of the monarchy and the introduction of the liberal-democratic 'Weimar Republic' demanded too much.

Germans were not used to so much freedom and when confronted with economic collapse and political confusion in the late 1920s they were only too willing to accept the order and discipline promised by the Nazis.

*Remarque wrote the sober and accurate anti-war novel, *All Quiet on the Western Front*.

Definitions

The vocabulary of Authoritarian government is full of confusingly similar words which are often used to mean slightly different things:

Absolutism . . . *The doctrine of 'absolute' rule usually by one person. The word is now slightly archaic and is most often used to describe the dictatorial rule of monarchs without any check on their actions from representative assemblies. 'Limited' or 'Constitutional Monarchy' is the development of absolute monarchy in which the monarch is controlled or limited by the conditions of a constitution.*

Dictatorship . . . *The condition under which a single person, who does not claim to be a monarch, governs. The problem with both absolutism and dictatorship is that, in neither case, is the ruler really governiong alone. It is difficult to find examples of monarchs or dictators who rule without the need for support from powerful individuals or groups and who, therefore, can take decisions without consulting or considering anybody else.*

Authoritarian . . . *A form of government in which one or more persons govern and under which their decisions are enforced by institutions which they, themselves, control. Absolute monarchs and dictators are Authoritarian but, note, they need not necessarily, be Totalitarian.*

Autocracy . . . *An older word for a dictatorial system. An 'autocrat' is one who rules alone.*

The Authoritarian state is usually justified on the grounds that it enables society to be managed efficiently. Mussolini was always, slightly ironically, known in Italy as 'The man who got the trains to run on time'! Almost all dictators, both of the left and of the right justify autocratic rule in terms of a more disciplined and ordered society, a better run economy, and – of course – a more effective response to any outside threats.

The State is All

The effect of Totalitarianism in action is to ignore the conditions in which people live. Their wealth or poverty, their health or sickness, their ignorance or education, their freedom or lack of it, everything becomes subject to the ultimate decision of the State. Economics, Justice, Freedom, Equality, Welfare, etc. are concepts which are either alien to the Totalitarian concept or are treated *absolutely* differently.

> *The State is not only present, it is also past and, above all, future.*
>
> Mussolini

> *What is life ? Life is the nation. The individual must die anyway.*
>
> Hitler*

On the left of the political spectrum, Stalin's views of individual life were just as clear cut as Hitler's. Human life was merely a means to an end and his fundamental belief had always been that 'ends justify means'. During the 1930s Stalin had several millions of his own countrymen, the Kulaks (or better-off peasants), executed or sent to their deaths in labour camps because they stood in the way of his 'collectivisation' programme. In the 1940s officers were executed for 'failing' in military assaults against the Germans and, in the late 1940s and early 1950s, many Soviet soldiers returning from prisoner-of-war camps in Germany were sent directly to Soviet labour camps. Their only 'crime against the State' being that they had been captured and might have learned too much about the Western way of life in the brief months since their release by the Allies.

Pol Pot, the Communist leader of Kampuchea in the 1970s, had several million people executed out of hand in order to cleanse the State of 'bourgeois' elements.

The fundamental difference between Totalitarianism and other concepts is that there are ideas which are more important than human beings either individually or collectively. Humans exist merely to serve these ideas and have fulfilled themselves *only* if they have served.

*In a speech delivered to a public dinner after news of the surrender of the German forces in Stalingrad. Of the 250,000 men of the German 6th Army who were trapped in the city by the encircling Russians over 150,000 were killed in the fighting. Hitler refused their General permission to surrender and ordered them to fight to the last man. In the end Von Paulus surrendered anyway and 100,000 Germans were captured. Of these only about 6,000 ever returned to Germany alive.

Classes of Humanity

Explicit in certain forms of Totalitarianism is the belief that mankind can be divided into distinct and ranked groups. In the nineteenth century this type of false 'science' was very popular. It resulted in many pseudo-sciences such as 'phrenology': the belief that it is possible to tell a person's character and intelligence from the physical shape of, and the position of bumps on, the head.

At the same time philosophers were attempting to develop ideas about the origins and subsequent development of mankind. Arthur de Gobineau 'discovered' that all Europeans are descended from a race known as the Aryans. This race has now been proved never to have existed, but the idea of a mystical race of super-beings who existed before us was also strengthened by people's interpretations of the ideas of Friedrich Nietzsche (1844–1900). Nietzsche believed that certain people and societies were superior to others. They derived their superiority from the fact, he thought, that they were directly descended from the Greek and Roman civilisations. Both Greece and Rome were superior, Nietzsche said, because they were intellectually and physically better than other societies. They were 'master' societies and kept slaves to undertake the menial work.

Another feature of Nietzsche's writings which was to have a significant impact was his argument that 'slave' races were inferior not only because they had lower intellectual and physical ability but also because they based their philosophies of life on 'weak' religions like Christianity. As a religion, Nietzsche felt that Christianity was 'unintelligent, servile and unhealthy'.

It should surprise no one that Nietzche died insane but his views were to have far reaching effects.

By the closing years of the nineteenth century the basic constituents of modern **racism** were in place:

- the belief that it is possible to link physical differences to differences of intelligence or intellect;
- the belief that Europeans, especially those descended from the original 'Aryan' stock (thought to be the 'Nordic' type: fair hair, blue eyes, fair skin) were superior to all other 'races'.

Anti-Semitism and Anti-Zionism

For centuries one specific race was hounded from country to country and city to city. Although middle-eastern in origin the people of the Jewish faith had no homeland of their own and did not 'integrate' into other societies very well.

Not only did the Jews *look* different, but their religion was a demanding one, even more so than Christianity (the fundamental difference, of course, between the Jewish faith and the Christian ones is that the Jews see Jesus Christ as merely another Prophet of God). In most European cities where the Jews settled they kept themselves to themselves and were feared and despised for so doing. As long as times were good the Jews were left alone to get on with their lives, but, if things began to go wrong, the population always had an easily identifiable scapegoat – the Jews – to blame:

- in 1349 the Jews were persecuted in Germany
- in 1492 all Jews were expelled from Spain
- in 1495 all Jews were expelled from Portugal
- it was 1858 before Jews were admitted to Parliament in Britain
- in 1882 all Jews were made to live in just 15 provinces in Russia
- in 1903 Jews were massacred at Kishinyov in Russia.

▼ *A German newspaper cartoon, 1930. The cartoon vilifies the Jews. The sign in the butcher's shop advertises 'Today's speciality' as minced meat.*

In the Europe of the early twentieth century the Jews were still an isolated and easily identifiable group and they still had the same skills which had earned them the hatred of generations of Europeans: they were good business people! The Jews have had a long tradition of success in running businesses and, consequently form an attractive target if things go wrong and someone has to be blamed.

A further contribution to twentieth century political history came when the **Zionist** movement was founded by Theodor Herzl (1860–1904) in 1897. Herzl, like many fellow Jews, wanted a Jewish state to be established and Zionism was the movement which he established at a Congress in Basle in 1897 to pressure world leaders for such a state.

Zionism provided the racists with yet another target and a further 'bogey-man' with which to frighten the people of Europe. Books began to emerge which spoke of the 'international Zionist conspiracy' and which then blamed most of the troubles of the world on the Zionists and on Jews in general.

Fascism

Fascism is not based on a single, cohesive set of ideas. There is no 'Fascist Manifesto', merely a collection of writings and speeches which have become recognised as the basis of this political creed.

Strangely enough, Fascism developed from the ideals of a convinced Marxist! Before World War I, Benito Mussolini was a Marxist committed to the idea that the working class was united across national boundaries by virtue of its class relationship. He accepted the Marxist notion that 'nations' were a creation of the ruling classes and that wars were essentially arguments about capitalism which were fought out using the lives of the workers. Mussolini believed that no worker should ever kill a fellow worker simply because a member of the ruling class told him to do so.

These notions were rudely shattered by the events of World War I. Mussolini was discouraged by the fact that the workers seemed to believe more in their own country than in their links with fellow workers who just happened to be in a different and opposing army. Mussolini developed, therefore, his idea that it must be possible to achieve Socialism and Nationalism at the same time.

Mussolini formed his 'party', the 'Fascia di Combattimento' – in 1919 – the same year in which Adolf Hitler joined the German Workers Party. By a combination of the poor state of the Italian economy and an audacious 'March on Rome', Mussolini actually gained power many years before Adolf Hitler, in 1922 as opposed to 1933 for Hitler.

Fascism was a combination of many different political ideas; some appear to be 'Socialist', while others were extremely right wing. Mussolini had constructed a new political system in Italy called a 'Corporate' state (see Chapter 14) but its underlying rationale is difficult to identify. Fascism stood for:

- reducing the hours worked by workers – the 8 hour day
- abolishing class privilege
- the state control (although *not* the state ownership) of industry
- the expansion of the Italian 'empire'
- abolishing trade unions.

However, by 1929 Mussolini had developed almost the full extent of his 'fascist' ideology. It was characterised by an irrational belief in the 'glory' of Italy and in Italy's 'destiny' (which was to become, once more, a world power with its own large empire). The system became, at least in theory, – Totalitarian: Italians were required to obey their leaders (and especially, *the* leader, *Il Duce*, Mussolini himself). The Fascist state was extremely elitist: one's rank in the party determined one's privileges and it was also based on a **militarist** view of the world.

The Italians were never, however, subjected to the same degree of supervision and control as the Gemans and Fascism did not involve the persecution of Italian Jews.

Benito Mussolini (1883–1945)

Born the son of a blacksmith, Mussolini, was a Socialist and a journalist until he was disillusioned by the events of World War I.

He founded his 'Fascist' Party in 1919 (taking as his emblem the bundled sticks and axe (called the *Fasces**) of the Roman Empire) and, after failing to win more than 35 seats in the Italian Parliament, marched on Rome in 1922 with somewhere between 10,000 and 30,000 followers. Although the government wanted to use the army to disperse the Black-Shirts, the King, Victor-Emmanuel III, was sympathetic and appointed Mussolini Prime Minister.

In 1924 he had a Liberal opponent, Matteotti, murdered and, by 1929, had imposed a full Fascist state on Italy.

On 28 April 1945 (just two days before Hitler's suicide) Mussolini tried to escape from Italy to Switzerland. He was caught and shot by Italian partisans.

Mussolini attempted to solve Italy's economic problems through a programme of public works and by building up an immense army, a modern and well equipped navy, and a large air force. He used these armed forces to conquer Abyssinia (Ethiopia) in 1936.

He believed that war was 'glorious' and that people could do nothing which was of greater service to their country than to fight and die for it.

Mussolini's quotations are an effective way of demonstrating both the irrationality and the power of the Fascist 'idea':

> *Feel don't think.*
> *Mussolini is always right.*
> *Believe – Obey – Fight.*

and

> *Fascism brings back colour, force, the picturesque, the unexpected, the mystical; in short, all that counts in the soul of the crowds.*

On the subject of war, Mussolini believed it to be the primary goal of any society. War was not simply something which happened if one failed to settle differences around a conference table; it was actually *necessary*. Mussolini believed that it was necessary for superior nations to dominate inferior ones. War was, therefore, a *duty*.

> *War alone brings up to its highest tension all human energy and puts that stamp of nobility upon the people who have the courage to meet it.*

> *War is the most important thing in a man's life; as maternity is in woman's.*

NAZISM

The ideology, if it can be so called, of Nazism differs in a few very important ways from that of Fascism. Both were 'National Socialist' and combined a veneer of 'Socialist' objectives with a mass of authoritarian doctrines. Nazism, however, was:

- more irrational – it depended more on myth and legend;
- more Totalitarian (or more effectively so) – it created a very large system of secret police and informers to control the people;
- more racist – Hitler's hatred of the Jews guided much of the Nazi's activities even before they came into power.

**Fasces*: literally Latin for 'bundles'. When Mussolini established his political party he deliberately chose, as its symbol, the *Fasces* due to its strong and direct link to Italy's Roman past. The *Fasces* were bundles of rods tied together with an axe in the middle. They were a symbol of authority in Rome and were carried in front of important people to signify their status; the more bundles that preceded the person, the more important they were.

A poster of Benito Mussolini and dolf Hitler in 1938.

Myth

Part of Hitler's achievement in establishing the Nazi Party at the head of the German State was his creation of a whole mythology about Germany which became the basis of much of the belief of a generation of Germans.

There were two people who assisted in this process: one was a German composer and the other an English writer. Richard Wagner (1813–83) is famous for his powerful operas based on the German legends of ancient heroes. Those heroes (who occupy the same sort of position in German culture as King Arthur in British culture) were immortalised as super-beings. Brunhilde, Hegan and Kriemhild were the 'supporting cast' for the ultimate hero: Siegfried (who was also ideal for the role which later Nazis gave him of the ultimate blonde Aryan superman).

Houston Stewart Chamberlain (1855–1927) married Wagner's daughter, Eva, and he combined Wagner's Teutonic mythology with the racism of writers like Gobineau to produce a book which is said to have had a great deal of influence on Hitler, *Grundlagen des Neunzehnten Jahrhundert* (The Foundations of the Nineteenth Century).

The basis of Chamberlain's work was that Germany was the location of the majority of the remaining Aryans; that the Aryan race was superior to all others; and that it should, by right, rule the world:

> *. . . the Aryans are pre-eminent among all peoples; for that reason they are by right . . . the Lords of the World.*

Hitler used these myths and legends to create a powerful cultural background for his party and for the 'New Germany'. The famous documentary by the great German film director Leni Riefenstahl 'The Triumph of the Will' opens with Hitler shown descending from the clouds in his private aeroplane. The impression is meant to be one of the links between Hitler and the legendary gods and heroes.

Adolf Hitler (1889–1945)

Born in Austria, Hitler failed as an art student in pre- World War I Vienna and, in the process, developed a life-long hatred of Communists and Jews.

He rose to the rank of corporal (with Iron Cross) in the German Army during World War I and joined the German Workers' Party in 1919. Hitler changed the policies of the German Workers' Party and changed its name in 1921 to **Nationalsozialistische Deutsche Arbeiterpartei** (the National Socialist German Workers' Party).

Even the Germans quickly shortened the name to the **Nazi** party.

In 1923 Hitler led an unsuccessful revolt (The Munich *putsch*) against the government (known as the Weimar Government after the post-war agreement which set it up). He was given a light jail sentence of five years of which he served just nine months.

While in prison he began writing the book for which he is best known and which set out his beliefs and his intentions: *Mein Kampf* ('My Struggle').

By 1930, and using a variety of techniques including violence, the Nazis had become the second largest party in the German Parliament (the Reichstag). By 1932 they had become the largest party and in 1933 Hitler was made Chancellor.

He led Germany throughout World War II and, facing total defeat, committed suicide in Berlin in April 1945.

Totalitarianism

Hitler's Germany was a state in which the people were supervised more tha in any other state ever before with the exception only of Stalinist Russi Hitler abolished all other political parties and imprisoned, in concentratio camps, their leaders and chief sympathisers. He created links between th party and almost every facet of German life; workers' savings schemes an holidays were organised by the party; school-children could belong t separate 'Youth' sections of the party; eventually Hitler ordered his speciall selected SS (Schutz Staffel) to inter-breed in order to create a 'super-race German women were viewed as having an extremely submissive an secondary role. They were there to provide homes and to bear and bring u the new super-race of 'Nordic' Germans. For the first few years of the wa and in spite of the advice of his industrial ministers, Hitler refused to allo German women to be conscripted into the factories (unlike their counterpar

► *Communists are rounded up in Berlin in March 1933.*

in Britain who did much to increase production and to release men for the fighting services).

Control of the population was exercised through a massive system of secret police together with undercover police and informers. Children were encouraged to (and some did) inform on their parents if they expressed opposition to Hitler.

Racism

Of all the identifying characteristics of Nazism, it is racism which is the most powerful. Hitler developed a virulent (many would say, plain evil) account of the racial system.

According to Hitler there were three 'classes' of humanity:

A Culture creating humanity These were the cream of the human race; the most intelligent, the strongest and the healthiest. According to Hitler they consisted of those peoples who came from (originally) the 'Nordic' countries of Scandinavia, Germany, the Netherlands, and Britain. The heritage of these countries was pure 'Aryan' (based on the civilisations of India, Persia, Egypt, Greece and Rome) and, therefore, they had the only chance of reviving the Aryan race. Each of these societies had been 'diluted' by foreign stock (some beyond redemption such as Persia, Egypt and Greece). The only way in which the super-race of pure Aryans could be re-established was from a 'Nordic' base and by careful selection from amongst even those populations.

> *Take away the Nordic Germans and nothing remains but the dance of the apes.*
>
> Adolf Hitler, *Mein Kampf*, 1924

B Culture Bearing Humanity These were racially inferior. They could be 'civilised', according to Hitler, but only as long as they were led by superior races and were not 'corrupted' by lesser races. The peoples of the 'Latin' countries (Spain, Portugal, Italy) were amongst this group as were the Slavs and all Orientals.

C Culture Destroying Beings Into this category Hitler placed Negroes, gypsies and Jews. They could not be called human and, therefore, need not be treated as such. This evil idea eventually led to the deliberate murder, by Hitler's 'supermen' of an estimated nine million people: over six million of them were Jews. The others were Slavs, Russians, gypsies, negroes and European Socialists from Germany and occupied countries.

Little more needs to be said about the ultimate ends of racist ideas but a final quotation from *Mein Kampf* will demonstrate not only the depth to which such ideas can sink but also the mixed metaphors with which Hitler expounded his 'theories':

> *The Jew is a maggot in a rotting corpse . . . a germ carrier . . . a drone that slowly sucks a people's blood out of its pores . . . the people's vampire.*

STALIN'S RUSSIA

In Soviet Russia Stalin used the full power of state police and military strength to impose his view of Russia's future.

At the top the State Planning Commission (GOSPLAN) decided on the production of every product from electrical power stations to shirts and from aircraft to toys. It initiated a series of five year plans which controlled and regimented Soviet production. The result was that, between 1927 and 1939 the Soviet Union overtook Britain as an industrial producer.

НЕ ПОСТУПИМОСЬ У ЛЕНІНОВІЙ СПРАВ

► *Stalinist industrialization poster.*

The Soviet citizen was made constantly aware of Stalin's central objective

> *We are fifty or one hundred years behind the advanced countries. We mus make good this lag in ten years. Either we do it or they crush us!*

Any citizen who failed to live up to the exacting standards required of ther might find themselves in a Labour Camp run by the secret police, th NKVD. At one point it was estimated that the Labour Camps contained ove 10 million people.

Stalin withdrew Lenin's reforms which, although the Land Decree of 191 had never intended it, allowed the peasants to own and to work their ow land. The objective was to make agriculture more efficient by creating ver large State farms on which the best mechanised methods of moder agriculture could be used. In order to make the changeover to 'collectivised agriculture work, he had millions of the richer farmers (the Kulaks) sent t Labour Camps, deported to remoter parts of the country, or put to death Stalin's Russia was a brutal, terrorised society in which the merest hin of opposition to Stalin would be reported through the network of informer and police agents and would result in imprisonment, forced labour or eve death.

At the top of the Communist Party Stalin began, from 1934, a ruthles series of purges of his opponents. Bukharin, Kirov, Kamenev, Zinoviev and abroad, Trotsky, were all assassinated or executed. From the 139 member of the 1934 Central Committee 98 were arrested and many were shot; of th 1,966 delegates to the Party Congress of 1934, 1,108 were arrested and 'deal with' in similar fashion. Stalin treated the Red Army in the same way, h had 13 out of 15 Generals executed as well as removing almost two-thirds o the senior officer grades.

Stalin's Russia became an almost completely Totalitarian society. Fron the purges of the 1930s the control necessary during the 'Great Patriotic War (World War II) meant that, by 1945, the population were subject to extensiv and all-pervading control. The Christian and Muslim religions wer proscribed, economic life totally controlled from the centre, social life rigidl controlled, entertainment strictly censored, and internal travel restricted b the use of 'internal passports'. Every block of flats, every street, every hamle had its political commissars and its network of informers. Little went o without the authorities becoming aware of it and people 'disappeared' o became 'non-persons' for the slightest degree of protest or dissent.

It should be noted, however, that the tendency towards Totalitarianism i Russia did not begin with Stalin. The country had been noted for its rigi control of its citizens since the middle ages and the brutality of its rulers wa widely recognised long before 'Uncle Joe' controlled the Soviet Union. As onl one example, Tsar Nicholas II (ruled 1894–1917) and his powerful Tsarina, Alexandra, were determined to eradicate all ideas, beliefs and customs with which they disagreed.

OTHER TOTALITARIAN REGIMES

Totalitarianism has yet to be practised in its purest form. In the sense of 'total' control of a society and its people's lives only fiction has yet demonstrated the true Totalitarian state.

In *Animal Farm* and *Nineteen Eighty-four* George Orwell painted pictures of the Totalitarian society and what it entailed. His nightmare view of a world in which the state saw and heard everything and in which the population was misled in order to perpetuate the system was slightly more extreme than Nazi Germany or Stalinist Russia.

Only 'slightly' because, in both those societies, the governments made sure that they received the maximum possible feedback about the thoughts and actions of individuals. Those who opposed were 'dealt with'. In both societies, also, the personality cult of the leader was taken to extremes. 'Big Brother' in *Nineteen Eighty-four* was given a benevolent, avuncular image (until a citizen opposed him that is). In Nazi Germany and Stalinist Russia the leaders were shown as strong men, whose wills could not be denied and who were always right.

Scene from the film of George)rwell's Animal Farm. *Major peaks to the other animals after his dream'.*

There is, however, one further example of a state in which the leader attempted to control *everything*, to guide every aspect of not only the political arena but every facet of the people's lives.

In Cambodia (now Kampuchea) in the 1970s Pol Pot tried to change and control an entire society of millions of people. He attempted to obliterate their past culture and everything that the old society stood for. He decided that cities were the source of all modern culture and that, therefore, they should be destroyed. In consequence every inhabitant of the cities was forced to march out into the countryside. Pol Pot decided that humour was a way of continuing a culture and part of the way people were socialised. He, therefore, ordered that humour was banned. Anyone seen laughing or even smiling was killed and all middle-class professionals were either killed or were sent to work as peasants on the land. Millions died during Pol Pot's brief span of power.

TOTALITARIANISM IN BRITAIN

If Totalitarianism represents a belief that the entire population should exis solely for the greater glory of the State and, if it entails the supervision of a activity from sport to business and from family life to humour and music then Britain has never even come close to experiencing a Totalitarian regime

During the Interregnum which followed the end of the English Civil Wa Oliver Cromwell banned most pastimes and closed theatres. These were see as 'sinful' practices. At the same time Cromwell's men were sent throughou the country to destroy any images or statues in churches and Catholics wer persecuted wherever they were found. This was not, however, a 'Totalitaria regime in the modern sense.

In modern times the British Union of Fascists under Sir Oswald Mosle tried to imitate the 'success' of Mussolini's Fascists. They organised meeting and, like today's neo-Nazis, employed Black-Shirted thugs to expel anyon they did not think ought to attend or to break up rival meetings. The battle between the Communists and the Fascists during the early 1930s became s widespread that the government passed the Incitement to Disaffection Ac of 1934 and the Public Order Act of 1936. The Fascists were almost identic to their Italian model and never achieved any real support in the UK. Whe World War II began Sir Oswald Mosley was imprisoned but was released i 1943.

The Extreme Right in Modern Times

Mosley's Fascists went into an understandable decline after World War I but the bulk of the movement survived in the form of 'loyalist' an 'nationalist' groupings. One of them, the League of Empire Loyalists, wa led by A.K. Chesterton, the editor of Mosley's party newspaper *Th Blackshirt.*

In early 1967 a number of these right wing groups came together to form the **National Front.** They were:

League of Empire Loyalists
British National Party, and the
Racial Preservation Society.

In 1968 these were joined by the Greater Britain Movement.

The peak membership of the National Front was attained during the mid 1970's when it is estimated that it had around 20,000 members. Since the the movement has split into several different organisations some of whic have chosen to go the paramilitary route (SS Wotan 88, etc.).

The National Front's policies have usually centred on a deep racialist cor and may be listed as follows:

- a complete end to coloured immigration,
- compulsory repatriation of all non-whites,
- racial segregation in schools while these policies are being implemented,
- abolition of trade unions,
- withdrawal from the EEC and from NATO,
- massive expansion of military strength,
- a steady dismantling and eventual end of the Welfare State.

The policies have included, at various times, such additional features as th proposal that blacks should not have either jobs or homes while there ar any white people without them; and the proposition that trade union leader who 'sabotage national recovery' should be jailed without trial.

The Front developed its own 'Honour Guard' of tough fighters and use them to police its own meetings and to break up those of opposing group (especially those of the extreme left). It also attempts to recruit young peopl with special literature distributed at the gates of some schools and makes a point of trying to recruit football hooligans (the latter are employed as wha the NF leaders have called 'shock troops').

The movement has all the elements of a potentially Totalitarian system. It believes in the myth of British supremacy, it has developed the usual outside enemies (blacks and Jews), it stresses feelings rather than rationality, and it demands total obedience from its followers.

> *The day that our followers lose their capacity to hate will be the day that they lose their power and their will to achieve anything at all.*
>
> Martin Tyndall; Leader of the National Front (at a rally in Tunbridge Wells in 1974).

The Future

The fact that no single, Totalitarian movement of either the right or the left has ever taken power in Britain is, however, no guarantee that a *trend* towards Totalitarianism would not occur. It is possible that a series of Governments of both left and right might increase the degree to which they control the lives of the population and the influence which they have on all aspects of economic, political and social affairs.

George Orwell thought that he could discern such a trend in the tendency of modern technology to allow greater power to reside in the centre. In *Nineteen Eighty-four* Orwell predicted that technology would allow a single ruler to have almost unlimited power to govern the lives of people and, more importantly, to keep them unaware of the true situation in the world. The technology of the late 1980s is, in reality, much more dangerous than even Orwell could have imagined.

Miniaturisation of electronic components means that people's lives can be spied upon without their being aware of it. Computers of immense power are either available or are in development which can listen to hundreds of telephone conversations at a time and automatically record only those in which key words are mentioned. Similar computers can keep track of every citizen from the cradle to the grave.

It is a long way from having the *potential* to establish a Totalitarian state to actually creating one, but the ideology of Totalitarianism: of the subjugation of the individual to the state, of the glorification of war, and of the right of the people who hold power in the state to make use of other people, must never be taken lightly. There may be room for debate about the way in which countries are governed and about the economic and social goals which they set themselves but there can never be any doubt that human beings remain the central concern of the state and that the state exists to serve its inhabitants not the other way round.

> *If you want a picture of the future, imagine a boot stamping on a human face – forever.*
>
> George Orwell, *Nineteen Eighty-four*

EXAMINATION QUESTIONS

1 Nazism and Communism have the same collectivist roots. Discuss. (London, June 1983,3)

2 What were the theoretical fundamentals of Nazism as an ideology? (London, June 1982,3)

3 Do the terms 'left' and 'right' have any significance in classifying totalitarian regimes? (London, June 1980,3)

4 Do you agree with the Marxist interpretation of Fascism as the political form of Capitalism in crisis? (London, Jan 1980,3)

5 Had the Nazis any right to call themselves National Socialists? (London, June 1983,3)

NOW READ ON . . .

Leonard Schapiro *Totalitarianism* Macmillan, 1972
A classic on the subject.
S. G. Payne *Falange: A History of Spanish Fasicsm*
The Falange was the Fascist movement in Spain which supported Franc
in power longer than any other Fascist leader
Eugene Weber *Varieties of Fascism New English Library, New York, 196*
A comprehensive survey of the varieties from Italy to Japan, and fron
Germany to Rumania.
Stan Taylor *The National Front in English Politics* Macmillan, 1982
One of the few good surveys of the NF's activities and role.

There are a variety of books which give graphic accounts of thes Totalitarian systems and all of us should be aware of the dangers presente by those who seek to impose them. Read one or more of the following:

I. Solzhenitzyn *One Day in the Life of Ivan Denisovitch*
George Orwell *Animal Farm; Nineteen Eighty-four*
William Shirer *The History of the Third Reich*
provides rich detail of the inner workings of a state which came clos to the Totalitarian *ideal.*
Adolf Hitler *Mein Kampf*
Benito Mussolini *Opera Omnia* (extremely lengthy); *My Autobiography*
R. Wilford 'Fascism' in R. Eccleshall *et al. Political Ideologies* Hutchinson 1985

16 Constitution

BASIC PRINCIPLES

Key Concepts

Power	A constitution is a set of rules for the exercise and distribution of power and a means of restraining the use of power through written rules together with unwritten conventions.
Authority and Legitimacy	The conferring of authority and the establishment of legitimacy may be achieved by constitutional methods.
Sovereignty	This is raised in the constitutional principle of the supremacy of parliament, or other ruling body, or of the Constitution itself, as in the USA.
Equality and Freedom	These concepts are raised in constitutional guarantees of political freedom and equality.
Rights and duties	These can be seen in arguments over whether Britain should now have a Bill of Rights.

DISCUSSING THE ARGUMENTS

Power

Today many political scientists reject the whole idea of studying constitutions for they argue that constitutions do not provide a clear account of, or guide to, actual political practice in any country.

It is said that extra-constitutional influences, such as pressure groups, political parties, the armed forces, etc., are vital to an understanding of political pressures, but usually their functions are not covered by constitutions. Nearly all states have written constitutions but this is seen to be no safeguard against them being ignored in the actual *conduct* of politics.

However, without knowing at least what the rules are supposed to be, it may be hard to judge governments on their record of ensuring justice, freedom, electoral choice etc. It may also be helpful to know which of the rules are being broken and with what justification.

Written/unwritten Constitutions

Definition

Constitution

The word 'constitution' for an American citizen would imply a single document drawn up and ratified at a particular point in history, although subsequently amended. A constitution, however, need not necessarily be written. Constitutional arrangements in a country may be widely accepted and explicitly followed but not set out in a single specific document.

So long as the essential elements are deeply ingrained in the thinking of those who practise politics, then, although they may only be established in common law or observed by tradition, they can still act as effective checks on the operation of government.

The trend towards written constitutions since the eighteenth century has, however, influenced most countries, with Britain as the only major one which has resisted this influence. In Britain, however, although there is no single constitutional document, most of the principles are to be found in written form in ordinary legal statutes.

Flexibility/Rigidity

The 'flexibility' or 'rigidity' of a constitution is measured in terms of how easily the provisions contained in the constitution can be amended. The concept of a constitution implies a degree of rigidity or stability because the aim is often to create safeguards for political practices and values that are considered fundamental. One of the usual safeguards is to make it ver difficult to change these practices without considerable deliberation.

In countries with a written constitution, if conflict arises between ordinar statutes and the constitution, then the latter will always prevail. Fc example, the American constitution is the 'supreme law of the land'.

In order to ensure the survival of fundamental constitutional practices mos written constitutions can only be amended by a set of special procedure separate from those for changing the ordinary law of the land. This wi usually be a specific majority in the legislature and more than a simpl majority, perhaps two thirds or three quarters.

Some constitutions can only be changed by the same resolution bein passed more than once and, even then, possibly subject to popula ratification by a referendum. In a federal system, such as the USA, th constituent states are also involved in the process of constitution amendment.

Distribution and Limitation of Power

Most written constitutions contain provisions which set out the relativ powers of each branch of government and how this power will be limited The lack of a written constitution does not necessarily change this feature for the establishment of limitations on the exercise of political power will b developed by historic tradition and custom, and may well be observed a rigidly as in written constitutions.

The rules also generally include a statement about who is to perform th executive, legislative and judicial functions of government, in what form, an sometimes, includes sets of rules for their enactment. These arrangements i many countries have led to a clear and formal **separation of powers** betwee the three branches. (See Legislatures Chapter 17.)

Constitutional Constraints of Power in Britain

A major element in the debate on the nature of the British constitution i whether one exists at all.

If a constitution consists of a single written document which sets out:

- rules and procedures of government
- allocation of power to various institutions
- establishes relationships between institutions
- identifies rights and duties of citizens.

Then on this basis the British constitution does not qualify.

This is not to imply that Britain does not possess established procedure for the conduct of political affairs through its institutions of government. I is just that they are not set down in a single document.

As we have established, much of the British constitution is, in fact, written There are many great statutes which lay out the mode of conduct of politica affairs and establish the rights and freedom of British citizens. Example range from Magna Carta up to recent legislation outlawing discriminatior on the grounds of race or sex.

The lack of a single written constitution can be accounted for, to a large extent, by historical reasons. The constitution has developed over a long period and has altered as political circumstances have demanded.

Written constitutions have a fairly short history dating back to the US Constitution (1787) and since then have been adopted in many countries. In Britain, in spite of major constitutional changes, no completely new system or set of values has been adopted in the form of a written constitution in a single document.

The result is that a large proportion of the British constitution is the outcome of 'evolutionary' rather than 'revolutionary' change and the need for a concise 'rule book' to dictate the play of the political game has not arisen.

Constitutional Change in Britain

Written constitutions have been associated with the development of modern democracy, and are generally seen as safeguards against the exercise of arbitrary power. The essential features of constitutions however vary considerably.

Constitutions may be:

- written or unwritten
- republican or monarchical
- presidential
- federal or unitary
- flexible or rigid.

One of the 'essential features' of the British constitution is claimed to be its flexibility. The procedures to alter or repeal a piece of legislation which is held to be of great constitutional significance are exactly the same as for any other legislation. A bill to amend voting rights or change civil liberties would have to go through exactly the same legislative procedures as ones to change levels of taxation or allow more flexible Sunday trading.

There is simply no distinction made between legislation which is seen as 'constitutional' and therefore requires careful consideration before any change is made to it, and any other Acts of Parliament. So it may be difficult to decide when a government is acting 'unconstitutionally'.

A government could well produce a list of Acts which it considers essentially 'constitutional' and pledge itself to interfere with them only with the greatest reluctance. However, different governments would certainly have different items on that list.

Even if the list was not so different from one government to another, the relative importance of the items probably would be. All elements in a constitution will not be considered equally important and, therefore, reaction to changing one element will not necessarily be the same as changing another. There will also always be arguments over what comprise 'good' change and 'bad' change.

Britain is unique, for most states do have a written constitution although the existence of such is no guarantee of the freedom, liberty, etc. that may be mentioned in the document. Nor do written constitutions necessarily last any longer. France, for example, has had over a dozen constitutions since the revolution of 1789.

By contrast Britain, despite the ease of constitutional change, takes a pride in the fact that many principles have remained untouched for centuries.

Example

Some demands were heard during the 1987 General Election campaign for a reduction in the voting age from 18 to 16 years. Sixteen year olds have to pay tax if they work, so should there be taxation without representation? Others argue that most young people by the age of 16 are not mature enough to understand the political choices presented by an election.

Disadvantages of Written Constitutions

It must also not be assumed that all written constitutions are a clear and concise statement. Some are remarkably vague about the allocation of power and the rights and duties of the citizens.

Another difficulty for written constitutions, in comparison to the British constitution, lies in how they are changed. Too much rigidity may result in the system becoming outdated and leading to the necessity for its complete overthrow. How should a balance be struck between maintaining, say, vital civil rights and yet not allowing a small obdurate minority to hold up necessary social change by claiming the protection of the constitution?

Another problem surrounds the selection of which rights to include as 'constitutional' and therefore protect from change by the constitution. Should the right to go on strike be a constitutional 'right', even if it is exercised in circumstances that could threaten the security of the nation? Also at what point does an issue that was not relevant when the constitution was formulated take on such significance that constitutional change is required?

Example

The US constitution is vague about the powers of the President and has led to the situation where much Presidential power is based upon established practice, not written rules.

For example, the question of votes for women and young people, as well a issues such as equal rights for minorities have been raised in this context.

Further questions about written constitutions also arise in terms of wha aspects of life should be considered important enough to be included in th constitution and given protection against change by government.

Example

In the USA public opinion has long favoured tighter control on the sale of guns but one difficulty in achieving this is the constitutional right to 'bear arms' which is cited by lobbies wishing to preserve the status quo.

Example

In Eire abortion has become a constitutional issue. The Eire constitution has been amended to make it impossible for any future constitutional amendment to be passed allowing abortion. In other countries such an issue would be seen as a matter of personal conscience and not a question of constitutional debate.

The US constitution was also amended at one point in order to regulate activities normally thought to be a matter of personal choice. The 18th amendment was passed to prohibit the production, sale and consumption of alcohol: this however was repealed by the 21st amendment.

► *Police making a haul from bootleggers during prohibition in the USA.*

Advantages of Written Constitutions

If many problems can be associated with written constitutions, why is it tha nearly all countries with the notable exception of Britain, accept the need t have a political 'rule book' to regulate the conduct of policies?

The advantage of a written constitution is that it should make it possibl to identify clearly the framework of power within which the politica institutions operate. In this way arguments over the 'rules of the game' ca be reduced.

As we have tried to establish, in Britain it is sometimes very difficul to come to a clear understanding of when a government is actin 'constitutionally' or not. By highlighting certain institutions and identifyin their importance in a written document, a significant constitutional status i attached to them, and, it is hoped, this will encourage a sense of reluctance when citizens contemplate change.

A written constitution also provides a definite yardstick against which the performance of governments can be measured. Written constitutions have often been drawn up in new nations or where an existing one has undergone a major political upheaval, such as a revolution. The introduction of a code of political behaviour is often an attempt to restore political order and generate a climate of political stability. Not that this always works of course!

A constitution that is drawn up after a revolution may merely be a way of consolidating the position of the victors in the political struggle and, therefore, be unlikely to constitute a recipe for national solidarity. A constitution which reflects the aspirations of only one group or class is likely to fail. The need to generate a feeling of national unity has been particularly acute for emergent nations in Africa in the period of post-colonial independence.

Example

To change the US constitution three-quarters of state legislatures in addition to two-thirds of the Congress have to accept a constitutional change. In effect it is very hard to introduce successful amendments with both sides able to exercise a veto.

Written constitutions in federal political systems often have, as their major objective, the establishment of the relationships between national government and the governments of the constituent states. Unlike Britain's unitary system, political power is shared with neither side able to impinge upon the sphere of activity of the other, with the constitution there to codify the division of labour. In these circumstances the constituent region or states will have a say in constitutional amendments to guarantee their position.

Change can be brought about in the US constitution by the Supreme Court without formal amendment, through its power to interpret the meaning of the constitution.

Example

Racial segregation in US schools was declared to be unconstitutional in 1954, in the case of Brown versus Topeka Board of Education. The Supreme Court in its judgement overturned several earlier interpretations which had taken a different view. This change in constitutional interpretation, however, had little impact on social and political practices in many parts of the USA. For, despite such a ruling by the Supreme Court, a long campaign had to be fought by civil rights protestors to ensure an end to institutionalised educational discrimination on racial grounds.

Stable political systems will be more likely to guarantee human rights, adult suffrage, liberty, equality, etc. whether they have a written or unwritten constitution. The content of the constitution may not be so important for what really matters is how much is accepted by the people. Public opinion will be the ultimate factor that decides constitutional rules and practices.

THE SURVIVAL OF THE BRITISH CONSTITUTION

The unwritten British constitution has survived possibly because the political struggles that have affected other countries were fought out much earlier in Britain. The conflict between Crown and Parliament was settled by a civil war in the seventeenth century, and the rules that have developed since for the settling of political disputes have become well established. Political contestants have generally not attempted to challenge the fundamental rules through a preference for violence over constitutional methods. Britain is perhaps just fortunate in not having undergone traumatic political upheaval, revolution or foreign invasion over a long period, thereby allowing relatively stable political development to take place. There is nothing inherently superior in Britain's constitutional arrangements: they should be judged in relation to her political past.

The unwritten constitutional arrangements have proved to be largel successful in maintaining political institutions, and as a result they have bee retained. This can provide no absolute guarantee for the future success c Britain's constitutional arrangements, and growing political tension in som areas of political life have led to calls for the institution of a writte constitution.

Conventions of the Constitution

Most governmental systems, even those with written constitutions, observe number of unwritten and non-legal rules in the conduct of political affair: Often those rules have arisen as a way of clarifying the application of th written parts. In Britain the unwritten rules are called 'conventions' and pla a central part in the theory of the constitution. Exactly which practices cour as a 'convention', however, is open to debate. The acceptance of convention does help fill the gap in the exercise of discretionary power where no writte rules exist, and many important areas of the British constitution are subje to the working of conventions. The exercise of the prerogatives of the Crow are in many instances dictated by **convention** not law.

The importance of constitutional conventions is widely recognised an accepted as necessary for the effective functioning of government. Th problem lies in identifying which 'working practices' of government can b separated out and given this status. By implication those which *are* shoul not be readily abandoned but considered to be as important as rules lai down in constitutionally important legislation.

Just because politicians and public officials have always acted in a certai way does not necessarily imply they will always continue to do so, or that i is the best way to act. Perhaps it is only when they feel that their actions ar guided by a convention that their practices become established as convention.

Precedent will obviously be a primary factor in deciding which practice count as a convention, but it may be simply that those involved considere it appropriate to adopt a particular way of working and that no grea unwritten constitutional rule has developed. Some conventions are simpl negative, in that they have developed as a means of preventing certain type of behaviour.

A breach of a convention, however, does not involve any breach of the law so no redress would be available through the courts. Political solutions wil have to be used in dealing with any such breach and any subsequent brea with convention will probably just demonstrate that it is no longer relevant One or two breaks with a convention, however, will not necessarily mean i has ceased to be applicable.

Example

The Royal Assent for Acts of Parliament is governed by convention, as are practices of appointing and dismissing ministers and the dissolution of Parliament.

Most of the functioning of the office of the Prime Minister and the Cabinet are not determined by statute but by convention, as is the conduct of the relationships between ministers and civil servants.

Example

Although Parliament possesses sovereign power it is a well established principle of the British constitution that it is not used to abuse the rights of minorities.

Example

In 1932 the convention of 'collective responsibility' in cabinet decision making whereby all ministers share responsibility for, and publicly defend cabinet policy was suspended. The suspension applied only to one issue and was reintroduced after the matter was settled.

A similar suspension occurred in 1975 when Labour cabinet ministers, who disagreed with Britain's membership of the EEC, were allowed to publicly say so during the campaign on the referendum which was held to decide on the Labour Government's renegotiated terms for continued entry.

Constitutional or Unconstitutional?

The question of 'constitutionality' was raised during Mrs Thatcher's secon term of office 1983–87, in relation to the appointment of senior civil servants

The convention followed by most Prime Ministers was that, although they were constitutionally empowered to make civil service appointments, their choice followed very closely the names recommended by the civil service itself. Mrs Thatcher however expressed dissatisfaction with some of the people suggested to her, particularly senior appointments in Treasury. So she exercised her established constitutional powers and made several changes to the recommended list.

Critics of this action claimed Mrs Thatcher had acted 'unconstitutionally' in breaking with convention. Mrs Thatcher said she had simply exercised the constitutional powers invested in the office of prime minister. The Leader of the Opposition, Mr Neil Kinnock, promised that if he were Prime Minister he would return to the former practice and accept the recommended list.

Why are Conventions Obeyed?

These unwritten, non-legal rules are generally obeyed because they make sense to the people who are governed by them. The problem with breaking them is that the results of doing so will be unpredictable and could turn out much worse than observing the convention.

Many other aspects of life are not controlled by the application of written rules, so why should this not apply in politics? Providing the established conventions reflect existing practice and they work, why break them or change them? There is still the problem however in obeying conventions of deciding exactly which practices constitute a 'convention of the constitution'.

One way of solving this problem would be to write them down and give them legal status. The process of doing so would lead to politicians and constitutional lawyers having to address the problem and come up with an agreed set of principles. These could then be enforced by the courts, who could quickly identify any transgressions of the rules. The assumption is that with a legal status for conventions, politicians and public officials would be less likely to break them. A major difficulty, however, lies in the fact that many conventions are quite general in nature.

Example

'Ministerial responsibility' makes an individual minister responsible to Parliament for the conduct of civil servants in his department. It also implies that if things have gone badly wrong, the minister may be called upon to resign.

What the convention does not do is to establish much predictability about the circumstances under which a minister should resign. Other than a successful vote of 'no confidence' in a minister by the House of Commons, it seems hard to see what circumstances for resignation could be written into a set of rules.

Example

It is a convention that the Monarch should grant a dissolution of Parliament to a Prime Minister so that a general election can take place. However, would it be wise to say that this must now be a legal requirement? Such a situation could cause a problem for a Monarch who might wish to restrain a Prime Minister from calling an election in circumstances that could damage the national interest.

The prerogative powers of the Crown would also throw up problems in codifying conventions.

The problem in identifying and understanding the working of the unwritten rules of the constitution is that unpredictability is nearly always present. A rule, if it is to be effective, whether it is written down or not, should give an indication of what should happen if it is applied. Conventions often do not.

AUTHORITY AND LEGITIMACY

As we have tried to establish, a constitution is a device which sets limits on the exercise of power by government, and outlines the distribution of that power between various institutions of government. A constitution will also give authority to the government when exercising the power granted and thereby give legitimacy to its actions. In order for this to come about, the constitution will, however, have to reflect and incorporate the essential political values of the people.

In considering whether a constitution does this, we have to return to the question of flexibility. In order to sustain its claim to have authority and legitimacy, the principles of the constitution may have to change.

The authority that the constitution can bestow upon a government cannot be fixed for all time. Political practices must change if necessary, and governments have to be prepared to accept changing views on the nature of the constitution.

This is what supporters of British constitutional arrangements claim to be its real strength: constitutional principles evolve and change in accordance with the changing political values and desires of the British people.

The benefits for government are great in terms of enhanced authority if it is seen to act in concert with the widely accepted values that are enshrined in the constitution. Conversely the charge of acting 'unconstitutionally' although hard to prove, and carrying no legal penalties, is one which governments will always seek to strongly rebut.

Constitutionalism

A distinction should also be drawn between 'constitutionalism' and 'constitution'. Most states possess a constitution, but this is no indication of the type of political system that the constitution will sustain.

A constitution may imbue government with power, but the power should not be so tightly roped in by checks and balances and prohibitions as to cripple its effectiveness. A balance has to be struck between the need to prevent the abuse of power with subsequent threat to political freedoms and the need to have an effective system of government which allows a degree of discretion in the exercise of constitutional powers. In Britain a compromise has been found in the development of the concept of responsible government.

Definition

Constitutionalism
Constitutionalism has fairly specific connotations and is associated with the concept of the rule of law. It implies that government should not solely pursue its own wishes, but should conduct its affairs in an equitable manner.

Example

The US constitution was drawn up with the object of preventing the abuse of power. The President can veto legislation from Congress, Congress holds the 'purse-strings' of American government and can thereby limit presidential activity, and the Supreme Court can sit in judgement on the 'constitutionality' of all their actions.

Responsible Government

Although the British constitution puts considerable power into the hands of government, nonetheless, we expect our politicians to exercise their duties in a responsible manner. This implies more than just being 'responsive' to the dictats of public opinion.

In Britain we feel that politicians have a duty to look after the interest of the whole nation, which will in itself imbue a sense of responsibility and caution in the exercise of power. This concept of responsible government, it is claimed, to a large extent, removes the need for the checks and balances and vetoes that are applied in other constitutions, which are intended to prevent politicians taking advantage of the constitutional power granted to them.

The concept of responsibility in the British constitution is seen clearly in the notions of 'individual ministerial responsibility', and 'collective responsibility'. (See Chapters 18 and 20 on The Executive and Administration.)

Rule of Law

Restraints are a core element in a constitution for, simply by establishing a power structure for governments, any constitution will thereby impose restraints. The establishment of certain procedures for governmental action in itself rules out others. However, constitutions usually go further in specifically limiting power by creating fixed and fair ways of conducting government.

One of the traditional ways the British 'constitution' ensures equitable behaviour lies in the Rule of Law. The assumption is that every person who holds office is subject to the limitations of the law that provides the authority for that office. The actions of the official can then be subjected to scrutiny by an independent judiciary and judged to be justified, or not, by law. So in this way the Rule of Law can act as restraint on government, with the courts being able to ensure that standards of adjudication are the same. The Rule of Law can then, one hopes, ensure certainty and predictability.

The impact of the Rule of Law as a limitation of government can be questioned however. A difficulty arises with the discretionary power which is often given to officials in order to make it possible for them to carry out their duties. Legislation which grants authority to officials rarely can be very precise in laying down exactly how that power is exercised. Discretion has to be allowed. The courts, as a result, are not the best place to deal with such matters. Ordinary judges will not have the knowledge of, often very detailed, administrative rules and procedures, to make a judgement in cases involving a dispute between a citizen and the state. One answer to this problem would be to introduce a separate system of judicial control to deal with disputes of this nature.

Example

In France there is a separate system of administrative law with its own courts. It is headed by the 'Conseil d'Etat' and has judges who are skilled in public administration and public law.

In Britain disputes between the citizen and the state are not normally settled in the ordinary courts but through a variety of independent tribunals. Critics of this practice say that it lacks uniformity, and the citizen cannot always be guaranteed that his or her problem will even have a tribunal to deal with it.

Appeals from such tribunals are not uniform and are sometimes heard by the government minister whose actions prompted the case originally. There is a Council of Tribunals which attempts to extend uniformity, but in Britain, there is nothing that could be confidently described as a 'system' for the redress of grievance.

The idea of an independent means of conciliation between citizen and the state was expanded by the creation of the Parliamentary Commissioner for Administration or 'Ombudsman' in 1967. He has the job of settling disputes when 'maladministration' is alleged in the actions of civil servants. The Commissioner has no formal legal powers to enforce his decisions, but generally government departments have responded positively to any criticisms in his reports.

This experiment has now been extended by the creation of similar Commissioners for the National Health Service and for local government. Critics, however, claim their sphere of activity is far too limited. The NHS Commissioner cannot, for example, investigate matters involving 'clinical judgement' and there is a large area of local government activity which is outside the ambit of the local government commissioners.

Sovereignty

The law in Britain assumes that Parliament possesses the power to enact, amend, or repeal any legislation whatsoever. Parliament is even empowered to introduce retrospective legislation. No court in Britain has the ability to question the validity of an Act of Parliament and all other law making bodies are subservient to Parliament. Although Britain is a unitary state there are special legal provisions that apply to Ulster, Wales and Scotland, but ultimately all can be amended or repealed by Parliament. Parliament possesses all executive, legislative, and judicial authority, which stands in sharp contrast to countries such as the USA, which have separated these powers in three institutions.

Even though executive power in Britain is exercised by the Prime Minister and Cabinet, they have to command a parliamentary majority in order to guarantee that their wishes are implemented. No Act of Parliament can be restrained by higher law with the exception of European Community laws to which Britain is bound by the Treaty of Rome.

There is, however, potentially nothing to prevent a future government taking Britain out of the European Community and thereby 'regaining' this sovereignty for Parliament. This is possible for, despite the importance that can be attached to Britain's continued membership, no Parliament can 'bind its successor'. This 'legal' view of sovereignty is rather limited and must be contrasted with 'political' sovereignty.

The legal view, as we have seen, implies that potentially no restriction exists on Parliament's ability to make law. Political sovereignty implies that sovereignty is constrained by public and electoral opinion. The overall responsibility of Parliament is to act in the best interests of the nation and this, therefore, places a political limit on sovereignty. So the argument is that, if Parliament enacted law which was so awful and unacceptable to the majority of the people, Parliament would simply be ignored.

The problem with political sovereignty is that it is much less easy to identify than legal sovereignty. For under what circumstances can the people take in the right to resist legislation which has been passed by Parliament through established constitutional procedures? The courts certainly would find it difficult not to accept legislation for the concept of legal sovereignty implies that they merely have to accept what parliament hands down.

The Rule of Law doesn't help either because, even if a court ruled that it had been breached, Parliament could just merely change the law or even abolish the courts. At present some legislation is not even subject to interpretation by the courts because the appropriate Act says so and consideration of it may be undertaken by a quasi-judicial body such as an administrative tribunal.

Equality and Freedom

Most constitutions have, as a fundamental aim, the guarantee of political equality, freedom and rights for citizens. These may clearly be stated and possibly involve an institutional apparatus for the protection of such constitutional rights. For example, one of the major functions of the Supreme Court in the USA is to protect the individual citizen's constitutional rights from any attack.

In Britain, with its unwritten arrangements, there is no such situation. This is not to say that there is not a strong body of opinion which would like to see the introduction of legislation which clearly identifies what rights British citizens should enjoy. These demands have become more frequent over the last 20 years from groups who feel that some civil liberties have come under threat, and that present institutional arrangements have increasingly been unable to ensure that citizens enjoy protection against abuse by the state.

Up until the 1960s there was fairly widespread confidence in the British constitution which appeared to allow flexibility and change, ensuring equality for all before the law. Britain after World War II adapted well to major changes in economic and social policy without recourse to significant changes in the constitutional arrangements. Human rights and civil liberties, although not incorporated into a single document or Act of Parliament, did not appear to be in any danger, for the courts were there if problems arose. Nonetheless, Britain has remained alone amongst its European neighbours in not adopting a Bill of Rights or written constitution.

Rights

A British Bill of Rights?

The most recent attempt to introduce a Bill of Rights in Britain occurred in February 1987 in the form of a Private Member's Bill. The Human Rights Bill, was sponsored by Sir Edward Gardner, and enjoyed all-party support.

The bill passed through the House of Lords supported by Lord Hailsham, the then Lord Chancellor, and was given a free vote in the House of Commons by the Conservative Government, yet failed. Only 94 MPs voted for it in the House of Commons, six short of the number it required to gain a second reading. It was discussed on a Friday afternoon and most members had returned to their constituencies for the weekend.

The aim of the bill was to allow citizens to take action in British courts for breaches of the freedoms contained in the European Convention on Human Rights of which Britain is a signatory. The Convention was established between 1945 and 1950 as a reaction to the horrors of Nazi persecution. The lawyers and politicians who created it wanted to prevent the rise of a dictator like Hitler ever occurring again by setting out basic human rights which must never be infringed.

Advantages of a Bill of Rights

In Britain citizens possess few 'positive' rights in the sense that they are conferred by Parliament through legislation. Liberties and rights tend to be identified by what the individual or state *cannot* do, not the reverse. Critics argue that this situation results in many cases involving disputes between the individual and the state in Britain having to be settled by the European Court of Human Rights in Strasbourg.

In fact Britain is the only one of the 21 signatories which does not allow its citizens to have the rights set out in the Convention guaranteed by domestic courts. All others ensure these rights in their written constitutions, or have incorporated them in domestic legislation. In Britain, if the rights are not established in statute or common law, the individual may have to go to Strasbourg to ask for the court's judgement. This can prove to be a very lengthy and expensive process, for the individual has firstly to show that no remedy exists in Britain through court action.

British law, it can be argued, is inadequate in providing such guarantees against the abuse of power by the state. The evidence for this is claimed to be that Britain sends more cases to the European Court than any other country and has lost more than any other. To incorporate the European Convention into British law, it can be said, would not increase the jurisdiction of judges, as some claim, and therefore would pose no threat to parliamentary sovereignty.

The advantage of having these rights on the statute book may not be that an absolute insurance would be established against them being removed, but that very serious consideration would need to be given to any attempts to do so.

The advantages claimed for such a bill would be:

- The present patchwork of legislation involving constitutional rights would be drawn together and any missing pieces completed.
- It would provide immediate redress for anyone whose rights were infringed.
- It would increase public awareness of the potential for abuse of power and in its turn would increase parliamentary vigilance in preventing any abuse.

Example

The instances of inhuman methods of interrogation for suspected terrorists in Northern Ireland between 1971 and 1973 were stopped when the government discovered they had been employed, and before the court ruled upon them.

Arguments Against a Bill of Rights

The main argument against such a constitutional change is that, simply, it is not needed, because the record of Britain in protecting human rights since the signing of the Convention is very good. Even when abuses have been identified the reaction has been such as to bring about change before the European Court has ruled upon it.

The actual working of the Convention has also come in for some criticism. It is claimed that the majority of cases involving Britain that have come before the Court have not been ones involving gross violations of human rights, but merely disputes between individuals and the state. Critics of a new Bill of Rights argue that most of its provisions already exist in British law and if Parliament feels the need to create more protections then it is at liberty to enact them.

There also exists the fear that an extension of the power of judges to reach decisions would in effect mean they could dictate to Parliament. Two rulings of the European Court angered some Conservative politicians for they appeared to directly challenge British sovereignty.

These were the questions of corporal punishment, 'birching' in the Isle of Man in 1978, and the use of corporal punishment in schools in 1986. In both cases the European Court ruled that corporal punishment was a breach of the Convention.

The second case was particularly annoying, for some Conservatives wished to see the option of corporal punishment retained in state schools, but the government was obligated, as a signatory of the Convention, to legislate in response to the ruling. The best guarantee for human rights, it is argued, rests with the political process and the ballot box, not with pronouncements from non-elected judiciary.

Judges, however, have taken account of the Convention when interpreting legislation passed since Britain ratified it, and have favoured interpretations which are in line with the Convention.

Any analogy with the position of the Supreme Court in the USA is questionable, the traditions of the judiciary in Britain are that it is non-political. In the USA appointments to the Supreme Court are made by the President on the basis of the political orientation and convictions of the appointee, not usually through a consideration of distinguished judicial ability. The effect of introducing a Bill of Rights into Britain, critics argue, would be to offer a temptation to governments to follow American practice.

It is also asked what the position of a court would be in enforcing a judgement on the basis of the Bill of Rights, which rejected a government decision endorsed by the electorate through the ballot box. Normally British judges are not placed in such a situation and have only to interpret the intentions of Parliament as laid down by law.

The major difficulty for the introduction of a Bill of Rights rests with parliamentary sovereignty. Given the doctrine that 'no parliament can bind its successors' would it be possible to make special arrangements for alterations to the Bill of Rights different from other laws? For example, a two-thirds vote in the House of Commons or a referendum? The difficulty lies in whether Parliament could, by ordinary methods, remove the act which provides for the special measures.

The answer to this question for the supporters of the Bill of Rights is, why would Parliament want to do away with such legislation if it were so important? Other major civil liberties have existed for a very long time in Britain without a threat from Parliament, so why not this one?

▸▸▸▸▸▸▸▸▸▸▸▸▸▸▸ EXAMINATION QUESTIONS

1 What advantages and disadvantages would follow from the introduction of a written constitution in Britain? (University of Cambridge, Special Paper, Politics and Government, 1982)

2 Consider critically the case for the enactment of a Bill of Rights in the United Kingdom. (AEB, Government and Politics, A-Level, 1980)

3 How is the constitution changed in Britain? Illustrate your answer with examples drawn from this century. (University of London, Government and Political Studies, 1981)

►►►►►►►►►►►►►►►► NOW READ ON . . .

J. Jowell and D. Oliver (eds) *The Changing Constitution* Oxford University Press, 1985
A collection of essays covering several aspects of constitutional theory.
N. Johnson *In Search of the Constitution* Methuen, 1977
An interesting approach and set of conclusions.
K. C. Wheare *Modern Constitutions* Oxford University Press, 1966
A comparative study of constitutional theory.

17 The Legislature

BASIC PRINCIPLES

Key Concepts

Power	Associated with Parliament's ability to govern and to fulfil the role the Constitution sets for it.
Authority	The sources of the authority of Parliament; traditional and legal.
Legitimacy	The role of the House of Lords as an unelected chamber; and of the House of Commons elected on the plurality system.
Justice	The role of the House of Lords as a court of final appeal and of the existence of elected law officers in the House of Commons.
Rights	The ability of the House of Commons to amend or withdraw them at will.
Representation/ Participation	The fairness and effectiveness of the system by which citizens are represented in the House of Commons; the Lobbying system; the House of Lords.

Key Theories

Democracy	How credible is the House of Commons as a democratic institution and is the continued existence of an unelected House of Lords compatible with our ideas of democracy?
Liberalism	Centralised legislatures versus devolved power; embedded large majorities due to the operation of the plurality system.
Conservatism	The pace of change in methods of representation; the role of the British Parliament.
Socialism	Elites in the legislature; the effectiveness of popular pressure and influence on the legislature.
Corporatism	By-passing Parliament with new formal systems of cooperative group representation.

DISCUSSING THE ARGUMENTS

The English people think that they are free, but in this belief they are profoundly wrong. They are free only when they elect Members of Parliament. Once the election has been completed they revert to a condition of slavery. They are nothing.

Jean-Jacques Rousseau *The Social Contract* 1762

Legitimacy and Democracy

It is clear that the Parliament, in both its Houses, is a *legal* body. It has a considerable history behind it and a great many legal documents are in existence which state, confirm, expand or reduce the powers of the two

Houses. The most recent, the Parliament Acts of 1911 and 1949 define the relationship between the Lords and the Commons in a way which seeks to avoid the constitutional battles of the late nineteenth and early twentieth centuries.

Example

The British Legislature

HOUSE OF COMMONS	HOUSE OF LORDS
650 members	1,175 members (1987)
Directly elected on a geographical basis	Hereditary peers (790) Life peers (338) Law Lords (21) Bishops (26 – incl. 2 Archbishops)

In essence, the Parliament Act of 1911 became necessary when the Lords were felt to be obstructing a Liberal Government. In more modern times it has become the habit of certain Labour supporters to assert that the upper House obstructs only Labour governments but, before World War I this was the attitude taken by the Liberals:

> *When the Conservative Party is in power there is practically no House of Lords . . . but, the moment a Liberal government is formed, this harmless body assumes an active life and its activity is entirely exercised in opposition to the Government.*
>
> Lord Rosebery, 1894 – quoted in S T Miller *British Political History, 1784–1939* MacDonald & Evans, 1977

The House of Lords in session.

The Lords rejected many Liberal Bills during the years between 1906 and 1910, but the affair came to a head with the upper House's rejection of Lloyd George's 'Budget' of 1909. By convention the Lords did not reject Finance

Bills. It was felt, even during the eighteenth and nineteenth centuries that the upper House did not carry sufficient legitimacy to reject finance bills passed by the 'popular' chamber.

The House of Lords had, therefore, not rejected a Finance Bill since the time of Queen Anne and it took a General Election, in 1910, which returned the Liberal Government to persuade the Lords to pass the Finance Bill of 1909. The Liberal Government then prepared an Act which limited the powers of the Lords and, by means of a threat from the King to create enough Liberal peers to push it through, the Parliament Act of 1911 was passed.

The Act

- required the Lords to pass all 'Money Bills' within one month of their being sent to them;
- restricted the Lord's power to delay other legislation to two years or two sessions of Parliament

The latter restriction was reduced to one year by the Parliament Act of 1949.

Example

Legislation Relating to the House of Lords

1911 Parliament Act: restricts power of Lords to delay legislation to 3 sessions or two years; Lords must pass 'Money Bills' within one month

1949 Parliament Act: power of delay reduced to one year or two sessions

1958 Life Peerage Act: allowed women hereditary peers to sit in the Lords; allowed the creation of non-hereditary peerages (Life Peers)

1963 Peerage Act: allowed peers to disclaim their peerages within a short time limit. Passed primarily to allow Earl Home to disclaim his hereditary title in order to become Prime Minister as Sir Alec Douglas-Home. Other peers who disclaimed their titles at that time were Viscount Stansgate who became Anthony Wedgewood-Benn, and Viscount Hailsham who became Quintin Hogg.

The fundamental reasoning behind these Acts, and behind attempts to abolish or further curtail the activities of the Lords since 1949 was that the Lords have no legitimacy upon which to base opposition to a popularly elected lower chamber. The Commons is directly elected by the people and, therefore, has a greater right to have its own way than the hereditary and appointed House of Lords.

Controlling an 'Illegitimate' Chamber – Three suggestions

1 The Salisbury Doctrine First recognised by the Conservative peer, Lord Salisbury, in 1900, it holds that the Lords should not attempt to prevent the Second Reading of a Bill which is based upon any proposal which was contained in the election manifesto of the governing party (or parties). Essentially following the doctrine of the 'Mandate'.

2 The 'Alliance' Doctrine Until such time as it is reformed into an elected second chamber the Lords should not prevent the passage of any Bill which has been passed by the House of Commons (1986).

3 The 'Labour' Doctrine Until such time as the second chamber is abolished the powers of the Lords to delay legislation will be entirely removed, excepting only with respect to its power to prevent the extension of the lifetime of a Parliament.

> *Labour will take action to abolish the undemocratic House of Lords as soon as possible and, as an interim measure, will introduce a Bill in the first session of Parliament to remove its legislative powers, with the exception of those which relate to the life of a Parliament.*
>
> Labour Party Election Manifesto, 1983

More Legitimate than the Commons?

> *. . . the House of Commons is unrepresentative. It is not only unrepresentative of the political attitudes of the people, it is unrepresentative of the composition, structure and occupations of our society. The Commons, as well as the Lords, is in need of legitimacy.*
>
> Lord Houghton address the Politics Association, 19 September 1977

It may well be, however, that the Lords have a few counter-arguments at their disposal. In the first place the Commons has explicitly recognised the right of the upper House to continue to have a veto over **constitutional change** where such change would involve extending the lifetime of a Parliament beyond five years. In the second place there is an increasing sense in which the House of Lords is becoming more representative of the people.

A supporter of the Lords would argue, today, that most of the work in the Chamber is actually done by appointed Life Peers and that these tend to come from much wider social and economic groups than the MPs of the lower House. Life Peers come not only from ex-politicians of the Commons but from business people, voluntary organisations, the professions, the trade unions, the nationalised industries, and from the public services. In addition they are not as constrained as their fellows in the Commons by party discipline, their debates are freer, and they have more time to consider matters in depth.

The greater legitimacy of the Lords in certain areas has been illustrated in recent years by the tendency of Governments to give over important social legislation for consideration by the upper House before it comes to the Commons. Not only do the Lords have more time to debate these important matters in great depth but the composition of the House brings a tremendous amount of experience to bear on the subjects.

Example

Examples of the Backgrounds of Peers in the House of Lords:

Lord Allen	ex-Head of the Civil Service
Baroness Cox	Senior Nurse and academic
Lord Raynor	Chairman of Marks & Spencer
Lord Todd	Chairman of the Royal Society
Lord Sandford	President of the Association of District Councils
Viscount Ridley	President of the Association of County Councils
Lord Beloff	ex-Professor of Government at Oxford
Lord Wilson	ex-Prime Minister
Lord Ezra	ex-Chairman of the National Coal Board
Lord Gormley	ex-General Secretary of the National Union of Mineworkers
Lord Tonypandy	ex-Speaker of the House of Commons, George Thomas

The issue, therefore, is not simply one of a basic definition of **democracy** or **legitimacy**. In both cases simple definitions would result in the Lords being found to be both undemocratic and illegitimate. Democracy means more than just functional representation, however. True democracy means that the real wishes of the people are being transmitted into laws. It is a sobering thought that, in some instances, we have an unelected chamber which is better able to discern the wishes of the people than one which is supposedly representative.

Example

Comparison of the percentage support for Political Parties in the Commons, Lords and among the voters of 1983

Party	Lords 1983	Commons 1983	Commons 1987	Voters 1983	Voters 1987
Conservative	48.9	61.6	58.1	42.4	43.3
Labour	15.9	32.2	35.3	27.6	31.5
Alliance	9.6	3.6	3.2	25.4	23.1
Other	25.6	3.2	3.4	4.6	2.1

These percentages have been calculated in the following manner:

1. LORDS: % of peers who have not applied for leave of absence and who, therefore, are able to attend.
2. COMMONS: % of seats won in the 1983 & 1987 General Election.
3. VOTERS: % of votes cast in the 1983 & 1987 General Election.

Source: Peter G. Richards 'The House of Lords – Recent Developments', *Teaching Politics*, May 1985, page 182 and 1987 election results

Example

Proposals for the Reform of the House of Lords

1. 1918 Bryce proposed a two tier House of Lords:
   - 246 nominated or elected by the House of Commons
   - an equal number elected by single transferable vote (STV) in large multi-member constituencies
2. 1969 Crossman
   Richard Crossman's famous Parliament (No. 2) Bill which actually reached the stage of full scale debates proposed a two tier House:
   - 230 peers who would be able to vote
   - plus all the hereditary peers who would be able to speak but not to vote
   - the delaying power of the Lords would be reduced to just six months
3. 1977 Champion
   The Labour Peer Lord Champion suggested: a single tier system consisting of just 250 nominated voting peers.
   - The delaying power would be reduced to six months.
4. 1977 Bow Group
   The Conservative Bow Group suggested that a **senate** be created consisting of:
   - 300 elected peers (on the regional list system)
   - 100 life peers nominated by the House of Commons

   The delaying power of the Senate would be for the life of the Parliament.
5. 1978 Home
   A Committee under the Conservative peer Lord Home proposed a two tier system:
   - 288 members elected by Proportional Representation (system not specified)
   - 142 members nominated by the House of Commons

   The delaying power would be extended to two years.
6. 1978 *The Guardian*
   The Guardian newspaper in a lengthy article entitled 'Scrap the Lords – bring on the Senators' proposed that a new Senate should be created with:
   - 243 voting members elected by the regional list system
   - 121 non-voting members nominated by the Commons
   - 81 European MPs
7. 1980 Rhys-Williams
   Sir Brandon Rhys-Williams (Conservative) introduced a Private Member's Bill which simply wanted:
   - 243 members elected by STV for a five year term which would coincide with the terms of the European Parliament.

Reform

Reform of the House of Lords remains the extremely contentious issue that it was back in 1909 when the Liberal government took the first steps towards curbing its power.

The issue divides neatly into those who believe that the Lords ought to be completely abolished and not replaced; and those who wish to see the House either radically amended or replaced with a new second chamber.

Those who wish simply to abolish the House of Lords argue that several other countries (New Zealand, Sweden, Finland, Denmark, etc.) have *unicameral* (one chamber) systems and that the House of Commons alone is perfectly capable of governing.

Those who wish to see the Lords amended or replaced argue that *bicameral* systems were originally established for the prime purpose of providing a check on each of the two chambers and that Britain, in particular, needs such a check. They argue, also, that, without either a Supreme Court or a Bill of Rights, Britain would be too vulnerable to the whims of a government whipped House of Commons. Only the House of Lords currently prevents the lower House from being able to extend its own life beyond five years, for example.

The Labour Party chose in the 1970s to take the first of these courses. Its 1977 Conference decided, by the incredible majority of 6.5 million votes to just 91,000, to abolish the upper chamber. That policy was amended by the 1989 Policy Review to replacement by an elected assembly.

The Conservative Party prefers to avoid the issue if at all possible, at least at the most official and senior level. However, in the same way as with electoral reform, there are a great many Tory backbenchers who believe that the upper House should be reformed or replaced. As can be seen from the list above, several of the most constructive suggestions for reform have come from Conservative sources (Bow Group, Home, Rhys-Williams).

The SLD sees the reform of the Lords, along with electoral reform, as a major element in its policy. The preferred solution is for a Senate which is partly elected, partly appointed, but with representatives from the European Parliament and, if possible, from any devolved Parliaments within the UK.

One interesting, if understandable, feature of the entire debate has been the reluctance of the Commons to share its power with a reformed Lords. The main reason for limiting the amount of time which the Lords can delay a piece of legislation is that it has no legitimate right to delay legislation passed by an elected chamber. One would think, therefore, that, if one increased the legitimacy of the House of Lords, the delaying power should be extended or even abolished. Neither the Crossman nor the Champion reforms took any real notice of the fact that they were, at the same time, both extending the legitimacy of the upper House and further restricting its powers vis-à-vis the Commons.

Example

The Problems of Reform of the Lords

It is an interesting game to play around with ideas for reforming the Lords:

- How many upper House representatives are required?
- Should they all be elected or could some be appointed?
- By what system should they be elected?
- Who should appoint the appointed peers?
- Should the new House/Senate include representatives of various interests in society: religious minorities, trade unions, voluntary organisations, youth, women, etc?
- What term should the upper chamber have? Should the term of office coincide with Commons terms or, like the US system, overlap?
- How much power should the upper chamber have to oppose the lower one?
- Should the upper chamber be elected on different constituencies (European constituencies, regional ones, etc.)?
- Where would the highest court of the land be if one replaced the Lords with something different?
- Would one need a Bill of Rights or a written Constitution?

LEGITIMACY OF THE COMMONS

The legitimacy of the House of Commons is, itself, not above question. As Lord Houghton's statement, quoted above, says, the House may well be unrepresentative in a social and economic as well as a political sense.

The 'first-past-the-post' (**plurality**) system of voting used in Great Britain tends to over-emphasise the majority of the vote gained by any particular party in the country so that a Government can have a very strong majority in Parliament based upon a minority of the vote. The table on page 214 shows the position after the 1983 and 1987 General Elections. In 1983 Mrs Thatcher's government acquired 61 per cent of the seats in the House of Commons on the basis of just over 42 per cent of the votes. Another way of looking at it is to say that she achieved a very strong position in Government on an electoral result in which almost 60 per cent of the people who voted *did not want* a Conservative Government.

As long as Britain had a true 'two-party' system this imbalance probably did not matter. In the 1950s and 1960s the Conservative and Labour Parties, between them, regularly accounted for well over 80 per cent of the votes (in 1951 the two parties gained no less than 96.8 per cent). In 1983 just 70 per cent of the voters voted for these two parties.

The voting figures are one possible argument but there is another aspect to the changes in the old two-party system. It could be argued that, during the 1950s and 1960s, there was a consensus among the leaders of the Labour and Conservative Parties about most aspects of British life. They agreed on the fundamentals of the welfare state, on the importance of nuclear weapons, of NATO, and, eventually, of Britain's joining the EEC. The Conservative governments of the 1950s did not denationalise most of what the Labour Party had nationalised in the late 1940s and they built vast numbers of council houses.

In the 1970s this post-war consensus broke down with the effect that the difference between one party or the other forming the next government has become extremely wide. The electoral system can give us more of the 'radical' Mrs Thatcher or it can give us a Labour government pledged to overturn much of what her government has done and replace it with Labour's own version of 'radical policies'. The important thing is that, in both cases, it is highly unlikely that the government will have anything like a majority of the voters on its side.

In 1974 the Labour Government entered office as the official government of the United Kingdom with the support of just 37.2 per cent of the voters (the Conservatives actually had greater support with 38.1 per cent). If the electorate as a whole is taken into account this meant that the February 1974 Labour Government had the positive support of less than a third of the electorate!

Mrs Thatcher's 1987 government was in a much stronger position – 43.3 per cent of the voters placed their crosses against Conservative boxes. This is still less than half of the voters, but it translated into 58 per cent of the seats in Parliament. But, it has to be remembered that only 70 per cent of the electorate bothered to turn out to vote: a lower percentage then in almost any other developed country except the United States which also uses the plurality system.

Mrs Thatcher's support in 1983, resulting in the greatest election victory since World War II, represented just 30.8 per cent of the electorate.

No British government since 1945 has ever been brought to office with the support of a majority of the voters (the nearest was the Conservative Government of 1955 with 49.7 per cent) and the effect of this has been, particularly in recent years, to undermine the legitimacy of those governments and of the Parliament through which they operate. People who live in a democracy are taught that the *essence* of democracy is that one should always bow to the will of the majority. Why then, they might ask, is it necessary to obey laws passed by a Government which patently does not command the support of a majority of the voters?

In 1971 the Labour Party (which, under the leadership of Harold Wilson in the 1960s had done most of the work to get Britain into the EEC) questioned the right of a Conservative Government to use its majority in Parliament to pass the Act of Accession to the European Economic Community. Labour Party MPs questioned the legitimacy of Parliament to take such a decision and pushed a demand for a referendum through the Labour Party Conference.

Similarly, in 1971, the Trades Union Congress questioned the legitimacy of a Conservative dominated Parliament pushing through the Industrial Relations Act. The TUC decided not to obey such a law and, for many months afterwards, a legally instituted law of this country was disobeyed by a significant section of the population.

Leader of the National Union of Mineworkers, Arthur Scargill's attempt to defy the Thatcher Government during the lengthy miners' strike of 1984–5 also found him denying the legitimacy of a government which had been elected by a smaller percentage of the vote than he had himself. (See Chapter 7, Representation.)

▶ *Which arrangement of seating is ikely to create the least adversarial ınd antagonistic, and the most 'onstructive and cooperative, liscussions?*

▶ *The British House of Commons.*

▶ *The European Parliament.*

The Institutional Structure

The British legislature consists of two 'Houses' of Parliament. This bicameral structure is divided into an elected 'lower' chamber called the **House of Commons** and an unelected 'upper' chamber called the **House of Lords**.

The House of Commons is directly elected by the people (all those over 18 years of age* with a few legal exceptions) on the basis of single-member constituencies. There are 650 Members of Parliament to represent around 4[illegible] million voters and, once elected, those MPs sit in party groups and, by and large, they obey party instructions as to how they should vote.

The House of Lords consists of a mixture of hereditary peers, life peers, bishops and 'law lords'. The last two categories are Church of England bishops who, by law, are given automatic representation (as leaders of the country's official 'established' church) and senior justices who have traditionally been given seats in the Lords so that they might, when necessary, hear cases brought to the Lords as the final court of appeal.

The legislature is responsible, under the Constitution, for making policy; it is **'sovereign'**. In theory, Parliament decides what policies to follow and then passes legislation allowing those policies to be put into effect. The executive, headed by Ministers appointed by Parliament, then puts those laws into effect aided by paid employees in the **'Civil Service'.**

Legislation is passed using a series of pre-set steps:

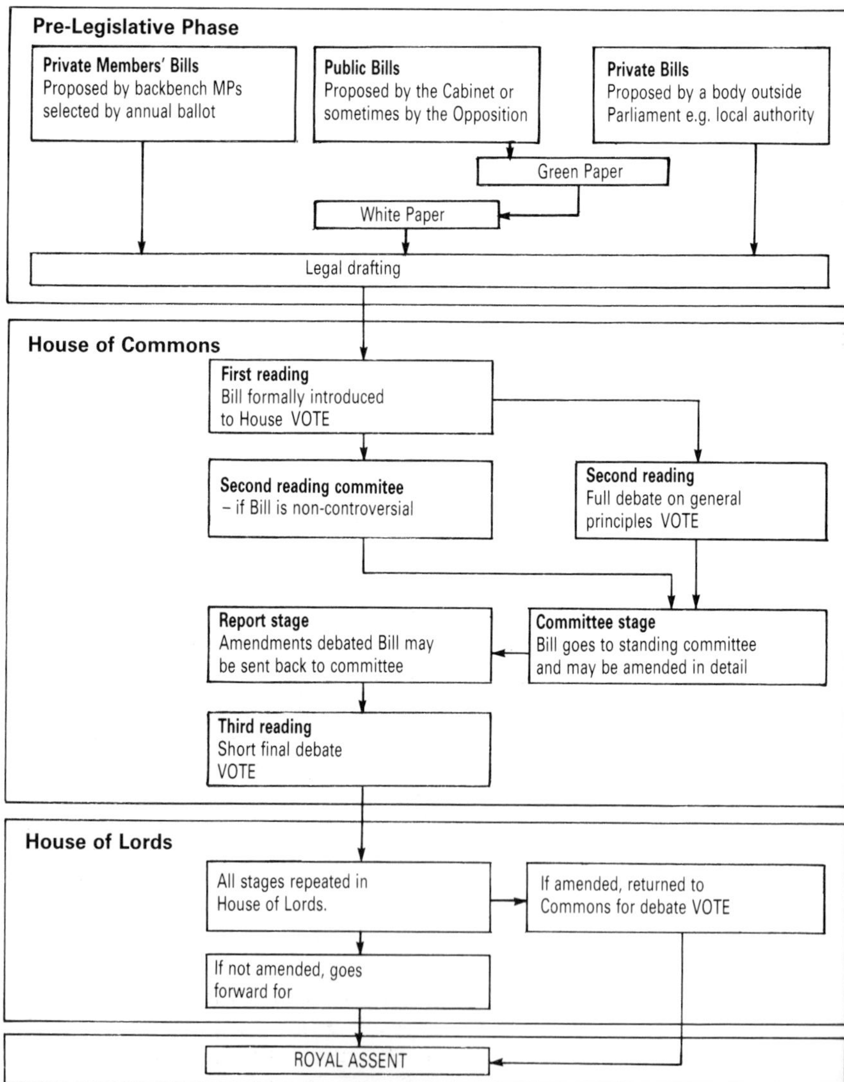

Source: Pye & Collier *The Organization in its Environment*, 1984

* Those over 18 were given the vote by the Representation of the People Act, 1969.

Unlike many legislatures the British Parliament operates almost wholly as a full chamber. Most of the deliberations and debates which precede a Bill's enactment are conducted on the 'floor' of the House. Many other legislatures (notably the US Congress and the European Parliament) conduct most of the debate in a series of specially formulated Committees.

Parliament has just two types of major committee:

Standing Committees whose role is to examine proposed legislation in depth and to amend where it is felt necessary
Select Committees are of various types; some have been set up to control the domestic affairs of the Parliament (both Houses have Catering Committees, and Privilege Committees, for example), whereas the main type of Select Committee watches over Government departments. These 'departmental' Select Committees were formed in 1979 and, although they have little real power, are widely felt to have been more effective than the 'general' Select Committee system which preceded them.

Example

'Departmental' Select Committees:		Other Select Committees:	
Agriculture	Home Affairs	European Legislation	Selection
Defence	Industry & Trade	House of Commons Services	Sound Broadcasting
Education	Social Services	Members' Interests	Statutory Instruments
Employment	Transport	Parliamentary Commissioner	Private Bills
Energy	Treasury	Privileges	Chairman's Panel
Environment	Welsh Affairs	Public Accounts	
Foreign Affairs	Scottish Affairs		

Power and Sovereignty

It is a well known conundrum that Parliament is all powerful because it can change any aspect of the British constitution at will but that it is also extremely weak because it cannot bind its own successors to continue those changes!

There is little doubt in anyone's mind that Parliament is the seat of power in the British system of government. The problem is to distinguish between legal sovereignty and power and *actual* sovereignty and power. The idea of Parliament is that decisions should be taken by 650 individuals after each has had a chance to make his or her views known. The reality is that those individuals operate almost entirely as 'blocks' of votes controlled by the party machines which enabled them to get elected in the first place.

How much true power does an institution possess when it cannot initiate legislation without the sanction of the Government? Private members' legislation is severely limited both in time available for it and in the matters which it can deal with. (These Bills cannot involve the spending of public finance, for example.) It is also increasingly the case that Parliament is delegating much of its legislative power to the executive in the form of **delegated legislation** (Statutory Instruments and Orders in Council being the two main types).

In addition, it is increasingly evident that the sheer workload of the House of Commons means that it is having to devolve responsibilities to committees and to individual Ministers. In the 1930s Parliament produced around 450 pages of legislation per year. In the 1980s it is producing about 3,000 pages of legislation, almost 10,000 Statutory Instruments and a large number of EEC regulations and directives (which have to be placed into law by Parliament).

Parliament's ability to control the executive is now extremely weak **Question Time★** allows only a brief period during which to question very wel prepared Government Ministers; Select Committees are kept short of financ and administrative assistance and, anyway, have to rely on the kin cooperation of the Government before persons or papers may be laid befor them. On only one occasion in living memory has the Commons succeede in acquiring papers (by *subpoena*) which it wanted to see but which th Government did not wish to be made public at that time.

Example

In November 1977 the Commons wished to know what the losses of the British Steel Corporation were going to be. The Select Committee had been informed that they would be huge. In spite of attempts by the Select Committee to question both the then Chairman of the Corporation and the Secretary of State concerned, Eric Varley, they were unable to get at the figures.

At first the Select Committee on the Nationalised Industries (SCNI) tried to acquire the relevant documents from the Secretary of State.

The Committee presented an 'Address to Her Majesty' for the approval of the Commons (this is one technique by which Committees can request the Crown to order its servant (the Secretary of State) to comply with a request). This placed Parliament in an unusual position and the 'Address' was delayed while legal opinions were sought.

In the end the SCNI used its power to issue 'Orders' to people outside Parliament. In this way they effectively sidestepped the legal controversy surrounding their attempt to order a Government Minister to produce papers by turning the order into one which was directed at the British Steel Corporation itself.

The Warrant Officer to the Sergeant-at-Arms served the Order on the Chairman of British Steel – Sir Charles Villiers – on 19 January 1978 and Sir Charles gave in and turned over the books and relevant documents.

It was subsequently found that the losses of British Steel were even larger than had been originally thought and that it did appear as though the Secretary of State and the Chairman of British Steel had deliberately tried to prevent that situation from becoming known to the SCNI and the general public.

It must be said of this exercise in Parliamentary power, that no one knows what would have happened had Sir Charles simply refused to obey the Order. It is likely that the only reason he did obey it was because the Government at the time was in the minority in Parliament and if it had been seen to be openly resisting the will of the elected representatives the result would almost certainly have been a vote on the original 'Address' which the Government would have lost.

There have been several occasions since the founding of the new 'departmental system of Select Committees on which the Government has successfully prevented the Committees in question from finding out information which they felt that they needed in order to do their job, of checking the **Executive** properly. The best remembered of these occasions was that of the enquiry into the Westland Affair (see pages 54-5) during which Government Ministers and Civil Servants either did not answer questions or did not appear before the Committee.

In view of the fact that these new Committees were set up in order to make the work of the House more effective in overseeing the Executive, these successful attempts to block investigations sit uneasily with the pledge of the then Leader of the House, Mr Norman St John Stevas, when he reassured

---

★ 'Question Time' is the period of approximately one hour from 2.30 p.m. to 3.30 p.m. each day of the Parliamentary Term which is allocated for questions to Government Ministers. The questions can come from backbenchers of the governing party or from the members of the opposition parties. Notice must be given of the questions to be asked and most are answered in written form. For those asked orally, in the Chamber of the House of Commons, one supplementary question, after the Minister's initial answer, is allowed.

The Prime Minister has two Question Times each week (on Tuesdays and Thursdays) while the other Ministers have a rota to share the remaining periods. It should be noted that Question Time is not the only opportunity for MPs to ask questions of the Government. There are several other ways, of which 'Motions for Adjournment' (at 10 p.m. each day) and 'Standing Order No. 9' motions are the most common.

the House in 1979 that there was really no need for the new Committees to have the power to *subpoena** the presence of people or papers:

> *There need be no fear that Departmental Ministers will refuse to attend Committees to answer questions about their Departments or that they will not make every effort to ensure that the fullest possible information is made available to them.*
>
> House of Commons Debates (HCDebs; 969,45)

RIGHTS

The development of theories of rights over the centuries has, in Britain at least, been pursued initially through Parliament and for the benefit of that body.

'Freedom of speech' was initially the result of the attempts by Parliament to protect itself against despotic monarchs. The Speaker of the House of Commons was originally chosen by the King and was required to speak *for* the King as well as to report to the monarch on the proceedings of Parliament. It was not until the battles between Parliament and the Stuart monarchs in the seventeenth century that the role of the Speaker was clarified as being one which was totally that of a servant of the House who *protected* the right of that House to freedom of debate.

In 1642 the then Speaker of the House took up the concept of freedom of speech for the House of Commons when he told King Charles I:

> *I have neither eyes to see nor tongue to speak in this place but as the House doth direct me whose servant I am.*

The Civil War, which saw many thousands of deaths in pitched battles between the King and his Parliament, decided the issue for all time. In the Bill of Rights of 1689 Parliament won the right to freedom of speech and debate. There may, however, be some question, in the late twentieth century, of whether this right still exists given the overwhelming power of governments with large majorities to control the schedule and the outcome of debates in Parliament.

Protection of the Rights of the Citizen

The central problem for students of British politics has to be the effectiveness of Parliament in guaranteeing the rights of the people against Parliament or Government. It is clear that Parliament won its own battle with the Crown during the seventeenth century and that, since then, legislation has been passed which gives certain rights to the people; but, if Parliament is sovereign and can abolish previous legislation at will, what is to stop Parliament from removing some or all of these rights whenever it, or, more to the point, a government, chooses?

As was seen in the chapter on Rights (Chapter 6) it is possible to identify certain documents which have been given Statutory force and which are regarded as the basis for the rights of British citizens:

The Magna Carta, 1215
The Petition of Right, 1628
The Bill of Rights, 1689

---

* *Subpoena:* Latin for 'under penalty', means a legal writ which demands a person's attendance in court.

At the basic level, however, Parliament has only begun to legislate *positiv* rights in the last twenty years and most of the rights of British citizens ar in the form of 'negative' rights. That is to say:

1 We have freedom of speech *except* where the law restricts that freedom (v the Official Secrets Acts or the laws against libel, slander, obscen language, etc.).
2 We have freedom from arbitrary arrest and have the right to be told wha charge we are being held under *except* where the law describes othe conditions (e.g. The Prevention of Terrorism Act, 1974 under which peop may be arrested without charge and held for up to seven days withou charge).
3 We have the right to privacy of our letters and telephone calls *except* whe the Royal Prerogative (as exercised by the Home Secretary) decide otherwise. (The Diplock Report of 1981 concluded that interception of ma and telephone calls had been decided and conducted within the bounds o the ruling of a Committee of Privy Councillors in 1957 which ruled that should only be done to detect serious crime or to protect the state.)
4 We have the right to freedom of assembly *except* under conditions impose by the Public Order Act, 1986 and the Race Relations Act, 1976.
5 It is felt, today, that there is a 'right' not to have the death penalty visite upon us. The 'right' appears to have developed from various statemen by international jurors and from the Abolition of the Death Penalty Ac of 1965 but capital punishment still remains on the Statute book under th Statute of Treasons, 1351. This statute, amended in 1702, 1707, 1795 an 1817 is still in force and allows the death sentence for treason.

It is clear that most British rights are merely conventions which have bee partially validated and restricted by Acts of Parliament. Only in recent time have positive rights been enacted in the form of the Race Relations Act (1965, 1968 and 1976), the Equal Pay Act (1970) and the Sex Discriminatio Acts (1975 and 1987). For the most part, including these positive Act conferring rights, Parliament remains absolutely sovereign; any act may b stricken from the Statute book at any time, and any conventional 'right' ma be amended or abolished by a new Act.

Given the domination of the Government over most Parliaments thi situation leaves British citizens in the position of relying upon tradition an political culture for their rights.

There have been many attempts during the 1980s to incorporate int British law either a new Bill of Rights (notably in 1980 and 1981) or the ful text of the European Convention on Human Rights.

The UK has recognised the jurisdiction of the European Court of Huma Rights since 1950 and, since 1966, individual citizens have been allowed t bring cases to its attention (the cases are brought before the Human Right Commission which then decides whether there is a case to answer before th Court of Human Rights).

In cases brought before the Court from Britain it has ruled:

- against the use of torture against prisoners in Northern Ireland (1976)
- in favour of the British government's policy of internment in Norther Ireland (1976)
- against the use of the closed shop to exclude new workers in British Rai (1981)
- against the use of corporal punishment in schools (1982)
  (See Chapter 7, Representation.)

In spite of this, however, the Convention remains a separate body of 'law which has never been integrated into the UK legal framework.

The Role of Parliament

Parliament fought for and has guarded its rights with respect to th monarchy ever since the mid-seventeenth century but, as yet, there is no supra-Parliamentary protection for the citizen against Parliament.

The Acts of positive rights mentioned above and the acceptance of the European Court of Human Rights are no guarantee to the individual UK citizen, for Parliament is sovereign: any of these rights can be abolished at any time by a single resolution of Parliament.

Any attempt to establish a supra-Parliamentary guarantee of rights would carry with it the need to dispose of Parliament's right to sovereignty (just as the enactment of Parliamentary rights in the seventeenth century carried with it the end of the absolute sovereignty of the monarch). Any new system would require that institutions be established to guard the rights of the people which were not subject to control by Parliament. Up to now the British constitution has remained free of entrenched conditions; if people's rights are to be guaranteed that would have to end. The guarantees would require that those rights be entrenched beyond the reach of mere Parliaments and under the protection of something akin to the Supreme Court of the United States.

Representation

In order to mean anything the concept of 'representation' has to involve the freedom of the representative to vote in ways which his or her conscience tells them to vote. They are not delegates and are not tied, at least in theory, to particular policies which their electorate has demanded.

Whether a 'pure' system of representation ever existed or not, we now appear to have a system in which the representative concept has been amended so that the electorate actually elects a *party* with its *policies.* The individual MP is then required to support that party and its policies because it is assumed that the electorate have given that set of policies their **mandate.**

This may well be a perfectly valid interpretation of the concept of representation, but it leaves many questions as to how the mandate is determined, whether the party conferences can change the mandate once the party is in office, and to what extent individual MPs are entitled to oppose party policy if they feel it to be wrong or in contravention to the wishes of their electorate.

At the Blackpool Conference of 1980 the Labour Party decided that all MPs should be subject to 'mandatory reselection' before each General Election. This decision raises many questions about whether it represents an extension of democracy by allowing the rank and file of the Labour Party much greater say in who their candidate shall be or whether it is the thin edge of a new delegatory wedge. Labour MPs cannot now feel as free to follow their own conscience as they once did (if they wish to retain their seat in Parliament).

Another aspect of representation involves the problem of 'representativeness'. Is it possible in a system, such as the British one, for MPs from a specific socio-economic group to truly represent people from different ones? Parliament is clearly not representative in this sense (as stated by Lord Houghton in the quotation on page 213):

MPs are:
- generally male
- usually university graduates (around 60 per cent at present)
- disproportionately from the professions (there are only a handful of ex-manual workers)
- over 40
- from the upper socio-economic groups
- very largely white.

To what extent can these people seek to represent the aspirations and attitudes of the bulk of the population? A further question might be to what degree these people constitute a genuine 'elite' no matter which party they come from? (See Chapter 7.)

Lobbying

(See, also the Case Study in Chapter 4: Influence and Persuasion.)

In a further questioning of the efficiency of the representative process on might point to the role of **pressure groups** (see Chapter 21) and the **lack c support** given to individual MPs. The finance which is provided to MPs fc administrative assistance usually just about covers secretarial help. Few MP can afford to have paid researchers working for them (unlike the US Congres in which the generous research allowances of Congressmen allow them t employ several skilled researchers each). This lack of resources not only limi the extent to which MPs are able to question government proposals and t examine the progress or implementation of Government policy, it also open the door to pressure groups who have the time and money to undertak detailed research and who provide the results of that research free of charg to MPs.

It may be that this research is of a very high standard and c unimpeachable quality (indeed, this is certainly so for many pressure group which provide MPs with information and backing) but the system does nc *guarantee* the independence of the MP and places our representatives in position in which they are dependent upon outside bodies each having an ax to grind.

Corporatism

In this context, corporatism means the extent to which policy is made b groups or bodies outside Parliament. The National Economic Developmen Council (NEDC) of 1962 was the first attempt to institutionalise a corporat structure in Britain. Harold Macmillan, the late Earl of Stockton, had lon supported some kind of cooperative decision-making forum in whicl business, the unions and government could discuss and decide futur economic policy.

The NEDC was never a success as a policy-forming body but it certainl represented an attempt to take a proportion of this activity away fron Parliament. The reasons may have been sound. Macmillan wanted to creat a structure which would reduce the need for damaging industrial action; t create a culture of shared aspirations between workers and owners rathe than one of continual conflict, but it remains the case that the effect c creating the NEDC, if it had fulfilled its role properly, was to by-pas Parliament.

The NEDC still exists, although diminished in both responsibilities an status. It could be argued today that it creates more conflict than it resolves The forum provided by the NEDC is often used for attacks by one side upo the other and for getting publicity for their respective attempts to embarras each other or the government.

There are, of course, other bodies which now operate on this tripartit basis. The Health and Safety Commission (1975) and the Advisory Conciliation and Arbitration Service (ACAS, 1976) were also set up wit representatives from both sides of industry as were the Industrial Trainin Boards. The important thing is that none of these could truly be calle 'corporatist' because all are *administrative* or *quasi-judicial* bodies rather tha *policy making* ones. Corporatism is an attempt to by-pass Parliament and, t date, has not been terribly effective in Britain. The main problem fc Parliament has come from the **executive** itself.

Liberalism/Conservatism

Liberalism has always regarded the individual as being of prime importance. The representative system which has grown out of liberal theories of democracy has also been one in which the individual voter had preeminence.

Burke (see Chapters 7 and 11) brought to this tradition the concepts of 'representation': the idea that a Member of Parliament must represent the constituents but not necessarily do everything that they would wish. Liberal-democratic theory requires, therefore, that the people elect someone whose ability, intellect, and general approach to life is satisfactory. The representative then takes his or her own decisions.

Parliament, today, is strongly founded on these traditions. The tendency towards delegatory-democracy which is inherent in the Socialist tradition does not, therefore, rest easily with Parliamentary practice and the Constitution of which it forms a part.

The individual MP is responsible to the electorate but only in a general sense. It is made very clear to sponsored MPs, of the union type, that they are *not* required to follow, without question, the decisions of their sponsoring unions.

EXAMINATION QUESTIONS

1 If pressure groups are so powerful, can Parliament be sovereign? (London, June 1979,1)

2 When a government enjoys a large Parliamentary majority effective opposition comes only from within the ranks of its own party. To what extent has this been the experience of governments since 1945? (AEB, June 1986)

3 Evaluate the claim that Parliamentary party committees are the most effective way for backbench MPs to influence frontbench policy. (AEB, June 1985)

4 To what extent have backbenchers managed to regain control over the activities of the government and administration in recent years? (Cambridge, June 1984)

NOW READ ON . . .

Jean-Jacques Rousseau *The Social Contract*
See Chapter 1

Richard Crossman *Diaries of a Cabinet Minister* Magnum Edition, 1979
Still the only detailed look at the workings of government by someone who actually worked in it.

18 The Executive

BASIC PRINCIPLES

Key Theory and Concepts

Power	Elective dictatorship and the power of the Prime Minister; the power of non-elected members of Cabinet Committees
Authority	The sources of the authority of the Prime Minister; the question of Ministerial responsibility
Legitimacy	– of the doctrines of collective and ministerial responsibility; of 'kitchen' Cabinets; of various conventions
Influence	– of outsiders on Cabinet Committees; of political advisers on Ministers and the Prime Minister
Representation	Degree of representation in a system dominated by the Prime Minister, the Cabinet and Cabinet Committees; representation of the people on Cabinet Committees
Democracy	Implications for democracy of the current executive structure

DISCUSSING THE ARGUMENTS

The British executive comprises:

- the Prime Minister together with all other Ministers, both senior and junior
- the Civil Service,

and all other arms of these bodies which put Parliamentary policy into force or which oversee the progress of Government activities.

This chapter will deal only with the senior levels of the executive, those elements which are elected. The administrative base will be examined in Chapter 20.

It should be noted right at the start that Britain is an unusual country in that it combines executive and legislative roles at the very highest levels. The doctrine of the **Separation of Powers**, most clearly stated by Montesquieu and put into practice by the founding fathers of the United States, has never been practised in the UK (in spite of the fact that Montesquieu regarded Britain as the origin of the doctrine).

It has long been recognised that certain elements of the state have to be kept separate. The Established Church and the state are kept fairly well separated except at the very top. The Queen combines the role of Head of State and Head of the Church of England, and no priest or vicar is allowed to become a Member of Parliament (although some 2 Archbishops and 24 bishops are members of the House of Lords)*. The clearest separation, however, and, perhaps the most important, has been between the law and the other two aspects of government. The Lord Chancellor as Head of the Judiciary, is a member of the executive (being a member of the Cabinet) and of the legislature (as a member of the House of Lords), but no judge is allowed to become an MP and the appointment and payment of judges is

*The clergy of the Church of England, the Church of Scotland and the Church of Ireland, as well as Roman Catholic priests, are disqualified from sitting as Members of Parliament although other, non-conformist, clergy are free to become MPs (e.g. The Rev. Ian Paisley).

supposed to be kept clear of political prejudice and Government interference.

The situation is far from simple and many would argue that there are far too many links between the three main components of government in the UK.

Fig. 18.1 **The Separation of Powers**

THE LEGISLATURE	THE EXECUTIVE	THE JUDICIARY
Parliament	Government	Judicial System
	PM/Ministers	
		Appointments of Judges
		Law Lords
		Lord Chancellor

The links between the various arms of government illustrated in Figure 18.1 enable the British system to function but give rise, in some quarters, to great concern.

The power of the Government to dominate Parliament, through its combination of the roles of government with leading the majority party in Parliament, is a major area of concern. Both Judges and Churchmen have the ability to influence legislation from within the legislature by virtue of their positions in the House of Lords. The Lord Chancellor is a member of all three sectors of government and certain MPs have great responsibilities towards upholding the law which sometimes appear to place great strains on the system, specifically the Home Secretary, the Attorney-General, the Solicitor-General and the Home Secretary (see Chapter 19).

The most important of the links, however, has to be that between the legislature and the executive.

Fig. 18.2 **The Foundations of the Executive**

The majority party (or parties) in the House of Commons forms the Government		
	of the 120 or so MPs in the Government up to 22 are invited to join the Cabinet	
		the leader of the majority party becomes Prime Minister

Fig. 18.3 **The Government**

The Prime Minister Secretaries of State	CABINET RANK
Ministers of State	Sometimes in the Cabinet
Under-Secrataries of State (Parliamentary Under-Secrataries)	Only very rarely in Cabinet
Parliamentary Private Secretaries	Never in Cabinet

The Power of the Prime Minister

This is a topic which is usually very well covered by other text books and i does not need to be rehearsed in depth here (see Now Read On . . .).

Arguments concerning Prime Ministerial power usually centre on the powe to:

- control their party in Parliament,
- dominate the proceedings of the Cabinet,
- select the date of an election,
- construct and use informal groups of Ministers (Inner or Kitche Cabinets),

but there are many other sources, some of which are frequently ignored.

Appointments and Dismissals

One of the most important of these is the power to appoint and to dismis members of the Government from the most senior Cabinet Minister to th most junior Parliamentary Private Secretary (PPS).

When an MP enters Parliament he or she has a choice of two possibl careers which are, to a large extent, mutually exclusive. They can opt for a government career and attempt to be noticed by the Whips and given th first step up the promotion ladder: a job as a PPS to one of the Ministers Later, if the MP does reasonably well, it is possible that a post will be foun for him or her in the ranks of the junior ministers. Eventually, the MP migh hope for a senior Cabinet post at the peak of his or her political career. Al of this advancement is, of course, dependent upon the goodwill of senio people in the party who have to put names forward to the Prime Minister fo promotion. The need to 'keep one's nose clean' is paramount.

The other career path is that of 'professional backbencher'. The MP take a decision (or is forced into it by the views of the senior people in the part at that time) to forget the glory and publicity of government posts and t concentrate, instead, on the much less publicised world of the House o Commons and its Committees.

Even on this second career path MPs know that their positions on th Committees in which they are most interested depend on the goodwill o senior people in the party. However, with so many Committees to staff, mos MPs who want to serve on them will be able to get a place. Often they wil build up a reputation as a good Committee-member while their party i in opposition and will then carry on harrying the executive from th backbenches even when their own party is in power.

The Prime Minister has the power to appoint and dismiss all governmen members (but not those MPs who sit on House of Commons Committees). A difficult Cabinet Minister can be relegated to the darkest corners of th backbenches if they get on the wrong side of a strong Prime Minister.

Against this seemingly invincible power has to be set the fact that Prim Ministers only possess it under special circumstances. In 1962 Harol Macmillan sacked 7 of his Cabinet Ministers and made 24 other governmen changes overnight. The so-called 'Night of the Long Knives' led to a backbench protest meeting of some 70 MPs the following day. In spite of thi meeting, and partly because none of those sacked were serious contenders fo Macmillan's job, the Prime Minister remained in office for a further yea until he resigned on the grounds of 'ill-health' (he had earlier told the Part Conference that he would be leading the party at the next general election).

Prime Ministers have a great deal of power but cannot exercise it in complete isolation from the realities of the need for personal support from the party. Mrs Thatcher has been able to reshuffle or dismiss many Minister without apparent harm to herself, but the reason for this has not been an inherent power of the office but the personal support of her party MPs.

If a Prime Minister ever loses that support – as did Macmillan in 1962–3 as had Eden in 1956 – then all the 'power' of the office of Prime Ministe will not save him or her.

Mobile Ministers

Another foundation of Prime Ministerial power which is often overlooked is the effect of the continual swapping around of Ministers from one job to another. The average lifespan of a senior Minister in a government department is only about 18 months and this is hardly time to build up either a reputation or a fund of expertise.

The list (see page 292) of Cabinet members and changes during the three Conservative governments from 1979 to 1989 demonstrates this clearly.

Constant shuffling means that the ability of the Prime Minister to be the sole member of the Cabinet to have an overview of everything that is going on is enhanced.

Cabinet Committees

It should not be forgotten, though, that much of the power of a modern Prime Minister derives from the system of Cabinet Committees without which modern government would quickly become bogged down in a mass of detail and very lengthy meetings. The necessity for Cabinet Committees does not, however, mean that their constitution and proceedings are free from theoretical disabilities.

Cabinet Committees are usually built around one or more Cabinet members chosen by the Prime Minister. Their meetings are supposed to be reported back to the full cabinet which has the ultimate responsibility for policy making. In fact, Cabinet Committees rarely report back in any detail (time is usually too constrained to allow this). Many decisions appear to be taken in these smaller groupings without the full Cabinet being able to do more than 'rubber-stamp' them.

The process appears to be quite inevitable. Just as the Cabinet developed from the need for a smaller policy making group than the party in Parliament, so, as the workload expanded, Cabinet Committees became necessary to relieve the full cabinet of work.

If this was the only problem then, perhaps, it could be set aside as an inevitable, but reasonable, result of the expansion of Government responsibilities. There is, however, a further aspect of the system which is even more disturbing, and that is the use of officials and unelected people on these Committees.

Most Cabinet Committees, which, incidentally, were supposed not to exist until recently, are made up of a core of Cabinet and other Ministers. There is reason to believe, however, that some of them may also have a number of civil servants, officers of the armed forces and others on them to give 'expert' advice. In theory the non-elected people on these Committees are there to advise the elected members who then take the policies through the full Cabinet and to Parliament for final approval of the democratically elected assembly.

The system of Cabinet Committees probably dates back to the formation of one called the 'Committee on Imperial Defence' in 1903. Today there are key Committees which appear to do a great deal of the work which the full Cabinet used to do. Amongst the almost permanent Cabinet Committees are:

- Economic Affairs
- Overseas Policy and Defence
- Public Expenditure Survey
- Social Services
- Home Affairs
- Future Legislation

In 1982 an incomplete list of 41 Cabinet Committees was leaked to, and published by, *The Economist* (*The Economist*, 6 February 1982). The list showed, in addition to those mentioned above, Committees dealing with nuclear deterrent policy, the then 'rate support grant', EEC policy, and the overview of intelligence matters. The JIC or Joint Intelligence Committee is said to include a number of civil servants and military personnel among its

► *'All we need now is to discover that Willie Whitelaw is on the board of Gay News.'* Daily Express, 27 July 1982.

members and was a key Committee in the policy setting and coordination for the Falklands conflict.

Each government is not allowed to know of the structure of the previous government's Cabinet Committees, or, of course, their names and personnel. The principle of secrecy from one government to the next cannot but enhance the power of civil servants to fudge or obscure issues.

The principle of *ad hoc* Cabinet Committees is that one Government creates them under the title of MISCs while the next will create them under the title of GENs (for General).

The Economist revealed in its article that Clement Attlee created no less than 396 GENs during his term of office, Harold Wilson created 118 between 1974 and 1976, and James Callaghan 158.

If Parliament was truly free to accept or reject Government policy then there would be no problem because the elected representatives of the people would be the final arbiters of policy and legislation. Instead, Parliament is usually controlled by the Government and the Government is controlled by the Cabinet. If the Cabinet has ceased to truly make policy, then where does that leave democracy in the UK – or, indeed, the concept of civil service neutrality?

Legitimacy of the Cabinet

The question of the illegitimacy of Cabinet Committees as policy-making institutions depends on whether the Cabinet itself is a legitimate arena for policy making.

The convention has always been that policy can be made in the confines of the Cabinet because only members of the legislature (both Commons and Lords) can be members of the Cabinet. This would appear to tie the right to make policy firmly to membership of the legislature where such policy is decided, and this convention appears to have been upheld over the years. When people have been nominated for Cabinet positions they have usually been Members of Parliament. Whenever such nominees have not been from Parliament, it has been the rule that they should very quickly present themselves for election. If defeated in the subsequent election the Cabinet member has, traditionally, resigned.

The examples which support this convention would include those of Patrick Gordon Walker and Frank Cousins during the Labour Governments of 1964–70. The Labour MP, Patrick Gordon Walker, lost his seat at the 1964 General Election but was asked by the Prime Minister to become, nevertheless, a member of his Cabinet as Foreign Secretary. Gordon Walker was found a suitable by-election to fight but, unfortunately, lost it. He then resigned his seat on the Cabinet.

Frank Cousins, then General Secretary of the Transport and General Workers Union, was also asked to become a member of the Wilson Cabinet. He accepted and successfully fought a by-election in order, effectively, to legitimise his seat on the Cabinet. (Cousins subsequently resigned in 1966 when he found himself unable to agree with the proposed Prices and Incomes legislation.)

So strong is the convention of representatives in the Cabinet that, in order to make places for Cousins and Gordon-Walker two Labour MPs were put under some pressure to accept peerages and thereby to create two by-elections.

In 1970 Edward Heath wanted to appoint John Davies, an ex-Director-General of the CBI, as Industry Minister. Again, a safe seat was found for him so that the convention on membership of Parliament could be observed.

Strong Prime Ministers, such as Mrs Thatcher, may not only place great faith in their Cabinet Committees but may also devolve policy-making to those Committees and to 'policy' groups within Downing Street. One is left without any genuine understanding of who is making policy in the British system (and we must never lose sight of the fact that, in the British system, 'making policy' is virtually identical with making laws).

In such a system, who is to be held responsible for those decisions which are taken by groups other than the Cabinet? (See the Westland Affair case study (page 54) in which, not only did it appear that policy was being made outside the Cabinet but also that Civil Servants were used for political purposes (to leak letters and to discredit colleagues). See, also, the Falklands War in which the progress of the war was monitored and led from a small group of people around Mrs Thatcher; the full Cabinet only rarely being more than simply informed of what was going on.)

Inner Cabinets

There have been 'inner Cabinets' in British politics for a very long time. Many nineteenth century Prime Ministers had their circles of close colleagues with whom they consulted and discussed policy.

In the twentieth century these inner groups have broken down into two main types:

- formal **inner Cabinets**
- informal **'kitchen' Cabinets**

The formal variety are by far the easiest to catalogue: Lloyd George and Churchill both had official 'War Cabinets'; Harold Wilson had his 'Parliamentary Committee' and, later, his 'Management Committee' (Cabinet Committees which appear to have operated as inner Cabinets).

Example

Inner Cabinets and Super-Cabinets

1951 Churchill established a Super-Cabinet consisting of himself plus three 'Overlords' – Lords Woolton (for Agriculture & Food), Leathers (for Transport, Fuel & Power), and Cherwell (for Research & Scientific Policy).
The idea was criticised because the Overlords were not responsible to the House of Commons and it was withdrawn in 1953.

1968 Lord Gladwyn suggested a Super-Cabinet of the Prime Minister plus five 'Great Officers of State'.

1968 Harold Wilson established an Inner-Cabinet of himself and nine senior Cabinet Ministers in the 'Parliamentary Committee'.

1969 Wilson established a smaller Inner-Cabinet called the 'Management Committee'.

During the Labour Government of 1964–70 Richard Crossman had a great deal of time and opportunity to study the workings of Cabinet Committees. As the author of a highly respected introduction to Bagehot, Crossman was particularly well suited to this analysis and his conclusions gain additional weight as a result.

Crossman was the first writer to document, from the 'inside', the extent to which Parliamentary government had become Cabinet government and the degree to which this, in turn, had become 'government by official Committee':

> *I was also right to recognise the importance of Cabinet Committees . . . The really big thing I completely failed to notice was that . . . in addition to the Cabinet Committees which only Ministers normally attend, there is a full network of official committees . . . This means that very often the whole job is pre-cooked . . . to a point from which it is extremely difficult to reach any other conclusion than that already determined by the officials in advance.*
>
> Richard Crossman *Diaries*, 18 April 1965 (Magnum Edition, 1979)

Although Crossman was careful to point out that *only* Ministers normally attend Cabinet Committee meetings, it is still the case that senior civil servants and senior members of the armed forces have been known to take part. Ministers on the full Cabinet have complained that the Committees undercut the value of having a Cabinet at all. Many specialist decisions are taken by the Committee and the rest of the Cabinet are given very little opportunity to debate or to question them.

The Authority of the Prime Minister

While the power of the Prime Minister is relatively easy to discuss (one can point to fairly easily defined sources of and limitations on that power), it is much more difficult to identify the sources of Prime Ministerial authority.

Authority is the right to wield power and, as such, has been identified by Weber* as deriving from three possible sources: tradition, law, and charisma.

As there is no law on British statute books which gives authority to the Prime Minister, we must look to tradition and to charisma for the sources.

The role of 'prime' Minister developed over the years as it became necessary, and probably inevitable, that one Minister would both dominate the others and be required to represent them with outside interests: the Monarch, the people, the rest of Parliament, or foreign governments. Even so, the system resisted the idea of a 'Head of Government' until very recently. The office of 'Prime Minister' was not recognised for salary purposes until 1937 and the doctrine of '*primus inter pares*' ('First among equals') was doggedly promoted. It may well be that certain Prime Ministers like to see themselves in this light, but most seem to take up a dominant if not a supreme position.

> *Harold Wilson . . . has certainly allowed some of us a great deal of Ministerial freedom in forging our own Departmental policies. Nevertheless . . . he has completely dominated foreign affairs and defence as well as the main economic decisions. Here the Cabinet has been excluded . . .*
>
> *Well, there's the Prime Minister: not 'primus inter pares' – not at all. He is Prime Ministerial in his supreme authority.*
>
> Richard Crossman, *Diaries*, op.cit.

---

*Max Weber (1864–1920) was one of the founders of modern sociology. His best known work is *The Protestant Ethic and the Spirit of Capitalism.*

It is interesting that, in confirming Prime Ministerial dominance, Crossman uses the word 'authority'. For it is evident that such is what it is. It derives mainly from tradition and role; the question remains as to how much weight should be given to Weber's 'charisma.'

CHARISMA AND AUTHORITY

Personality and its effect on others has long been recognised as a major feature of the exercise of power. Some people are 'born' leaders; they have the ability to have people obey them simply by virtue of their 'presence'.

This book is not the place for a study of 'charisma'; suffice it to say that it may well play a role in supporting the actions and decisions of the Prime Minister.

During World War II it was well understood that Winston Churchill often got what he wanted simply by the force of his personality. In the United States both John F. Kennedy and Lyndon Johnson in their different ways exerted strong influence over people by virtue of 'charisma'. More recently Mrs Thatcher's personality is seen as being an extremely important factor in her Government's success in winning three General Elections in a row and maintaining a quite remarkable degree of popularity.

Mrs Thatcher's opponents may call it 'stubbornness' and call her 'narrow-minded' and 'inflexible'. Her supporters would view it as 'decisiveness', 'determination', 'persistence' and 'courage'. Whichever view one accepts it remains the case that, as the longest serving Prime Minister this century, she has left an almost indelible stamp on British Government.

The key to the concept of 'charisma' would seem to lie in the degree to which poor decisions and reverses can lead to the downfall of a Prime Minister or a Government. There can be no greater contrast than between Mrs Thatcher and Mr Edward Heath. The Heath Government ran into a series of quite serious problems: the economic recession, the increases in oil prices, and the troubles with the National Union of Mineworkers in both 1972 and 1973, but, although severe, these were no greater than many other Governments have had to face. The Heath Government's reaction to these problems, however, led, eventually, to its defeat at a General Election in 1974 which had been called at the almost sole behest of the Prime Minister himself.

▼ *John F. Kennedy – one of the USA's most charismatic Presidents.*

Mrs Thatcher's periods of office have been bedevilled by similar problems: the severe recession of 1981–2; the Miners' strike of 1984–5; continual problems with Ministerial embarrassments (the resignations of Heseltine, Carrington and Parkinson being only a few); a tripling of unemployment (some would argue that it quadrupled); the 'Westland Affair'; and the promotion of a series of extensive pieces of trade union legislation.

One wonders, also, whether the Falklands Crisis would have turned out to be the electoral bonus it was if it had been dealt with in a different way by a different Prime Minister. There were many at the time, for example, who wished simply to begin negotiations with the Argentinians for the return of the islands. It was Mrs Thatcher's determination to go to war to retrieve the islands (a quite considerable gamble) which led, in the end to military and electoral success.

Another test of charisma must be the extent to which an individual Prime Minister can overcome mistakes which are obviously theirs. Mr Heath was thoroughly blamed for his decisions to make economic 'U-turns' and, in the end, to call a General Election in 1974. Mrs Thatcher, on the other hand, has made as many, if not more, errors of judgement and has not seemed to have them held significantly against her.

In the first few months of office, in 1979, she took a decision to maintain gas prices at their then level. She did this in spite of strong advice from her Ministers and advisers that such a move would be economically wrong, and so it turned out. Within twelve months her Government was forced to introduce two separate rises (one of over 30 per cent) in gas prices. In more recent times she refused Roy Jenkins, then leader of the SDP, permission t lay a wreath on the Cenotaph during the annual Remembrance Day servic (1983) and she took up a public position of support for Mr Cecil Parkinso when it was clear to almost everyone else that public opinion would not b in favour of his retaining office. She also made the mistake of almost formall offering the Speakership of the House of Commons to Mr Francis Pym whe George Thomas retired.

Similarly, errors which could be attributed directly to Mrs Thatche continued during her second and third terms of office. One of the mos potentially damaging was the lengthy and extremely expensive legal pursui of Mr Peter Wright during the 'Spycatcher' affair. Wright, an ex-MI5 officer had published an account of his experiences within MI5 which, th British Government argued, was a breach of his commitment to lifelon confidentiality as an officer of the security services. Wright's book, *Spycatche* was effectively banned in the UK but he arranged to have it publishe abroad. It was said, at the time (during 1987–8) that the attempts to hav the book banned in Australia and the United States were continued long afte it became clear that they would fail only because of the persona determination of Mrs Thatcher herself.

Perhaps the most direct comment on Mrs Thatcher's authority within he own Government comes from her own lips. She was reported by *The Observe* as having said:

> *As Prime Minister I couldn't waste my time having any internal arguments*
> *The Observer* 9 December 198

It might be that this comment, taken out of context, gives a misleadin impression of Mrs Thatcher's force of personality but, taken with the othe examples above it demonstrates, at the very least, a strong case for charism as being a major foundation for Prime Ministerial authority.

COLLECTIVE RESPONSIBILITY

The notion of collective responsibility is now well established in Britis political life. In essence, as every student of politics knows, it requires tha every member of the Cabinet be bound, *collectively*, by decisions which ar taken by that body at its meetings. Individual ministers do not need to agre with the policy in question but, once it has become Government policy, the must support it (or, at least, not oppose it) in public.

George Brown resigned from the Cabinet in 1968 when it became clear tha he could not support the official government line on the respective roles o the Department of Economic Affairs and the Treasury. More recently Michael Heseltine resigned from Mrs Thatcher's government when he foun that he could not support that administration's policy on the future of th Westland Helicopter Company.

The Range of Collective Responsibility

One of the basic problems about the concept of Collective Responsibility i the range of people that it is supposed to cover.

In theory and, increasingly, in practice it is held to cover all members o the Government no matter how junior they may be: indeed several PPS' (Parliamentary Private Secretaries) have been sacked for speaking ou against policy with the formation of which they had no part.

It has also become clear over the past decade or so that the concept is now held to apply to the 'shadow cabinet' of Her Majesty's Official Opposition Tony Benn was sacked from his position on the Labour shadow-cabinet fo publicly disagreeing with official party policy.

The Effectiveness of Collective Responsbility

The doctrine has been enforced largely against those whom the Prime Minister or the rest of the Cabinet wanted to see the back of. Those who ha a strong position in the party or who were protected in other ways found that they were able to get away with isolated examples of public opposition.

Those who were extremely careful about the way they went about opposing the Government's policy could sometimes get away with much more than the odd, isolated act of opposition. The secret of this latter, guerrilla opposition is the use of the 'leak'.

In 1968 James Callaghan was Home Secretary and made it very clear that he did not support the Labour Government's official policy to reform the trade unions, which was centred on the policy document 'In Place of Strife'. It is plain that the support of the party's paymasters, the unions, was sufficient to make his position virtually impregnable. Callaghan was not required to resign and, in reality, it was the Government itself which was forced to back down and to abandon reform of the unions!

Agreement to Differ

On the whole, Ministers have to resign when they disagree with Government policy, but there have been occasions when a 'holiday' has been granted for all. On these occasions the Prime Minister or the Cabinet as a whole has determined that issues which would, otherwise, have brought the Government down must be fought outside the doctrine of collective responsibility.

For a few months in 1932 there was such an agreement in the then newly-formed National Government over the issue of tariffs (customs duties). In order to preserve the government and to avoid the need for a general election (and on a single, well-defined issue) Ministers were allowed to take up positions which were not the 'official' Government ones.

In 1975 this 'agreement to differ' principle was revived for the issue of membership of the EEC. The bulk of the Labour Cabinet supported Britain's membership under the terms which had been renegotiated by Harold Wilson, but a minority did not. If the Prime Minister had insisted upon the principle of collective responsibility under the prevailing political conditions (in which he did not have an overall majority in Parliament) it would have entailed another General Election, the fourth in five years! Wilson decided, therefore, to hold a national **referendum** and that, for the duration of the referendum campaign, Ministers could speak on whatever side of the issue they wanted *as long as they did so outside Parliament.*

The 1975 EEC Referendum Campaign treated us to the unique spectacle of politicians like Enoch Powell, Eric Heffer and Tony Benn speaking on the same 'No' platforms while Mrs Thatcher, Harold Wilson and David Steel spoke on the same 'Yes' platform.

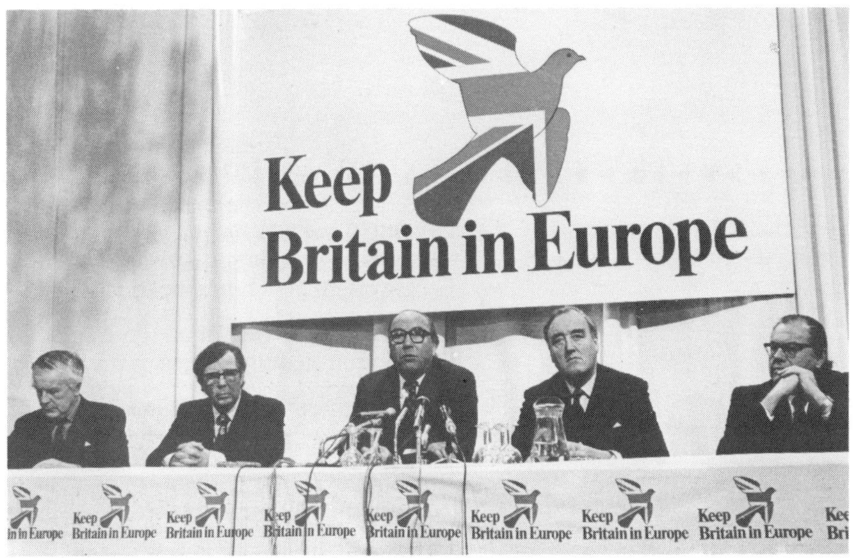

Left to right on the 1975 'Yes' campaign platform: Jo Grimond (Liberal), Cledwyn Hughes (Labour), Roy Jenkins (Labour), William Whitelaw (Conservative), Reginald Maudling (Conservative).

MINISTERIAL RESPONSIBILITY

The concept of Ministerial Responsibility is, if anything, even less clear tha that of Collective Responsibility. In theory it is supposed to imply th Minister's personal responsibility in both a *legal* and *political* sense for th acts and omissions of his Department.

Underlying this concept is the parallel concept of the anonymity of Civ Servants. The latter are deemed to be *advisers* and not *policy-makers*. Th person who must take responsibility for mistakes is, therefore, the person wh is directly accountable to the public through Parliament: the Minister. Thes ideas have become hopelessly confused over the past decades; if, indeed, the were ever very clear. It has always been rare for Ministers to resign due t personal errors or to acts or omissions of their Departments but it is becomin rarer.

Other textbooks list all the standard examples of Ministerial Responsibilit in action: Hugh Dalton's budget leak of 1947, Crichel Down and Sir Thoma Dugdale in 1954, and Lord Carrington after the invasion of the Falklan Islands in 1982.

What is clear, however, is that it seems as if the personal preference of th Minister concerned, and the ability or desire of the Prime Minister to suppor the Minister, have as much to do with the final resignation as does th existence of an error in the Department.

On the surface it would appear that Hugh Dalton's 1947 indiscretion i revealing the main budget points to a correspondent just as he was about t enter the chamber of the House to give the Chancellor's Budget Speech wa a clear case of absolute responsibility. He knew the purpose of the conventio of budget secrecy and the mistake was his alone. The result was that London newspaper was able to get an edition on the streets giving the mai points on the Budget before the Chancellor had finished his speech. There i no doubt that Dalton made a mistake, but it certainly does not follow tha he necessarily needed to resign.

In 1983 Mrs Thatcher tried, for a long time, to protect Mr Cecil Parkinson whose affair with his secretary and her widely publicised pregnancy ha resulted in grave embarrassment for the Government.

On a slightly different level it is also recognised that Ministers cannot b held responsible for *everything* that happens in their Departments. In 197 the Vehicle and General Insurance Company collapsed with massive losse to its customers. The Department of Trade and Industry had known of th company's problems for some time but had never made them public Although voices were raised asking for the Minister to resign, there was neve any serious attempt to enforce the doctrine.

▶▶▶▶▶▶▶▶▶▶▶▶▶▶▶ EXAMINATION QUESTIONS

1 Did the Parliamentary agreement between the Labour and the Libera parties in March 1977 offend against the principles of responsible government? (London, Jan 1980,1)

2 Discuss the view that the Cabinet is simply the 'clearing house' for top decision-making bodies in the British government today. (AEB, June 1980)

3 'The power of the Prime Minister is only as great as the success of the policies with which he/she is identified.' Comment. (Cambridge, 1982)

4 What evidence is there, if any, for the claim that the power of Parliament over the Executive has declined in the past 25 years? (Cambridge, 1982)

5 Do we still have Cabinet government in Britain? (Cambridge, 1987)

►►►►►►►►►►►►►► NOW READ ON . . .

Richard Crossman *Diaries of a Cabinet Minister* Magnum Edition, 1979
Although dated the *Diaries* show a picture that is probably as true now as it was during the 1960s.

Peter Jenkins *Mrs Thatcher's Revolution: the Ending of the Socialist Era* Cape 1987
One man's view – take with care.

Bernard Donoughue *Prime Minister: The Conduct of Policy under Harold Wilson and James Callaghan* Cape, 1987
Another man's view of a different government; treat with equal care.

John Cole *The Thatcher Years* BBC Books, 1987
A further journalistic view; a close reading is necessary.

Anthony King *The British Prime Minister* Revised Edition Macmillan, 1985
The classic on the office of the PM.

19 The Judiciary

BASIC PRINCIPLES

Key Concepts

Legitimacy	Of the Magistrates (in view of their background); of jurors; of the Courts acting to control elected Ministers.
Power and Authority	The legal profession as a pressure group; role of the Law Society; lawyers as MPs.
Justice	Differences in treatment of offenders in different areas; Northern Ireland Courts; the fairness of the overall system in Britain to minorities.
Equality	Access to legal aid; equality before the law of minorities, the poor and the uneducated; juries and trial by peers.
Freedom	Bail and the remand system; Prevention of Terrorism Act.
Rights	'Radical law' and the rights of tenants, of minorities and of the employed; the question of a Bill of Rights.

DISCUSSING THE ARGUMENTS

A Ministry of Justice?

This must be one of the oldest chestnuts of the British judicial system and one which has formed the basis of a great many exam questions over the years. It is an important question because, at the moment, the judicial system is directed from many different headquarters:

The Home Office	Deals with the police (the Metropolitan Police directly and the police in the provinces indirectly), the prison service, public morals, race relations and with the introduction of criminal law.
The Lord Chancellor	Deals with the administration of the courts and the appointment of judges and magistrates.
The Law Officers Department	Consisting of the Attorney-General and the Solicitor-General, both of whom are Members of Parliament, and act as legal advisers to the Crown and the Government.
The Scottish Office	Deals with the judicial system in Scotland

There are a number of Ministers who have responsibility within the system: the Home Secretary, the Lord Chancellor, the Secretaries of State for Northern Ireland and for Scotland, the Attorney-General and the Solicitor-General and, of course, the Prime Minister who 'recommends' judicial appointments to the Monarch.

It is also the case that each separate Ministry is responsible for its own legal affairs and for promoting its own laws in Parliament. Each has a Legal Officer and a team of civil servants responsible for drafting and amending laws in consultation with Parliamentary Counsel.

A separate Ministry of Justice would combine most of these functions within one administrative organisation and would enable other Ministries to look to a central team to prepare and to oversee legislation.

Although this sounds, superficially, like a reasonable idea, it is more justified from an administrative than a judicial point of view. Administratively, such a Ministry would probably save both time and money. Judicially, however, it might have several unlooked-for effects.

At present all of the Law Officers and, of course, the Lord Chancellor, have to be qualified lawyers. In the case of the Lord Chancellor it is usually a very senior lawyer. A Ministry of Justice might well not require such qualifications (after all, no one insists on the Minister of Defence being an ex-soldier, or the Secretary of State for the Social Services being an ex-doctor, nurse or social worker).

The concern over creating a Ministry of Justice always seems to have been centred on whether such an organisation would allow sufficient separation between the executive and the judicial system. The sinister impact of the words 'Ministry of Justice' seems to carry additional connotations of Orwell's *Nineteen Eighty-Four*. On the other hand one has to ask whether, in the light of the sorts of things discussed below, there is sufficient separation at the moment and whether the system operates properly with MPs (as Attorney- and Solicitor-General) acting as their own government's legal advisers.

Trial by Combat

Any analysis of the British legal system would be incomplete without an attempt to question one of its aspects which is most taken for granted: the way in which the courts operate.

The essence of the system is a sort of 'trial by combat' in which the accused and the accusers each put forward 'champions' to do battle on their behalf. Each side has its legal champion who is responsible (in court) for establishing which side wins. The umpires are the judges or magistrates together, in some cases, with a band of lay-people called a jury.

Whether a case is won or lost often depends not on whether 'truth' is on one side or the other, but on the debating skill of the respective champions. Many people have used the skill and status of the best barristers to represent them in fairly minor cases in Magistrates' courts and have, perhaps, benefited from such high quality representation.

Although the system is almost invariably taken for granted, it does not always produce the right results. There have been too many prisoners released in recent years when it was found that they were, in fact, innocent, for us to be sanguine about the effectiveness of the court system. In many other countries the system is not '*adversarial*' as it is here but, rather, '*inquisitorial*'.

In France and Italy, in particular, the courts operate on a system which requires a lawyer to *investigate* the crime alongside the police. This lawyer will then attempt to find out the truth of the case and will present these findings to the court. There are no real court-room battles-of-words such as occur in British courts. It is often said that the European system takes longer but can be relied upon to produce better results.

Police Prosecutions

Up until 1986 it was the practice for the police in England and Wales to make their own decisions as to whether to bring a prosecution in a criminal case (in Scotland the decision was taken by the 'Procurator Fiscal', an independent lawyer).

It became clear over the years that the police, who worked with local 'prosecuting solicitors', tended to enter into court cases which were somewhat weak. It was said, not without some justification, that the police tended to be optimistic about many cases because they were blinded by the fact tha they themselves had carried out the investigation.

Many police officers became convinced by their own evidence or tha gathered by their subordinates, and others tended to enter into prosecution on the basis that they 'knew' who had committed the crime. This may wel have been the case. Police officers of some years experience are sometime able to 'solve' cases on the basis of their local knowledge and experience This is not, however, the same as *proof*, and the courts were often forced t throw out cases which had been brought by the police on the basis of to little firm evidence. In 1984 over a quarter of all criminal cases brought b the police were thrown out of courts for these reasons.

In 1985 the Government introduced the Prosecution of Offences Act, whic took the responsibility for deciding whether to prosecute away from the polic and gave it, instead, to local Prosecuting Solicitors who are independent o the police.

THE SYSTEM OF CIVIL JUSTICE

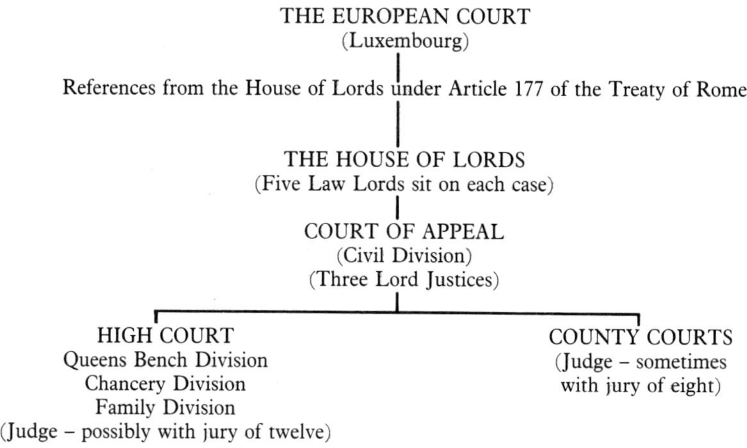

NOTES:
1. In Scotland appeals may be heard in the Court of Sessions and, if necessary, may be further hear by the House of Lords.
2. Northern Ireland appeals may also be heard by the province's Court of Appeals and by the Hous of Lords.

THE SYSTEM OF CRIMINAL JUSTICE

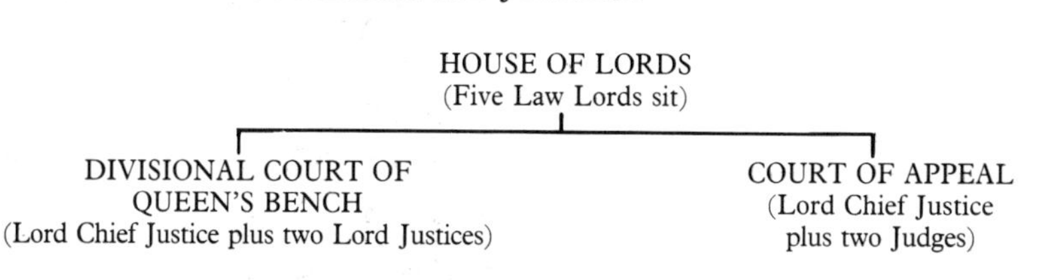

CROWN COURT
(In the first instance a Judge plus a Jury of twelve; for appeals, a Judge plus between 2 and 4 Magistrates)

MAGISTRATES COURT
(For an indictable offence two Magistrates, – for a summary offence three Magistrates)

NOTES:
1. An Indictable Offence is more serious than a Summary one and it is generally believed that the Magistrates Court acts, essentially, as a filter and that the trial itself should be heard before higher courts in front of a Jury.
2. The highest court of appeal in Scotland is the High Court in Edinburgh. There is no appeal from there to the House of Lords.
3. In Northern Ireland there may be an appeal to the House of Lords from the Northern Ireland Court of Appeal.

Equality Before The Law

Access to Law

In theory all are equal before the law, no matter what one's position in society or one's wealth. It would be fair to say that most of our Magistrates and judges would agree with and uphold this ideal to the best of their ability, but it is also true that it does not operate without problems.

The most obvious problem is that of *access to law*. The Legal Aid system covers the requirements of most of the poorest section of the population and the richest section can almost always afford their own legal representation. There are, however, about a quarter of the population who are not rich enough to afford their own representation but who are well-off enough to fall outside the boundaries of the Legal Aid system. Access to law for these people is difficult and relatively expensive.

A single day of legal activity in the High Court can cost around £5,000: a figure which is, obviously, outside the means of any but the richest amongst us.

The question, therefore, becomes one of fairness and justice. Should part of the population be treated differently as far as access to law is concerned?

If the answer to this question is 'No', then the solution lies in one of two different directions: either the Legal Aid system must be extended to include everybody but the most wealthy (and how are they to be determined?) or the legal profession must be 'nationalised' and their charges (and salaries) reduced.

The latter solution is not quite as far-fetched as it sounds, in as much as the medical profession was virtually nationalised in 1948 and operates largely on state determined salaries. Are there any good reasons why the legal profession should be any different?

Should access to law be made easier and more widely available there might well be significant implications for the level of demand on already over-stretched courts.

Different Treatment

Equality also means that people are treated in the same way for the same offences or in response to the same civil grievances. It is clear, however, that this need not be the case. Magistrates in certain parts of the country are notorious for treating certain types of offenders more leniently than their counterparts in other areas.

Even judges, who are professional lawyers, have been known to treat the same types of circumstances very differently. On one notorious occasion a judge was officially reprimanded for merely fining a rapist.

Whether it involves serious crime or parking offences, it is a fundamental part of the rule of law that a person should not receive treatment in one court which is different – *for the same offence or in the same circumstances* – as he would receive in another court.

The training of magistrates and judges is obviously one partial solution to this problem. At the moment judges (who are really senior barristers or solicitors) receive just a few days 'training' in sentencing. Any follow-up training is optional. Magistrates all receive mandatory training, but many experts believe that this is still inadequate.

The Jury System

Another foundation of the British legal system, since the Middle Ages, has been the principle that, for serious crimes, a person is entitled to be tried in front of a panel of his peers – called a **jury**. In the first instance the system was designed to protect the ordinary knight or commoner against the arbitrary justice of the King or the Lord of the Manor. The judge could pronounce sentence (because he was a professional lawyer and understood what punishments the law allowed and what the precedents were), but the question of a person's guilt or innocence was decided by a unanimous verdict of a panel of his 'peers'.

The jury system has come under increasing question in recent years on two main levels:

- with respect to the level of expertise available to juries in complex cases;
- with respect to the way in which the inherent bias of any one jury is dealt with.

Expertise

As a random selection of citizens, juries are expected to hear, understand and decide almost all serious crime. In most cases even the circumstances and the elements of proof of the most serious crime (murder) can be explained clearly to a jury; but these days of high technology and high finance are breeding new types of crime which involve the complex and arcane worlds of computers and finance. In these types of crime most juries are completely lost and it is impossible to give each jury the technical knowledge to be able to understand what happened.

For example, cases of 'insider dealing' or fraud involving millions of pounds may be extremely difficult to detect and even more difficult to prove. They require highly trained police officers who are themselves expert accountants or computer analysts. What chance does the average jury have of comprehending the intricacies of international share dealings, banking or company accounts?

Although it is not fashionable to speak of such things, there is also a question about the ability of juries to understand and decide even relatively simple cases. There is no qualification required to be a juror except the right to vote and many lawyers have questioned the ability of some jurors to comprehend the complexities of most criminal cases or to understand when a defendent or his lawyer is trying to pull the wool over their eyes.

Bias

It was possible, until recently, for lawyers to object to jurors without giving reasons and for jurors themselves to be excused if they believed that, because of firmly held personal beliefs, they could not hear the case with impartiality. A juror who claimed to have strong racist views would have to be excused, for example, from a trial in which a black person was a defendant. This has led to cases in which, it is thought, certain jurors have deliberately avoided jury service by inventing reasons why they would be unsuitable. It was felt, for a long time, that one only had to turn up for jury service in a suit and tie for the defence to object to you (as being too likely to take the side of the police or authority).

Jury Picking

A similar problem is that of jury-picking. In theory juries are selected at random from the list of voters and they take their decisions by a majority vote in which 10 to 2 is the lowest acceptable majority. Up until 1987 the lawyers could object to up to three jurors but could not question them in order to make these objections. Most of the objections were done on the basis of the way the juror looked, or on their colour, race or sex. In 1987 the Criminal Justice Act abolished this right.

The judge can, however, still allow the pre-trial 'screening' of a jury; a power which is little known and whose effect on the judicial system is unpredictable. In 1978 a judge allowed the screening of a jury panel of 82 members by the Special Branch. The jury was required for a case in which Official Secrets would need to be revealed to the court.

More worryingly perhaps, a judge in York in 1979 allowed the police to screen a panel of 60 for prison records. The jury was required to hear the case against 13 Hull Prison Officers concerning their treatment of prisoners after a riot in 1976. It was felt, probably with some justification, that people who had been in prison would be biased against prison officers. The precedent could be seen as one which then justified the screening of women out of rape trial juries, of bank employees from trials of alleged bank robbers and house owners from trials of burglars . . .

The Authority and the Power of the Judiciary

The authority of the judiciary rests on two main foundations:

- the *precedent* set by Common Law and by previous decisions
- the *provisons of Statutes.*

These have established the role of the judiciary as the judges of whether the letter of the law has been put into effect or not.

All students know, however, that judges not only rule on the application of the strict letter or **construction** of laws (**constructionism**), but that they also **interpret** the meaning of the law and, in some cases, actually extend the laws into new areas (**creative judging**).

The best known example of the latter was the famous Supreme Court of the USA under the command of Chief Justice Earl Warren. The 'Warren Court' made a long string of decisions between the early 1950s and the late 1960s which extended the laws of the United States in a wide variety of social areas including the rights of black people, the rights of offenders, and the powers of the Federal and State governments. In this activity the Warren Court excited a great deal of opposition from Congress and from some Presidents who believed that it was not the role of the Supreme Court to act as a source of 'back-door' legislation. In the USA, however, the Supreme Court was in a position of great power. The Constitution implied (and later Court decisions confirmed) that the role of the Supreme Court was to guard and to interpret the meaning of the Constitution. The Justices of the Warren Court era used this power and the legitimacy it gave them to change not only the laws of the USA but also the whole approach to some critical social problems.

In the UK the role of the judiciary is much more constrained by the fact that Parliament has the sovereign right to make law and the fact that there is no written constitution which the courts can claim to be guarding.

This has not prevented several judges from claiming the right to develop and interpret laws however. The best known of these, in recent years, being Lord Denning who, as Master of the Rolls until 1982, tried to interpret laws in the light of what he felt was Parliament's *intention* in creating the law and what he felt were the requirements of society.

Even judges who feel less radical about the role of the law than Lord Denning have found that the dividing line between a 'neutral' judiciary, which merely adjudicates on disputes over the law, and a 'political' judiciary, which makes politically and socially 'loaded' decisions, is extremely thin. Society expects judges not only to hear and decide criminal cases (which, in themselves, can be fraught with problems) but to sit on cases involving matters about which society itself is heavily divided: sex discrimination, racial discrimination, trade union matters, the role of local government, etc. It is no wonder that judges, being human, make decisions which draw criticism from one side or the other.

Like teachers, our judges and magistrates take their own upbringing and social values to work with them. In theory they should not allow those values to influence what they do, but how many human beings can deny their own strongly held beliefs in order to do this? The best that we can hope for in the classroom is that society will accept whatever values the teacher brings. Most parents have a view of what they would wish their children to learn about the world (based, of course, on their own values), and will only become disturbed if the school appears to be teaching their child something greatly different.

To a large extent it is the same in our courtrooms. Only when the decisions of judges appear to differ greatly from the norms which society expects of them do the public become concerned. In the case mentioned above, about the convicted rapist who was merely fined £2,000, the values of society appeared to have been flouted by the judge. The reactions of the general public and the press were extremely critical.

POLITICS AND THE LAW

The separation of our legislature and executive from the judiciary is designe to minimise the possibility of the judges being corrupted by either politica ideology, bribery or blackmail. The salaries of judges are paid directly fron the Consolidated Fund and cannot be stopped or amended by th Government, and judges hold their offices by very strict tenure which ca only be withdrawn by a vote of both Houses of Parliament.

One must try to distinguish, however, between the open political bias of judge either inside or outside the courtroom and the application of the judge' values to a case. The most frequently mentioned area of dispute here i usually the judiciary's attitude to the trade union movement. Many left-win trade unionists believe that the judges are 'on the side' of the governmen and are so patently right-wing that their decisions lack legitimacy. The mos commonly heard cry is that of 'Tory Courts'.

Example

The Disciplining of the Judiciary

It is possible for judges to be sacked but examples are very rare.

In 1983 a judge was removed from office for smuggling, with an accomplice, large amounts of whisky and cigarettes from the Channel Isles. The Lord Chancellor was able to remove him, under the terms of the Courts Act 1971, for misbehaviour.

In 1977 the Scottish Secretary sacked the Sheriff of South Strathclyde, Dumfries and Galloway (a Scottish judge), Mr Peter Thomson, for using his judicial position in his campaign in favour of a referendum on home rule for Scotland. Mr Thomson had used his title of Assistant Returning Officer in a pamphlet supporting a referendum and had been openly involved in the campaign since 1974. Under the Sheriff Courts of Scotland Act of 1971 the Secretary of State for Scotland has the power to dismiss a Scottish judge on the recommendation of two senior Scottish law officers. In this case, Mr Thomson had been investigated by Lord Emslie, Lord Justice General of Scotland, and Lord Wheatley, Lord Justice Clerk. Both officers recommended Thomson's dismissal.

TRADE UNIONS AND THE COURTS

Example

The Gouriet Case

In January of 1977 the Post Office Union (the Union of Post Office Workers – UPOW) made a decision that, in support of the anti-apartheid movement, it would 'black' the delivery of mail between the UK and South Africa.

The Director of the right-wing 'Freedom Association', Mr John Gouriet, argued that as holding up the Royal Mail was a criminal offence, the Attorney-General should prevent the ban taking effect.

The Labour Attorney-General, Mr Sam Silkin, refused to do this and Mr Gouriet brought an action before the Court of Appeal asking that they prevent the UPOW from initiating the ban.

The Court of Appeal agreed that the union's action was illegal and placed an injunction on the UPOW preventing it from beginning the blacking of mail. The union then called off the ban.

Mr Silkin, however, called on the House of Lords to make a ruling on what he considered to be a matter of great legal importance: whether Mr Gouriet, who was a private citizen and not directly involved in the dispute, could seek legal action when the Attorney-General had used his discretion not to intervene.

In July 1977 the House of Lords ruled that the discretion of the Attorney-General was 'absolute and non-reviewable' (by the courts) and they overturned the Appeal Court's injunction.

In this case the Lords ruled, apparently, in favour of trade union rights, but for the perfectly sound legal reason that they felt that the courts had no right to question the discretion of the Attorney-General, who claimed that he was answerable to Parliament only. The earlier decision by the Appeal Court, however, had been seen by the trade unions as a patently political and anti-union decision by the 'Tory Courts'.

The question has to be: are the courts expressing an unjustified political bias against trade unions, are they simply interpreting the law as passed by Parliament rigidly, or are they also expressing their own values? If the last, then there must also be a further question about whether the values of the judges match those of the society in which they operate. A series of examples should provide sufficient initial basis for consideration of these questions:

Example

Conservative Trade Union Legislation

Since the Conservative Government of 1979 began introducing legislation concerning the activities of trade unions (the Employment Acts of 1980 and 1982 and the Trade Union Act of 1984) the Courts have been brought even closer to the 'political' arena.

The Miners' Strike of 1984–5 brought some of the bitterest disputes between the unions and the courts, and these were made even more bitter by the fact that the courts were not only asked to adjudicate disputes between the union and the employers but also between the union and its own members and ex-members.

Early in the dispute the High Court ruled that the strike was unofficial (not because it contravened the Employment Acts but because it contravened the National Union of Mineworkers' (NUM) own rules on ballots before strikes).

In October 1984 the same court imposed a fine of £200,000 on the NUM for contempt in defying the earlier ruling that the strike was unofficial. (The NUM had continued to claim that it was official and had tried to prevent miners going to work by threatening them with disciplinary action.)

The NUM refused to pay the fine of £200,000 and the High Court ordered the sequestration of the union's entire assets, estimated at around £10m.

Both of these examples illustrate the difficulty of analysing the 'political' bias of the judges. Most of our judges come from a public school background, all of them, of course, from a university background. Most of our magistrates come from a middle-class background and they are predominantly white, male and elderly. It is not difficult to show examples of genuine bias towards certain values. The problem is whether that bias is of significant importance in our system or whether it is merely superficial.

EXAMINATION QUESTIONS

1 Should the courts play a larger role in the control of government? (London, Jan 1983,1)

2 Should judges be able to reject provisions of Parliamentary statutes, as Lord Denning has suggested? (London, June 1982,1)

3 Can judges stay out of politics? (London, June 1983,1)

4 Can judges be impartial in their application of the law, and do you think they are? (London, Jan 1980,1)

NOW READ ON . . .

Lord Gifford, QC *Where's the Justice?* Penguin, 1986
Part of Lord Gifford's case (he is a Labour peer) involves a call for a Ministry of Justice.

J. A. G. Griffith *The Politics of the Judiciary* Fontana 2nd Edition, 1985
Professor Griffith's excellently argued and controversial thesis begins with his analysis of the backgrounds of our judges and examines the track record of the courts across a wide range of legislation

Lord McClusky 'The Reith Lectures on Law, Justice and Democracy' *The Listener* (beginning 6 November 1986).
Lord McClusky is a Scottish Judge and claims to have been a Labour Party supporter for some years. The six lectures bring out many of the most important themes of the modern judiciary.

'English Justice' *The Economist* 30 July–3 Sept 1983 (six part series).

In his Monday column Peter Hennessy examines the career of Sir Robert Armstrong

Swan-song of a public civil servant

WHITEHALL WATCH

by Peter Hennessey

SIR ROBERT Armstrong has three weeks to go as Cabinet Secretary and head of the home Civil Service. There will, no doubt, be a warm tribute from Margaret Thatcher at the end of the last Cabinet meeting at which he takes the minutes. But last week saw his public swan-song. It took the form of two statements, both of which were entirely in character.

The first was a refinement of the rules of conduct for civil servants who believe that ministers are acting improperly. The chain of complaint was laid down up to and including the head of the service but no further, with confidentiality about the grievance to be maintained unto the grave.

The second was a speech on the Government's management reforms on Friday at Regent's College in London as part of a seminar organised by the Royal Institute of Public Administration and Peat Marwick McLintock.

His theme – the drive for greater efficiency in Whitehall – was as dry as it was important. But it gave way at the end to a statement of personal values which was genuinely poignant given Sir Robert's public trials in the past two years.

Speaking of the public service ethic, he delivered the quote which "I can never get out of my mind", the words Elizabeth I used when she appointed William Cecil as her Secretary of State: "This judgement I have of you: that you will not be corrupted with any manner of gifts, and that you will be faithful to the state, and that without respect of my private will you will give me that counsel that you think best."

Sir Robert added: "One of the abiding strengths of the British Civil Service is that it retains a strong sense of the values of public service and of its importance and worth, which gives civil servants pride in the discharge of their duties and sustains them when the going is rough."

None of the five Cabinet secretaries who preceded Sir Robert have had it rougher. He has faced, as a fellow permanent secretary put it, "this awful series of stinkers – GCHQ, Ponting, Westland and Wright". For a man who has admitted his preference for being in the backroom, it has been a public torment.

Sir Robert's personal aspirations shone through in the obituary of his predecessor but two, Burke Trend, which he prepared for *The Independent* earlier this year. "He [Trend] was a private person, who did not become, or aspire to be, a public figure," he wrote. "He was content to be appreciated by his peers and by the ministers whom he served with self-effacement for so many years."

For Sir Robert it was not to be. For him the nightmare of every traditional civil servant – becoming associated by name with political controversy – became an abundant reality.

It has happened before during his century. Sir Horace Wilson was destroyed by his association, as one of the "guilty men" who pursued appeasement, with Neville Chamberlain. And Sir William Armstrong never recovered from being dubbed the "deputy prime minister" to Edward Heath during the economic and industrial crisis of the 1970s.

Yet the notoriety of Wilson and William Armstrong was largely confined to the political nation – those who find the ins and outs of Westminster and Whitehall a subject of fascination.

Sir Robert's travails at the hands of Malcolm Turnbull and Judge Powell in the Sydney courtroom last year made him a household name and his typically self-ironic admission that he had been "economical with the truth" has entered the popular lexicon. To discover anything comparable one has to go back more than 450 years, beyond Elizabeth and Cecil, to the fall of Cardinal Wolsey, to find a more public public servant. Sir Robert, even before his retirement, has found the kind of niche in history to which no civil servant aspires. Quite apart from the celebrity factor, there is the danger of distortion in the historical memory. It stems partly from the fact that Sir Robert, unlike many of his predecessors, has served only one prime minister.

But he is not the Thatcherite he is sometimes dubbed. On specific issues she has often acted contrary to his advice – the naming of Anthony Blunt as a spy in 1979, the deunionisation of GCHQ in 1984. He was horrified at her insensitivity in handling the inner city riots of 1981 and was keen on Michael Heseltine's ambitious plans for urban regeneration. Sir Robert was and remains a one nation man, close to the ideas of the late Harold Macmillan, for whom he retains an abiding affection.

Source: *The Independent*, 7 December 1987

One of the major features of the British civil service is its wish to avoid any public association with political controversy. There exists a well established tradition of service to the government of the day, whatever its political colour. Increasingly in recent years the civil service has become a target for critics of both 'left' and 'right' in British politics, and its established traditions are criticised as being a threat to radicalism and change. Civil servants have been criticised further for exercising undue control over their ministers yet any public disclosure of this is prevented by an alleged cloak of secrecy. Since 1979 in particular there has been growing concern in the Conservative government over the efficiency of the Civil Service, which has resulted in attempts to change some aspects of the traditional relationship between officials and ministers.

BASIC PRINCIPLES

Key Theory and Concepts

Influence and Persuasion: The lack of formal power may not prevent civil servants having considerable influence over the way in which government policy is implemented.

Representation Administrators in government are often criticised for being drawn from too narrow a segment of society and in effect of forming an elite group.

Responsibility Public servants have a duty to act in a way which puts aside personal preferences in response to an almost 'ethical code' which entreats them to act in the public interest. Responsibility also implies that civil servants should answer to the public for their actions.

Democracy The effectiveness of controls upon government officials and their accountability to both parliament and public.

DISCUSSING THE ARGUMENTS

'No, minister': The 'Threat' of Bureaucracy

Public servants are often described as 'bureaucrats'. The term bureaucracy has its origins in the French word 'bureau' which is used to describe a government office or a department. It was the fear that the employees of these 'bureaux' were gaining too much power and influence that led to the term 'bureaucratic' being used often in a derogatory way. In popular usage 'bureaucracy' has been associated with inefficiency, insensitivity, and complicated and lengthy administrative procedures.

The possibility that power may be concentrated and centralised in the hands of officials has come to be seen as a threat to liberty, in that non-elected state officials are felt to take decisions which affect the lives of individual citizens. However, in Britain, administrative power is more greatly dispersed than in some other European countries and, therefore, the 'threat' of bureaucracy has not been felt so widely. The potential danger, however, is still recognised. The 'antidote' is seen as lying in the limits that are placed upon public officials by elected representatives.

The need for an administrative machinery of paid officials, to organise and run the services provided by the modern state, is similar to the need for paid employees in any large organisation. The specialised skills and the complexities of the tasks of full time officials has led to the criticism that they are separate and distant from the general public, and that this has assisted them to gain and retain power.

Government administrators may appear to be isolated because of the nature of their job, for, as in any other organisation, administration involves inspecting, supervising, organising, etc rather than directly producing goods or services. The work of the administrator will usually be governed by a set of rules and regulations, often statutes, although inevitably not all eventualities can be anticipated.

Policy-making or Discretion?

Example

There is little point in a government minister deciding to introduce major reforms in welfare provision if administratively it is impossible to do so. Even if it can be done, the administrator still needs to know when and who will be included, excluded, etc. So the method of implementation can in itself be a policy decision.

Administrators usually require a degree of discretion in running an organisation. Not all situations that occur can be dealt with by established rules and, on occasions, regulations may be waived, if good grounds exist for them to be put aside. The exercise of discretion by a public official can produce problems for it may appear that 'policy' is actually being produced. Policy is supposed to be the responsibility of politicians and the job of the public servant is to implement (i.e. to administer) the wishes of the policy makers. The distinction is, however, extremely difficult to sustain, because much policy will be determined by the practicability of implementing it. Politicians implicitly rely upon their administrators to help them form policy and much policy is the result of ideas being developed by administrators and endorsed by politicians. In many instances though, 'policy' is based on feedback from the administration of previous policies. This dependence has grown as the size and complexity of the administrative machinery has expanded during the twentieth century.

The responsibilities of the **state** (see Chapter 2) were minimal at the beginning of the nineteenth century, and largely restricted to defence and law and order functions. As the century progressed the need to legislate on hours of work, factory and mine safety, the employment of women and children, town planning, etc. meant a gradual increase in the number of public servants.

The contemporary British state provides a plethora of services (such as health and education), direct to the citizen, and it also attempts wide ranging regulation of many economic activities. As the range of state activity grew so did the number of people employed.

Today the state is by far the biggest employer with nearly 6.4 million engaged in public employment. By 1987 1.2 million people were employed by the National Health Service, 1.8 million in local government and there were 594 000 civil servants. The proportion of the Gross Domestic Product now consumed by the public sector runs to 40 per cent, even though attempts have been made since 1979 to reduce levels of public expenditure.

It is not just the 'size' of the 'empire' run by public officials that is felt to enhance their power, but also the increasingly complex nature of the functions they undertake. The result is that public officials have become more and more specialised in areas such as management, economic planning, and cost benefit analysis, which would have been unknown even 40 years ago.

THE 'SECRET' CIVIL SERVICE

Another feature of the alleged power of the central administration is its ability to conduct its affairs with little public scrutiny. A prohibition on the unauthorised disclosure of information by civil servants has existed since 1911. The 1911 Official Secrets Act covered all information no matter how trivial even the menu in the Home Office canteen was secret! Every civil servant had to sign the Act and a deliberate infringement could result in prosecution and imprisonment for the offender. They were bound by the Act in the following way:

> . . . *I am aware that I should not divulge any information gained by me as a result of my appointment to any unauthorized person, either orally, or in writing, without the previous official sanction in writing of the Department appointing me, to which written application should be made and two copies of the proposed publication be forwarded. I understand also that I am liable to be prosecuted if I publish without official sanction any information I may acquire in the course of my tenure of an official appointment (unless it has already officially been made public) or retain*

Example

Dame Evelyn Sharp, Richard Crossman's Permanent Secretary, at the Ministry of Housing and Local Government came in for particular criticism. He claimed she effectively ran the department without consulting him, and constantly took decisions with which he disagreed. In her defence, she claimed that Crossman simply misunderstood his role as a minister in that he expected to be able to take administrative decisions which had to be left to civil servants.

without official sanction any sketch, plan, model, article, note or official documents which are no longer needed for my official duties, and that these provisions apply not only during the period of my appointment but also after my appointment has ceased . .

Kellner and Crowther-Hunt *The Civil Servants* Macdonald, 1980 (page 264)

The legislation covering official information became the subject of a good deal of criticism and demands were made for major changes to the Act, or for its replacement by a 'Freedom of Information Act' similar to that in the USA and Australia. It was argued that the range of official material covered by national security considerations should be reduced considerably and thereby allow a more 'open' form of government. In 1984, a parliamentary campaign was mounted to get the government to change the law and this won the backing of civil service unions and several former senior civil servants.

One of the reasons why some civil servants wished to see this 'cloak' of secrecy lifted was a reaction to the revelations contained in the *Crossman Diaries* in which some civil servants were publicly named and criticised. This breach of trust and anonymity by Richard Crossman was considered by many civil servants to be a serious betrayal of established conventions.*

The Conservative Government announced plans in 1988 to review the Act and consider changes to it. The major objection to it was that it is ridiculous to classify *all* official information under the umbrella of the Act, no matter how trivial. There was also the question of what was meant by 'intentional' disclosure of information which led to a situation in which some instances of disclosure resulted in prosecution, whereas others did not.

The Act

The Official Secrets Act of 1911 was passed very hurriedly in response to an alleged threat of German espionage and, although it was amended in 1920 and 1939, for 70 years the substance of the Act remained unaltered.

Its workings were, however, reviewed in 1972, by a Government appointed committee. The **Franks Committee** called for major reform. It argued that a much narrower definition of 'secret' was required and before any prosecution under a new 'Official Information Act' could take place the relevant minister should have to prove that the information had been correctly classified. The findings of the Franks Committee were included in a 1978 White Paper, but the 1979 general election prevented any further progress.

Conservative attempts after 1979 to introduce a new act produced considerable criticism. Many argued that it would be worse than the 1911 Act in that it outlawed all discussion of British security services. The Protection of Information Bill, as it was called, was dropped partly as a result of the publication of a book by Andrew Boyle, *Climate of Treason*, which named an art advisor to the Queen, Sir Antony Blunt, as a former Soviet Agent. The provisions of the bill, if in force, would have made the publication of Boyle's book illegal.

---

*The diaries of Richard Crossman were published in a series of books in the late 1970s. They contained an often candid account of the life of a Cabinet minister. Crossman had held several ministerial posts in the Wilson governments of 1964–6 and 1966–70. He described, often very critically, not only his relations with his Cabinet colleagues but also his relations with senior civil servants. One of the objections that was raised to the publication of the diaries was that many named politicians and civil servants were still active in public life.

A new Official Secrets Act, passed in 1989, attempted to give a cleare definition of when unofficial disclosure of information might be a crimina offence. Harmful disclosures relate to defence, international relations interception of communications, and confidential material given by othe governments. The Act caused some controversy by making it an offence fo former members of the intelligence and security services to reveal anythin about these services. Also it is unnecassary in any cases that arise for th prosecution to prove that the disclosures were damaging. All unauthorise disclosures of this kind are treated as harmful to national security. Critic say that the Act gives the public 'no right to know' and fails to reduce th powerful tendency towards secrecy in government.

Ministerial Responsibility

The justification for civil service anonymity and secrecy involves th relationship between civil servants and ministers. The convention o ministerial responsibility implies that it is the minister who is held responsibl by Parliament for the administration of his department.

The minister takes responsibility for the decisions reached, and an subsequent blame or praise is directed at the minister.

In order for civil servants to be frank and open with ministers when givin advice, they need to be sure that they will not be publicly associated with it If the advice offered was to become subject to public scrutiny by the remova of anonymity and secrecy then, it is argued, civil servants would be less ope and frank with ministers. They would tend to withhold advice if they felt i would be unpopular and could reflect badly on their careers if revealed t the general public.

Openness in Local Government

The apparent secrecy of central administration can be contrasted with greater degree of openness in the conduct of local affairs. Public officials an politicians in local government are not covered by the Official Secrets Act and they have been urged for many years by central government to be fa more open in their dealings with the public.

The public and press have the right to attend almost all committe meetings of a local authority, and have access to all relevant papers. Th right of the public to attend full council meetings has been established fo many years. The right to prior consultation in local authority decisio making for the public is continuing to grow, as is the growing need for publi officials to explain 'why' in many areas of local administration.

Much more information is available about the activities of loca government compared to central government. Local authorities have t produce a good deal of information in their annual reports, and eac ratepayer receives a breakdown of spending with annual rate demands Professional bodies such as the Chartered Institute of Public Finance an Accountancy also publish reports on local government. By comparison littl information is produced for the consumers of services provided by centra government. There is no similar central annual spending and incom statements for health, social security, or education!

The end-of-the-year audited accounts of local authorities have to be mad available for public inspection and, if a ratepayer feels that certai expenditure is not proper, he or she, can demand that the auditor explai why no action has been taken.

The accounts of a local authority can also be challenged in the courts, bu such an undertaking would prove very difficult for an individual taxpaye who attempted to examine the expenditure figures of a central governmen department.

Citizens also have rights of participation in a variety of local authorit functions especially those that relate to planning decisions, land usage, and the compulsory purchase of land.

Example

In education, parents are now able to serve as school governors, schools have to publish examination results, and parents have the right to take a school out of local authority control altogether, if sufficient numbers of them are unhappy with local education policy. Very few comparable opportunities exist for taxpayers in respect of central government functions.

► *Mothers demonstrate on behalf of their children's nursery outside the Law Courts in 1980.*

'Yes, Minister': Influence and Persuasion

Constitutionally the relationship between a civil servant and the minister is clear. The minister is responsible for the development of policy and the civil servant carries out the lawful decisions of Government, as passed by Parliament.

The 'power' of the civil service is, therefore, formally limited to working for the minister, but the ability of top administrators to affect policy decisions may be better assessed in terms of their capability to persuade and influence. Some would argue that it is this capability which is the 'real' strength of the civil service in determining the course that a government might take.

Civil servants have limited 'power' to force a government or individual minister to do what they might not otherwise desire, but critics argue that, nonetheless, they can largely get their own way. The argument centres on the respective abilities of civil servants and ministers to perform their tasks. The most jaundiced view of this relationship is that top departmental advisors are so influential that ministers have little choice but to accept the advice they are offered, and have hardly any opportunity to produce alternative strategies.

These civil service 'mandarins' are displayed by some writers as so expert in the management of government that they can exploit their often relatively inexperienced political 'masters'. The argument for this viewpoint is that the skills required to reach the top in politics are not necessarily those appropriate to the running of such a large and complex organisation as a government department.

This problem may be even greater for a party gaining power after many years in opposition. For example, the Labour Party in 1964 were returned to power for the first time since 1951 (after 13 years of opposition) and only two of the new ministers had ever held a government office before (both of them in a junior capacity). If the current (1989) Conservative Government runs to its full term, Labour will have been again in opposition for 13 years. Additionally few ministers remain in office for the whole period of government. Resignation and reshuffles mean that on average ministers are in a department for less than two years. (See Chapter 18 on the Executive.)

Civil servants, by contrast, although they may move between departmen to gain experience in the early years of their careers, remain in seni positions in the same department for much longer periods. The result of thi it can be argued, leads to the development of a 'departmental' view of mar issues which ministers find hard to resist when it is explained by top advisor

The 'departmental view' may have developed over a number of years an will, in effect, be the accumulated 'wisdom' of the top civil servants in th department. Following the departmental view may appear to the minister be the most convenient way for the successful implementation of policy, an will also be the most acceptable to his civil servants. The temptation to acce what is offered by the top civil servants may prove irresistable to a politicia keen to make his mark and enhance his ministerial prospects, or simply have a quiet life.

Example

Emmanuel Shinwell, a veteran Labour politician, explained in his autobiography how he had campaigned all his adult life for the nationalisation of the coal mines. Yet when given the responsibility to do so as a minister in the 1945–50 Labour Government, discovered virtually no plans had been drawn up by the party to this end. He had to rely upon his civil servants to complete the task.

Political parties usually produce only general programmes prior to a election and expect, if they win, that civil service expertise will be used plan out the details.

It is noteworthy that the civil service tradition of drawing up plans to me the manifesto promises of both major contenders in General Election mea that the nationalisation of much of British industry went ahead relative quickly and smoothly after 1945. It can be argued, indeed, that the influen of the civil service stems from the policy process itself. Much of what endorsed by the Government, and the Cabinet in particular, is the result civil servants examining and analysing existing policy and suggestin changes to the relevant minister.

The idea of a master/servant relationship in this analysis does not appe to be very appropriate. The limitation on ministerial control of civil servan may also be highlighted by the fact that ministers have comparatively litt time in which to dispense their duties within a particular department. Th calls made upon the time of leading politicians are many and include:

- constituency business
- parliamentary debate
- parliamentary committees
- parliamentary question time
- public speaking events
- appearances on television and radio
- party functions and rallies.

and for some more senior ministers:

- Cabinet meetings
- Cabinet Committee meetings.

After all of these, the minister also has to be responsible for a large an possibly very complex government department.

To Change or not to Change?

One of the most critical views of the alleged ability of civil servants influence the course of events in government is contained in the diaries Richard Crossman, who served as a minister in the Labour Government 1964–70 (see pages 232 and 249). Most civil servants, however, would argu that a weak minister is of little help to his department for, if he can be easi influenced and led by his senior advisors, then he will probably also be unab to defend departmental interests in Cabinet discussions.

Other arguments also run counter to the Crossman analysis and relate the role the civil service assumes. Employees in any large organisation wi not necessarily welcome change, particularly if it could result in more wor for them. In this way it can be argued that civil servants will not necessari be keen to enthusiastically pursue new policy initiatives that the ministe opposes. A more realistic criticism of the civil service may well be that i ability to 'influence and persuade' will be directed at avoiding change rath than seeking to implement it.

Civil servants have traditionally not considered their primary function to lie in the field of policy making; they have felt that their job is to implement the wishes of the minister. Civil servants have also argued that their efficiency is often judged by ministers on the basis of their ability to implement policy expeditiously rather than to formulate it.

Senior civil servants, like ministers, are also very busy and spend a great deal of time undertaking the routine day-to-day administration of the department. They are concerned with personnel matters, financial control, negotiation with outside interests and the preparation of policy briefs and answers to ministerial questions. Consequently they do not have much time for policy planning.

The Fulton Committee (which reported on the workings of the civil service in 1968) recognised this fact and, although it argued that civil servants should be engaged in long term policy planning, saw that the burden of their departmental responsibilities often prevented them from doing so. There is, however, some controversy concerning the exact role of the Committee of Permanent Secretaries* as to whether this body is merely a coordinating machine or one which 'shadows' and attempts to steer government policy.

ADMINISTRATION IN LOCAL GOVERNMENT

The opportunities for administrators in local government to influence the course of events is potentially greater than in central government. At local level politicians are unpaid 'amateurs' who discharge their responsibilities whilst often having full time employment. The officials, by contrast, are full time salaried employees of the local authority and will usually have specialist professional qualifications in their field of responsibility. The advice they proffer to their political 'masters' may therefore carry a degree of authority and expertise which is hard to counter.

In 1974 a major reorganisation of local government took place with the number of local authorities being reduced and the number of councillors halved. The outcome was a sharply increased workload for the remaining 26,000. However, attempts to introduce salaries for councillors have been resisted, although attendance allowances and expenses are claimed. One criticism of this arrangement is that local councillors often are not representative of the local population and that there is a preponderence of middle class, middle aged, self-employed, or retired, men.

The Committee System

The executive function (see Chapter 18) differs between central and local government in that there are no 'ministers' in local government. Decisions are taken in a system of committees that have all-party representation. The political balance of the committees reflects the balance of the whole council, but there are no 'backbench' councillors, as usually all will serve on at least one committee.

The advantage of such a system is that responsibility falls onto more shoulders and differing political viewpoints. It could be argued, therefore, that the ability to influence and persuade a committee could be quite a difficult task. Principal administrators are, however, present at committee meetings and they are expected to give advice and guidance to committee members during the formal deliberations. Overall committee deliberation on council policy does assist the councillor in making policy and can result in a councillor building up a considerable knowledge of at least one area of the local authority's work.

---

*A Permanent Secretary is the senior civil servant in a government department, and works closely with the Minister, advising him or her on all aspects of the department's work.

The role of the committee chairman in drawing up the agenda wit officials and guiding the direction of discussion in committee is ver important. Committee chairmanships will usually only be attained after councillor has had many years of council service.

The committee system, therefore, can act as a limitation on the influenc of officials for they do consider matters in considerable detail with gener policy left to the full council. It must be said, nonetheless, that decisior taken will frequently reflect the advice the committee receives from the ful time officials. The opportunity for the officials to influence decisions in loc government may still, therefore, be quite considerable, but where a loc council is dominated by a single party with a precise policy programme, th opportunity may be reduced.

It must also be noted that many of the services provided and much of th money spent locally, are effectively controlled by central, and not, loc government. Although the financial dependency of local government upo central government has fallen in percentage terms in recent years, the larges source of local authority income still comes in grants from centr government. They amount on average to over half the income loc authorities receive.

REPRESENTATION

Critics of the British civil service claim that, as a group, top officials ar extremely 'unrepresentative' of the population as a whole, in that they ar drawn from a narrow social and educational background. The result of thi is said to be that such officials act as a cohesive 'conservative' bloc and resis any programme of radical reform by a British government whether it b radicalism of the 'left' or 'right'. Tony Benn, the left wing MP who held offic in five Labour governments, has argued that the civil service had tremendous influence on economic policy and in fact reversed the policy o the 1964 Labour Government.

The methods of recruitment and the people recruited, it is argued, increas this tendency and strengthen the position of the civil service in dealing wit

► *Tony Benn at the Anti-Nazi League carnival in London in 1978.*

Example

The Fulton Committee reported that 85 per cent of top civil servants had been recruited from only two universities, Oxford and Cambridge. The 'unrepresentativeness' being even more noticeable in that over half of them were graduates in either history or classics.

Fulton felt this to be undesirable, but by the mid 1970s still over 60 per cent of top civil servants were recruited from 'Oxbridge', although this had fallen to 50 per cent by 1985.

governments. Most civil servants who reach senior positions are recruited directly from university and although some leave the service to go into industry or commerce, few 'outsiders' are brought into the civil service.

The evidence available has been used by critics to point to the 'unrepresentativeness' of the civil service. Critics claim that this tendency increases the solidarity of the civil service and helps to 'socialise' new recruits into accepting departmental thinking and civil service 'philosophy'. The result, it is argued, is the formation of an elite group that can, in effect, ensure the protection of its own interests irrespective of 'passing' governments.

In defence of the civil service it can be said that not only has the pattern of recruitment changed in recent years, but that, even if a significant proportion of the new recruits who are expected to achieve senior positions are drawn from Oxbridge, then this, in itself, need not necessarily result in an inbuilt bias. To draw future senior civil servants from amongst the most talented and able individuals may be logical and rational if it is accepted that these people tend to go to 'Oxbridge'. Lord Simey in a memorandum of dissent to the Fulton Committee certainly took this view although he was not out of step with many of the other findings of the committee. (see pages 258–260).

Also it is not merely a British phenomenon that senior public servants are drawn often from a fairly narrow educational and/or social background. The social background of many top French civil servants, for example, is markedly elitist, and the elitism extends to top positions in government, commerce, industry, and education as well.

RESPONSIBILITY

The concept of civil servants acting 'responsibly' is well established in British government. It is closely associated with the idea that civil servants are politically non-partisan servants of the Crown, and responsible for the good government of the country. In this sense, civil servants are seen to have a 'public duty' to execute their responsibilities efficiently and honestly within an almost 'ethical' code of conduct which is self-imposed and into which civil servants are socialised during their careers.

To an extent, therefore, the lack of direct and immediate political accountability is compensated for by this concept of 'responsibility' in the civil service, which is a self-imposed culture of service and high ethical standards. Misgivings about the philosophy and workings of the civil service have led several government ministers in recent years to question this 'ethos' of impartiality and import 'political' advisors into their departments from their own party political machinery.

Example

In 1982, Mrs Thatcher brought in a former British ambassador to the United Nations, Sir Anthony Parsons, to act as an advisor on foreign policy, although it was only a short term appointment. In effect, she was questioning the reliability of the advice she was receiving from the Foreign and Commonwealth Office.

Sir Derek Raynor, joint managing director of the Marks & Spencer chain stores, was used by the Prime Minister, Edward Heath, in 1970, to advise the Ministry of Defence on procurement policy. He also worked for Mrs Thatcher in 1979 to conduct an efficiency drive in the civil service.

The policy of using political advisors to produce 'alternative' viewpoints to those offered by the civil service was also evident during the 1974–9 Labour Government when over 35 were employed and the Prime Minister set up a policy unit. Mr Tony Benn, for example, employed Frances Morrell as a political advisor. She herself entered politics in London shortly afterwards.

The main challenge to the established position of the civil service, however, has come in recent years from the right in British politics. The reputation of the civil service was damaged, for some elements of the Conservative Party, by a period of industrial action in 1981. Since then the Civil Service Department, which was created in 1969 as a result of the Fulton proposals, has been scrapped, manpower sharply reduced, and a drive for greater efficiency instigated by Derek Raynor has been implemented.

Civil Servants and GCHQ

In the case of civil servants working at the government communicatio headquarters in Cheltenham (GCHQ), which is part of the Foreign Offic trade union membership has been banned since 1985. GCHQ has a important security function but was not excluded from the 1981 industri action.

Those civil servants who were not willing to give up trade unic membership were offered the chance to move to other posts, but those wh gave up membership had an *ex gratia* payment in compensation. The civ service unions opposed to the government moves took legal action an claimed they had not been consulted prior to the decision and as such th this was an infringement of 'natural justice'. The High Court upheld th unions' claim, but both the Court of Appeal and the House of Lorc overturned the original decision. Their rejection was on the grounds that national security was involved then such decisions must rest only wi government ministers and not with the Courts under 'normal' industrial lav

Example

The Sarah Tisdall and Clive Ponting Cases

Questions concerning the ultimate responsibility of civil servants in carrying out their departmental duties were raised by the separate court cases of civil servants Sarah Tisdall and Clive Ponting.

The case of Sarah Tisdall was less controversial than that of Clive Ponting. She was a junior Foreign Office clerk who sent details of the timing of the arrival of Cruise Missiles in Britain to *The Guardian* newspaper. She also disclosed the way in which the Government would attempt to handle the parliamentary debate on the subject. The Government instituted a successful prosecution against Miss Tisdall for a breach of the Official Secrets Act. She accepted that she had breached the Act but considered it a matter of conscience. Nonetheless, she received a short prison sentence.

The case of Clive Ponting involved the way in which the Conservative Government handled the debate over the sinking of the Argentinian warship *General Belgrano* during the Falklands War of 1982.

Critics of the Cabinet's decision to sink the ship, which resulted in a large loss of life, claimed that it was unjustified. The British government had drawn an exclusion zone around the Falkland Islands and declared that any Argentinian warship entering zone would be liable to attack. The *Belgrano*, it was claimed, was sunk by a British submarine not only outside the zone, but when heading away from it. The other major allegation was that the Government had attempted intentionally to deceive Parliament by not disclosing all the facts surrounding the incident.

Ponting, a civil servant in the Ministry of Defence, gave relevant documents to the Labour MP, Tam Dalyell, who passed them on to the House of Commons Select Committee, which was investigating the *Belgrano* affair. An inquiry was instituted by the civil service to find out how these documents had been leaked and, when Ponting was identified as the source, he was prosecuted under the Official Secrets Act.

Critics of the decision to prosecute claimed that the Attorney General, who had discretion as to whether to institute proceedings under the Act, did so, not in the public interest, but in order to serve the interests of the Government. The inference was that the Attorney General had been influenced to start proceedings as a result of pressure from Cabinet colleagues, thus compromising his position as a law officer of the Crown. The Attorney General denied this strongly, however.

Ponting's defence was that giving the information to Tam Dalyell did not constitute an offence under the Act as an MP could be considered to be an authorised person and thus legitimately receive it. He also claimed that the public interest was not being served, if he, as a civil servant, concealed the truth for the convenience of ministers.

The judge at his trial, however, ruled that the public interest could only be determined by the government of the day and not by the civil servants. The ruling appeared to make it certain that Ponting would be convicted and probably receive a prison sentence. The jury, however, chose to ignore the judge's views and Ponting was found not guilty.

Clive Ponting during his trial.

Since the Sarah Tisdall and Clive Ponting cases 'Notes of Guidance' have been issued to civil servants declaring emphatically that they are servants of the Crown, which, for all practical purposes, means the government of the day. The possibility therefore of a civil servant interpreting his or her 'responsibilities' as extending beyond the wishes of the incumbent government and escaping prosecution may appear to have been removed.

DEMOCRACY

Democratic control and accountability of the administration in Britain is not achieved, as it is in some countries, by the election or political appointment of top officials. In the USA, for example, the heads of most federal bureaux and agencies are political appointments. They are made by the President in his role as the head of the executive branch. On the election of a new President the top 2,000 US civil servants stand down, and the President may reappoint them or place new people in their positions.

In Britain, democratic control of government civil servants is exercised by parliamentary process known as **ministerial responsibility** (see chapter 18). It simply implies that the relevant minister is held responsible for the actions of his or her civil servants, and has to, if necessary, explain to Parliament. If problems have arisen which Parliament considers serious enough, the minister may be called upon to resign. It must be said, nonetheless, that few ministers have resigned in deference to this convention. Lord Carrington, the Foreign Secretary, however, did resign as a result of criticisms of the Foreign and Commonwealth Office in the period prior to the Argentinian invasion of the Falkland Islands in 1982.

The convention has been criticised on the grounds that it protects incompetent civil servants from having to face the full public consequences of their actions. However, if it is accepted as desirable to have a permanent non-partisan civil service, then it seems hard to see how officials could be held publicly accountable for policies over which they have had little control and with which they may disagree privately.

Ministerial responsibility, as well as requiring ministers to account for failures in their departments, also gives them the credit for the successes that have been achieved through the hard work of civil servants.

Since 1979 the expansion of the system of all-party **Parliamentary Select Committees** of the House of Commons (see chapter 17) has increased the ability of MPs to highlight shortcomings in the operations of the government departments scrutinised by the committees. Civil servants have been requested to give evidence to Select Committees and some Committee reports have been very critical of what they have found.

Problems have arisen, however, for civil servants in giving evidenc because they have, on occasions, found themselves facing questions whic although they were capable of answering, strictly came within the ambit ministerial responsibility. Since the Select Committee investigation in t conduct of the Westland Helicopter affair (see the chapter on the Executiv the Conservative Government has become less willing to allow civil servan to appear in person because, in answering questions on Westlan embarrassing information was disclosed.

One suggestion of the Fulton Committee was to increase civil servi accountability by the introduction of accountable management. It w envisaged that, although civil servants would not be held responsible for t format and content of policy, which must remain with the minister, th could, nonetheless, still be held responsible for the subsequent manageme and implementation of policy. In this way the administrative performan of departments, or sections of departments, could be scrutinised, and prai or blame allocated.

We should not assume necessarily that the civil service would be oppos to greater public scrutiny for all the problems of government cannot be la at their door. Perhaps the politicians might have more to fear?

THE QUEST FOR 'EFFICIENCY'

The Northcote-Trevelyan Report (1853) was highly critical of the civil servic and led to the first concerted attempt to improve its organisation. In 1855 **Civil Service Commission** was established which led, in 1870, to th introduction of recruitment by competitive examination. Various oth reforms followed the lines advocated by the Report and for many years aft the civil service enjoyed a reputation for honesty, efficiency, and fairness.

From the 1950s the service increasingly became a focus for criticism of a alleged lack of management skills, the elite nature of its senior officials, an its power over ministers. In short, many argued that its values and practice were outdated and that senior officials lacked the necessary skills to ru modern complex government departments efficiently. It was as a result such criticisms that the Labour Prime Minister, Harold Wilson, in 1965, s up a committee to investigate the organisation of the home civil service.

The Fulton Committee 1966–8

An investigation of the working of the civil service was begun in Februar 1966 by a committee under the chairmanship of Lord Fulton. The repo (cmnd 3638) published in June 1968, was sharply critical of civil servic organisation and suggested significant changes should be introduced.

The Findings

> *The Home Civil Service today is still fundamentally the product of th nineteenth century philosophy of the Northcote Trevelyan Report. Th problems it faces are those of the second half of the twentieth century. Th is what we have found; it is what we seek to remedy.*

This is the opening paragraph of the report, and sums up concisely what th committee felt was the underlying problem of the civil service. One member Lord Simey, felt this analysis to be unfair and wrote a memorandum o dissent to that effect, but, nonetheless, he accepted the need for 'far reaching changes.

The report argued that the role and scope of government has change tremendously, but the structure and practices of the service had not. Th defects in the service which were outlined were nearly all attributed to thi and the report concluded that 'fundamental change' was needed.

The Criticisms

The civil service was based on the philosophy of the amateur (or 'generalist' or 'all rounder') administrator, especially amongst those in the Administrative class to which senior civil servants. belonged Top civil servants were gifted laymen expected to have, as a primary qualification, a knowledge of the governmental machine which could be brought to bear on problems, irrespective of subject matter. The committee argued that the 'cult is obsolete at all levels and in all parts of the service.' Other criticisms were:

- Too few civil servants were skilled managers.
- Not enough scientists, engineers and specialists were allowed to enjoy administrative responsibilities appropriate to their positions.
- The system of civil service classes (1400 in total), grouped into three broad categories of Administrative, Executive and Clerical, impeded its work and should be scrapped.
- The civil service lacked adequate personnel management.
- Generally the civil service had insufficient direct contact with the community it served.

The Remedies

- A Civil Service Department should be created with the Prime Minister as its head.
- More appropriate and lengthy in-service training was needed to generate greater professionalism.
- More specialists, such as accountants, doctors and scientists, should be recruited as administrators.
- More attention needed to be paid to the relevance of the academic qualifications of potential recruits.
- A Civil Service College should be created to provide more training courses.
- The system of civil service classes should be abolished and replaced by a new career structure.
- More 'outsiders' should be recruited from industry and commerce.
- More serving civil servants should be given opportunities to gain experience working outside government for fixed periods.

The Results

There has been a good deal of argument over how successfully the Fulton proposals were implemented. A Civil Service Department was created in 1969, but abolished in 1981 by Mrs Thatcher, who had become increasingly dissatisfied with its work. The method of recruitment was reformed and a new career structure introduced to replace the system of classes. A Civil Service College was also created, although the in-service training of civil servants is still less than is generally given to public servants in many other countries. Few new recruits have been brought into government departments from industry or commerce and the large majority of civil servants still enter the civil service after graduating from university.

Politicians do not often take an interest in the problems of administering the civil service, as the article below claims. Since 1979, however, significant attempts have been made to reform the administration of central government. In line with the Government's overall strategy of reducing public expenditure, civil service numbers have fallen. Plans were drawn up to reduce numbers from 732,000 in 1979 to 630,000 by April 1984, with future cuts to achieve a total of 593,000 by April 1988. The figure by April 1986 was actually 594,300.

A further change can be seen in attempts to secure greater 'efficiency'. Most of the effort has centred upon financial and operational planning, which was established by the Treasury in the form of the Finance and Management.

Other methods employed have included efficiency scrutinies and aud under the direction of a central unit headed by the Prime Minister. T overall philosophy of the Government sees a need for officials to concentr more on management and less on policy advice to ministers. The prima task for the civil servant in a time of limited resources is seen to be t efficient and effective management of the resources available.

The Fulton Committee (see page 258) had come to similar conclusio but, since 1979, there has been a notable determination in the Conservati Government to carry through reforms. The appointment of Sir Derek Rayn (now Lord Raynor) as a political advisor to Mrs. Thatcher was an examp of this process of increasing civil service efficiency.

Raynor's unit was given the responsibility, working in cooperation wi government departments, of carrying out efficiency reviews. From 1979 1982 a large number of scrutinies and departmental reviews were conduct which, it was claimed, produced potential savings of over £300 millio Critics of this approach, however, argued that the work was limited in outlook and concentrated too much on *costs* with insufficient account bei taken of *benefits*. Other changes in the civil service have involved t scrapping of the established system for negotiating pay and the abolition the Civil Service Department.

A notable example of this trend can be seen in the administrative chang implemented by Michael Heseltine during his time as a minister in M Thatcher's cabinet.

Mr Heseltine's Reforms

(See the article on the opposite page.)

The management information system for ministers (MINIS) w introduced into the Ministry of Defence after Michael Heseltine succeed John Nott as Defence Secretary in 1983. MINIS had first been used by hi in 1981 whilst he was Secretary of State at the Department of t Environment. The exercise at the Ministry of Defence (MOD) involved M Heseltine interviewing all his top civil servants about their objectives for t department and the ways in which they were attempting to achieve ther This process produced for him information about MOD structures and t changes that were needed.

MINIS also gave him a picture of the range of responsibilities covered b his department and identified which officials were in charge of each. 1 senior officials were each allocated an area of responsibility and asked analyse administrative structures, resources used, staffing, proposed plan and major objectives. The results of the exercise were analysed by M Heseltine and other Defence Ministers, with senior officers questioned abo efficiency and cost effectiveness. The results of the whole process, togeth with the report of a firm of management consultants on the defence account led to a significant reorganisation of the MOD.

The changes created a new unified Defence staff to replace separate to level Service Staff and the Chiefs of Staff (senior military advisors in th MOD) were relegated to the status of senior advisors. An Office Management and Budget was created in the MOD, so as to give th Government greater control over the establishment of priorities f expenditure, and to control the allocation of resources.

The Chiefs of Staff protested vigorously to Mrs Thatcher about th reorganisation and their reduced status, but nonetheless, the proposals we implemented.

Government policy overall has led to stricter financial limitations on th civil service with a more critical assessment of cost and efficiency in th activities of government together with a questioning of whether servic should be provided by government at all.

PERMANENT GOVERNMENT

Tarzan in the Whitehall game park

Peter Hennessy

ICHAEL HESELTINE is, in both ıses of the term, a Whitehall freak. : is fascinated by the machine, avid to m it and supercharge it simulta- ously. And I can think of no other litician who would devote the first o chapters of his political testament* the subject. Not even that supreme hnician-of-State, Mr Heseltine's hero, vid Lloyd George (whose portrait he rted round from department to partment) would have placed so avy an emphasis on Whitehall.

Just how unusual an animal he was in : Whitehall game park was apparent a No. 10 dining room in 1982 when, the Prime Minister's request, Mr seltine outlined before his less than miring colleagues the beauties and ricacies of MINIS, the management ormation system for ministers (a kind modern, departmental Domesday ok) he had pioneered at the Depart- nt of the Environment.

'he Heseltine plan is back, if ot to Victorian values, at least a tiny Victorian Whitehall'

'My fellow Cabinet Ministers,' writes r Heseltine, in his *Where There's a ill*, 'sat in rows while I explained my ainchild, each with his sceptical per- anent secretary behind him muttering jections, or so I suspected. Any litician knows when he is losing his dience's attention, and I knew well ough. When I had done there were w takers and absolutely no enthu- sts.'

What Mr Heseltine doesn't record is w the Prime Minister, confronted th collective Cabinet ennui and dis- in for the idea of the minister-as- anager, pleaded for 25 minutes with r colleagues to take MINIS seriously d to emulate it in their own ministries an intriguing sidelight on an allegedly er-mighty premier when faced with the departmental baronies. 'She who must be obeyed,' as Mrs Thatcher is called in the environs of Downing Street, eventually had her way. A White Paper declaring the government's Financial Management Initiative in 1982 instructed each ministry to develop its own management system along MINIS lines.

Heseltine an arch privatiser. He now wants to denationalise as much of Whitehall as possible.

First of all the concept of a unified Civil Service run from the Treasury and the Cabinet Office would go. Individual departments should have the right to run their own pay and personnel policies offering market rates to attract the people they need. Large blocks of executive functions – not just cleaning and catering – would be put out on contract. Only a small policy-making elite would remain as a core Civil Service with hefty tranches of new blood transfused at regular intervals to invigorate it.

In its way, the Heseltine plan is back, if not to Victorian values, at least to a tiny Victorian Whitehall with the functions of the big 20th century state hived off and supervised by a highly paid *grand corps* of Civil Service guardians. It's the most radical plan for Whitehall reform since the Northcote-Trevelyan report of 1853 drew up the job specification for the prototypical guardians of the 'night-watchman state'. For that reason it has nil chance of adoption unless fate projects Mr Heseltine himself into No. 10 – and even then the resistance and the battles would be terrifying to behold.

The history of Whitehall reform shows that it only succeeds in peacetime if its patron and pacesetter is in No. 10. The serious implementation of Northcote-Trevelyan had to wait nearly 20 years till Gladstone, who commissioned the report, reached the premiership. In wartime, matters can move faster, as Lloyd George found in 1916. The last person who thoroughly reformed Whitehall was that well-known public administrator Adolf Hitler, who forced the British Civil Service to admit the skilled and the capable on the grand scale in 1939–50**. World war is a high price to pay for such shake-ups.

ON THE LESSER scale there is one service Mr Heseltine is uniquely placed to perform now. In his book he recommends the building of a model which would draw together on a trans-Whitehall basis all the versions of MINIS. It would take a month at most, he says, to do this: The benefits? It would 'ensure that the best information is available, regularly updated, the tightest disciplines applied and comparability between departments achieved. The information should be published'.

Why doesn't he undertake the job himself and do for Whitehall efficiency what Lloyd George tried to do from the wilderness for the economy with his famous *We Can Conquer Unemployment* pamphlet of 1929? He knows where to find help, the equivalents of Keynes and Hubert Henderson in LG's case. They can be found among recently departed officials with excellent efficiency track records like Clive Priestley at British Telecom, Ian Beesley at Price Waterhouse, David Edmonds at the Housing Corporation, Norman Warner at Kent County Council or Gerry Grimstone at Schroders. A scheme handcrafted by such as these would be hard to ignore if sent not only to No. 10 and the Management and Personnel Office but to the Commons Select Committee on the Treasury and Civil Service as well. □

*Michael Heseltine, *Where There's A Will*, Hutchinson, £12.95.

**Peter Hennessy and Sir Douglas Hauge, *How Adolf Hitler Reformed Whitehall*, (Dept of Politics, Strathclyde University, 16 Richmond St, Glasgow G1 1XQ, £4.50).

Peter Hennessy is a Visiting Fellow at the Policy Studies Institute.

Source: *New Statesman*, 27 March 1987

EXAMINATION QUESTIONS

1 'The Official Secrets Act is designed to protect officials rather than prote secrets.' Discuss. (Cambridge GCE Special Paper Govt. and Pol. 1982)

2(a) Assess the extent to which senior civil servants may exercise politic power.

(b) What are the major limitations upon such power? (AEB GCE A-Lev Govt. and Pol. 1986)

3 'Whatever party is in office the civil servants are always in effective powe Comment. (Cambridge GCE A-Level Pol. and Govt. 1980)

4 In what sense is the civil service a pressure group? (London GCE A-Lev Govt. and Pol. Studies 1986).

NOW READ ON . . .

G. Jones and J. Stewart *The Case for Local Government* G. Allen ar Unwin, 1985
A strong set of arguments for a vigorous system of local government.

H. Young and A. Sloman *No Minister* BBC, 1982
A useful insight into the process of decision making.

R. Norton-Taylor *The Ponting Affair* Cecil Woolf, 1985
A good analysis of the problem of a civil servant's responsibilities.

21 Pressure Groups

The industry of influence in the corridors of power

Political lobbying has become big business, worth at least £10 million a year in fees. Labour MP Bob Cryer believes the industry is out of control and in need of regulation. David Rose lks to the people – including Andrew Gifford – who make a living out of making friends and influencing people

R BOB Cryer, Labour MP for Bradrd South, asked Mrs Thatcher during ime Minister's questions last month ether she would set up a register of e political lobbyists who met members the Civil Service on behalf of private siness interests. Her reply was sucict: "No."

She chose thereby to turn her back on expanding industry operating deep thin a myriad spheres of government.

The Government has been lobbied tensely on virtually every recent occaon when it has made difficult decisions volving business. The lobbyists were sy in the contested bid for Westland, e Guinness take-over of Distillers, the ce between Boeing's Awacs and EC's Nimrod for the £1 billion airrne radar contract, and the contest tween the Scandinavian SAS and itish Airways for British Caledonian.

In the United States, all 10,000 lobists on Capitol Hill must be regered. In Britain, no such safeguard ists. The only code of conduct is luntary and widely ignored – administred by a professional association ich most of the important firms oose not to join.

Since 1982, when Mr Cryer tried successfully to introduce a register by eans of a private member's bill, the litical lobbying industry has grown. en, a handful of tiny firms competed r a total fee income of less than £1 illion a year.

Now, more than 40 specialist comnies, one-person bands and subliaries of public relations firms, derive at least 10 times that amount.

As their operations have grown, their methods have changed. Mr Cryer's 1982 bill sought only to register firms which lobbied MPs and ministers: and at that time, Parliament was seen as the main field of lobbying activity.

But liquid lunches and cosy retainers for MPs have become peripheral. According to Douglas Smith, managing director of Political Communication, the House of Commons now represents "only the tip of the lobbying iceberg".

Expressing a view held generally by lobbyists, he says: "I don't want to minimise Parliament, I've got my friends there. But we are, as you know, living in an elective dictatorship.

"MPs can be useful to back Whitehall contacts: if civil servants can see you can get MPs to raise merry hell they're more likely to take you seriously. But the best lobbying is done by getting access to the right civil servant."

Andrew Gifford, a former political advisor to the Liberal leader, Mr David Steel, says he has "continual contact with civil servants, virtually every day." Mr Gifford is a partner in Gifford Jeger Weeks, a specialist firm which has grown from shoestring origins in his Lambeth basement flat in 1980 to being bought out by the advertising giant Lowe Howard Spinks for £6.5 million last July.

Like many of the bigger firms, GJW's staff includes former civil servants. Ms Claire Wenner once conducted EEC farm policy negotiations in Brussels for the Ministry of Agriculture. Now she lobbies officials from the ministry and the European Commission on behalf of GJW's clients.

Mr Gifford says: "There will be people in our office who know the various permanent secretaries quite well, either from the Civil Service or from working with senior politicians. We'll be on good, friendly terms."

Such contacts – coupled with an astute reading of political developments – can pay high dividends. Like other lobbyists, Mr Gifford emphasises that prevention is better than cure. Last-minute lobbying in reaction to measures which have already been publicly announced is always extremely difficult, and clients are more likely to benefit from a steady intelligence service forewarning them of Government activity in their field, when action can be taken early.

Some firms, like Mr Smith's Political Communication, operate mainly in the purely political sphere. One of his conspicuous successes was to persuade the Environment Secretary, Mr Nicholas Ridley, to drop plans for the storage of radioactive waste. Mr Smith's year-long campaign was conducted on behalf of three of the counties selected as test sites.

Other companies, however, concentrate on the commercial field. Their clients come from foreign and domestic big business. The objective here may be to modify legislation likely to affect a company, or to improve a firm's chances of obtaining government contracts.

Source: *The Guardian*, 8 January 1988

The activities of pressure groups in British politics raise many important questions. Some would argue that their influence has grown too much and that the democratic and representative institutions are being by-passed. The close working relations that some groups enjoy with government may be mutually beneficial, but it could also be claimed that the result is th relatively small groups are able to exercise an influence over government th is out of all proportion to their size. What may also be disturbing is that the relationships are conducted outside the more public arenas like Parliament.

Others argue that pressure group activity is a vital and unavoidab consequence of modern political activity which enlivens democracy an makes government more responsive to the wishes of the people. Some woul say that, collectively, pressure groups are now the most effective means communication between citizens and government and have as such surpasse political parties in this task.

BASIC PRINCIPLES

Key Theory and Concepts

Power The use, size, finance, connections, and even forms of direct actic to achieve the objectives of the group.

Representation The degree to which each group represents the wishes and desir of its members or of any section of society.

Freedom Freedom of action, meeting and expression are necessa preconditions of pressure group activity as it is understood in th western world.

Legitimacy Some forms of pressure group activity may not be considered lega civil disobedience, breaking the law during sit-ins, strikes, protest etc.

Influence and Persuasion The methods used by groups to influence government and th characteristics of group activity are critical to those processes.

Democracy Arguments arise over the effects of group activity upon democrat processes and the possibly 'anti-democratic' features of them.

Corporatism The degree to which groups have become incorporated into th decision-making processes of government.

Pluralism The importance of groups to the functioning of the politic system and the competition between them to win the support government.

DISCUSSING THE ARGUMENTS

Range of Pressure Group Activity

Example

Age Concern claims to speak for the elderly and Shelter works to help the homeless and poorly housed. The formal 'members' of these pressure groups are the workers and the organisers, while the people they attempt to represent are not limited to the pressure groups directly.

The number of pressure groups active in British politics is vast and today majority of people belong to a pressure group of one sort or another. Fo example, there are over 1,000 employers' organisations in Britain, and trad unions claim to represent nearly half of the working population.

Outside their working lives many people belong to organisations whic reflect their cultural, leisure, sporting, religious interests, etc. Many pressur groups claim to speak for, and attempt to protect, the interests of quite larg sections of the community even though many of the people concerned ma not be formal members of the group.

What this means for government is that there is virtually no area of it activities which will not be subject to some form of pressure group activity Even if such an area existed, as soon as government took an interest, pressur groups would almost certainly emerge from amongst those affected b governmental activity. Given the large number of groups and the size of som of them it may be argued that they possess the power to determine the course of political action.

Pressure groups do not, however, usually seek to gain political power directly by entering candidates in elections. Some local pressure groups, like the Ratepayers Associations, do occasionally run candidates in local elections, and trade unions sponsor half of the Labour MPs, but, by and large, pressure groups seek to influence affairs indirectly.

The reason most pressure groups do not attempt to gain political office is that it would require them to draw up, in effect, a complete party manifesto to appeal to the majority of the electorate. By their nature, pressure groups are concerned to articulate the interests of their members, or a section of the community they claim to represent, and not appeal to a majority on a wide range of issues. Pressure groups therefore concentrate mainly on influencing those who hold office even though some groups have strong links with particular political parties.

The Green Party in Britain, is, however, slightly different. It developed from the Ecology Party and has run candidates in General Elections. The 'Greens' have now developed a 'green' approach to almost every aspect of life, especially economic policy, where they advocate new forms of taxation, transport, etc, which adds up to a different way of running society.

Example

The links between the British trade union movement and the Labour Party are formalised. The unions have representation at many levels of the Labour Party and strong links also exist between sections of British industry and the Conservative Party, but these are mainly to be seen in financial contributions rather than institutionalised arrangements.

Aims of Industry has spent money on advertising campaigns at general elections to emphasise its belief in free enterprise, this they argue, can be best achieved by voting Conservative.

The Growth of Pressure Groups

Pressure groups have always been a feature of British politics but, since 1945, there has been a rapid growth in their numbers and range of activities. One reason for this expansion can be seen in the growth of the activities of government itself. The founding of the welfare state and increased governmental intervention in the economy had resulted in more interests being affected (see Chapter 14 Corporatism).

The outcome has been that a greater number of people have become prepared to demand a say, through specific pressure groups, in the way in which governmental responsibilities are exercised. Pressure groups have developed as an effective means for people to articulate, collectively, their views and bring them to the notice of government in the hope of a positive response.

The growing willingness of people to join pressure groups as a means of influencing policy making has caused concern to the leaders of the political parties. The Labour Party, in particular, has become concerned over this trend of people joining pressure groups rather than working through the traditional political parties to gain influence. The worry is that people may no longer regard membership of a political party as the best way to achieve their ends, and that this can be seen in the steady fall in individual party membership.

The drift away from political parties since 1945 has been significant and today only about 5 per cent of the electorate are formal party members, but even fewer will be active members. This has led some writers to conclude that there is a direct correlation between the fall in party membership and the growth in pressure groups.

The growth has been noticeable since the 1960s for many more groups are now prepared to enter the political arena. 'White collar' trade unions, which represent managerial and administrative staff, for example, have become more militant over the past 20 years.

New groups have also entered the competition. Organisations that represent homosexuals, promote (or oppose) liberalisation of abortion laws, pursue sexual equality, defend welfare recipients, protect ethnic minority interests, campaign for more liberal drug laws, and care for the homeless have all entered the competition.

The most rapid increase in group members has taken place in the environmental lobby. In Britain today about 2.5 million people belong to environmental groups. Organisations like Friends of the Earth, founded in 1970, and Greenpeace, founded in 1972, have come to prominence through active campaigns on a variety of environmental issues.

Other older established environmental groups have become willing to take a more active role in lobbying government. Organisations like the Council for the Protection of Rural England, and the Ramblers Association have taken part in vigorous campaigns to counter what they feel to be a growing threat to the countryside.

Many more single-issue groups also have emerged in British politics and this may be seen as further evidence of a growing willingness of people to engage in direct political action rather than work through political parties. The siting of airports, the building of motorways, the expansion of nuclear power stations, tours by South African sports teams, the closure of hospitals and schools, are all examples of the kind of issues that stimulate people to protest.

Definition

Pressure groups
Pressure groups are organisations which aim to influence governmental policy making but can be distinguished from political parties in that they generally do not attempt to hold formal office.

The activities of pressure groups in British politics have raised major questions about the nature of political power, democracy, and the effectiveness of representative institutions. Many writers argue that pressure groups are an inevitable feature of political life and that political institutions cannot function effectively without their participation. Whether this view will need to be reviewed, given the apparent changes in governmental pressure group relations since 1979, is open to debate.

Types of Pressure Group

Lengthy academic debate has taken place over how pressure groups can be categorised and which of the subsequent divisions are most 'powerful'.

One well established method of attempting this task is to draw a distinction between:

- sectional/economic groups
- cause/ideas/promotional groups

Sectional/Economic Groups

The basis of association for this type is said to be a shared economic, professional, business, trading, or industrial interest.

Example

Most people join a trade union because they share in common with other members, a similar form of employment, and hope that collective strength can be used, amongst other things, to secure improved pay and working conditions.

Most solicitors belong to the Law Society which represents their interests.

Many companies engaged in motor vehicle construction belong to the Society of Motor Manufacturers so that they can, as a group, highlight the problems and needs of the industry. An equivalent role in the clothing industry is performed by the British Clothing Industry Association.

Cause/Ideas/Promotional Groups

The basis of association for this type of group is said to be a shared set of ideas or beliefs amongst the members. The group's objective will be to promote these ideas.

Example

Members of the RSPCA share a belief in the need for animal welfare and members of Friends of the Earth have an interest in a wide variety of environmental issues.

Other approaches involve distinguishing between **protectional** and **promotional** groups. Protectional groups are said to have the primary objective of 'protecting' the interests of their members. Examples of this type of group are trade unions, employers' associations, professional bodies, etc.

Promotional groups are distinguished, as we have tried to establish, by them aiming to 'promote' the interests of their members through various campaigns to influence government policy and legislation. Groups such as the Child Poverty Action Group and the Council for the Protection of Rural England, are examples.

The problem with this type of classification is that it tends to lump together large numbers of groups that may be very different in size, nature, levels of political activity, organisation, financial capacity, ideological orientation, etc.

Further subdivisions must also be taken into account for, some groups are single-issue *ad hoc* groups, others are permanent with an interest in a wide range of problems. Some single-issue *ad hoc* groups are established to fight one particular campaign (perhaps the proposed construction of a motorway or airport) and once the issue is resolved they cease to function.

Other groups which might be involved in the same campaign could be permanent groups with an established membership and national or local organisation. The campaign of opposition to the extension of Stansted Airport in Essex has involved such a combination of local *ad hoc* groups and national environmental groups.

Further complications for categorisation arise with the establishment of occasional *ad hoc* alliances of permanent groups, with groups pooling resources and organisational skills over a particular issue. Sectional groups also sometimes promote causes. For example, the Royal College of Physicians supports the anti-smoking lobby, Action on Smoking Health (ASH).

It is also sometimes difficult to decide whether an organisation is actually a pressure group or not. For example, institutions such as the Church of England may launch campaigns on social issues in order to evoke a response from government. Some parts of the political system itself act as pressure groups. Local authorities regularly lobby government either individually or through the associations that represent them.

Overall the ability of pressure groups to have an impact upon government policy making is, to a large extent, determined by the effectiveness of their methods of influence and persuasion rather than by possessing 'power' to force government into a particular type of action. The 'industrial power' of trade unions is often quoted as an example of certain interests being able to coerce government. It is however, a 'power' far more rarely exercised than might be imagined, for trade unions in Britain have instigated few strikes and industrial action for covertly political purposes.

Most industrial action that has generated concern over the 'industrial power' of unions has involved the Government as an employer and has not been a direct challenge to the state (although a small minority of union members may have attempted to use the action in this way). The 'industrial power' of the unions should not however be linked solely to political ends: it is also used for other purposes. Strikes are a method used by unions to try to force companies to concede to demands for improved wages and conditions.

Example

The formation of the Democratic Union of Mineworkers after the 1984 coal strike arguably reduced the 'representativeness' of the National Union of Mineworkers which previously had represented nearly all grades of workers in the mining industry.

One of the major difficulties for any pressure group in lobbying government is to prove that its views are representative of those it claims to speak for, or of widely held public opinion. Viewpoints which government consider 'unrepresentative' can easily be dismissed or ignored, but proving 'representativeness' presents real problems for many groups.

Where trade union leadership, for example, can demonstrate that its membership is fully behind its demands (perhaps by a ballot) and that its membership constitutes a large percentage of those employed in an industry, its case is given a great deal of weight. This of course does not apply to all unions.

Example

In the late 1960s the Ministry of Transport decided to introduce both the 'breathaliser' to test motorists who were suspected of drinking and driving, and a maximum 70 miles per hour speed limit.

These policies were criticised by several motoring organisations who claimed that public opinion was against such moves. Polls conducted by the Ministry, however, produced contrary evidence, thereby making it easier for the Government to ignore these groups by claiming they were unrepresentative.

Example

The Confederation of British Industry, the largest employers organisation in Britain, and the Trades Union Congress, to which 90 per cent of trade unionists are affiliated, both have difficulties.

The CBI has 12,000 member companies, representing most sections of the British economy, but this very diversity makes it difficult for it to produce a composite set of policies to present to government which will be supported by all its members.

The TUC has a membership of 9.6 million affiliated trade unionists, representing nearly half the workforce. But when the TUC claims to speak for workers in Britain, its claim might nevertheless, be regarded as unjustified.

REPRESENTATION

'Representation' is particularly difficult for those groups who claim to speak on behalf of others, who are not directly members of the group. For example, can the spokesperson of Age Concern prove that they represent the views of old people, or can those who work for Shelter know the true wishes of the homeless? Age Concern workers will not necessarily be 'old' and members of Shelter not homeless. This is not to deny that such groups may well reflect accurately the views of many of those they work to help, but the groups must always be aware of the need to demonstrate this by publicity, research, opinion polls, etc.

It is often claimed that, by responding to pressure group activity, government will be more representative of the views of the public. However, this is based upon the assumption that the total of all group views is equivalent to public opinion. So, if the Government is prepared to listen and respond to pressure groups, it can be argued that government policies will be 'representative'.

This, as we tried to establish in Chapter 14, is an essential principle of **corporatism.** Decisions in a corporatist society are reached through a process of consultation between the major organised interests, and government is only one of those elements. In this sense the role of major pressure groups is seen to be so important that they virtually become an institution of government and an integral part of the political system. Power in a corporatist society will be concentrated in a small number of groups who cooperate closely amongst themselves, as well as with the government.

Some writers felt that a trend towards close collaboration between government and economic interests was developing during the 1974–9 Labour Government and that Britain was becoming a corporatist state. (See Chapter 14.)

DEMOCRACY

The functioning of pressure groups raises questions about:

- the democratic nature of decision making within them
- the effects on democratic political processes of their activities.

The democratic nature of decision making within groups is closely tied to the question of the 'representativeness' of the leaders of groups and the views they express on behalf of their members, or the public.

The leadership and active membership of many groups is predominantly middle aged and middle class. It could be argued that it is precisely the people who are best equipped to look after their own interests that are very keen to join the groups which attempt to strengthen the individual's chances of success in influencing government.

A particularly controversial issue has been the attempts by Conservative Governments since 1979 to introduce a greater degree of 'democracy' into the decision making processes of trade unions.

The situation at present is:

- Trade unions are now required to hold secret ballots in advance of strike action because in the past strike votes were often taken by a show of hands at an open meeting.
- All executive members of trade unions are now required to be elected by the membership as a whole rather than by the executive.
- Any 'closed shop' arrangements are now subject to periodic ballots of the membership if they are to be instituted, or retained.

The government claimed these measures have given more power to ordinary union members in decision making and subsequently makes the decisions of the leadership more 'representative' of the views of the membership. The problem of ensuring that democratic methods exist to guarantee that decisions by group leadership conform to what the mass of the membership wants occurs in many large organisations.

The views of those who are the active members of pressure groups, and most likely to hold office, do not necessarily always reflect the views of the mass of the, largely passive, membership. This can lead to possible conflict when leaders speak out on majority policy issues.

On the more general question of the effects of pressure group activity on the political system, far from enhancing democracy, it may be rather that pressure groups pose a threat to democracy.

Anti-democratic?

Liberal democracy has, as one of its central concepts, the idea of majoritarian decision making, even though this may be coupled to a belief that minority interests should nonetheless be protected (see Chapter 10, Liberalism). Pressure groups, in this context, can be seen as representing only narrow, selfish interests and adoption of their ideas might well be at the expense of majority opinion. In this way groups can be seen to be undermining the democratic process by exercising a disproportionate influence over government given their size. The wishes of the majority, it can be argued, are by-passed through the ability of groups to gain the attention of government. This process could therefore be seen to be 'anti-democratic', in that the will of the majority may not prevail.

Pro-democratic?

A pluralistic view of pressure group activity sees it as enhancing democratic processes. Pluralism, like corporatism, sees pressure groups as vital to the functioning of government but (unlike corporatism) sees power as dispersed across a large number and wide range of groups. A competition between the groups takes place to win concessions from government, which itself remains neutral and acts as a final arbiter in the process.

This view of group activity assumes that all groups must be free to enter the competition for government favour and that the outcome will not be permanently predetermined. Democratic benefits are supposed to follow.

Pressure groups, it is argued, supply useful information for government, keep it aware of the wishes of the people, and enhance the liberal democratic principles of political competition, with the result that a tolerant, open society will be created where an over-riding objective is the establishment of widespread consensus.

The competition, it is argued, ensures that no permanent monopoly of power by any groups is established and, conversely, no permanent minority is created. The assumption is that the total of opinions expressed by pressure groups equals the total of public opinion.

Public opinion, however, will of course reflect a variety of conflicting claims. The Society for the Protection of the Unborn Child oppose abortion law reform groups, and the National Farmers Union, on occasions, find themselves opposed by environmental groups. The CBI and TUC dispute a variety of economic issues, the National Union of Railwaymen is at odds with the road transport lobby and the National Union of Mineworkers disagree with the Central Electricity Generating Board over nuclear stations and so on.

The number of conflicting voices that reach government may seem endless but, with a pluralistic view, it is still the Government that, in the end, has to decide between them. It must weigh up the competing arguments, information, statistics, appeals to conscience, etc. and come to a decision. Pluralists see this process in a liberal democratic society.

FREEDOM

The existence of political freedoms is essential to the proper functioning of pressure groups in terms of effective lobbying of decision makers. Groups will only be able to work if there exists freedom of association, freedom of speech, and freedom to publish.

INFLUENCE AND PERSUASION

The major objective of any pressure group is to bring pressure to bear on government to adopt policies in line with its wishes. Governments do not, however, like to be seen to be coerced into action by the 'threats' of pressure groups. Most groups are well aware of this and the effectiveness of a pressure group, therefore, may be gauged more accurately by their ability to influence and persuade decision makers. The way groups approach this task is very varied and flexibility will be necessary.

Direct contact with government ministers and civil servants can be the most effective means, but not all groups can enjoy immediate consultation with the decision makers in Whitehall. This is not to say that more public forms of campaigning will not prove effective, because the need to generate a favourable climate of public opinion is important to all groups.

Parliamentary lobbying and public campaigning may be the only effective means of pressurising ministers for the groups that do not enjoy ready access to government. The difficulty, as we have tried to demonstrate, lies in establishing whether public support for a pressure group is generally evident.

Protest marches, petitions, rallies, advertising, mass lobbies of MPs etc. are all good methods of attracting attention particularly from the media and, for many promotional groups, the media is their main source of publicity and can prove very helpful in highlighting group demands. If forms of public campaigning result in TV coverage, this can be useful because the government department or public authority concerned will always be given the opportunity to reply. In this way, at least the group involved will have provoked a public response from government to their demands. Even if the government rejects them, it will have to explain its reasons and thus generate public debate.

Single issue or *ad hoc* groups often may not have the time to establish close working relations with government and instead have to achieve a fairly

Example

The National Viewers and Listeners Association is an interesting example of a group who make good use of the media in promoting their campaigns.

The group was formed in 1965 by a schoolteacher, Mrs Mary Whitehouse, who felt that there was an undesirable amount of sex and violence on TV and radio. The group was created as a result of widespread media coverage of a campaign she launched in 1963, which included public meetings and a national petition calling for better broadcasting standards.

The NVLA has campaigned on a variety of issues and at one point, in October 1980, took legal action against Michael Bogdanov, for his version of the play *Romans in Britain* at the National Theatre. The play depicted scenes of homosexuality, which the NVLA considered obscene, but the trial lasted for only 3 days when the prosecution was withdrawn.

The NVLA also campaigned strongly in favour of a successful Private Members Bill, introduced by Graham Bright, MP to limit the public availability of so called 'video-nasties'. These video tapes often showed scenes of extreme violence, but were not covered by the legislation dealing with the public exhibition of films.

The strength of Mrs Whitehouse's NVLA is that she has always been able to attract a good deal of media coverage. The coverage has not always been supportive but it has meant that the group has remained in the forefront of debate over moral standards in the media.

immediate impact by more public forms of campaigning. If the government announces plans to close a hospital or build an airport it may prove essential to generate support quickly so as to oppose such measures. Public campaigning although perhaps quite effective in some situations does have its drawbacks.

Vociferous groups of protestors who engage in 'media-worthy' forms of activity will not enhance their reputation as a 'responsible' group with whom government does not mind being seen to negotiate. The more 'responsible' and well established groups will generally be welcomed by government in policy planning processes. Radical groups which publicly attempt to embarrass or cajole government may find the door of the ministry closed to them.

The ability of a group to be involved in policy planning can prove to be vital if they are to exercise any influence. It is far better for a group to have a voice in the planning of policies, rather than having to oppose them once they have been announced. A government that has invested a good deal of 'political capital' and time in a scheme which it has publicly launched, will be reluctant to change it in the face of hostile criticism by pressure groups. If it does, then it opens itself to the criticism of having 'given in' to organised interests.

The tactics of pressure groups may, therefore, be determined by the value the groups attach to the consultation procedures that all governments establish. A very wide range of such consultative bodies exist and appropriate groups are invited to take part in their deliberations.

Nonetheless, by becoming 'respectable' in the eyes of government and thereby being invited to engage in consultation, the group may face the possibility of losing its independence of action and of becoming too 'domesticated'. The result may be that the group will have to forgo the use of some of its best 'weapons'.

Example

The Howard League for Penal Reform has been able, over a number of years, to build up close working relationships with the Home Office. The Howard League is regarded by government to be a 'responsible' organisation which does not engage in public forms of campaigning. Instead it has developed links with Home Office officials who have come to value its research work on the penal system.

More radical prison reform groups, by contrast, have enjoyed much less access to civil servants and Home Office ministers.

Example

During the period of the 'Social Contract', 1974–8 (see Chapter 14 on Corporatism), some trade unionists felt that the close co-operation established between the unions and the Labour Government meant they had to pay too high a price in that they gave up free collective bargaining, backed if necessary, by forms of industrial action.

It can be argued that it is not the function of groups to help expedite th implementation of government policy, but to act as 'watchdogs'. To becom too closely involved in government policy making may mean the watchdo loses its teeth!

Despite these arguments, most groups are prepared to work wit government in areas of mutual benefit and it is often the usefulness of group to government that determines their influence. If the group has something t offer, then politicians will be prepared to listen. What politicians ofte require are statistics, technical information, and advice. This process has le to the establishment of close working relationships between some groups an the policy makers in government.

The process of consultation can be taken a step further, for some pressur groups can be crucial to the implementation of policy and not just it formulation. Groups in this position will be allowed many more opportunitie to talk to policy makers compared to those not so well placed.

The kind of close relations that can be established benefits not only th pressure group but the policy makers as well, for it can be of great assistanc to them to know that a principal pressure group in a particular area c activity supports their efforts. For example, if the National Union c Teachers supports government education policy, then it is helpful to th policy makers to know that the biggest union in the teaching profession wi be backing their efforts and lobbying its own membership to this end.

Example

The Department of Health and the British Medical Association work closely in many areas of health policy making. This has not, however, prevented the BMA from publicly criticising health policy on many occasions.

Example

The officials of the National Farmers Union are in frequent contact with civil servants in the Ministry of Agriculture, Fisheries and Food. They are involved in many areas of agricultural policy making.

The major area of interest for the NFU has moved since Britain joined the European Economic Community and agricultural policy planning became subject to the Common Agricultural Policy. So their major objective is now to pressurise government into 'protecting' farming interests during European negotiations.

The need to involve pressure groups in policy making, or at least to attemp to win their support for decisions reached, has been recognised by a governments. The difficulty arises when major groups do not endors government policy and actively oppose them. As we have tried to establis at the beginning of this chapter, very close links appeared to have develope between government and major economic groups during the 1960s and 197C and this led some to conclude that Britain was developing into a corporatis state. Since 1979, the close proximity of trade unions and industrial group to government appears to have lessened because Mrs Thatcher's governmer is less concerned to seek endorsement from them for economic policy.

The financial capacity of a group, necessarily, will help to determine ho influential they may be. The groups that are able to command considerabl resources both financially and organisationally will be in a strong position t present a sophisticated and rationally argued case to government. Jus opposing what government proposes, even if the opposition may be legitimat and reasonable, may not be enough.

The ability to suggest alternatives and to question the basis of governmer proposals in a rational manner often requires a good deal of expertise This in itself can cost a good deal of money and require considerabl organisational skill. All pressure groups have to be aware of the need to rais money for even the most local campaign needs a 'fighting fund' to pay fc posters, the hire of church halls for meetings, etc.

The NIMBY (not-in-my-back-yard) factor may be evident in th arguments of groups opposing proposals such as the disposal of low leve nuclear waste by burying it, but it is still necessary for groups to show wh it should happen in someone else's backyard, or no one's backyard, b rational argument. The ability of groups to do this has been highlighted b several cases involving major environmental issues.

Example

The public inquiry into the application by the CEGB to build another nuclear reactor at Sizewell in Suffolk, ran for two years, 1985–7.

The CEGB spent millions of pounds in presenting its case. It employed legal counsel and extra administrative staff, who were housed in temporary offices, erected outside the hall where the hearings took place. By comparison, many of the environmental groups that objected to the application had to raise money by jumble sales, and the like.

The CEGB considered its financial outlay justifiable in that the inquiry supported its case and ministerial approval for the scheme was given. The expenditure involved in presenting arguments at the Sizewell inquiry led to some calls for all groups to be given government funded financial assistance at public inquiries.

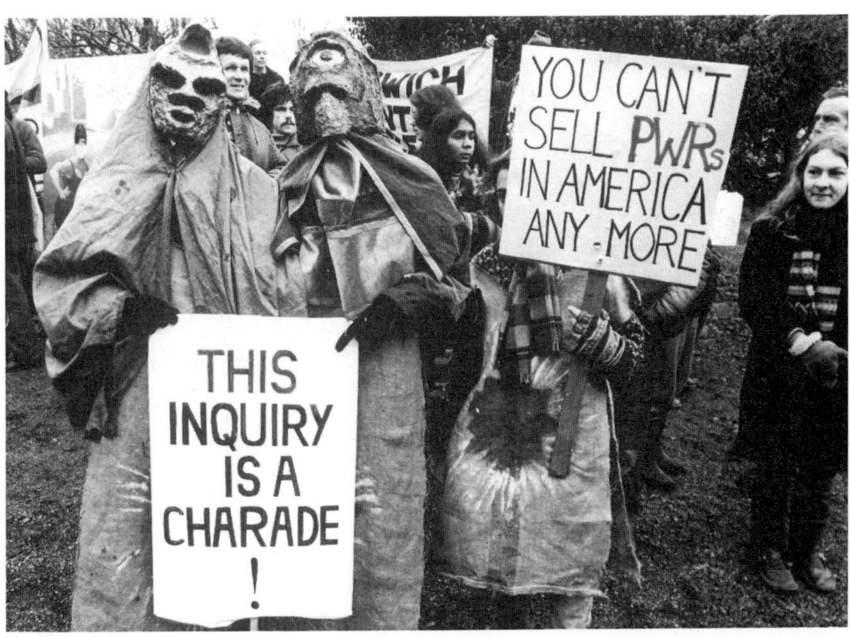

▸ *Pickets at the opening of the public inquiry into Sizewell 'B'.*

The recognition of some groups of the need to present sophisticated and well organised campaigns has led to an increasing use of public relations firms and professional lobby firms. As the example at the beginning of this chapter shows, this can be big business. Such firms are able to identify the right politicians, civil servants, and pressmen, to support the groups activities. Individual companies, as well as pressure groups, are clients of this growing industry. The aim is to generate a favourable image for the group engaged in lobbying as well as to 'educate' the appropriate politicians.

Example

The British record industry organised a sophisticated and expensive campaign in order to influence the Conservative Government to introduce a levy on the sale of blank audio cassette tapes. The revenue from such a levy, it was claimed, should be paid to the record industry in order to compensate for the loss of record sales due to people illegally taping records.

They appeared at first to have been successful, in that the government published a White Paper in 1986 which proposed a 10 per cent levy. It was estimated that £5 million would be raised for distribution to copyright owners and performers who had suffered from illegal copying. This proposal was opposed by consumer groups such as the National Consumer Council, and by the Tape Manufacturers Group, which represents the major blank tape producers.

The outcome was that in October 1987, the plans for the levy were not included in the Copyright Design and Patents Bill, when it was presented to Parliament. The Government said that the adverse effects of the levy on consumers and blind people, coupled with the costs of administering the scheme, outweighed the benefits it might bring.

The ability of a group to influence government still often depends upon th degree of importance attached by government to the demands of the grou A group that wishes to maintain the status quo in whatever field will hav an in-built advantage over a group that wishes to bring about chang Governments inevitably will be reluctant to respond to demands for chang especially if they have no great commitment to the area of interest of th pressure group. The skills of a group will have to centre around convincin government that positive good will result and, even better, that public opinio desires change.

Governments, however, do not always correctly anticipate the strength established practices and the groups attempting to preserve them. Fo example, in 1987, the Conservative Government, in the face of organise opposition in the House of Commons, withdrew its schemes to liberalise th laws in England relating to Sunday trading. The lessons of this episode we not lost on the Government, for its proposals to liberalise licensing laws i England, announced later in the year, notably did not extend to Sunda drinking laws!

RECENT TRENDS

Up until 1979 and the first Conservative election victory under Mrs Thatche the major pressure groups representing business and labour were considere to be welcome participants in national economic management. This triparti relationship is now largely gone, for both the Confederation of Britis Industry and the Trades Union Congress have lost a good deal of influenc with government.

The trade unions have suffered a loss of membership, to a great exten through economic recession, and their options for industrial action have bee reduced by industrial relations legislation. The CBI have also found increasingly difficult to influence the course of economic affairs.

Other pressure groups, however, have become more militant and have bee prepared to adopt tactics of civil disobedience, and in some cases, dire action to further their campaigns.

Example

The Womens Peace Movement, and in particular those who set up a camp outside the Greenham Common US Airbase in Berkshire, engaged in a long term programme of civil disobedience, in opposition to nuclear missiles being located in Britain.

Gay Rights protestors have employed direct action in their opposition to legislation such as section 28 of the Local Government Act 1987, which made it illegal for local authorities to give assistance to organisations that intentionally promote homosexuality. In one incident in May 1988, gay women protestors managed to avoid security at the BBC and to disrupt the broadcasting of a national news programme.

► *Greenham Common Women's Peace Camp, February 1982.*

Given the complexity and range of pressure group activity, it is unlikely that any group can win concessions continuously from government. Governments are always aware of the 'public interest' and the findings of public opinion polls in some cases.

Example

A factor in the Conservative Government's decision to make a number of concessions involving the National Health Service in 1987 and 1988, was the apparent widespread public support for a campaign waged by NHS pressure groups. The findings of public opinion polls showed growing concern over the NHS funding and sympathy for the nurses pay claims.

Nottingham health workers in an HS day of action in 1988.

The influence of particular pressure groups is not always constant and may vary from issue to issue. As the importance, or public awareness, of political issues varies, so too does the ability of pressure groups to influence events.

Example

The Campaign for Nuclear Disarmament, in the 1950s and early 1960s, was a major pressure group in the peace movement. At one point, in 1960, a CND campaign inside the Labour Party led to the party conference adopting a policy of unilateral disarmament. Thereafter, its influence declined notably only to be revived again in the 1980s.

The debate over the siting of American missiles in Britain helped the CND cause. CND membership doubled and public support, as measured by public opinion polls, grew, although a majority were never converted to its policy of unilateralism. The Labour Party, however, again adopted a unilateralist stance as its official defence strategy.

The Easter 1964 CND march to ie nuclear research station at ldermaston.

EXAMINATION QUESTIONS

1 To what extent are the respective roles of pressure groups and politic parties contradictory rather than complementary? (University of Can bridge, Politics and Government, Special Paper, 1982)

2 To what extent do pressure groups help promote the ideals of democra in the United Kingdom? (AEB Government and Politics, A-Level, 1980)

3 'Government by agreement with pressure groups is now an essential featu of British government.' Discuss. (University of London, Government an Political Studies, A-Level, 1983).

NOW READ ON . . .

G. Alderman *Pressure Groups and the Government in Britain* Longma 1984
A valuable analysis of pressure group activity.
W. Grant *Business and Politics in Britain* Macmillan, 1987
An assessment of the relationships between government and industry.
M. Davies *The Politics of Pressure* BBC, 1985
The 'art' of lobbying explained.

22 Political Parties and Electoral Systems

BASIC PRINCIPLES

Democracy substitutes election by the incompetent many for appointment by the corrupt few.

George Bernard Shaw in *Man and Superman*, 1903

Key Concepts

Influence and Persuasion	The image of parties and leaders; the role of the media; the role of opinion polls; parties as pressure groups.
Participation	Membership of the parties; the concept of 'active membership'.
Representation	Party channels of representation; role of party agents; the case for referendums; a 'recall' system; how representative are the parties?
Legitimacy	Why do MPs get elected? The legitimacy of the current electoral system and of current party structure.
Power	The power of large parties in the current system.
Law	The use of pressure group activities by political parties, some of which may involve encouraging people to break the law.
Democracy	Representative system versus a delegatory system; democratic implications of the electoral system.

DISCUSSING THE ARGUMENTS

Selection of Candidates

Most British parties select their candidates on a constituency basis but they vary as to the exact method of selection. The techniques are described at length in other textbooks and will not be repeated here.

The central issue would appear, however, to be the extent to which the means of the selection of political candidates enhances or detracts from the democratic process.

Parties which allow the selection of candidates by the constituency party itself are, in effect, allowing a small group of active party supporters to choose the candidate. In the Labour Party, in particular, this group of party activists can be extremely small. Conservative Party constituency memberships are usually higher, but are still relatively small compared to the numbers of voters who vote for the party at most elections.

The candidate is supposed to represent the constituency and the party in that order, but it is the party which will pay the deposit and the election expenses and it is the party activists who have shown themselves to be interested and dedicated enough to turn up to meetings and work for the party. From this point of view it would seem only right, therefore, for the activists to select the candidates.

The Social and Liberal Democrat Party (SLD) and the Social Democratic Party (SDP) allow their memberships as a whole to select candidates.

Parliamentary candidates are presented not to small groups of activists f interview but, by post, to the entire local membership of the party. The vot of all the members, as opposed to those of the minority who are 'active' party affairs, count towards who becomes the party's candidate.

An even greater extension of democracy would be to allow the electora as a whole to select candidates. In certain States of the USA **Prima Elections** are held in which the voters vote for candidates who will then sta in the General Election later. In most states which have this system t method allows all registered Republicans to vote in the Republican Prima (in which several Republican candidates will put themselves forward f possible selection as the eventual Republican candidate) and all register Democrats will vote in the Democratic Primary. There are several layers complexity to the 'Primary' system but the result is to select candidates wh will then stand in the General Election.

In theory a primary election system sounds extremely democratic. It allov the maximum number of the electorate to have a say not only in who the representative in the Legislature will be but which candidates will b standing. In practice the democratic nature of the system is limited by th extent to which the electorate will actually turn out and vote in yet anoth election. Primary turnouts in the USA tend to be very low: usually averagin about 15-20 per cent of those entitled to vote.

Reselection or Recall

It is possible in theory for every MP to have to undergo a process 'reselection' before an election campaign. The local party might decide th they do not like the MP's work or attitude and might require him or her stand for selection against a set of new 'shortlisted' candidates. The Labou Party, however, now requires automatic reselection before each electio Every Labour MP has to stand for reselection before each General Electic although not necessarily against a set of new candidates.

The object of reselection in the Labour Party is to ensure that MPs do n forget their ties to the local party or to the aims of the Labour Movement a whole. The aims of reselection in the other parties would be exactly th same but are not, at the moment, instituted automatically.

Reselection is a *party* matter and usually occurs if an MP consistently fai to follow the party line or commits some breach of good practice. In Brita there is no way that the electorate *as a whole* can change its mind about a MP. Once an MP is elected they are in office for the duration of th Parliament. In certain states in the USA there is the possibility of **recallin** the sitting member.

The 'Recall' system means a petition signed by a given proportion of th electorate can force a by-election and, in this way, enable the constituenc to 'sack' the representative before the full term has been served. Such Recal are not very common in the USA, but it is argued that their very presenc means that representatives are much more attentive to the needs and desir of their constituents (see Chapter 7, Representation).

The Deposit

In theory anyone over 21 who has the deposit of £500 and has been nominate by ten registered electors can stand for election to the House of Common and as long as they receive more than 5 per cent of the vote they will kee their deposit. In return the country will subsidise their election expenses b giving them free publicity (for their national party through 'Party Politica Broadcasts' on TV and radio) and free postage of election leaflets.

Should there be a deposit before one may stand as a candidate fo Parliament? The idea is, of course, to prevent frivolous candidates fron standing and from detracting from the seriousness of the political process For many years the deposit was set at £150 (it was so set in 1918 when th average wage was a lot less than this figure). It therefore constituted a significant financial barrier to parties and individuals wishing to present themselves to the people. The deposit was forfeit if the candidate did not achieve at least 12.5 per cent of the vote.

In 1984, for a very brief period, the deposit was actually raised to £1,000 but this was lowered to £500 in 1986. The 'qualifying percentage' was also lowered, in 1984, to 5 per cent of the vote. In the example of the Kensington By-Election of 1988 given below these rule changes meant that eleven of the fifteen candidates lost their deposits of £500.

Example

THE KENSINGTON BY-ELECTION 14 JULY 1988

Results:

Candidate	Party	Vote	%
D. Fishburn	Conservative	9,829	41.6
A. Holmes	Labour	9,014	38.1
W. Goodhart	SLD	2,546	10.8
J. Martin	SDP	1,190	5.0
P. Hobson	Green	572	2.4
C. Payne	Rainbow Alliance	193	0.8
Lord David Sutch	Monster Raving Loony Rock Music	61	0.3
J. Duignan	London Class War	60	0.3
B. McDermott	Free Trade	31	0.2
B. Goodier	Anti-Left Fascist	31	0.2
R. Edey	Fair Wealth	30	0.2
W. Scola	Leveller	27	0.2
J. Crowley	Anti-Yuppie	24	0.1
J. Connell	Peace	20	0.1
K. Trivedi	Ind. Janata	5	0.0

In the 1987 General Election the Conservatives took 47.5 per cent of the vote; Labour 33.2 per cent and the Alliance 17.2 per cent. The Green Party won 1.7 per cent.

At the General Election of 1987 there were only 6 candidates compared to 15 in the By-Election of 1988.

Of these 15 candidates no less than 11 lost their deposits.

Election Spending

The British electoral system also places a further restriction on the way in which finance may influence the campaign: candidates are limited, on a constituency basis, to spending an average maximum of about £5,000 on their campaigns. In theory this is intended to ensure that the candidates cannot use large sums of money to swamp their opponents. However, the restriction was invented at a time when campaigns really were 'local' and does not seem to be very logical in an age when the central party machines can legally spend an unlimited amount on publicity. Unless the national spending of the parties is similarly restricted there would seem to be little point in restricting spending at local level. The public's awareness of the views of the major parties is enhanced by continued exposure to advertisements in the press while the smaller parties cannot afford to compete.

On the other hand one could argue that a political party which had the finance to promote itself is already demonstrating its popularity and its ability to raise that finance. Small, poor parties are small and poor, the argument would continue, because they cannot raise the support for the ideas and objectives.

This argument would hold water in a democratic sense if it were the ca that the amounts of money raised by the parties were exactly proportion to the amount of individual support they received. This, of course, is n necessarily the case. It could be argued that a party which appeals to th upper and middle classes begins life with an automatic advantage. It is al the case that some parties receive their finance not from individual supporte but from large organisations. One has to weigh the democratic implicatio of, for instance, three large trade unions giving the Labour Party a total £100,000 or two large companies giving the Conservative Party £50,0 apiece against three individuals giving the Green Party £100. Does this mea that the Labour Party or the Conservative Party can claim 1,000 times mo support or democratic legitimacy than the Green Party?

Individual Candidates

A further problem of the financial aspect of elections and parties is that the effect on individual candidates. The rules place limits on the amount money which even a very rich candidate can spend on his or her own beha in an election but do not restrict the spending of parties from the centre. local candidate of a large party receives an automatic boost from the centr advertising and from the image of the party which has been projected (great expense) over the years preceding an election.

This might be held to place local independent candidates at disadvantage and one might, therefore, consider why it is that this should b the case. Independent candidates are free to represent their constituency views. A constituency which elects such a person usually does so because the *do* represent the local point of view better than any of the national part candidates. Democracy, therefore, would seem to be enhanced by allowin the system to produce more independent candidates.

The problem, of course, arises with the necessity to govern the country: th need for efficient and effective government. It may well have been th difficulty of forming and maintaining effective governments which led to th formation of the strong, centralised party system in the first place!

Law

The extent to which one should abide by the law even when one believes i to be wrong has always been a difficult matter but it is usually believed tha political parties are **Constitutional** bodies and, as such, should remain withi the law.

As the mainstay of the Parliamentary system the parties, it is felt, ough to demonstrate their commitment to the system by remaining within the law

On several occasions, however, British parties have publically supporte breaking the law in order to make political points or to create pressure fo changes in the law or the constitution.

1. **Provisional Sinn Fein** The Northern Irish political wing of the Provisiona IRA has usually taken the line that opposition to the British governmen can take any form including the use of violence although Sinn Fein, itself claims never to have taken part in such activities.

2. **Plaid Cymru** The Welsh Nationalist Party once encouraged the Wels people not to pay for their TV licences in order to try to pressure th government into creating a specifically Welsh fourth TV Channel Thousands of Welsh people did not pay for their licences and the the leader of Plaid Cymru, Mr Gwynfor Evans MP, went on hunger strike The government eventually gave in to these demands and created th Welsh Channel 4.

3. **Labour Party** Certain elements within the party have always felt that disobeying the law is a justified technique towards achieving change. This viewpoint goes back to the earliest days of the Labour movement but has been seen in 1989 in the encouragement by certain politicians of disobedience of the Poll Tax laws. One of the most famous examples of 'party' disobedience of the law took place when, in 1972, the Labour councillors of a place called Clay Cross refused to implement a Conservative Government law on the imposition of 'Fair Rents'. These councillors claimed that the then Conservative Government lacked legitimacy. They were surcharged but few people asked themselves who *really* had the legitimate right to decide on what constituted a 'fair rent'.

4. **Scottish Nationalist Party** This party actively encouraged Scottish householders not to pay the new Poll Tax when it was introduced in Scotland in 1989.

The Electoral System

The British system is called the **Plurality System** or, more commonly, **First-past-the-post.** The person who gets the largest number of votes in a constituency is elected, even though a majority of the voters might *not* have voted for that candidate for example:

Candidate A – 15,000 votes = 31.9%
Candidate B – 12,000 votes = 25.5%
Candidate C – 10,000 votes = 21.4%
Candidate D – 5,000 votes = 10.6%
Candidate E – 5,000 votes = 10.6%

Total Votes Cast – 47,000 = 100.0%

In the example above, candidate A has been elected as MP for this constituency with just under 32 per cent of the votes cast. Over two-thirds of the voters did *not* want this MP.

A party which attempts to form a government in Parliament is expected not simply to have a plurality of the seats but an **absolute majority** of them. This need not, however, be matched in terms of votes. No British government since 1945 has ever had a majority of the votes cast in a General Election.

There have been 'minority' governments (in terms of seats) during the period since 1945, but they have usually been extremely brief or have been shored up with disguised coalitions such as the **'Lib-Lab Pact'** of 1976–8. In October 1974 the Labour Party was returned to government with an absolute majority of just three MPs over all the other parties. This was soon reduced to a minority situation by deaths and resignations, and the Callaghan Government was forced to enter into an agreement, known as the 'Lib-Lab Pact' with the Liberals and the two Nationalist parties in order to remain in power between 1976 and 1978. It might surprise some people to know that, since 1900, there have been around 20 years of 'coalition government' in the supposedly 'single party government' system in Britain.

The table on General Elections and the associated graphs overleaf illustrate the situation since 1945. Although most governments have had an absolute majority of the seats in Parliament there has not been a single one which has enjoyed an absolute majority (more than 50 per cent) of the votes actually cast. In October 1974 Labour's 39 per cent of the vote won 50 per cent of the seats in Parliament; in 1983 Mrs Thatcher's 42 per cent of the vote won 61 per cent of the seats, and, in 1987, the same government's 43 per cent of the vote gained them 58 per cent of the seats in the House of Commons.

General Elections 1945–87 Main political parties only

Year	Seats Won			%Vote			%Seats		
	Con	Lab	All	Con	Lab	All	Con	Lab	Al
1945	213	393	12	39.9	48.0	9.0	33	61	2
1950	298	315	9	43.5	46.1	9.1	48	50	1
1951	321	295	6	48.0	48.8	2.6	51	47	1
1955	345	277	6	49.7	46.4	2.7	55	44	1
1959	365	258	6	49.3	43.8	5.9	58	41	1
1964	303	317	9	43.4	44.1	11.2	48	50	1
1966	253	363	12	41.9	47.9	8.5	40	58	2
1970	330	287	6	46.4	42.9	7.5	52	46	1
1974(F)	296	301	14	38.1	37.2	19.3	47	47	2
1974(O)	276	319	13	35.7	39.3	18.3	44	50	2
1979	339	268	11	43.9	36.9	13.8	53	42	2
1983	397	209	23	42.4	27.6	25.4	61	32	3
1987	375	229	22	43.3	31.5	23.1	58	35	3

Note: The numbers of seats in this table may not add up to the total number of sea in the appropriate Parliament because only representation for major partie Conservative, Labour and those for Liberal, Social Democrats and Social a Liberal Democrats (under 'Alliance') are provided.

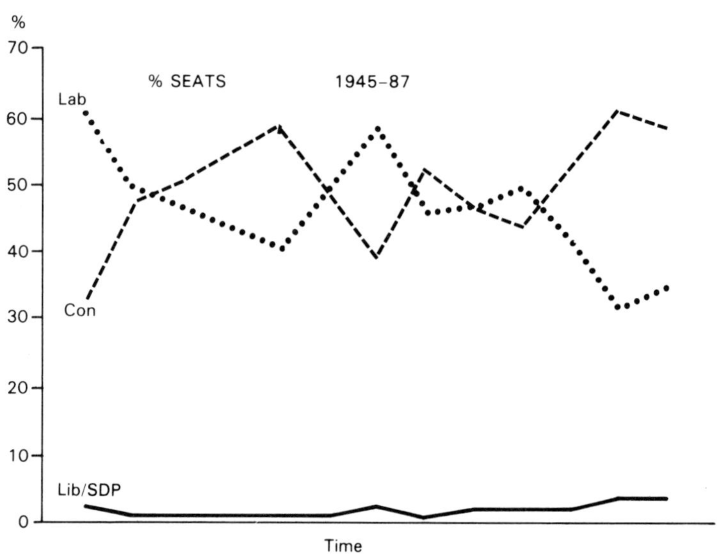

► *Percentage shares of seats won at General Elections 1945–87.*

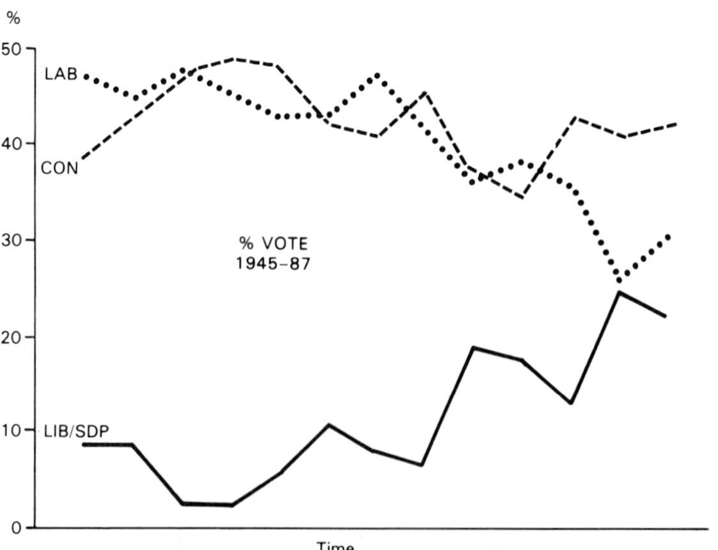

► *Percentage shares of General Election votes 1945–87.*

The main argument in support of the current electoral system has always been that it produces 'strong' governments rather than the 'weak' governments which, its supporters argue, are produced by proportional systems.

The concept of 'strong' and 'weak' government is extremely problematic: on the surface a strong government is one which can govern without too much hinderance from the Parliament; laws are passed quickly, decisions are taken relatively easily and efficiently, and policy is expressed and pursued clearly and openly. 'Weak' government, on the other hand, entails lengthy negotiation between coalition partners, laws tend to be compromises between the partners and take a longer time to argue through Parliament, and the coalitions themselves tend to be unstable and to break down thereby creating a need for frequent elections and producing a much less coherent set of long term policies.

The case against **Proportional Representation** (PR) systems is usually predicted upon their leading to 'weak' governments. The term 'weak' is not very clear, however, but is taken to mean things like 'indecisive', lacking force or direction, etc. It has always been difficult to assess the validity of these arguments precisely because the terms are so loose and the variables so many.

The example which is most often put forward as representing all that is bad in proportional systems is that of Italy with its frequent elections and even more frequent need to change Prime Minister and government.

It remains the case, however, that even Italy has performed better than the UK since 1945 in economic terms. In spite of frequent changes of government (and Italy has, in fact, had fewer General Elections since 1945 than Britain), Italy has created for its citizens a standard of living which is now so close to that of the UK that there are frequent arguments about whether it should replace the UK on the major economic councils of the world. In relative terms the performance of Italy under a fairly chaotic system of PR has been much better than that of the UK.

Example

BRITAIN'S OTHER PARTIES

Scottish National Party (SNP)

Founded in 1928, it merged, in 1933 with the 'Scottish Party'. Its first MP was returned at a by-election in April 1945 but the seat was lost very quickly (at the General Election of the same year). **Main aims**: Self-government for Scotland within the Commonwealth.

The party achieved its first post-war MP in 1970 on 11.4 per cent of the Scottish vote. Over the next two General Elections the party built up its representation until it had no less than 11 MPs and 30 per cent of the vote in Scotland (after the October 1974 election).

In 1979 the SNP lost most of its MPs, reducing from 11 seats to just two and had its share of the Scottish vote cut to 12 per cent. Although in 1987 the SNP still retained two MPs the party's share of the vote was reduced to under 10 per cent.

Since 1979 the party has been through a traumatic period of reappraisal of its aims. The left of the party, led by such figures as Margo MacDonald, was defeated in its attempts to steer party policy towards complete independence for Scotland. The SNP has also had to deal with a militant section called 'Siol Nan Gaidheal' (Seed of the Gael).

Plaid Cymru (Welsh National Party)

Plaid Cymru was founded in 1925 with the objective of achieving self-government in some form for Wales. It's first MP, Gwynfor Evans (Leader of the party until 1981), was elected for Carmarthen in 1966 and the party peaked in popularity before the SNP (probably due to the fact that the latter's support depended to a large extent on the large deposits of oil which were found in the early 1970s in 'Scottish' waters).

Plaid Cymru's vote peaked at 11.5 per cent of the Welsh vote in 1970 and polls over the years (to 1988) showed its support at less than 6 per cent. It achieved three MPs, however, in the October 1974 General Election. Since then, and including the 1987 election it has consistently returned two MPs.

Unlike the SNP, Plaid Cymru lost the 1979 Devolution Referendum by a very substantial margin. Only 12 per cent of the electorate of

Wales and 20 per cent of those actually voting supported the idea for Wales.

In many ways, though, Plaid Cymru has been more successful than its Scottish counterpart. Over the years, a combination of militancy and Labour Party fears for its own vote in the Labour strongholds of Wales has given Plaid Cymru a number of 'victories'. Noteworthy have been the agreements by various UK Governments to provide dual-language signposts in the Welsh-speaking areas of the country, and the almost incredible agreement to give Welsh speakers their own TV channel (Channel 4 Wales).

Green Party
Established as the 'Ecology Party' in the late 1970s, the Green Party changed its name so that it could be more closely identified with those of similar title on the continent.

Unlike its continental counterparts, the British Green Party does not have the advantage of proportional representation and has not achieved representation in Parliament (although it has won many local council seats).

In many ways the 'Green' movement represents a totally new and radical approach to politics. Unlike most conventional parties (which tend to present their policies in economic terms) the Green Party argues that the economics and politics of **capital** are no longer important. Instead they would argue, we should be moving towards smaller units, devolved political power, more responsibility for the environment, and a greater sense of responsibility for the rest of society.

National Front
The National Front was formed, in 1966, from a merger of two older right-wing parties: The League of Empire Loyalists and The British National Party. The new party was joined in 1967 by the 'Greater Britain Movement'.

The party has never won a Parliamentary seat in post-war times and its share of the national vote peaked in 1979 at just 0.6 per cent.

Its policies are usually centred around law and order and nationalism. One of the most common threads over the years has been the call for 'humane repatriation' of all 'non-Anglo-Saxon immigrants'. The 'Front' usually opposes such things as the EEC, the UN, immigration generally, and Gay rights.

The NF split into four separate groups in 1980 and the effect of this has been to dilute its vote.

Communist Parties
Britain has several parties which might be termed 'Communist' including:

- **The Communist Party of Great Britain**: Established in 1920; it had representation in Parliament before 1939.
- **The New Communist Party**: Set up in 1977 to promote a hard-line 'Stalinist' form of Communism.
- **The Communist Party of England**: Another breakaway sect following a more traditional but still Russian-based Communist line.
- **The Communist Party of Britain**: Anti-Moscow; pro-Maoist.

Socialist Workers' Party
This party was formed by Paul Foot in 1977 out of the earlier 'International Socialists' which had been established in 1950 to promote a Trotskyist approach to Socialism and to oppose the authoritarian, State-socialism style of the Soviet Union.

Although limited in terms of numbers, the SWP has been much more active than the traditional 'Communist' groups. Its newspaper, **'Socialist Worker'** has a large circulation – estimated at about 20,000.

It is primarily a revolutionary party and does not believe that Socialism can be achieved through the ballot box.

Workers' Revolutionary Party
Another Trotskyist, revolutionary socialist group, the WRP are supported by a small but active membership. After the revolution the party believes that the police force should be replaced by a 'Workers' Militia'.

International Marxist Group
A small, intellectual grouping of Trotskyist supporters which has been closely connected to the SWP during recent years. Their main objective is to increase the awareness of the workers so that, as the IMG would have it, they will be able to understand the way in which the Labour Party has actually acted in support of the capitalist system.

The *Other* Other Parties
Mebyon Kernow (the Cornish National Party)
Wessex Regional Party
Anarchists
United Country Party (founded by Patrick Moore)

It is necessary to point out that virtually every other country in Europe als has a system of proportional representation and that, far from ther exhibiting symptoms of weakness, almost all of them have stabl governments for lengthy periods of time, have consistent domestic and foreign policies and have now overtaken the UK in economic terms. Most of them have much more stable political systems if that stability is measured in terms of coherence of political, economic and social policy.

The economic argument is heard most clearly in one of the most famous criticisms of the British electoral system* in which the almost 180 degree changes in policy direction which occur when a different party takes office in Britain have been dubbed the 'Jekyll and Hyde Syndrome'.

Participation is usually put forward as one of the fundamental tests of a democratic system and the British usually point proudly to the 'high' average turnouts in their General Elections. The comparison is usually made between the British average turnout of about 77 per cent since 1945 with the average in the USA of nearer 60 per cent. While the British figure is undoubtedly high for a plurality system it is now dropping and has averaged only 74 per cent since 1970. Turnouts in proportional systems are rarely below 80 per cent and often average over 85 per cent (even in those countries which do not make voting compulsory).

Although measures of turnout are much too simple upon which to base a direct comparison between systems, they do give a broad indication of the extent of participation which *might* be possible under a British proportional system and this indication is supported by the increasing degree of apparent apathy among British voters under the current system.

The Vote-less Voters

If the franchise is an important element in democracy then the effective removal of a person's ability to cast an *effective* vote must be of paramount concern. The fact that each individual possesses the *right* to vote does not, in itself, constitute democracy. There may be many reasons why the vote is not *effective*.

In the mid nineteenth century the franchise was being widened, but the effectiveness of those new voters was extremely limited by the system of voting and the degree of corruption in the system. All votes were counted visually by means of a count of hands (meaning that the way a person voted could be noted and, if necessary, held against him) and it was common practice for the votes of the poorer elements of society to be bought with bribes of money and/or beer or forced by means of physical intimidation. The result was that most voters, although legally given the vote, were not effectively enfranchised.

The effect of the modern electoral system can be said to be somewhat similar in certain areas of the country and for certain individuals. Although corruption and intimidation have been all but eradicated by the use of the secret ballot, it remains the case that certain voters are virtually disenfranchised by the current system. Depending on where one lives one's vote either 'counts' or it does not and this applies as much to supporters of the major parties as it does to those of the minor ones.

The Conservative voter in northern industrial towns and the Labour voter in southern country towns know that their votes do not have any weight at all. They simply do not count at all and they might as well stay at home. Similarly, SLD voters in many areas have, hitherto, felt that their votes carry no weight.

The results of this 'effective disenfranchisement' have been extremely difficult to identify because it has been impossible to tell, for example, how many SLD voters have been voting for the other two major parties simply

---

*In the book *The Jekyll and Hyde Years* by Michael Stewart, 1968.

because they know that an SLD candidate does not have a chance of bein elected and that, therefore, they must vote for their second preference. Thi is usually called 'tactical voting' but it is, in essence, exactly the same as th **preferential systems** used in some countries on the continent. Ir constituencies which have strong permanent majorities for one particula party, the voters who support other political parties tend to express seconc preferences by voting in specific ways. A Conservative may vote SLD; o SLD voters may vote for one of the other two parties. A great many voter almost certainly recognise their 'effective disenfranchisement' and simpl stay at home.

Faced with the effective nullification of their preferred vote the voter use what has become known as 'tactical voting' to ensure that the vote has som value. As the British system has ceased being a two-party one and ha become, essentially, a three-party system, so the need for an electoral syster which adequately reflects the exact wishes of the electorate might be regarde as more important.

Example

THE ELECTORAL CONTROVERSY – PROS AND CONS

The Plurality System – Claimed Advantages
- 'Strong' governments with working majorities
- 'Stable' governments not needing frequent renegotiations of coalitions
- Simple electoral system which is easy for voters to understand
- Single member constituencies which strongly link MPs to their constituents

The Plurality System – Claimed Disadvantages
- Frequency of minority governments – no government since 1945 has ever had a majority of the votes cast
- Unfairness to smaller parties; no relationship between votes cast and seats gained
- Effective disenfranchisement of certain voters
- Illegitimacy of governments based on minority votes leading to lack of credibility and, possibly, to unrest (e.g. Miners' Strike)
- System works to the advantage of parties which have their voters concentrated geographically, such as the Nationalist Parties, and to the disadvantage of those which have their votes spread out across the country, such as the SLD, Green Party, etc.
- System encourages 'party' strength and prevents the establishment of independent MPs
- MPs themselves are elected on minority votes and lose legitimacy thereby

Proportional Representation – Claimed Advantages
- Ensures that all governments have the support of more than half of the voters – all governments are 'majority' governments
- Ensures that all MPs have the support of more than half of their constituents (depending on the system concerned).
- Results in a more accurate match between the votes cast for a party and the number of seats gained in Parliament
- Depending on the system chosen (single transferable vote, etc.) independent MPs would find it easier to stand and to win a seat
- Removes the problem of 'effective disenfranchisement' – all votes would count and would be effective in the final analysis.

Proportional Representation – Claimed Disadvantages
- Certain systems (the list system for example) would have the effect of increasing central party power at the expense of the constituencies
- Certain systems (the list system) would almost totally exclude the possibility of independent MPs standing and winning seats
- Most systems which result in almost pure proportionality (such as the list system and pure STV) result in a large number of parties being elected to Parliament with consequent problems of negotiating coalitions and unstable governments

Types of 'Proportional Representation'

The first thing which needs to be understood about '**PR**' as it is commonly known in the press is that the term is used to cover a wide variety of very different types of electoral system *each of which has its advantages and disadvantages*.

Electoral systems should properly be divided into:

1 Plurality systems such as those used by the UK and the USA
2 Preferential systems such as that used in Australia
3 Proportional or Near-Proportional systems such as those used in most of the EEC countries

It is with the latter two types of electoral system that we are concerned in this section and a brief list would include:

- the Alternative vote system
- the List System
- the Single Transferable Vote system
- mixed systems

The Alternative Vote System

This is really a preferential system which does not result in anything like proportionality, but which attempts to give the voter a choice and to enable them to express preference between candidates.

- candidates stand for single member constituencies
- voters complete a ballot paper by listing the candidates in order of preference (1,2,3, etc)
- a candidate who gets more than 50 per cent of the first preferences is automatically elected
- if no one gets this 50 per cent then the candidate with the lowest number of first preference votes is eliminated and his votes are redistributed among the other candidates
- this process continues until one candidate gets more than 50 per cent of the vote

The system results in almost the same degree of disproportionality between votes and seats as the plurality system.

It should be noted that, until very recently the French used a preferential system called the **Double Ballot System** in which two elections were held on successive Sundays. A candidate who got more than 50 per cent of the votes on the first ballot was elected. If no one in the constituency passed this hurdle then those who had got less than 12.5 per cent of the vote were eliminated and the rest went on to the next Sunday election where a simple plurality system applied.

Again, the system did not produce anything like a proportional result.

Example

The Labour Party and the Double Ballot

The British Labour Party used to use the Double Ballot for electing its leader. If no candidate was elected by more than 50 per cent on the first ballot then the lowest candidate was eliminated and a further 'run-off' held.

In the last election of this type before the institution of the Electoral College the results of the first ballot for Deputy-Leader were:

Denis Healey – 45.3%
Tony Benn – 36.6%
John Silkin – 18.0%

Mr Silkin was eliminated and the next ballot produced the following extremely close result:

Denis Healey – 50.4%
Tony Benn – 49.6%

The List system

These systems achieve the closest to true proportionality:

National List System

- The entire nation is treated as if it were a single constituency and each party draws up a list of candidates equal to the number of seats to be filled.
- Each voter simply votes for the party of his or her choice.

- The votes are counted up by parties and seats are allocated in proportion to the party's share of the vote above a certain 'threshold'.
  (In Israel, which uses this system, the threshold is just 1 per cent of the vote.)

Regional List System
- The object of this system is to try to introduce a personal vote into the party vote bias of the list systems
- In Finland, which is the best example of these systems the country is divided into a number of multi-member constituencies
- Parties put forward a list of candidates in each constituency which is equal to the number of seats to be filled
- The voter does not simply vote for a party but, instead, casts one vote for a **named candidate** who he or she would like to see elected. This vote counts as both a party vote and a personal vote.
- The votes are counted and parties are allocated seats on the basis of the proportion of the votes which they received
- The parties then allocate the seats to the most successful candidates on their lists
- There is usually a threshold in these systems of about 5 per cent of the vote.

Single Transferable Vote
This is a system which has the qualities of being both preferential and proportional. STV may seem extremely complex to the student but is, in fact extremely easy for the voter to understand and to use.
- The country is divided into multi-member constituencies
- The voter expresses his preference among the candidates on the ballot paper by listing them 1,2,3,4, etc.
- The system rests on the notion of the **quota** which is the lowest number of votes which a candidate has to get in order to fill all the seats in the constituency with the least number of wasted votes
- The quota is expressed by the formula:

$$\text{Quota} = \frac{\text{Total Number of Votes Cast}}{\text{Number of Seats}} + 1$$

in a constituency with 4 seats to be filled and 30,000 votes cast the quota needed to be elected to any one of the seats would be:

$$\frac{30000}{5} + 1 = 6{,}001 \text{ votes}$$

- Candidates are elected when they have reached the quota. If no one reaches the quota count, then the candidate with the lowest number of votes is eliminated and his or her votes are redistributed in proportion to the expressed preferences of his or her voters.
  The STV system is used in the Republic of Ireland and for the Australian Upper Chamber.

Mixed Systems
Strictly speaking the Regional List System counts as a mixed system because it allows the voter to express both a *party* vote and a *personal* vote at the same time.

The best known mixed system, however, is the West German one which enables the voter to elect a single member for the constituency and to express a party vote at the same time.
- The country is divided into single member constituencies (quite large ones): in West Germany there are 248 of them.
- In addition there are 248 'pool' seats which do not relate to constituencies at all.

- The voter casts two types of vote on the same ballot paper: on one half the vote is for a candidate for the constituency (in the same way as a British election); on the other half the voter can cast a vote for a party.
- The votes for candidates are counted and constituency members are elected on the simple plurality system just as in the UK.
- The votes for parties are counted on a national basis. This provides an idea of how many seats the party deserves in each region if it were to be represented proportionally. The actual number of single members elected for the party are then deducted from this number and the party is 'topped up' with seats from the pool. If a party ever won more seats than it was entitled to in a region (through the operation of the plurality voting system) then the total number of seats in the Bundestag would be temporarily increased by that number.

Example

Examples of Various Electoral Systems

National List (allowing no choice of individual candidates): Israel Turkey

Regional List (allowing some choice of individual candidates): Netherlands Denmark Italy Sweden Belgium Switzerland

Single Transferable Vote: Australia Eire India Malta

Mixed System: West Germany

The Hansard Society suggested, in 1976, a variation of this system for Britain which was called the **Additional Member System**. Under this system the voter would have only one vote (for a candidate representing a party). Constituency MPs would be elected in the same way as now, by plurality. Candidates who had fought but not won seats would then be placed on a regional list in descending order of their percentage vote and, based on the proportion of the votes gained by the party regionally, these candidates would be given 'topping-up' seats.

The Additional Member System would have the advantages of retaining the current style of constituency MP but would ensure that virtually all of the votes cast were effective in electing MPs.

PARTIES AND ELECTORAL SYSTEMS IN PRACTICE

Party Finances

The major parties all acquire part of their finance from their membership subscriptions and part from donations from friendly organisations.

- **The Conservative Party** gets most of its cash in a non-election year from the annual subscriptions and fund-raising efforts of its membership (given at about 800,000 nationally).

  Although the Conservatives receive a great deal of money (between £1m and £2m in a non-election year) from individual businesses and from other organisations representing business interests, the Party receives a much smaller *proportion* of its total income from organisational sources than does the Labour Party (in a non-election year the Labour Party receives only about 30 per cent of its income from individual members whereas the Conservatives receive around 70 per cent from the same source).
- **The Labour Party** gets most of its money in a non-election year from the trade unions. Membership appears, in recent years, to have dropped to around 250,000 nationally, perhaps even fewer. In 1981 Labour income totalled £3,070,000 of which over 81 per cent came from the trade unions.
- **The Social and Liberal Democrat Party** gets its funds from annual membership subscriptions, from members' fund raising efforts and from organisations (some from trade unions and some from businesses).

None of the parties, however, feels that it has enough finance.

During the 1983 election campaign the Conservative Party spent around £8m to £10m and the Labour and Alliance Parties spent about £3m each.

This discrepancy in funding means that the administrative and promotional effort of the parties is very different. The Labour Party can afford, just, to keep a central staff of about 150 plus about 50 agents whereas the Conservatives keep a total staff of 498 going.

The difference in wealth between the political parties in Britain raises a number of important questions:

- To what extent should the spending of the political parties be limited during election campaigns; locally, nationally or both?
- Should the state fund political activity, and, if so, on what basis should the funds be allocated? (See Now Read On . . . for the Houghton Report of 1976.)

or

- Does the difference in wealth merely reflect the amount of support which the parties attract?

EXAMINATION QUESTIONS

1 Is the British system of government rendered undemocratic by its electoral system? (London, June 1986,1)

2 Contrast the organisational structures of the Labour and the Conservative Parties with particular reference to the centres of power in each. (London, June 1980,1)

3 Is the British political system best described as a two-party, three-party, or a multi-party system? (Cambridge, June 1987)

4 Consider the view that the electoral setbacks of nationalist parties in the UK make unnecessary further discussions of devolution. (AEB, June 1981,1)

5 Should anti-democratic parties such as the National Front and the Communist Party be banned? (London, Jan 1980,1)

6 'Internal democracy within a party must give way when the party obtains office.' Discuss the arguments for and against this view. (London, June 1986,1)

NOW READ ON . . .

David Butler and Dennis Kavanagh *The General Election of 1987* Macmillan, 1988

The latest in the excellent series of books which was initiated by David Butler to review and analyse British General Elections.

An ABC of Electoral Systems Parliamentary Democracy Trust (01-235 3381)

An excellent little booklet which explains almost every system and which includes worked examples.

Electoral Reform The Speaker's Conference Conservative Action for Electoral Reform (CAER) (01-629 2791)

Speaker's Conferences are a way in which controversial, constitutional ideas can be discussed in an all-party forum. There have been five so far and this booklet describes some of the ideas put forward.

'Getting the Party you want' David McKie, *The Guardian*, 10 December 1981

An interesting survey of the options for Britain. See, also, the series of short articles on reform in *The Times*, by Julian Haviland, on 21, 22 and 23 February 1983

'Socialist Transformation through PR', Tariq Ali, *The Guardian*, 12 October 1981

A well written and well argued piece by one of the extreme left's ablest philosophers

The Report of the Committee on Financial Aid to Political Parties (Lord Houghton; Cmnd 6601), August 1966.

An independent report into the possibility of state aid for parties for their activities outside Parliament.

Dick Leonard and Richard Natkiel *The World Atlas of Elections* The Economist, 1987
Fascinating and useful.
Alan Ball *British Political Parties* Macmillan, 1981
Very dated now in its approach.
Richard Rose *Do Parties Make a Difference?* Macmillan, 1984
A thought-provoking essay.
David Held and Christopher Pollitt *New Forms of Democracy* Sage, 1986
An examination of different types of democratic organisation. Should set you thinking about many different levels of politics – from local government to trade unions.
H. M. Drucker *Multi-Party Britain* Macmillan 1979
The thesis which looked valid during the early days of the SDP/Liberal Alliance but began to pale a little during the massive Conservative majorities and weak oppositions of Mrs Thatcher's second and third terms.
Michael Stewart *The Jekyll and Hyde Years* Heinemann, 1968
The now classic theory that the major handicap faced by the UK, in economic, social, and political terms, lies in its electoral system.

Appendix

The Cabinet, October 1991

Prime Minister First Lord of the Treasury Minister of the Civil Service	John Major
Lord Chancellor	Lord Mackay of Clashfern
Secretary of State for Foreign and Commonwealth Affairs	Douglas Hurd
Lord Privy Seal & Leader of the House of Lords	Lord Waddington
Lord President of the Council and Leader of the House of Commons	John MacGregor
Chancellor of the Exchequer	Norman Lamont
Home Secretary	Kenneth Baker
Secretary of State for Defence	Tom King
Secretary of State for Education and Science	Kenneth Clarke
Secretary of State for Transport	Malcolm Rifkind
Secretary of State for Energy	John Wakeham
Secretary of State for Social Security	Antony Newton
Chancellor of the Duchy of Lancaster (Chairman of the Conservative Party)	Chris Patten
Secretary of State for Northern Ireland	Peter Brooke
Minister of Agriculture, Fisheries and Food	John Selwyn Gummer
Secretary of State for Employment	Michael Howard
Secretary of State for Wales	David Hunt
Secretary of State for Trade and Industry	Peter Lilley
Secretary of State for Health	William Waldegrave
Secretary of State for the Environment	Michael Heseltine
Secretary of State for Scotland	Ian Lang
Chief Secretary to the Treasury	David Mellor

The Cabinet stood at 22 members – the maximum number allowed to be paid unde existing legislation.

Cabinet Changes (1979–91)

Since the 1979 General Election, the Conservative Cabinet has been amended on 1 occasions. Four large scale reshuffles took place during the first administratio (1979–1983), six during the second administration (1983–1987), and nine times sinc the beginning of the third term of office in June 1987 (culminating in the resignatio of Mrs Thatcher in November 1990).

First Administration Changes

January 1981 – a limited shuffle of a few posts which included the promotion of Joh Nott to Defence; of John Biffen to Trade; and of Leon Brittan into the Cabinet.

Leavers at this early stage were Norman St John Stevas and Angus Maude.

Semptember 1981 – a more extensive reshuffle which brought Sir Keith Joseph t Education; Nigel Lawson to Energy; James Prior to Northern Ireland; Norma Fowler to Social Services; Norman Tebbit to Employment; and Patrick Jenkin t Industry.

Leavers were Load Soames; Sir Ian Gilmour; and Mark Carlisle.

June 1982 – following the Falklands War with Argentina Mrs Thatcher confirmed the promotion of Francis Pym to Foreign Secretary; promoted John Biffen to Lord President and introduced three 'new faces': Lord Cockfield at Trade; Cecil Parkinson as Chancellor of the Duchy of Lancaster; and Baroness Young as Lord Privy Seal.

Leavers were: Lord Carrington who had resigned as Foreign Secretary in April at the beginning of the war; and Humphrey Atkins.

January 1983 – John Nott resigned as Defence Secretary and was replaced with Michael Heseltine.

Second Administration Changes

July 1983 – a major shuffle following the election of June 1983.

New Boys: Peter Rees as Chief Secretary to the Treasury; and Michael Jopling as Minister of Agriculture.

Expelled: Francis Pym and David Howell.

Honours: Mr William Whitelaw was given the first hereditary peerage since 1964 and was created Viscount Whitelaw.

October 1983 – Cecil Parkinson resigned following the 'scandal' of his affair with his secretary and the revelation of her pregnancy. He was replaced by Lord Cockfield.

September 1984 – James Prior resigned from Northern Ireland, was replaced by Douglas Hurd. Lord Young entered the Cabinet as Minister without Portfolio responsible for 'job creation and enterprise'; the Earl of Gowrie also entered the Cabinet as Chancellor of the Duchy of Lancaster responsible for the Civil Service and the Arts. Selwyn Gummer was made Paymaster General but was not given a cabinet seat.

Leavers: Lord Cockfield (to the European Commission); and James Prior.

September 1985 – Norman Tebbit became Chancellor of the Duchy of Lancaster and took on the Chairmanship of the Conservative Party.

Moves: Brittan to Trade and Industry, Hurd to the Home Office, King to Northern Ireland, Lord Young to Employment

New Boys: Clarke became Paymaster-General with a Cabinet seat. Baker came in to the Environment; MacGregor became Chief Secretary to the Treasury.

Leavers: Earl of Gowrie; Patrick Jenkin; Peter Rees.

February 1986 – Following the inter-Cabinet squabbles of the 'Westland Affair' both Michael Heseltine and Leon Brittan resigned. George Younger was given Defence, Rifkind got the Scottish Office and Paul Channon was introduced to the Cabinet at Trade & Industry.

May 1986 – Sir Keith Joseph resigned and was replaced at Education by Kenneth Baker. Ridley was given Environment.

New Boy: John Moore at Transport.

Third Administration Changes

June 1987 – after her third General Election win in a row, Mrs Thatcher said goodbye to Lord Hailsham (after eight years as Lord Chancellor in this Government); Norman Tebbit (the most reliable reason for his departure appears to have been the pressures of his work and of the severe disabilities of his wife who was very badly injured in the Brighton hotel bombing at the Conservative Party Conference of 1984); Michael Jopling; John Biffen and Nicholas Edwards.

She then said hello (again) to Cecil Parkinson in his rehabilitated form as Secretary for Energy and 'hello' for the first time in the Cabinet to John Major as Chief Secretary to the Treasury; Sir Michael Havers as Lord Chancellor; and John Wakeham as Lord Privy Seal and Leader of the House of Commons.

Moves: Lord Young to Trade and Industry, MacGregor to Agriculture, Clarke to the Duchy of Lancaster with Minister of Trade & Industry, Fowler to Employment, Channon to Transport, Moore to Health & Social Services, Walker to the Welsh Office.

January 1988 – Viscount Whitelaw, after 33 years in politics, was forced to resign due to ill health from his positions of Deputy Prime Minister, Leader of the House of Lords and Lord President of the Council.

Lord Belstead was appointed Leader of the House of Lords while John Wakeham was asked to pick up Lord Whitelaw's role as Lord President of the Council.

July 1988 – A surprise reshuffle was performed in order to split the over-lar Department of Health and Social Security. Kenneth Clarke was given the Heal part while John Moore was left with Social Security. Tony Newton was brought in the Cabinet to take over Clarke's old job at the Department of Trade and Industry.

During the previous year Lord Mackay became the first Scot to be Lo Chancellor when Lord Havers had to give up the job after only 4½ months.

July 1989 – PM announces the biggest cabinet shake up since 'Night of the Lo Knives'.

Mrs Thatcher was widely credited with a major coup in surprising everyon including the victim himself, with the sideways demotion of Sir Geoffrey Howe fro the Foreign Office to Leader of the House and Deputy PM. Sir Geoffrey was repute to have enjoyed the Foreign Office job and was seen as a success in it. His increasin disagreement with Mrs Thatcher over the European Community and the EM sealed his fate. He made way for the new heir-apparent John Major (46) as the ne Foreign Secretary.

Other moves: Tom King ended his stint in Northern Ireland and moved t Defence; Nicholas Ridley was moved to Trade and Industry; Kenneth Baker becam Chancellor of the Duchy of Lancaster and Chairman of the Conservative Party John MacGregor went to Education; Cecil Parkinson took another step on the lon road to rehabilitation by becoming Transport Secretary; John Wakeham was move to Energy; and Antony Newton went to Social Security

New boys: Christopher Patten to Environment; Peter Brooke (ex-Chairman c the Party through the disastrous 1989 European Elections) to Northern Ireland John Gummer to Agriculture; and Norman Lamont became Chief Secretary to th Treasury.

Leavers: George Younger (after over ten years in the Cabinet); Lord Young (t return to business); Paul Channon; John Moore (once tipped as a future leader of th Conservative Party).

October 1989 – In the first major crisis since Westland, Nigel Lawson resigned. Like S Geoffrey Howe, he was regarded as a success in the job of Chancellor – in spite o economic reverses during 1989. He left after a series of disagreements with the PM over the European Monetary System and control of Sterling. However, the mos publicised reason for his resignation was the conflicting advice being publicly give to the PM on economic affairs by her Economic Adviser, Sir Alan Walters.

Moves: John Major had one of the briefest ministerial careers at the Foreig Office – about 3 months – as he was shifted to the Exchequer. Douglas Hurd, who – i was reported – had been overlooked for the Foreign Office in July 1989, now got hi dearest wish. He was moved from the Home Office to the Foreign Office.

New boy: this term's new boy was David Waddington – promoted from Chie Whip to Home Secretary.

January 1990 – To prove that there was a voluntary way to go, Norman Fowle resigned as Employment Secretary. He had been in the Cabinet since the ver earliest days and had reached the peak of his career at the Department o Employment.

The reshuffles of July and October 1989 had shown that he was not bein considered for promotion to one of the high offices of State and he took th opportunity to leave the Government.

The reason given was that he wanted more time with his young family. H departed amicably and was given a knighthood for his trouble.

New boy: Michael Howard joined the Cabinet as Employment Secretary from a junior ministerial role.

March 1990 – After almost eleven years as the only "wet" in the Thatcher Cabinet Peter Walker announced his decision to resign.

He was replaced as Welsh Secretary in May 1990 by David Hunt who had been Minister for Local Government.

July 1990 – Nicholas Ridley, never known for his tact, chose this month to give an interview to the "Spectator" in which he called the move to European Economic and Monetary Union "a German racket designed to take over the whole of Europe".

He resigned. The new Trade & Industry Secretary was Peter Lilley.

November 1990 – The fall of Mrs Thatcher.

Sir Geoffrey Howe handed in his resignation on November 1st. Mrs Thatcher reshuffled and brought in a new boy – William Waldegrave.

On November 13th Sir Geoffrey gave a powerful statement to the House on his reasons for resigning.

The annual opportunity to challenge the Party Leader was then upon them and Michael Heseltine decided to stand against Mrs Thatcher. When nominations closed on November 15th only Thatcher and Heseltine's names were in the ring.

The first round ballot took place on November 20th:

Thatcher	-	204
Heseltine	-	152

Mrs Thatcher had failed by just 4 votes to get the necessary 15% margin over the nearest rival.

After first announcing that she would fight on Mrs Thatcher announced, on November 22nd, her decision to resign as Party Leader and PM.

Both John Major and Douglas Hurd decided to enter the second ballot. This took place on November 27th 1990. The result was:

Heseltine	-	131
Hurd	-	56
Major	-	185

Although Major was 2 votes short of the absolute majority required by the rules the other two candidates both conceded to him.

Mrs Thatcher officially resigned as Prime Minister on November 28th 1990.

In the following Cabinet reshuffle John Major brought in Michael Heseltine as Environment Secretary together with two new boys - David Mellor and Ian Lang.

Mrs Thatcher was accompanied in her departure by Cecil Parkinson and Lord Belstead (although the latter stayed in the Government in a non-Cabinet post).

Absent Friends

The following is a list of those who have been members of the Conservative Cabinets since 1979 but who are no longer:

Norman St John Stevas	- Chancellor of the Duchy of Lancaster (1979–Jan 1981)
Angus Maude	- Paymaster-General (1979–Jan 1981)
Lord Soames	- Lord President of the Council (1979–Sept 1981)
Sir Ian Gilmour	- Lord Privy Seal (1979–Sept 1981)
Mark Carlisle	- Education Secretary (1979–Sept 1981)
Lord Carrington	- Foreign Secretary (1979–April 1982)
Humphrey Atkins	- Northern Ireland (1979–Sept 1981) Lord Privy Seal (Sept 1981–April 1982)
John Nott	- Trade (1979–Jan 1981) Defence (Jan 1981–Jan 1983)
Francis Pym	- Defence (1979–Jan 1981) Leader of the House (Jan 1981–April 1982) Foreign Secretary (April 1982–July 1983)
David Howell	- Energy (1979–Sept 1981) Transport (Sept 1981–July 1983)
Cecil Parkinson	- Duchy of Lancaster (April 1982–July 1983) Trade & Industry (July 1983–Oct 1983)
Parkinson was out of the Cabinet from October 1983 until June 1987	
Baroness Young	- Lord Privy Seal (April 1982–Oct 1983)
James Prior	- Employment (1979–Sept 1981) Northern Ireland (Sept 1981–Sept 1984)
Lord Cockfield	- Duchy of Lancaster (Oct 1983–Sept 1984)
Earl of Gowrie	- Duchy of Lancaster (Sept 1984–Sept 1985)
Patrick Jenkin	- Social Services (1979–Sept 1981) Industry (Sept 1981–July 1983) Environment (July 1983–Sept 1985)
Peter Rees	- Chief Secretary to the Treasury (July 1983–Sept 1985)
Michael Heseltine	- Environment (1979–Jan 1983) Defence (Jan 1983–Feb 1986)
Heseltine was out of the Cabinet from February 1986 until November 1990	
Leon Brittan	- Chief Secretary to the Treasury (Jan 1981–July 1983) Home Secretary (July 1983–Sept 1985) Trade & Industry (Sept 1985–Feb 1986)

Sir Keith Joseph	– Industry (1979–Sept 1981)
	Education (Sept 1981–May 1986)
Lord Hailsham	– Lord Chancellor (1979–June 1987)
John Biffen	– Chief Secretary to the Treasury (1979–Jan 1981)
	Trade (Jan 1981–June 1982)
	Lord President of the Council and Leader of th
	House (June 1982–Oct 1983)
	Lord Privy Seal & Leader of the House of Common
	(Oct 1983–June 1987)
Michael Jopling	– Minister of Agriculture, Fisheries and Food (Oc
	1983–June 1987)
Norman Tebbit	– Employment (Sept 1981–June 1983)
	Trade & Industry (June 1983–Sept 1985)
	Duchy of Lancaster (Sept 1985–June 1987)
Nicholas Edwards	– Welsh office (1979–June 1987)
Lord Havers	– Lord Chancellor (June–Oct 1987)
Viscount Whitelaw	– Home Secretary (1979–July 1983)
	Leader of the House of Lords
	Lord President of the Council and Deputy Prim
	Minister (July 1983–Jan 1988)
George Younger	– Secretary of State for Scotland (1979–Feb 1986)
	Defence Secretary (Feb 1986–July 1989)
Lord Young	– Minister without Portfolio (Sept 1984–Sept 1985)
	Employment Secretary (Sept 1985–June 1987)
	Secretary for Trade and Industry (June 1987–July
	1989)
Paul Channon	– Trade and Industry Secretary (Feb 1986–June 1987
	Transport Secretary (June 1987–July 1989)
John Moore	– Transport Secretary (May 1986–June 1987)
	Secretary for Health and Social Services (Jun
	1987–July 1988)
	Social Security Secretary (July 1988–July 1989)
Nigel Lawson	– Secretary for Energy (Sept 1981–Dec 1983)
	Chancellor of the Exchequer (Dec 1983–Oct 1989)
Norman Fowler	– Secretary of State for Social Services (Sept 1981–
	June 1987)
	Secretary for Employment (June 1987–Jan 1990)
Peter Walker	– Minister of Agriculture, Fisheries & Food (June
	1979–Dec 1983)
	Secretary for Energy (Dec 1983–June 1987)
	Secretary for Wales (June 1987–May 1990)
Nicholas Ridley	– Secretary for Transport (Dec 1983–Nov 1986)
	Secretary for the Environment (Nov 1986–July
	1989)
	Secretary for Trade & Industry (July 1989–July
	1990)
Sir Geoffrey Howe	– Chancellor of the Exchequer (June 1979–Dec 1983)
	Foreign Secretary (Dec 1983–July 1989)
	Lord President of the Council & Leader of the Lords
	(July 1989–Nov 1990)
Mrs Margaret Thatcher	– Prime Minister (June 1979–Nov 1990)
Cecil Parkinson	– Secretary for Energy (June 1987–July 1989)
	Secretary for Transport (July 1989–Nov 1990)
Lord Belstead	– Leader of the House of Lords (July 1988–July 1989)
	Lord Privy Seal and Leader of the House of Lords
	(July 1989–Nov 1990)

A total of 59 people have held senior office (Cabinet positions) during the Conservatives' three administrations between 1979 and 1991. These include the 22 in the 1991 Cabinet (but do not count Cecil Parkinson or Michael Heseltine twice!).

Acknowledgements

The authors and publishers are grateful to the following for permission to reproduce material.

Barnaby's Picture Library, pages 152, 170, 200
Bristol United Press Ltd, page 131
British Film Institute, page 193
Bundesarchiv, West Germany, page 190
Camera Press Ltd, pages 44 (left: Peter Francis; Right: Richard Open), 141 (Ashley Ashwood), 189 (Sven Simon), 211 (Geoffrey Shakerley)
Central Office of Information © Crown, page 217 (top)
The Daily Telegraph, pages 10, 82
David King Collection, pages 151 (left), 165, 192
Deborah Marley, page 126
The Economist, pages 31, 56, 64
France Presse, page 48
The Guardian, page 263
The Independent, page 246
International Freelance Library (John Harris), pages 83, 84
Labour Party Photograph Library, pages 45, 254
The Liberal Party, page 122
Liverpool Daily Post and Echo Ltd, page 105
London Express News and Features Service, page 230
Macdonald/Aldus Archive, page 151 (right)
Martin Jenkinson, pages 13, 63, 76, 93, 102 (both), 275 (top)
Mary Evans Picture Library, pages 80, 97, 99, 110, 118, 123, 124, 125, 129, 136, 144, 146 (both), 164
National Economic Development Office, page 179
The New Statesman, page 261
Photo Co-op, pages 16 (Bill Thorndycroft), 140 (Crispin Hughes), 177 (Vicky White), 251 (Gina Glover)
Popperfoto, pages 51 (Reuter), 74, 233
Report, pages 39 (Derek Speirs), 116 (Andrew Wiard), 235 (Chris Davies), 257 (Andrew Wiard), 273 (Andrew Wiard), 274 (Andrew Wiard), 275 (Romano Cagnoni)
Saatchi and Saatchi Advertising, page 47
Social and Liberal Democrat Party, page 130 (Gemma Levine)
Swiss National Tourist Office, page 109
Times Newspapers, page 95
UK Press and Information Office of the European Parliament, page 217 (bottom)

Every effort has been made to contact copyright holders and we apologise if any have been overlooked.

Index

BARRY COLLEGE
LIBRARY
COLCOT ROAD